OXFORD WORLD'

A MEMOIR OF JA

AND OTHER FAMILY R

JAMES EDWARD AUSTEN-LEIGH (1798–1874), the only son of Jane Austen's eldest brother James and his second wife Mary Lloyd, was born at Deane parsonage, Hampshire, and moved the short distance to Steventon rectory in 1801, aged 2, when his father became rector there on his grandfather's retirement to Bath. Thus he spent his childhood and youth in the same house in which Jane Austen had spent hers. After school at Winchester he went to Exeter College, Oxford, was ordained in 1823, and, like his father and grandfather, became a country clergyman. As a schoolboy he wrote verses and even began a novel, which Jane Austen encouraged. He represented his father at her funeral in 1817. Upon his great-aunt Jane Leigh Perrot's death in 1836 he inherited the estate of Scarlets, taking the name of 'Leigh' in addition to Austen. In 1852 he became vicar of Bray, near Maidenhead, where he lived until his death. A keen huntsman, it was his late success as a published writer with *Recollections of the Vine Hunt* (1865) which encouraged him to begin the *Memoir* in the Spring of 1869, in which he drew upon the memoirs of his sisters Anna Lefroy and Caroline Austen, and of his uncle Henry Austen.

KATHRYN SUTHERLAND is Professor in Bibliography and Textual Criticism at St Anne's College, Oxford. She has published widely on fictional and non-fictional writings of the Scottish Enlightenment and Romantic periods. Her editions include Jane Austen's *Mansfield Park* (for Penguin Classics). Her book *Jane Austen's Textual Lives: From Aeschylus to Bollywood* was published in 2005 (paperback 2007).

OXFORD WORLD'S CLASSICS

For over 100 years Oxford World's Classics have brought readers closer to the world's great literature. Now with over 700 titles—from the 4,000-year-old myths of Mesopotamia to the twentieth century's greatest novels—the series makes available lesser-known as well as celebrated writing.

The pocket-sized hardbacks of the early years contained introductions by Virginia Woolf, T. S. Eliot, Graham Greene, and other literary figures which enriched the experience of reading. Today the series is recognized for its fine scholarship and reliability in texts that span world literature, drama and poetry, religion, philosophy and politics. Each edition includes perceptive commentary and essential background information to meet the changing needs of readers.

OXFORD WORLD'S CLASSICS

J. E. AUSTEN-LEIGH

A Memoir of Jane Austen

and Other Family Recollections

Edited with an Introduction and Notes by
KATHRYN SUTHERLAND

OXFORD
UNIVERSITY PRESS

Great Clarendon Street, Oxford OX2 6DP

Oxford University Press is a department of the University of Oxford.
It furthers the University's objective of excellence in research, scholarship,
and education by publishing worldwide in

Oxford New York

Auckland Bangkok Buenos Aires Cape Town Chennai
Dar es Salaam Delhi Hong Kong Istanbul Karachi Kolkata
Kuala Lumpur Madrid Melbourne Mexico City Mumbai Nairobi
São Paulo Shanghai Singapore Taipei Tokyo Toronto

Oxford is a registered trade mark of Oxford University Press
in the UK and in certain other countries

Published in the United States
by Oxford University Press Inc., New York

First published as an Oxford World's Classics paperback 2002
Reissued 2008

British Library Cataloguing in Publication Data

Data available

Library of Congress Cataloging in Publication Data

Data available

ISBN 978–0–19–954077–8

6

Typeset in Ehrhardt
by RefineCatch Limited, Bungay, Suffolk
Printed in Great Britain by
Clays Ltd, St Ives plc

ACKNOWLEDGEMENTS

In preparing this edition I have incurred many debts and received advice and assistance from several sources. My greatest debt is to Deirdre Le Faye, who generously shared with me her Jane Austen scholarship and knowledge of the archives; she also checked my text of Caroline Austen's *My Aunt Jane Austen: A Memoir* against the manuscript in Jane Austen's House, Chawton. I am grateful to the staff of the Hampshire Record Office, Winchester; to the staff of the Heinz Archive, the National Portrait Gallery; to Judith Priestman of the Modern Manuscripts Room, Bodleian Library; and to the staff of Balliol College and St Anne's College Libraries, Oxford. My thanks for specific and general advice go to Geneviève Baudon Adams, Claire Harman, Tom Keymer, Claire Lamont, Hermione Lee, Matthew Leigh, and Jim McLaverty; to my sister Moira Wardhaugh for helping me think about family memories; and to Judith Luna for her enthusiasm for the project.

I am grateful to the Archive Department of the Hampshire Record Office and to the Heinz Archive and Library, the National Portrait Gallery, for permission to publish manuscript materials in their possession. I would also like to thank Brian Southam and the Jane Austen Society for permission to reprint Caroline Austen's *My Aunt Jane Austen: A Memoir*. For permission to reproduce images of family members, my thanks go to Katharine Beaumont, T. F. Carpenter of the Jane Austen Memorial Trust, and to Maggie Lane.

CONTENTS

LIST OF ILLUSTRATIONS

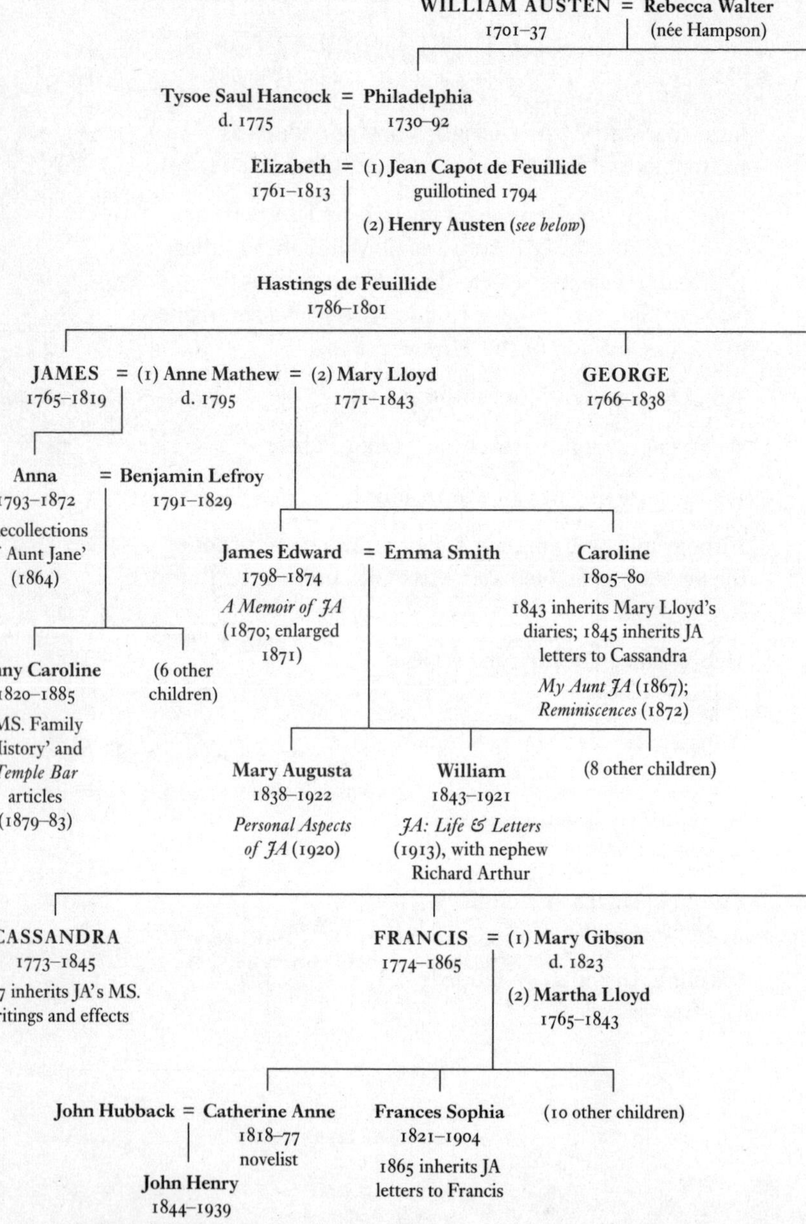

WILLIAM AUSTEN = Rebecca Walter
1701–37
(née Hampson)
Tysoe Saul Hancock = Philadelphia
d. 1775
1730–92
Elizabeth = (1) Jean Capot de Feuillide
1761–1813
guillotined 1794
(2) Henry Austen (see below)
Hastings de Feuillide
1786–1801
JAMES = (1) Anne Mathew = (2) Mary Lloyd
1765–1819
d. 1795
1771–1843
GEORGE
1766–1838
Anna = Benjamin Lefroy
1793–1872
1791–1829
'Recollections of Aunt Jane' (1864)
James Edward = Emma Smith
1798–1874
A Memoir of JA (1870; enlarged 1871)
Caroline
1805–80
1843 inherits Mary Lloyd's diaries; 1845 inherits JA letters to Cassandra
My Aunt JA (1867); Reminiscences (1872)
Fanny Caroline
1820–1885
'MS. Family History' and Temple Bar articles (1879–83)
(6 other children)
Mary Augusta
1838–1922
Personal Aspects of JA (1920)
William
1843–1921
JA: Life & Letters (1913), with nephew Richard Arthur
(8 other children)
CASSANDRA
1773–1845
1817 inherits JA's MS. writings and effects
FRANCIS = (1) Mary Gibson
1774–1865
d. 1823
(2) Martha Lloyd
1765–1843
John Hubback = Catherine Anne
1818–77
novelist
Frances Sophia
1821–1904
1865 inherits JA letters to Francis
(10 other children)
John Henry
1844–1939
JA's Sailor Brothers (1906), with daughter Edith

THE AUSTEN FAMILY TREE
AND DESCENT OF BIOGRAPHICAL MATERIALS

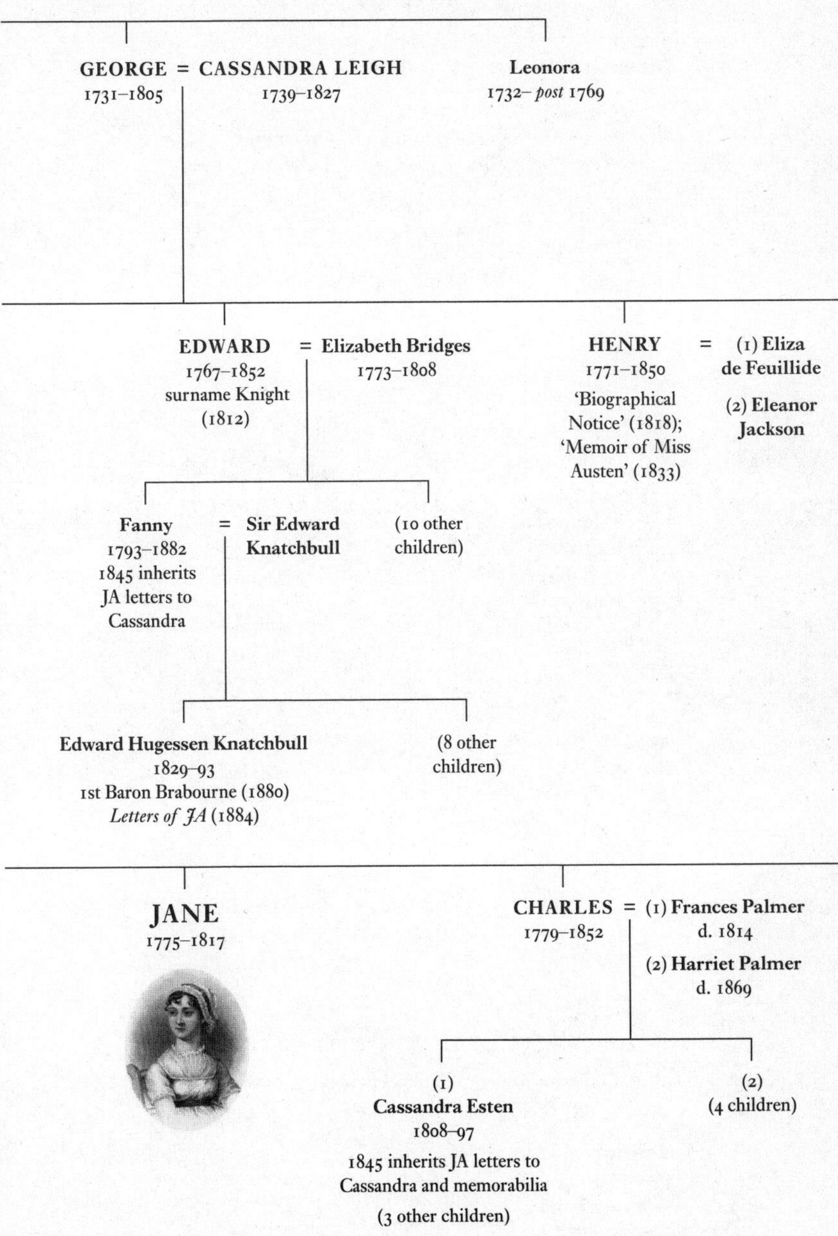

INTRODUCTION

The Business of Biography

When in 1926 Robert Chapman published his edition of James Edward Austen-Leigh's biography of his aunt Jane Austen the *Times Literary Supplement* chiefly welcomed its reissue not for the life it recorded but for the manuscripts described in it. Under the heading 'Manuscripts of Jane Austen', it concentrated on that feature of the *Memoir* which 'makes it necessary to the complete Austenian . . . the particular account, in Mr Chapman's introduction, of the manuscripts of Jane Austen's letters and of her other writings'. The reviewer continued: 'Here we may find . . . the last word about Jane Austen manuscripts, which not only is a thing to welcome for its own sake but may help to bring to light other manuscripts which are known to exist, or to have existed, but have been lost to sight'.[1] In 1926 the manuscript notebook of juvenilia, *Volume the First*, was known outside Austen family circles only by the two scenes of the spoof play 'The Mystery', printed by Austen-Leigh in 1871 and perhaps written as early as 1788 (when Jane Austen was 12 or 13). After 1871 and Austen-Leigh's second edition of the *Memoir*, enlarged with early or unfinished manuscript drafts of several 'new' Jane Austen works (the cancelled chapter of *Persuasion*, *Lady Susan*, *The Watsons*, and a synopsis of *Sanditon*), there was no further printing of such material until the 1920s; readers had to wait until 1951 for the first publication of *Volume the Third*, the last of the juvenile manuscript books. There was an important exception to this silence, in the edition in 1884 of Jane Austen's *Letters* by her great-nephew Lord Brabourne, which brought to public light eighty-four autograph letters in the possession of Lord Brabourne's mother, Jane Austen's niece, Fanny Knight (Lady Knatchbull), and a minor

[1] *Times Literary Supplement*, 17 Mar. 1927, p. 177.

exception in the printing in 1895 of *Charades . . . by Jane Austen and her Family*.

But in the 1920s Chapman was busy distinguishing life from works and extending the Jane Austen canon beyond the six major novels on which her reputation so far rested. He had published or was planning separate and handsomely produced editions of the non-canonical writings that Austen-Leigh had chosen, after family consultation, to stretch out his biography, and it did not seem impossible that more manuscripts might come to light, especially as materials in family ownership were now beginning to appear in the auction rooms. Chapman was particularly concerned at this time with tracing *Volume the First* and the whereabouts of surviving Jane Austen letters. This explains his slant on the *Memoir* in his brief introduction: its importance to him is as a frame on which to hang the extant literary remains and as a guide to the reconstruction of writings which may or may not still exist. Even now this aspect of Austen-Leigh's work cannot be disregarded; in some cases the *Memoir* provides the only documentary authority—for certain letters and for the mock panegyric to Anna Austen ('In measured verse I'll now rehearse').[2] But more subtly at work on Chapman's own Austenian ambitions in 1926 was the influence of later generations of the family as biographers and keepers of the archive. In 1913 James Edward's grandson Richard Arthur Austen-Leigh had published with his uncle William Austen-Leigh an expanded biography, *Jane Austen: Her Life and Letters. A Family Record*, enlarging the 1871 account with materials drawn from other branches of the family. Substantially updated and largely rewritten by Deirdre Le Faye in 1989, *A Family Record* remains the 'authorized' reference or 'factual' biography. The absence of biographical notice or speculation from Chapman's introduction and appended notes to his edition of the earlier Austen-Leigh memoir not only registers a reticence to engage critically with what in 1926 was still family business, it was also the prudent act of a scholar and publisher eager to claim

[2] e.g. those letters printed as nos. 111, 118, and 131, in *Jane Austen's Letters*, ed. Deirdre Le Faye (3rd edn., Oxford: Oxford University Press, 1995). For the verses to Anna Austen, see p. 75 of the *Memoir* and note.

the literary remains in family hands for his own shaping. Chapman was Secretary to the Delegates at Oxford University Press, which had as recently as 1923 issued under its Clarendon imprint his pioneering edition of the six novels—not only the first accurate text of Jane Austen's novels, after the careless reprint history of the nineteenth century, but the first major textual investigation of the English novel as a genre.

Since 1926 there has been no serious editorial engagement with the *Memoir* and little critical attention paid to it.[3] Yet James Austen-Leigh here assembled a major work of Austenian biography which stands unchallenged as the 'prime source of all subsequent biographical writings'.[4] This is even clearer when, as in Chapman's edition and in the edition printed here, the *Memoir* is cut free from the manuscript writings which in 1871 threatened to overshadow it. What is left is an account of a life shaped and limited by the recollections, affections, and prejudices of a very few family members who knew her. But it is worth dwelling on those drafts a little longer because, by attaching *Lady Susan* and *The Watsons* to the *Memoir* text of 1871, James Austen-Leigh, by this time an elderly and respectable Victorian clergyman, may be said to have undermined his overt purpose. 'St. Aunt Jane of Steventon-cum-Chawton Canonicorum', as Austen-Leigh's hagiographic portrait has been wittily dubbed, is a comfortable figure, shunning fame and professional status, centred in home, writing only in the intervals permitted from the more important domestic duties of a devoted daughter, sister, and aunt. 'Her life', her nephew summarized, 'had been passed in the performance of home duties, and the cultivation of domestic affections, without any self-seeking or craving after applause' (p. 130). To such a meek spirit, writing was of no more value than needlework, at which she equally excelled: 'the same hand which painted so exquisitely with the pen could work as delicately with the needle' (p. 79). Indeed, when Austen-Leigh

[3] An exception must be made for D. W. Harding's edition, issued as an appendix to *Persuasion* (Harmondsworth: Penguin Books, 1965).

[4] As stated by David Gilson in his introduction to the facsimile reprint of the 1870, first edition of the *Memoir* (London: Routledge/Thoemmes Press, 1994), p. xiii.

describes her writing it is her penmanship and the look of the page that concerns him, as it concerns her brother Henry ('Every thing came finished from her pen') and niece Caroline, who records somewhat curiously that 'Her handwriting remains to bear testimony to its own excellence' (p. 171). But the unpublished manuscripts speak a different story—of long apprenticeship, experiment and abandonment, rewriting and cancellation, and even of a restless and sardonic spirit. They provide unassailable evidence to upset some of Austen-Leigh's chief statements about Jane Austen the author; considered by the light of these irreverent works her steady moral sense looks more ambiguous, her photographic naturalism ('These writings are like photographs . . . all is the unadorned reflection of the natural object' (p. 116)) less trustworthy. The unpublished writings challenge Austen-Leigh's image of the writer who is first and foremost 'dear Aunt Jane', whose novels are the effortless extensions of a wholesome and blameless life lived in simple surroundings:

> [Steventon] was the cradle of her genius. These were the first objects which inspired her young heart with a sense of the beauties of nature. In strolls along those wood-walks, thick-coming fancies rose in her mind, and gradually assumed the forms in which they came forth to the world. In that simple church she brought them all into subjection to the piety which ruled her in life, and supported her in death. (pp. 24–6)

On the contrary, the manuscript pieces, both early and late, show a rawer, edgier, social talent (of the major Romantic-period writers she is the least 'natural'), and reveal that the artlessness of the finished works is the result of laboured revision, of painful inner struggle, rather than unconscious perfection. Bound together, they irresistibly implied a new Austen novel; once read, they even suggested a new Jane Austen. Chapman reminds us that, 'by inadvertence or cunning', the publisher Richard Bentley had the spine of the second edition of the *Memoir* printed to read *Lady Susan &c*; and this is how it was subsequently issued in the six-volume Steventon set of Jane Austen's Novels (1882), where volume 6 is *Lady Susan, The Watsons, &c.* (With a Memoir and Portrait of the Authoress).[5]

Since 1926 the emphasis has shifted—the manuscript writings have been absorbed into the canon, changing our readings of the six novels and, more pertinently here, literary biographers have appropriated the 'family record', discovering or imposing psychological and aesthetic forms to explain and expand the little we know of Jane Austen's life. But a better way to describe literary biography, caught somewhere between the 'facts' of historical documentation and the competing 'truth' of imaginative association, might be to say that biography is not so much an attempt to explain as an attempt to satisfy. In a now notorious review of Deirdre Le Faye's revised edition of the *Letters*, Terry Castle wrote that the reader of Jane Austen's fiction is 'hungry for a sense of the author's inner life'.[6] If this is so—and the number of Austen biographies even since the revised *Letters* of 1995 argues that our appetites remain keen—then it is not facts or explanations we crave but intimacy and identification. Writers themselves have regularly expressed distaste or fear at the hunger for biographical detail which their own creativity has fuelled and which threatens to invade every private corner. George Eliot viewed biography as a 'disease', complaining to her publisher John Blackwood of the posthumous fascination with the details of Dickens's life: 'Is it not odious that as soon as a man is dead his desk is raked, and every insignificant memorandum which he never meant for the public, is printed for the gossiping amusement of people too idle to re-read his books?'[7] But, as theorizers of biography regularly note, it is the novel itself—more particularly, the nineteenth-century realist novel, with its illusion of the comprehensive and comprehensible life—which is the biographer's readiest model. It is not that we are too idle to reread

[5] *Memoir*, ed. R. W. Chapman (Oxford: Clarendon Press, 1926), p. viii. The advertisement for the Steventon Edition of the novels, printed in the second volume of *Letters of Jane Austen*, ed. Edward, Lord Brabourne (2 vols., London: Richard Bentley and Son, 1884), attaches the notice of the *Memoir* in brackets after *Lady Susan, The Watsons, &c.*

[6] Terry Castle, 'Sister-Sister', *London Review of Books*, 3 Aug. 1995, p. 3.

[7] *The George Eliot Letters*, ed. Gordon S. Haight (9 vols., New Haven: Yale University Press, 1954–78), vi. 23, Eliot to Blackwood, 20 Feb. 1874.

works of literature, but rather that one powerful consequence of reading certain kinds of literature (and especially novels) is our wish to extend and bring closer to us the illusion of knowing and of knowingness they create. The novel-writer is by association the inevitable victim of the hunger her imagination has stimulated and appeared to appease. And, as John Wiltshire suggests, 'of all writers in the canon, Jane Austen is the one around whom this fantasy of access, this dream of possession, weaves its most powerful spell'.[8] Because she is more than usually retiring, because there seems so little to know, because her plotless fictions, themselves the subtlest and most tactful of biographies, present human beings in the fascinating light of their trivial and essential moments, we long to know more. Her novels absorb us deeply and, in a genre where absorption is a conventional expectation, even uniquely. We cannot believe that they will not lead us back to their author. Against this natural longing, artfully stimulated, we should set that other, more sceptical knowledge which novels try to teach us: 'Seldom, very seldom, does complete truth belong to any human disclosure; seldom can it happen that something is not a little disguised, or a little mistaken', the narrator of *Emma* warns the naïve reader; while, for the narrator of *Flaubert's Parrot*, biography is 'a collection of holes tied together with string'.[9] But biography, like novels, is built on paradoxes.

If we look in James Austen-Leigh's memoir for the kinds of encounter with the individual life that we have come to expect from literary biographies of the twentieth century we will be disappointed. While his account remains the printed authority for so much of what we know, it is marked by a lack of candour that frustrates reinterpretation. There are several reasons for this, but all can be summed up by the family constraints on its construction. The details of the life of no other famous individual are so exclusively determined through family as are those of Jane Austen. Not only is it the case that surviving letters, manuscripts,

[8] John Wiltshire, *Recreating Jane Austen* (Cambridge: Cambridge University Press, 2001), 17.

[9] *Emma*, vol. 3, ch. 13; and Julian Barnes, *Flaubert's Parrot* (London: Jonathan Cape, 1984), 38.

and other material witnesses remained largely in family hands for a hundred years after her death, but there is no non-fictional evidence for a 'self' other than that constructed within the bounds of family. No diaries or personal writings have come down to suggest the existence of an inner life, a self apart. If there is no autobiographical record, there is also very little by way of a non-familial social or public record. The archive of her later publisher John Murray has yielded nothing but the barest details of a professional relationship conducted with respect and good will on both sides—no hints of literary parties at which Miss Austen might have been a guest. Henry Austen, in his second, 1833 'Memoir', can only mention as noteworthy the meeting with Germaine de Staël which did not take place, while the introduction to the Prince Regent's librarian, James Stanier Clarke, becomes significant chiefly as it is transformed into the comic 'Plan of a Novel'. What are left are family memories, which if not totally consensual in the 'facts' they collectively register, are sufficiently convergent and mutually endorsing to determine the biographical space as only familial. The modern biographer, for whom the interest of a life generally increases in proportion to its inwardness, is defeated by this absence of a resistant private voice.

The comparison that Austen-Leigh invites us to make is with Charlotte Brontë, and it is more interesting than at first appears. Elizabeth Gaskell's *Life* of her friend and fellow-novelist had been published as recently as 1857, setting a standard for the simultaneous memorializing and effacing of its difficult subject, the female writer, that proved influential on Austen-Leigh. In Chapter 7 he compares his aunt's seclusion from the literary world with the details Gaskell revealed of Brontë's shunning of public applause. That the Jane Austen we encounter in Austen-Leigh's account is as inadequate to the novels we now read as is Gaskell's Brontë can be explained in each case by the Victorian biographer's project of domestication. But there is an added twist whereby the novelist whom Brontë found too 'confined', and from whose 'mild eyes' shone the unwelcome advice 'to finish more, and be more subdued', becomes liable to a biographical constraint which in some part derives from Gaskell's earlier authoritative presentation of Brontë as herself the respectable and unpushy lady novelist. Austen-Leigh quotes (at p. 97), via Gaskell, Charlotte Brontë's now famous denunciation of Jane Austen's quiet art; but Gaskell's elevation of the ideal domestic woman, modest spinster daughter of a country parson, one not 'easily susceptible' to 'the passion of love' in which her novels abound,[10] is clearly instructive for his later presentation of an equally saintly heroine whose emotional and intellectual life never ranged beyond the family circle, and whose brushes with sexual love were so slight as to warrant hardly a mention. Where Gaskell's Brontë walks 'shy and trembling' (p. 91) through the London literary scene, Austen-Leigh's Aunt Jane refuses any and every public notice with an energetic determination that transforms rural Hampshire into a farther retreat than Siberia, let alone Gaskell's exaggeratedly remote Yorkshire parsonage. Jane Austen lived (we are told), with unnecessarily shrill emphasis, 'in entire seclusion from the literary world: neither by correspondence, nor by personal intercourse was she known to any contemporary authors' (p. 90). Austen-Leigh's biography presents what it cannot (or will not) know about creative genius in terms of a withdrawal of imaginative speculation, a deflection of enquiry into anything as intense, familially disruptive, or counter-social as writing. When he equates Jane Austen's literary creativity with her other forms of manual dexterity—her use of sealing wax, her games with cup and ball and spilikins—he conceals within domestic pastime what must also have been a profoundly undomesticated, self-absorbed activity. Beyond a certain point the familial perspective is irrelevant, even dishonest.

Origins

The decision to prepare a biography of Jane Austen was taken by the family in the late 1860s. Admiral Sir Francis Austen, her last

[10] Mrs Gaskell, *The Life of Charlotte Brontë*, ed. Alan Shelston (Harmondsworth: Penguin Books, 1975), 443. For a recent, metabiographical examination of the treatment of Charlotte and Emily Brontë by their biographers, see Lucasta Miller, *The Brontë Myth* (London: Jonathan Cape, 2001).

surviving sibling, had died in August 1865, aged 91. His death marked the end of her generation and therefore a moment for gathering the family record in written form. In addition, those nieces and nephews who had known her in their childhoods were also now old and wished to hand on, within the family, some account of their distinguished relative. 'The generation who knew her is passing away—but those who are succeeding us must feel an interest in the personal character of their Great Aunt, who has made the family name in some small degree, illustrious' (p. 166), wrote Caroline Austen in her 1867 essay, subsequently published as *My Aunt Jane Austen*. Significantly too, at about this time, the public interest in Jane Austen's novels, mounting gradually since the 1830s, showed signs of developing in at least two ways that provided cause for concern. One was the anxiety that a non-family-derived biography might be attempted; and the other was the equal risk that another branch of the family might publish something injudicious. As the only son of the eldest branch, James Edward Austen-Leigh assumed the task as a duty and in a spirit of censorship as well as communication. Before him, the public biographical account necessarily derived from Henry Austen's 'Notice' of 1818 or its revision as the 1833 'Memoir' (both printed here), where even Henry, purportedly Jane Austen's favourite brother, eked out his brief evaluation with lengthy quotation from the views of professional critics. According to Brian Southam's estimate, there were only six essays devoted exclusively to Jane Austen before 1870; but from the 1840s Lord Macaulay, George Henry Lewes, and Julia Kavanagh were publicly attesting to her importance. In private, in his journal in 1858, Macaulay noted his wish to write a short life of 'that wonderful woman' in order to raise funds for a monument to her in Winchester Cathedral.[11] The correspondence, in 1852, between Frank Austen and the eager American autograph hunter

[11] *Jane Austen: The Critical Heritage*, vol. 2, *1870–1938*, ed. B. C. Southam (London: Routledge and Kegan Paul, 1987), 12. Southam prints extracts from the pioneering, pre-1870 appraisals by Kavanagh, Lewes, and Macaulay in *Jane Austen: The Critical Heritage*, vol. 1, *1811–70* (London: Routledge and Kegan Paul, 1968). See, too, *The Life and Letters of Lord Macaulay*, ed. George Otto Trevelyan (2 vols., London: Longmans, Green, and Co., 1876), ii. 466.

Eliza Susan Quincy, referred to by Austen-Leigh in the *Memoir*, suggests a ready circle of devotees as far away as Boston, Massachusetts.

James Edward Austen-Leigh was supported in his decision to write the official family life of Jane Austen by his two sisters and several of his cousins. As early as 1864 his elder, half-sister Anna (Jane Anna Elizabeth Austen) Lefroy (1793–1872) was writing down her memories in response to his enquiries ('You have asked me to put on paper my recollections of Aunt Jane, & to do so would be both on your account & her's a labour of love' (see p. 157)). They are printed in this collection as 'Recollections of Aunt Jane'. His younger sister Caroline Mary Craven Austen (1805–80) provided her reminiscences, as noted above, in 1867. These, too, are included in this collection. As the children of Jane's eldest brother, Anna, James Edward, and Caroline had inhabited her natal home of Steventon, after their father James took over as rector there on the retirement to Bath of his father George Austen. All three were closer to Jane's Hampshire roots (socially as well as geographically) than other branches of the family, notably the grander Knights of Godmersham, Kent, the descendants of her third brother Edward. Of the numerous nephews and nieces (of her six brothers, Edward, Frank, and Charles produced eleven, ten, and eight children respectively), James's children had unique personal knowledge of their aunt and were of an age to remember her. Anna Lefroy had known her aunt from earliest childhood when she was brought to live at Steventon after the death of her mother, James Austen's first wife Anne Mathew. Caroline, though much younger and only 12 when her aunt died, stayed often at Jane Austen's later home at Chawton, while James Edward (known as Edward in the family) was the only one of his generation present at his aunt's funeral. Of the other nieces to have known their aunt, Cassandra Esten Austen (1808–97), Charles Austen's eldest daughter, and Mary Jane Austen (1807–36), Frank's eldest daughter, were both regular visitors to Chawton in their childhood. Mary Jane was now dead, but Cassy Esten was her aunt Cassandra Austen's executrix for her personal effects, and since her own father's death had inherited many papers belonging either to Jane or Cassandra. She shared information, recollections, and copies of Aunt Jane's letters with her cousin James Edward. Another promising source of memories and archival materials should have been Fanny Knight, now Lady Knatchbull (1793–1882), Edward Austen Knight's first child who, just three months older than Anna, was Jane Austen's eldest niece. At the division of their aunt Cassandra's papers after her death in 1845, Fanny had inherited the bulk of those letters from Jane to her sister that Cassandra had chosen to preserve. But by the 1860s Fanny's memory was confused, she was senile, and other family members were unable or reluctant to trace the whereabouts of the letters. His cousin, Fanny's sister, Elizabeth Rice (1800–84), wrote to Austen-Leigh at this time: 'it runs in her head that there is something she ought to do till her brain gets quite bewildered & giddiness comes on which of course is very alarming—I really do not think that it is worth your while to defer writing the Memoir on the chance of getting the letters for I see *none*.'[12] Lady Knatchbull's daughter Louisa returned the same reply to requests for letters, adding 'I only wish the "Memoirs" had been written ten years ago when it would have given my Mother the *greatest* pleasure to assist, both with letters and recollections of her own'.[13]

The gap which these unforthcoming letters and recollections suggest for our retrospective understanding of Austen-Leigh's account is worth considering. Fanny Knight has been represented to posterity as the favourite niece, in Jane Austen's own words 'almost another Sister' (to Cassandra, 8 October 1808).[14] It was a bond strengthened by the death of her mother when Fanny was only 15. As Anna Lefroy, another motherless niece, records in her 'Recollections of Aunt Jane': 'Owing to particular circumstances there grew up during the latter years of Aunt Jane's life a great & affectionate intimacy between herself & the eldest of her nieces;

[12] NPG, RWC/HH, fo. 23, National Portrait Gallery, London, a file of correspondence between R. W. Chapman and Henry Hake, containing typescripts made from 'letters addressed to James Edward Austen-Leigh about the date of the composition & publication of the Memoir and preserved by him in an album'.

[13] NPG, RWC/HH, fo. 25.

[14] *Jane Austen's Letters*, ed. Le Faye, 144.

& I suppose there a [*sic*] few now living who can more fully appreciate the talent or revere the memory of Aunt Jane than Lady Knatchbull' (see pp. 158–9). But in the same place Anna also writes that Fanny's family, the Knights of Godmersham, felt a general preference for Cassandra Austen and that they viewed Jane's talent with some suspicion—intellectual pursuits and a passion for scribbling did not fit with their finer family pretensions. Though Jane was welcome at Godmersham, she stayed there less frequently than Cassandra, was less intimate in the family circle, and expressed some unease with its ways. Time undoubtedly dulled Fanny Knight's earlier attachment to Aunt Jane; so much so that Anna's recollections quoted above assume a wonderful inappropriateness when set against the record we do have of Fanny's opinion in 1869. Senile or not, she had energy enough to write down this memory for her sister Marianne when she in turn raised Austen-Leigh's enquiries:

Yes my love it is very true that Aunt Jane from various circumstances was not so *refined* as she ought to have been from her *talent* & if she had lived 50 years later she would have been in many respects more suitable to *our* more refined tastes. They were not rich & the people around with whom they chiefly mixed, were not at all high bred, or in short anything more than *mediocre* & *they* of course tho' superior in *mental powers & cultivation* were on the same level as far as *refinement* goes—but I think in later life their intercourse with Mrs. Knight (who was very fond of & kind to them) improved them both & Aunt Jane was too clever not to put aside all possible signs of 'common-ness' (if such an expression is allowable) & teach herself to be more refined, at least in intercourse with people in general. Both the Aunts (Cassandra *&* Jane) were brought up in the most complete ignorance of the World & its ways (I mean as to fashion &c) & if it had not been for Papa's marriage which brought them into Kent, & the kindness of Mrs. Knight, who used often to have one or other of the sisters staying with her, they would have been, tho' not less clever & agreeable in themselves, very much below par as to good Society & its ways. If you hate all this I beg yr. pardon but I felt it at my *pen's end* & it chose to come along & speak the truth.[15]

[15] *Fanny Knight's Diaries: Jane Austen through her Niece's Eyes*, ed. Deirdre Le Faye (Alton: Jane Austen Society, 2000), 38–9.

The discrepancy between Anna Lefroy's confidence in Fanny Knight's reverence for her aunt's memory and the details of Fanny's own late outburst, both recovered across a fifty-year gap, exposes something important about biographical truth—it is not just that Anna's sense of what Fanny will remember and hold dear is sharply at odds with what Fanny does indeed retain as significant, but that the two impressions are based on different readings of the same basic ingredients—the long visits to Godmersham, the value placed on talent and cleverness, social distinctions, and the Knights' powers of patronage within the wider Austen family.

In other words, Austen-Leigh's memoir of his aunt is not just a family production, it is the production of a particular family view of Jane Austen, and against it might be set other, different family recollections and therefore different Aunt Janes. Here we have Jane Austen as remembered by the Steventon or Hampshire Austens, for whom she is nature-loving, religious, domestic, middle class. The Godmersham (Knight-Knatchbull) or Kentish Jane Austen was not to be made public until 1884. When in that year Lord Brabourne, Fanny's son and Jane's great-nephew, published his mother's collection of Jane Austen letters, he attached to them a short introduction whose chief purpose appears to be to oust Austen-Leigh's biography and assert his rival claims to the more authentic portrait. Not only is Brabourne's Jane Austen located in Kent as often as in Hampshire, she is a more emotional figure, inward and passionate, and of course more gentrified, improved willy-nilly by contact with her fine relations. These letters, mainly Jane's correspondence with Cassandra, 'contain', he promises, 'the confidential outpourings of Jane Austen's soul to her beloved sister, interspersed with many family and personal details which, doubtless, she would have told to no other human being'. More pointedly, these letters 'have never been in [Mr. Austen-Leigh's] hands' and they 'afford a picture of her such as no history written by another person could give'. To settle the matter of significance, the collection is dedicated to Queen Victoria and proceeds by way of a hundred-page biographical prelude, just under half of which situates its subject in relation to

Godmersham, the Knights, and other Kent associations. '[B]efore one can thoroughly understand and feel at home with the people of whom Jane Austen writes . . . one should know something of the history of Godmersham.'[16]

Competition to shape the record also came in another form, from Frank Austen's daughter, Catherine Austen Hubback (1818–77), who had already stolen a march on the senior branch of the family. Aunt Cassandra frequently stayed with Frank, since 1828 married to her long-time companion Martha Lloyd, and during these visits would read and discuss Jane's manuscript writings with his family. In 1850 Catherine Hubback had published a novel, *The Younger Sister*, with a dedication 'To the memory of her aunt, the late Jane Austen'. The first five chapters are based quite closely on the Austen fragment 'The Watsons', and it appears that Mrs Hubback simply remembered the opening, from Cassandra's retelling, and completed it. Writing to her brother on 8 August 1862, Anna Lefroy fears that their Hubback cousin, now with several more novels to her credit, is ready to do the same with the fragment known in the family as 'Sanditon'. 'The Copy [of 'Sanditon'] which was taken, not given, is now at the mercy of M^rs. Hubback, & she will be pretty sure to make use of it as soon as she thinks she safely may.'[17] Not only did Anna Lefroy resent this appropriation by the lesser novelist of Aunt Jane's voice, *she* was now the legal owner of the 'Sanditon' fragment. Of all her family correspondents Anna, herself a would-be novelist, could claim to have had the deepest fictional communing with Aunt Jane, as letters included in Austen-Leigh's *Memoir* attest. It was, after all, with Anna that Aunt Jane discussed her views on novel-writing and, in any case, Catherine was born only after Jane's death. Here, then, is another reason why, when the *Memoir* was enlarged for a second edition, it sought to place some mark on the manuscript writings as well as the life, though as Lord Brabourne would tetchily observe in his edition of the *Letters*, the autograph copy of 'Lady Susan' belonged to *his* mother,

[16] *Letters of Jane Austen*, ed. Brabourne, vol. i. pp. xi–xiii and 6.

[17] HRO, MS 23M93/86/3c-118(ii), Hampshire Record Office, the Austen-Leigh Papers.

and when Austen-Leigh printed it he did so from a different copy and without his express permission.

One thing is clear, that without the Godmersham perspective Austen-Leigh's account cannot give proportionate space to the part played by Cassandra Austen in her sister's life. But it was Cassandra herself who had done much to obscure and fragment the record. As Caroline Austen observed to her brother: 'I am very glad dear Edward that you have applied your-self to the settlement of the vexed question between the Austens and the Public. I am sure you will do justice to what there *is*—but I feel it must be a difficult task to dig up the *materials*, so carefully have they been buried out of our sight by the past generat[ion]' (pp. 186–7). She herself supplied her brother with an intimate picture of Aunt Jane's daily routine at Chawton Cottage, punctuated with the kind of inconsequential visual detail that only a child would store up as significant. As my annotations to the *Memoir* point out, Austen-Leigh drew heavily on Caroline's essay, and when he does so his prose comes to life. Like him, Caroline was the child of James Austen's second wife, the Austens' family friend Mary Lloyd, and Caroline came into possession of her mother's pocket books, in which over many years she kept a brief diary of events as they occurred. Mary Lloyd Austen had been at her sister-in-law's bedside when she died, having travelled to Winchester to help nurse her. Caroline thus had her mother's recollections, written and spoken, to draw on as well as her own. As one of the unmarried nieces she also spent much time with Aunt Cassandra in her later years. On the strength of this, their older half-sister Anna reminds James Edward, Caroline must have some unique knowledge: 'Caroline, though her recollections cannot go so far back even as your's, is, I know acquainted with some particulars of interest in the life of our Aunt; they relate to circumstances of which I never had any knowledge, but were communicated to her by the best of then living Authorities, Aunt Cassandra' (p. 162).

Cassandra's Legacies

The major ingredients of the *Memoir*, as well as its reverent colouring, are owed, in one way or another, to Cassandra Austen. The closeness of the relationship between Jane and Cassandra has been the subject of much speculation among modern biographers, ranging through good sense, bizarre curiosity, and wild surmise. It is undisputed that theirs was the deepest and most sustaining emotional bond that either made; and as the guardian of her sister's reputation and material effects, Cassandra is the key to what tangibly remains. The sisters lived in close companionship, not unusually for the period sharing a bedroom at Steventon and again at Chawton. But they spent weeks and months apart, often when one or other was staying at the home of another of the large Austen family. It is this regular round of visits—to Godmersham to the Edward Austen Knights, to London to Henry Austen's various fashionable addresses—which accounts for the majority of the surviving letters, addressed from Jane to Cassandra. It was with Cassandra that Jane discussed her work in any detail; Cassandra was her chief heiress and executor of her will. As such she was almost solely responsible for the preservation (and the destruction) and subsequent distribution among brothers, nieces, and nephews of the letters, manuscripts, and memories. She decisively shaped—not only through stewardship of the archive but through conversation—what was available to the next generation. The point is significant (though surely unsurprising) that, through Cassandra's management, and not least through her apportioning of the inheritance, the nieces and nephews individually knew rather less than we might expect. Writing to James Edward in 1864 Anna speculates: 'There may be other sources of information, if we could get at them—Letters may have been preserved' (p. 162), but she does not know this with any certainty. A few years later she concludes: 'The occasional correspondence between the Sisters when apart from each other would as a matter of course be destroyed by the Survivor—I can fancy what the indignation of Aunt Cass[a]. would have been at the mere idea of its' being read and commented upon by any of us, nephews and nieces, little or great—and indeed I I [*sic*] think myself she was right, in that as in most other things' (p. 184). The collected letters of Jane Austen, as they are now available to us, only came together in 1932, and so the reconnection of the various parts of the epistolary archive considerably post-dates both the *Memoir* and the publication of the largest Knatchbull cache (in 1884). Of the 161 letters from Jane Austen now known to have survived, only six were addressed to Fanny Knight (Lady Knatchbull) in her own right; but Cassandra left to her keeping almost all of her own surviving correspondence with her sister, presumably because very many of these letters were written either to or from Fanny's childhood home of Godmersham. Without them, James Edward's memoir lacks significant information. For example, the sparseness of his record for the Southampton years and his vagueness about how long the Austens lived there (his calculation is out by about eighteen months) can be explained in part by the fact that the letters covering that period were, since Cassandra's death, with Lady Knatchbull.[18]

According to Caroline, who gives the fullest account of the treatment of the letters, Aunt Cassandra 'looked them over and burnt the greater part, (as she told me), 2 or 3 years before her own death—She left, or *gave* some as legacies to the Nieces—but of those that *I* have seen, several had portions cut out' (p. 174). Between May 1801 and July 1809 Jane Austen's life was, in outward circumstances at least, at its most unsettled—various temporary homes and lodgings in Bath and Southampton, holiday visits to the seaside, new acquaintances and friendships—and for all that potentially exciting period James Edward provides only four letters. When the Knatchbull cache is added in, there is still a long silence between 27 May 1801 and 14 September 1804. And there are earlier hiatuses in the record—from September 1796 to April 1798, for example. These gaps coincide with important personal and family events: in the earlier years, the death of Cassandra's fiancé Tom Fowle, James Austen's second marriage

[18] They are nos. 49–67 in *Jane Austen's Letters*, ed. Le Faye.

and Henry Austen's marriage to glamorous cousin Eliza, Mrs Lefroy's attempt at matchmaking during the visit of the Revd Samuel Blackall to Ashe, the writing of 'First Impressions' (the early version of what would become *Pride and Prejudice*), and its rejection by the London publisher Thomas Cadell; in the later years, between 1801 and 1804, almost all the romantic interest in Jane Austen's life of which we have any hints at all. We simply do not know the extent of Cassandra's careful work of destruction and whether it is this that accounts for the unyielding nature of the evidence—in particular, the difficulty we have in recovering anything more satisfactory than a partial and unconfiding life of Jane Austen. Lord Brabourne's description of the letters he edits as the 'confidential outpourings' of one soul to another is, from the evidence, wildly inaccurate, but perfectly explicable in terms of family rivalry—his claims to marketing another Jane Austen. Equally, Caroline's account of Cassandra's pruning of the correspondence may suggest secrets hidden and confidences suppressed, but it is just as likely that what remains is not atypical within a larger, censored record but fully representative of it. Cassandra may have chosen to preserve and apportion with such care these letters and not others chiefly because their addressees and internal details were of particular value to one branch of the family or another. It might be that there never was a confiding correspondence to hold back; on the other hand, there might have been.

Biography is suspicious of gaps and silences; the form has tended to assume a correlation between biology and chronology, to the extent that any break in this 'natural fit' supposes the suppression of information. This is all the more so when documentation is not available for periods of obvious psychological interest—love affairs and deaths—when events appear, inexplicably to hindsight, not to have been recognized as 'eventful' and therefore simultaneously translated into narrative form. Literary biography in particular is bound to the twinned assumptions that a life can be written and that its writing is pre-given, part of the natural fit, according to which its texts must already exist and be recoverable as the chronology of thought and feeling attending a sequence of events. Commenting on the paucity of textual clues to Jane Austen's response to the emotional crises of 1796–8, David Nokes despairingly asks: 'Why do we have no letters from this period? It can hardly be because Jane Austen did not write any . . . It can only be that Cassandra . . . chose to destroy them . . . she preferred to obliterate the memory of a period of such distress.' A favoured strategy among recent biographers has been to reconstitute empathetically such 'destroyed' textual traces. Accordingly, Nokes tells us that 'Cassandra received the news [of Tom Fowle's death] with a kind of numbness. Outwardly, she was strangely calm . . . Upon Jane the influence of this change in her sister's disposition was no less profound for being, at first at least, unacknowledged and unperceived.'[19] It is the biographer's duty, in the interests of recording the complete life, to recover not only what must have existed and been destroyed but what only appears to be 'unacknowledged and unperceived'. Biography's texts are thus almost endlessly recessive.

Partiality and Evasion, or Secrets and Lies

The family members whose labours around 1870 chiefly constructed the public record of Jane Austen—James Edward, his two sisters, and their cousin Cassy Esten—were alive equally to the fortuitous and the ethical dimensions of their task. The failings of memory and the shadow of old age as it falls across a later generation ensure that the *Memoir* opens on a note of elegy which contends perilously with annihilation: 'the youngest of the mourners' at the funeral, now in old age, will attempt 'to rescue from oblivion', 'aided by a few survivors', a life 'singularly barren' (pp. 9–10). Old age recovers childhood impressions of a life, itself empty of event, cut short in its middle years—the reader should not be deaf to the effects of an irony which runs throughout the *Memoir*. Accidents of survival, both personal and documentary, constitute what is known, while a more purposive dimension distinguishes what is known from what can be told.

[19] David Nokes, *Jane Austen: A Life* (London: Fourth Estate, 1997), 169–71.

The *Memoir* is a rag-bag, not the shaped life of the historio- or psycho-biographies of the late twentieth century, but an undesigned and unprioritized assortment of textual states. These range through the expansive contextualizing and 'costume' detail of Chapter 2, with its tansey-pudding, minuets, and eulogy of spinning; to the more relevant antiquarianism of Chapter 3, with its letter of 1686 to 'Poll' (Mary Brydges), Jane Austen's great-grandmother, and on to the digression on the Welsh ancestry of the Perrot family which opens Chapter 4; and, in Chapter 9, the roll-call of Jane Austen's famous readers and the student recollections of Sir Denis Le Marchant, Austen-Leigh's brother-in-law. The annotations to this edition give some sense of both the desultoriness and the indulgence of Austen-Leigh's clerical prosings. Against their background noise, voices from letters (though Austen-Leigh is careful to edit them), scraps of remembered conversation, and an occasional sharp vignette convince of their authenticity by the power of surprise—'There is a chair for the married lady, and a little stool for you, Caroline' (p. 128). At such moments, and there are many more of them in the unedited recollections provided by Anna and Caroline, it is as if text, as an aspect of its privacy (its recovery through private recollection), gives up to the reader the trace of real presence—Jane Austen's voice or look or gesture. In these cases, the partiality of the *Memoir* is also its strength.

In significant ways the declared partiality of the family record raises important issues concerning biographical truth and the terms in which all biography functions. Writing to her brother with memories and stories from the past, Caroline makes a distinction between what she has to tell and what she gives for him to print: 'I should not mind *telling* any body, at this distance of time—but printing and publishing seem to me very different from *talking* about the past'; and 'this is *not* a *fact* to be written and printed—but you have authority for saying she *did* mind it' (pp. 188 and 185). The stories she sketches here, got from Aunt Cassandra and from her mother Mary Lloyd, refer respectively to the marriage proposal from Harris Bigg-Wither in December 1802, and the Revd George Austen's decision late in 1800 to leave

Steventon and move to Bath. A century and more later, the boundaries between the private and public knowledge of Jane Austen no longer obtain. The living links with the past and the other sensitivities by which Austen-Leigh and his associates were bound are severed; and the 'right to privacy' of Jane Austen, her immediate family, and neighbours would now strike us as a surprising if not an absurd concept, easily overtaken by the competing 'rights' of history (in the form of accurate scholarship), or just the vaguer, modern 'right to know'. Biographers have since Austen-Leigh's time equipped themselves to probe the silences and evasions in these prime sources. It is now in terms of its secrets and lies that Austen-Leigh's *Memoir* might seem to be most profitably approached.

We now know that her nieces and nephew did not tell us the whole truth about Jane Austen and her family as they knew it. The existence of a second brother, the handicapped but long-lived George Austen, is concealed, and Edward, the third brother, is presented as the second (p. 16). There is no reference to the jailing of Jane's aunt Mrs Leigh Perrot on a charge of shoplifting in Bath. Neither piece of discretion is surprising; both are matters of honour and, for the time, of good taste. Austen-Leigh was his great-uncle Leigh Perrot's heir, adding Leigh to his name on his great-aunt's death in 1837. But the excitement and publicity of the imprisonment and trial, occurring only a year before the Austens moved to Bath, must have continued to hang in the air and to affect the family's social standing in the city. For this reason and others, we long to know more of Jane Austen's impressions of life there. As David Gilson tells us, Mrs Leigh Perrot's trial has the doubtful distinction of being 'the only public event involving a member of the novelist's family of which significant contemporary documentation survives'.[20] Over all the texts gathered in this collection, there hangs silence on this matter.

[20] David Gilson, Introduction to Sir F. D. MacKinnon, *Grand Larceny, Being the Trial of Jane Leigh Perrot, Aunt of Jane Austen* (1937); repr. in *Jane Austen: Family History* (5 vols., London: Routledge/Thoemmes Press, 1995), volumes are unnumbered.

The suppression of such circumstantial facts, it might be argued, is a limitation of frankness rather different from the unwillingness to probe the inner life of the biographical subject. It is evident, for example, from the fragments of correspondence which remain that nephew and nieces did speculate about the extent of Jane Austen's romantic attachments—to Tom Lefroy in the winter of 1795–6, to the Revd Blackall two years later, about the abortive seaside romance, and the proposal from her friends' brother Harris Bigg-Wither. There is confusion over how many attachments there may have been—seaside and other romantic clergymen blur and multiply. We detect disagreements, too, over who at this distance still needed to be protected, as well as over what it is proper to expose in public. One of the important revisions between the first and second editions of the *Memoir* deepens the sense that Jane Austen did, like most of us, experience romantic love and the pain of its loss. The sentence in the first edition which reads 'I have no reason to think that she ever felt any attachment by which the happiness of her life was at all affected' is removed from the second edition which now hints, though with conscious insubstantiality, at two possible romantic episodes before concluding: 'I am unable to say whether her feelings were of such a nature as to affect her happiness' (p. 29). The shift is small but it sanctions the reader's closer identification with the human subject of the *Memoir*.

In particular, the Tom Lefroy affair was not forgotten in family memory—Caroline had her version 'from my Mother, who was near at the time', while Anna, a Lefroy by marriage, has her own more highly charged story of events, coloured by internal family politics. As she does on other occasions, Caroline presses for discretion; Anna is generally less prudish. What the brother and sisters did not have access to, because they were now in Knatchbull hands, were the important letters from Jane to Cassandra in which she records the brief relationship and something of her feelings. Significantly or not, these are the first surviving letters. But it is possible to make out, without their excited mock-serious communications, that the attachment was more earnest and its end more painful than Austen-Leigh allows. In the late 1860s

Tom Lefroy was still living. Though his death, only months before publication of the *Memoir*, provided an opportunity to reconsider the story for the second edition, Austen-Leigh retained intact the guarded, even cryptic, paragraph which appeared in the first.[21]

This sense of reserve towards the subject of a posthumous biography is not just a matter of family respect, though the lines between what is accounted as for private or public knowledge will obviously be drawn differently depending on where the biographer stands. Rather, it is indicative of a discretion which separates mid-Victorian biographers from the prying accountability of our modern need-to-know stance. Reticence was a matter of moral responsibility for the Victorian biographer, but that does not mean that attention to the limits of what can or should be made known need prevent discerning speculation, or that the moral reading of a life cannot become its imaginative reading. One of the earliest and most insightful readers of the *Memoir* was the novelist Margaret Oliphant, whose review of the first edition appeared in *Blackwood's Edinburgh Magazine* for March 1870. Oliphant refuses to have any truck with Austen-Leigh's idealized portrait of a selfless spinster aunt, grateful sister, and uncomplaining daughter. To her mind Jane Austen the novelist is an altogether harder and more brilliant individual, the author of 'books so calm and cold and keen', whose portrayal of human behaviour is 'cruel in its perfection'. It follows that the sentimentality of her painted domestic environment will not do. She names the Austen family 'a kind of clan', their happy circle more like a prison, and 'this sweet young woman' of Austen-Leigh's construction a stifled figure, 'fenced from the outer world'.[22] But, though she questions the relevance and truth of his portrait, she does not suggest that the biographer should examine deeper into the details of the life. A little over ten years later, in 'The Ethics of Biography' (1883), she warned against 'that prying curiosity which loves to investigate circumstances, and thrust itself into the

[21] See p. 48 in this edition and my note for further details.

[22] [M. O. W. Oliphant], 'Miss Austen and Miss Mitford', *Blackwood's Edinburgh Magazine*, 107 (1870), 290–1, 300, 304.

sanctuaries of individual feeling'.[23] The partiality of Jane Austen's Victorian biography is explicable, then, not only in terms of the fragmentariness of the record and the prejudices and loyalties of the family, but also as a more principled rejection of that kind of disclosure which invades 'the sanctuaries of individual feeling', places immune from pursuit and exposure.

Speculation and Context

To the mind and sensibilities of the modern biographer, 'sanctuaries of individual feeling' can seem like caves of repression. Areas once out of bounds to ethical enquiry have become compelling sites of exploration to the clinically charged post-Freudian enquirer. Our validation is that by probing we rescue and in some way restore the life of the biographee now in our charge. In recent times this rescue-work has been seen as a special trust laid upon the female or feminist biographer by her female subject. So, for example, Claire Tomalin examines the *Memoir* account (p. 39) of Mrs Austen's system of child-rearing for clues to explain what she diagnoses as Jane Austen's emotional defensiveness in adult life. It was Mrs Austen's practice to breast-feed each of her numerous babies for the first three or four months of life and then foster-out the baby to a woman in the village for the next year or longer (until she/he was able to walk). In Austen's adult letters we encounter, by Tomalin's reading, not the passionate confidante of Brabourne's description, but 'someone who does not open her heart', a woman potentially traumatized by very early weaning and associated emotional withdrawal. Tomalin concludes that 'in the adult who avoids intimacy you sense the child who was uncertain where to expect love or to look for security, and armoured herself against rejection'. The early severance of a maternal bond will account not only for a subsequent guardedness in matters of feeling (the absence of acknowledged romantic attachment), and for the formality in Jane Austen's relations with

[23] M. O. W. Oliphant, 'The Ethics of Biography', *Contemporary Review*, 44 (1883), 84.

her mother, but also for the intensity of her feelings for her elder sister; there may have been something infantilizing in Cassandra's influence. Tomalin suggests that their relationship was not unlike that of many couples ('sisters can become couples'), while Terry Castle's sensationalized review of the letters, proclaimed 'the primitive adhesiveness—and underlying eros—of the sister–sister bond', provoking heated discussion and rejection of the dual charges of incest and lesbianism. The details of what strikes the modern reader as an odd practice (fostering-out) can be made to yield far-reaching consequences. But it is also worth considering how far biographers, too, might carry baggage from one project to another: is it possible that Tomalin's reading of Jane Austen's early life is in any way influenced by her earlier reading of Mary Wollstonecraft's jealous pursuit of the love her mother denied her?[24]

One moment of suspected intense repressed emotion has proved irresistible to all biographers. It is when Jane Austen hears the news that she is to lose her natal home, Steventon rectory, and be uprooted to Bath. The event must have occurred late in November or early in December 1800. Austen-Leigh provides the first public statement. He writes:

> The loss of their first home is generally a great grief to young persons of strong feeling and lively imagination; and Jane was exceedingly unhappy when she was told that her father, now seventy years of age, had determined to resign his duties to his eldest son, who was to be his successor in the Rectory of Steventon, and to remove with his wife and daughters to Bath. Jane had been absent from home when this resolution was taken; and, as her father was always rapid both in forming his resolutions and acting on them, she had little time to reconcile herself to the change. (p. 50)

His account is brisk but compassionate, and a little distant. He hints at his subject's strength of attachment, her exclusion from the decision-making process, and her powerlessness to reverse it, but he also notes that such is 'generally' the feeling of imaginative

[24] Claire Tomalin, *Jane Austen: A Life* (London: Viking, 1997), 6–7 and 211. Castle, 'Sister-Sister', p. 3. See also Claire Tomalin, *The Life and Death of Mary Wollstonecraft* (1974; Harmondsworth: Penguin Books, 1977), 14 ff.

'young persons'. It is perhaps worth remembering that the home from which the sensitive young Jane Austen was so swiftly exiled was also that to which the baby James Edward (aged 2 years) was, by the same decision, introduced. But after this brief paragraph he leaves the matter. His source was his younger sister Caroline, not then born, but subsequently in receipt of the details from their mother Mary Lloyd Austen 'who was present'. Caroline wrote to James Edward:

My Aunt was very sorry to leave her native home, as I have heard my Mother relate—My Aunts had been away a little while, and were met in the Hall ^on their return^ by their Mother who told them it was all settled, and they were going to live at Bath. My Mother who was present.[*sic*] said my Aunt Jane was greatly distressed—All things were done in a hurry by Mr. Austen & of course that is *not* a *fact* to be written and printed—but you have authority for saying she *did* mind it—if you think it worth while— (p. 185)

Caroline's disjointed, repetitive note-making unintentionally raises the painfulness of the story, but the raw elements of her version, smoothed out in her brother's more circumspect delivery, also convey the rush, the shock, and the distress of the event in a wholly convincing way. We almost hear Mrs Austen delivering her great news in the hall (to Jane and Martha Lloyd, the two aunts who had been away, and not to Jane and Cassandra, as is here implied). There was also another version, recorded by Fanny Caroline Lefroy in her manuscript 'Family History'; she got it from her mother Anna Lefroy, aged 7 at the time of the incident.

Repeating the story in 1913 in *Life and Letters*, Austen-Leigh's son and grandson transform it into drama and embellish it with what will become a familiar psychological coda—the mystery of the non-existent letters. This is their version:

Tradition says that when Jane returned home accompanied by Martha Lloyd, the news was abruptly announced by her mother, who thus greeted them: 'Well, girls, it is all settled; we have decided to leave Steventon in such a week, and go to Bath'; and that the shock of the intelligence was so great to Jane that she fainted away. Unfortunately, there is no further direct evidence to show how far Jane's feelings resembled those she attributed to Marianne Dashwood on leaving Norland; but we have the negative evidence arising from the fact that none of her letters are preserved between November 30, 1800, and January 3, 1801, although Cassandra was at Godmersham during the whole of the intervening month. Silence on the part of Jane to Cassandra for so long a period of absence is unheard of: and according to the rule acted on by Cassandra, destruction of her sister's letters was a proof of their emotional interest.[25]

What is new in 1913 is the melodrama—the fainting and the association of Jane Austen's behaviour with that of her hysterical heroine Marianne Dashwood (whose sorrows and joys, her narrator tells, 'could have no moderation') from the yet-to-be-published *Sense and Sensibility*.[26] Summing up the family traditions in 1948, R. W. Chapman presses them yet further:

Jane made the best of it. . . . Jane's local attachments were of extraordinary strength; they were no small part of her genius. We cannot doubt that the loss of her native county, and of the multitude of associations which made up her girlish experience, was exquisitely painful. Her feelings cannot have been less acute than Marianne's on leaving Norland, or Anne's on leaving Kellynch. Her return to her own country, eight years later, was the long-delayed return of an exile.[27]

Jane's love of the local Hampshire countryside is partly drawn from Fanny Caroline's account, but Chapman takes it on himself to strengthen the relationship of equivalence between author and fictions by extending the link, arbitrarily made to Austen's first heroine by later generations of Austen-Leighs, to incorporate her final heroine, Anne Elliot from *Persuasion*. It is, of course, the kind of recognition a certain sort of biography delights in, where fiction offers clues back to its author or demonstrably derives directly from personal experience. In his opening chapter Austen-Leigh had been at some pains to point out that if 'Cassandra's character might indeed represent the "*sense*" of Elinor',

[25] William Austen-Leigh and Richard Arthur Austen-Leigh, *Jane Austen: Her Life and Letters. A Family Record* (London: Smith, Elder, and Co., 1913), 155–6.

[26] *Sense and Sensibility*, vol. 1, ch. 1.

[27] R. W. Chapman, *Jane Austen: Facts and Problems* (Oxford: Clarendon Press, 1948; repr. 1949), 47.

'Jane's had little in common with the "*sensibility*" of Marianne' (p. 19). But Lord Brabourne played up the romance of a more susceptible Aunt Jane, as did Austen-Leigh's descendants. Now Chapman adds the finishing touch, and Austen transforms from Marianne Dashwood into Anne Elliot, enacting the whole gamut of emotions from hysteria to settled melancholy. Implicitly, we are told, Jane Austen's total achievement as a writer is to be explained in terms of the loss of Steventon. The trajectory of her fiction is determined by her need for reconnection with her natal environment. The suppression of those letters (which if they ever did exist can only be allowed, in the interests of biographical consistency, to witness to dispossession and a loss of self) and the equally apocryphal transformation of great distress into something greater, a temporary loss of consciousness (she fainted), provide the kind of discontinuities the biographer can turn to some purpose.

Why does this one distressing moment matter and why do subsequent biographers embellish it so enthusiastically?[28] It marks an end, but it might also mark a new beginning—the move to Bath and a wider social scene, with more variety and incident to fuel the aspiring novelist's imagination. But one purpose the moment has consistently served has been to foreclose on the future. The secret of, or clue to, Jane Austen's creativity lies, we are told, like DNA coding, in her original script. Though he would not recognize it presented in these terms, this is Austen-Leigh's view, and it explains his erasure of even the idea of struggle from his account of her writing life. 'Whatever she produced', he asserts, 'was a genuine home-made article' (p. 90). An intermittent subtext to his account links the careers of Jane Austen and her contemporary Walter Scott. Not only was Scott the best-selling novelist of the early nineteenth century, but the standards he set for the production of fiction—as saleable commodity and as large-scale social panorama—continued to shape the novel far

[28] Nokes, *Jane Austen: A Life*, 220–3 and 350–2, pores over the episode, using it to jump off in a quite different direction, to the robust (but unprovable) conclusion that after fainting or not fainting Jane went off to Bath to have fun and it is because she was too busy enjoying herself there that there is now a perceptible gap in the biographical record.

into the century, and in so doing to overshadow Austen's different contribution. The identity of artistic effort with economic worth, by which Scott laboured so vigorously to give significant value to the work of the novelist, is just as vigorously denied in Austen-Leigh's account of his aunt's unremarked (and little-remunerated) writings. Instead, what he does emphasize is that, settled in Chawton after the disruptions of the Bath and Southampton years, her habits of composition assumed identity with those he conjectures for the Steventon years, 'so that the last five years of her life produced the same number of novels with those which had been written in her early youth' (p. 81). The structure Austen-Leigh imposes here has been of profound significance for how critics have viewed Jane Austen's creative life. He suggests that the novels as we know them were the products of two distinct and matching creative periods—roughly Austen's early twenties and her late thirties—and that these were divided by a largely fallow interlude. But another interpretation of the same evidence and dates, one which has found less favour, might be that, with the exception of *Northanger Abbey* (sold, under the title of 'Susan', to a London publisher in 1803), all the finished novels were the products of the mature Chawton years, and that this intense burst of creativity between 1809 and 1817 was not necessarily the consequence of a return to emotional or environmental origins but the culmination of some twenty years of uninterrupted fictional experimentation. A case can be made for linking *Northanger Abbey*, possibly in a second drafting, *The Watsons*, and *Lady Susan* with the disrupted Bath and Southampton years, but there may also have been other draftings or revisions at this time. Given the hard critical gaze Austen turns upon homes and families in her fictions, can it be that they are exclusively the products of home and rootedness? In other words, what intervened between Steventon and Chawton may not have been just one long swoon of unconsciousness, a syncope of around eight years, from which she only recovered when time and events conspired to restore as nearly as possible those primal scenes.

The structuring device of home, and of Hampshire homes in

particular, sustains Austen-Leigh's account, with its emphasis on well-regulated domesticity and family harmony. The Austens were a close-knit and talented family. '[U]ncommon abilities . . . seem to have been bestowed, tho' in a different way upon each member of this family', wrote their cousin Eliza de Feuillide in 1792.[29] Their closeness, strengthened by marriages between cousins and within a small circle of long-time friends, and by the recurrence across generations of the same Christian names, can disorientate the reader attempting to separate the various threads of connection. It also impresses on our modern sensibilities an apprehension of confinement, of too much accord and correspondence. Austen-Leigh contributes much to this. Quoting from Anna Lefroy's manuscripts, Constance Hill, one of the earliest non-family biographers, writes that Henry, Jane's fourth brother, 'was the handsomest of the family, and, in the opinion of his own father, the most talented. There were others who formed a different estimate, but, for the most part, he was greatly admired.'[30] At last we glimpse a chink in the family's public presentation. But in the *Memoir* this other Henry's story is not told. Here he is the brother who 'cannot help being amusing' (p. 63), who acts informally and generously as his sister's literary agent, entertains her in London, and in the autumn of 1815 is nursed by her through a serious illness. That he was also an unsuccessful opportunist who managed to entangle various members of his family in debt, that his eventual bankruptcy may have had profound consequences for Jane's late publication plans and the course of her final illness—none of this is conveyed by Austen-Leigh's preliminary sketch, in which Henry 'had perhaps less steadiness of purpose, certainly less success in life, than his brothers' (p. 16). But hints in Fanny Caroline Lefroy's 'Family History' suggest that Anna, fiercely attached to her aunt, handed down within the family a more critical account, certainly of the bankruptcy and its effects on the family and Jane's health.

[29] *Austen Papers 1704–1856*, ed. Richard Arthur Austen-Leigh (London: Spottiswoode, Ballantyne, and Co., 1942), 148.

[30] Constance Hill, *Jane Austen: Her Homes and Her Friends* (1902; London: John Lane, 1904), 48.

Another aspect of the *Memoir*'s persistent familism is its preoccupation with genealogy. In fact, genealogy seems to have been a favourite Austen family pastime, and the appearance in the novels of names taken from the concealed, maternal line is evidence that Jane shared the pleasure in some degree. The complicated transference and transformation of names within the family—Leigh to Leigh Perrot, Austen to Knight, Austen to Austen-Leigh—would obviously stimulate what was in any case a convention of Victorian biography and a gentle clerical pursuit. Genealogy provides a scaffold for and helps plug the gaps in the record of the individual life. It assists Austen-Leigh in his self-conscious work of 'book-making' around the otherwise scanty figure of his aunt; and it also witnesses to his anxiety to secure the status of the Austen family. How else do we account for the 'very old letter' from Eliza Brydges to her daughter Mary, Jane Austen's maternal great-grandmother, included in Chapter 3? Austen-Leigh's explanation that anything two hundred years old and incorporating domestic details 'must possess some interest' (p. 44) is hardly compelling; nor are the letter's contents. But its circumstances give it significance. It was clearly a cherished family heirloom, handed down through the Leigh and Austen families. Anna Lefroy drew her brother's attention to its present whereabouts as he was collecting his materials. Not only does the Chandos letter (Mary Brydges was the daughter of James Brydges, eighth Lord of Chandos, and the sister of the first Duke) remind the reader of Jane Austen's distant aristocratic pretensions, it also gives a favourable gloss to the standing of her more immediate family. As Austen-Leigh is at pains to point out, Mary Brydges's father was a penniless aristocrat, while her grandmother was the widow of a rich merchant. In registering the periodic adjustments between rank and trade by which English society was secured in the course of the early modern period, he simultaneously underpins the fluid social group, comprising minor gentry, the professions, rentiers, clergymen, and trade, whose membership encompassed the diversely positioned Austen family in the late eighteenth century. Austen-Leigh's snobbish streak runs fairly wide through the *Memoir*, a recognizable if unattractive nervousness which at times descends into massive condescension and complacency—when confronting the absence of improvements in domestic arrangements, furniture, meals, and general living conditions during Jane Austen's lifetime. At such moments he comes perilously close to her own Mr Collins. Less specifically, however, the social anxiety his biography registers offers a valuable insight into a family who were, much like the fictional society of the novels, insecurely positioned in what has been described as 'pseudo-gentry'—in some cases upwardly mobile and with growing incomes and social prestige, and in others in straitened circumstances, but, in either case, aspiring to the lifestyle of the traditional rural gentry.[31]

According to his daughter's later account, Austen-Leigh began the *Memoir* on 30 March 1869 and it was finished, in a little over five months, early in September. During that time he made a short visit to Steventon to fix what impressions he could still trace of his own and his aunt's early home, and he corresponded with his sisters and cousins in the hope of collecting further information. The *Memoir* was published on 16 December 1869, though dated 1870, in a relatively modest edition of around a thousand copies.[32] It is, as its title states, a memoir ('a record of events, not purporting to be a complete history, but treating of such matters as come within the personal knowledge of the writer, or are obtained from certain particular sources of information': *OED*, s.v. 3a). To some extent, its discontinuous narrative guarantees authenticity. As Austen-Leigh's daughter notes: 'It could not relate that which none of them knew, respecting the details of her earlier life, nor could it describe many facts given in letters not then before him, to which later writers have had access.' Most importantly, this is Aunt Jane as her nieces and nephew came to know her in the Chawton years. 'Of her earlier and gayer experiences, he probably knew nothing, and still less

[31] On the 'pseudo-gentry', see David Spring, 'Interpreters of Jane Austen's Social World: Literary Criticism and Historians', in Janet Todd (ed.), *Jane Austen: New Perspectives* (New York: Holmes and Meier Publishers Inc., 1983), 61–3.

[32] Mary Augusta Austen-Leigh, *James Edward Austen-Leigh, A Memoir* (privately published, 1911), 263–4.

likely was it that, in spite of their strong mutual affection, he should have any knowledge of the intimate and private feelings of an aunt whose years, at the time of her death, numbered more than twice his own.'[33] In defending the partiality of her father's 'life' of Jane Austen, Mary Augusta Austen-Leigh hoped also to adjust its cultural impact. If the *Memoir* had the immediate effect of awakening general public interest in an author virtually forgotten outside select critical circles, it had done so, or so it seemed in 1920, on terms too narrow and comfortable. Certainly, Austen-Leigh's complacent presentation of his aunt had an incalculable influence on the popularization and critical reading of her novels far into the twentieth century. It was not seriously disturbed until 1940, when D. W. Harding, a psychologist rather than a literary critic, detected beneath the cosy domesticity a 'regulated hatred', declaring that her 'books are . . . read and enjoyed by precisely the sort of people whom she disliked'.[34]

One of the most comfortable ingredients of all was the frontispiece portrait of the author, based on a slight watercolour sketch made by her sister Cassandra in about 1810. After family consultation, Austen-Leigh commissioned a professional artist, James Andrews of Maidenhead, to execute a portrait from the sketch, and this then provided the model for a steel engraving. Its difference from Cassandra's original is evident to the most cursory glance. Her crude pencil and watercolour likeness is sharp-faced, pursed-lipped, unsmiling, scornful even, and withdrawn; in its Victorian refashioning, the face is softer, its expression more pliant, and the eyes only pensively averted. The greater attention to detail and finish in costume and seating (the chair the figure occupies is now elegantly Victorian) serves to assimilate the face to a whole, where in Cassandra's representation it expresses an energy at odds with its unformed context. As visual biographies the two tell quite different stories, whatever claim either might make to be representing a human original. At the time of the *Memoir*'s writing, Cassandra's sketch was the property of Cassy

[33] Id., *Personal Aspects of Jane Austen* (London: John Murray, 1920), 4–5.

[34] D. W. Harding, 'Regulated Hatred: An Aspect of the Work of Jane Austen', *Scrutiny*, 8 (Mar. 1940).

Esten, Charles's daughter, and was considered by Anna Lefroy to be 'hideously unlike'. Writing to her cousin on 18 December 1869, immediately after publication of the *Memoir*, Cassy Esten expresses her relief at how the picture has turned out: 'I think the portrait is very much superior to any thing that could have been expected from the sketch it was taken from.—It is a very pleasing, sweet face,—tho', I confess, to not thinking it *much* like the original;—but *that*, the public will not be able to detect.' Caroline records something similar, telling her brother 'there is a *look* which I recognise as *hers*—and though the general resemblance is *not* strong, yet as it represents a pleasant countenance it is *so* far a truth—and I am not dissatisfied with it.'[35] It is tempting to find in the story of the portraits a lesson for the biography reader.

Other Family Recollections

One of the purposes of this collection of family biographies is to help the reader of Jane Austen's life recover the texts and contexts from which it continues to be rewritten; and to help reconsider the steps by which we have moved from a reticent to a revelatory view of the individual life. Because of what we can now see it does not say, the early family record can also help us gain critical understanding of our own less perceptibly partial accounts. Recognized or not, Austen-Leigh's *Memoir* stands as pre-text for the large-scale Austen biography industry of the twentieth century. His sisters' less mediated recollections interpellate his narrative to provide its most particular, unshaped moments. Situated within his expansive prose, the vivid illuminations of their childhood memories, in themselves profoundly located, stand out as sharp dislocations—texts out of context. Caroline's is the more consciously crafted account. To her we owe the most intimate details of Jane Austen's daily routine at Chawton—how she looked at that time; her piano-playing; her

[35] NPG, RWC/HH, from typescript of a letter from Anna to James Edward, 'July 20' [1869], unfoliated; NPG, RWC/HH, fo. 15, typescript of part of a letter from Cassy E. Austen to JEAL, 18 December 1869; and Appendix, p. 192.

superintendence of the household supplies of tea, sugar, and wine; her stories about fairyland. From Caroline, who got it from her mother who was present, we also have the account of Jane Austen's final illness and death. Anna's memories reached back further, to Steventon days, and they are touchingly quirky. For her, aunts come in pairs, mysteriously distinguishable only by a forgotten detail of their bonnets, which otherwise were perfectly alike as to 'colour, shape & material'. Anna, sent to Steventon at the age of two to be comforted after her mother's death, remembers things that relate to her—the fuss made over her likely memory of hearing an early version of *Pride and Prejudice* read aloud, and in later years the co-operative storytelling that so exasperated Aunt Cassandra. Anna's recollections are the more persuasive and haunting for being voiced—her memory of Grandpapa enquiring 'Where are the Girls? Are the Girls gone out?' (p. 157) is the freshest, most startling, and most authentic detail the family biographies have to offer.

In contrast are Henry Austen's two formal notices of his sister from 1818 and 1833. 'Short and easy will be the task of the mere biographer', an opening remark from his 1818 'Biographical Notice', strikes the reader rather differently now. Himself recently refashioned as a clergyman of the Church of England, Henry first suggested that Jane Austen's religion be considered as relevant—a conventional gesture on his part, perhaps, but it has had far-reaching critical consequences. Here and in his later piece Henry gives the briefest details of a writer's life, habits of composition, and literary debts, and he sets the hagiographic tone for his nephew. But it was thanks to Henry's airy reference to the deathbed verses, 'replete with fancy and vigour' (p. 138), that his primmer Victorian relatives found themselves defending Aunt Jane from the potential charge of unseemly frivolity. It is also in Henry's two accounts that the long-running myth begins of effortless artistic originality, the morally irreproachable spinster who, entirely unconsciously, produced exquisitely finished novels ('Every thing came finished from her pen . . .' (p. 141)). His second account is the more considered—he removes all mention of those deathbed verses—and it is less narrowly grounded in family recollection. His purpose is far removed from that served by Anna and Caroline's whimsical conjuring of childhood memories. Now he supplements biography with professional critical assessment, incorporating passages from contemporary reviews. The larger motive for Henry's two notices, as it is for Austen-Leigh's *Memoir*, is our conventional assumption that books need authors. His first notice, written within months of Jane Austen's death, prefaces the posthumously published *Northanger Abbey* and *Persuasion*. Up to this point the novels had been published anonymously, or, more accurately, they had followed one another as an accumulating set of textual alliances—for example, *Mansfield Park: A Novel. By the Author of Sense and Sensibility and Pride and Prejudice*. In writing and reading the biographies of writers we may be tempted to work back from the writings to the subject and to find in the fiction the coherence that eludes 'real' experience. But another of the questions literary biography sets out to examine, if not to answer, is why books need authors. Why do the self-governing, independent states of fiction require to be referred back to a figure who fashioned them? Henry Austen's biographical notices cannot answer the question but, standing at the beginning of the Jane Austen life project, they help us to formulate it.

NOTE ON THE TEXTS

The text printed here of James Edward Austen-Leigh's *A Memoir of Jane Austen* is that of the second edition of 1871, but with significant omissions. Issuing it less than a year after the first edition, Austen-Leigh expanded the second edition in several ways, incorporating in the main body of his text further correspondence, family papers, and biographical recollections, much of it material which had only lately come to light. He also printed for the first time, and as a sequence of appendices to the biography, important fragments of unfinished or early drafts of his aunt Jane Austen's works. Those expansions which form part of the body of the text of the second edition (described in the preface as a 'narrative . . . somewhat enlarged', 'a few more letters', and 'a short specimen of her childish stories') are retained here. But the appended Chapter 12, consisting of the cancelled chapter of *Persuasion*, and Chapter 13, extracts from and a synopsis of *Sanditon*, still under the title of 'The Last Work', are omitted; omitted, too, are *Lady Susan* and *The Watsons*, both also published for the first time in 1871 as an appendix to the *Memoir*. In addition, I have restored some elements which were present in the first edition of 1870 but removed from the second edition: namely, the second postscript, dated 17 November 1869, defending Jane Austen from the attack in Mary Russell Mitford's newly published *Life*, and the set of five illustrations—a portrait of Jane Austen, a facsimile of her handwriting, and family drawings of Steventon Parsonage, Steventon Manor House, and Chawton Church—an important feature of the first and of subsequent editions, but unaccountably left out of the second. The effect of these cuts and expansions is to deepen the work as memoir and family record, an impression which the publisher's calculated marketing of the second edition did something to obscure. As Austen-Leigh remarked of the new edition to his American correspondent Susan Quincy: 'It will be smaller & less expensive than the former edition, being made to range with, & to form an additional Vol. to Bentley's last Edition of the novels.'[1] In token of this, the lettering on the spine of the binding of the second edition misleadingly read *Lady Susan &c.* Marketed as the sixth volume in Richard Bentley's 'Favourite Novels' reissue of the complete set of Jane Austen's novels, the *Memoir* became in outward appearance *Lady Susan &c.*, signalling the importance placed at this time on the appended fictions over biography. With editions of these previously unpublished writings now widely available, there is little justification for following what was in 1871 a commercial strategy. On the other hand, a modern market which in one recent year alone (1997) saw three substantial biographies of Jane Austen competing for attention, suggests that Austen-Leigh's account of a life 'singularly barren' of events compels ever more interest.

I have included with Austen-Leigh's *Memoir* four others: the account written by Jane's brother Henry Austen to accompany the posthumous joint publication of *Northanger Abbey* and *Persuasion* in 1818; Henry's reworking of the same materials to preface the edition of *Sense and Sensibility* issued by Bentley in 1833 as No. 23 of his 'Standard Novels' series; Anna Lefroy's 'Recollections of Aunt Jane', written in 1864 and first published in 1988; and Caroline Austen's *My Aunt Jane Austen: A Memoir*, written in 1867 and first published in 1952. Henry's two biographies are printed from the first editions of 1818 and 1833 respectively. Anna Lefroy's 'Recollections' are taken from the surviving autograph manuscript in the Austen-Leigh archive, Hampshire Record Office, and Caroline Austen's memoir is reproduced from the 1952 edition which R. W. Chapman prepared for the Jane Austen Society, corrected against the manuscript held in Jane Austen's House, Chawton. Further editorial and bibliographical information can be found in the headnotes accompanying the annotations to each text. An Appendix prints a few brief recollections, mainly from family letters preserved as

[1] From a letter of 28 Nov. 1870, included in M. A. DeWolfe Howe, 'A Jane Austen Letter With Other "Janeana" From an Old Book of Autographs', *Yale Review*, 15 (1925–6), 333.

autograph manuscripts or later typescripts. All are accounts, drawn up late in life, by members of Jane Austen's family or close connections who knew her personally. In their various ways, these further recollections represent the decomposition or pre-texts of the *Memoir*.

In the *Memoir* Austen-Leigh's footnotes appear at the foot of the page. A degree sign (°) indicates an editorial note at the back of the book. The only silent editorial change made to the texts of the shorter recollections and Appendix has been to replace double quotation-marks with single throughout, to accord with the practice adopted in the 1871 edition of the *Memoir*.

SELECT BIBLIOGRAPHY

Reference and Background

Austen, Jane, *Jane Austen's Letters*, ed. Deirdre Le Faye (3rd edn., Oxford: Oxford University Press, 1995), a revised and expanded edition of R. W. Chapman, *Jane Austen's Letters* (1932; 2nd edn., 1952).

Gilson, David, *A Bibliography of Jane Austen* (Oxford, 1982; rev. edn., Winchester, Hants: St Paul's Bibliographies, 1997).

Grey, J. David, Litz, A. Walton, and Southam, Brian (eds.), *The Jane Austen Companion* (New York, 1986); published in the UK as *The Jane Austen Handbook* (London: Athlone Press, 1986).

Littlewood, Ian (ed.), *Jane Austen: Critical Assessments* (4 vols., Mountfield: Helm Information Ltd., 1998).

Modert, Jo, *Jane Austen's Manuscript Letters in Facsimile* (Carbondale and Edwardsville, Ill.: Southern Illinois University Press, 1990).

Poplawski, Paul, *A Jane Austen Encyclopedia* (Westport, Conn.: Greenwood Press, 1998).

Roth, Barry, and Weinsheimer, Joel, *An Annotated Bibliography of Jane Austen Studies, 1952–72* (Charlottesville, Va.: University Press of Virginia, 1973).

—— *An Annotated Bibliography of Jane Austen Studies, 1973–83* (Charlottesville, Va.: University of Virginia Press, 1985).

—— *An Annotated Bibliography of Jane Austen Studies, 1984–1994* (Athens: Ohio University Press, 1996).

Southam, B. C., *Jane Austen's Literary Manuscripts: A Study of the Novelist's Development through the Surviving Papers* (1964; new edn., London: Athlone Press, 2001).

—— (ed.), *Jane Austen: The Critical Heritage* (2 vols., London: Routledge and Kegan Paul): vol. 1, *1811–70* (1968); vol. 2, *1870–1938* (1987).

Jane Austen: Family History (5 vols., London: Routledge/Thoemmes Press, 1995). The collection reprints, with new introductions by David Gilson, several of the standard reference and background works.

'Jane Austen Studies', listed regularly in the *Jane Austen Society Reports* (the journal of the Jane Austen Society, Chawton, Hants), provides an annual update on the main bibliography.

Jane Austen Society Reports (1949–) and *Persuasions* (1979–) (the journal of the Jane Austen Society of North America, JASNA) regularly include articles of biographical interest on Jane Austen and members of her family.

Persuasions On-Line has from vol. 22 (Winter 2001) updated bibliographies (http://www.jasna.org/index.html).

A Memoir of Jane Austen

James Edward Austen-Leigh, *A Memoir of Jane Austen* (London: Richard Bentley, 1870).

—— *A Memoir of Jane Austen, to which is added Lady Susan and fragments of two other unfinished tales by Miss Austen* (2nd edn., London: Richard Bentley, 1871).

—— *Memoir of Jane Austen*, ed. R. W. Chapman (Oxford: Clarendon Press, 1926): mainly a reprint of Ed.2, but omitting *Lady Susan* and *The Watsons*.

—— *A Memoir of Jane Austen*, included as an appendix to *Persuasion*, ed. D. W. Harding (Harmondsworth: Penguin Books, 1965).

—— *A Memoir of Jane Austen*, with an introduction by Fay Weldon (reprint of R. W. Chapman's 1926 edn.; London: Century Hutchinson, 1987; and Folio Society, 1989).

—— *A Memoir of Jane Austen*, with an introduction by David Gilson (facsimile reprint of 1870 edn.; London: Routledge/Thoemmes Press, 1994).

Contemporary Reviews of J. E. Austen-Leigh's Memoir, *Ed.1*

[Margaret O. Oliphant], *Blackwood's Edinburgh Magazine*, 107 (1870), 290–313 (reviewed with A. G. L'Estrange's *Life of Mary Russell Mitford*).

[Richard Simpson], *North British Review*, 52 (1870), 129–52.

[Henry F. Chorley], *Quarterly Review*, 128 (1870), 196–218 (with L'Estrange's *Life of Mitford*).

Contemporary Reviews of Ed.2

[Anna Isabella Thackeray], *Cornhill Magazine*, 24 (1871), 158–74.

Extracts from several of the above reviews can be found in Southam (ed.), *Jane Austen: The Critical Heritage*, vol. 1 (1968).

See, too:

Austen-Leigh, Mary Augusta, *James Edward Austen-Leigh, A Memoir* (privately published, 1911).

Other Family Biographies

Austen, Caroline, *Reminiscences of Caroline Austen*, ed. Deirdre Le Faye (written 1870s; Alton, Hants: Jane Austen Society, 1986).

Austen-Leigh, Mary Augusta, *Personal Aspects of Jane Austen* (London: John Murray, 1920).

Austen-Leigh, William, and Austen-Leigh, Richard Arthur, *Jane Austen: Her Life and Letters. A Family Record* (London: Smith, Elder, and Co., 1913).

Austen-Leigh, Richard Arthur (ed.), *Austen Papers 1704–1856* (privately printed; London: Spottiswoode, Ballantyne, and Co., 1942).

Brabourne, Lord (Edward Knatchbull-Hugesson), *The Letters of Jane Austen* (2 vols., London: Richard Bentley and Son, 1884).

Hubback, J. H., and Edith C., *Jane Austen's Sailor Brothers: Being the Adventures of Sir Frances Austen, G.C.B., Admiral of the Fleet, and Rear-Admiral Charles Austen* (London: John Lane, 1906).

Knatchbull, Lady, 'Aunt Jane', *Cornhill Magazine*, 163 (1947), 72–3.

Knight, Fanny, *Fanny Knight's Diaries: Jane Austen Through Her Niece's Eyes*, ed. Deirdre Le Faye (Alton: Jane Austen Society, 2000).

Lefroy, F. C., 'Is It Just?' and 'A Bundle of Letters', *Temple Bar*, 67 (1883), 270–84 and 285-8.

Non-Family Biographies

Caplan, Clive, 'Jane Austen's Banker Brother: Henry Thomas Austen of Austen & Co., 1801–1816', *Persuasions*, 20 (1998), 69–90.

Chapman, R. W., *Jane Austen: Facts and Problems* (Oxford: Clarendon Press, 1948; repr. 1961, 1963, 1970).

Fergus, Jan, *Jane Austen: A Literary Life* (Basingstoke and London: Macmillan, 1991).

Hill, Constance, *Jane Austen: Her Homes and Her Friends* (1902; London: John Lane, 1904).

Hodge, Jane Aiken, *The Double Life of Jane Austen* (London: Hodder and Stoughton, 1972).

Honan, Park, *Jane Austen: Her Life* (London: Weidenfeld and Nicolson, 1987).

Jenkins, Elizabeth, *Jane Austen: A Biography* (London: Gollancz, 1938; rev. edn., 1948).

Le Faye, Deirdre, 'Jane Austen and her Hancock Relatives', *Review of English Studies*, NS 30 (1979), 12–27.

—— *Jane Austen. A Family Record* (London: British Library, 1989), a revised and enlarged edition of W. and R. A. Austen-Leigh's *Life and Letters* (1913).

Nokes, David, *Jane Austen: A Life* (London: Fourth Estate, 1997).

Shields, Carol, *Jane Austen* (London: Weidenfeld and Nicolson, 2001).

Tomalin, Claire, *Jane Austen: A Life* (London: Viking, 1997).

Tucker, George Holbert, *A History of Jane Austen's Family* (Stroud, Glos.: Sutton, 1998), previously published as *A Goodly Heritage: A History of Jane Austen's Family* (Manchester: Carcanet New Press, 1983).

Criticism

Corley, T. A. B., 'The Earliest Non-Family Life of Jane Austen', *Notes and Queries*, 45 (1998), 187–8.

Kaplan, Deborah, *Jane Austen Among Women* (Baltimore and London: Johns Hopkins University Press, 1992).

Kirkham, Margaret, 'The Austen Portraits and the Received Biography', in Janet Todd (ed.), *Jane Austen: New Perspectives* (New York: Holmes and Meier Publishers Inc., 1983).

Le Faye, Deirdre, '*Sanditon*: Jane Austen's Manuscript and her Niece's Continuation', *Review of English Studies*, NS 38 (1987), 56–61.

Lynch, Deidre, 'At Home with Jane Austen', in Deidre Lynch and William B. Warner (eds.), *Cultural Institutions of the Novel* (Durham and London: Duke University Press, 1996).

—— (ed.), *Janeites: Austen's Disciples and Devotees* (Princeton: Princeton University Press, 2000).

Marshall, Mary Gaither (ed.), *Jane Austen's Sanditon: A Continuation by her Niece; together with 'Reminiscences of Aunt Jane' by Anna Lefroy* (Chicago: Chiron Press, 1983).

McAleer, John, 'What a Biographer Can Learn about Jane Austen from Her Juvenilia', in J. David Grey (ed.), *Jane Austen's*

Beginnings: The Juvenilia and Lady Susan (Ann Arbor, Mich., and London: UMI Research Press, 1989).

Mcdonald, Irene B., 'Contemporary Biography: Some Problems', *Persuasions*, 20 (1998), 61–8.

Oliphant, M. O. W., 'The Ethics of Biography', *Contemporary Review*, 44 (1883), 76–93.

Sabor, Peter, 'James Edward Austen, Anna Lefroy, and the Interpolations to Jane Austen's "Volume the Third"', *Notes and Queries*, 245 (2000), 304–6.

Townsend Warner, Sylvia, *Jane Austen*, British Council, Writers and their Work, No. 17 (Harlow, Essex: Longman, 1951; rev. 1957 and 1964).

Wiltshire, John, *Recreating Jane Austen* (Cambridge: Cambridge University Press, 2001).

Woolf, Virginia, 'Jane Austen', in *The Common Reader*, First Series (London: Hogarth Press, 1925), based on Woolf's earlier review, 'Jane Austen at Sixty', in *The Nation and Athenaeum*, 15 Dec. 1923.

Further Reading in Oxford World's Classics

Austen, Jane, *Catharine and Other Writings*, ed. Margaret Anne Doody and Douglas Murray.

—— *Emma*, ed. James Kinsley.

—— *Mansfield Park*, ed. James Kinsley

—— *Northanger Abbey, Lady Susan, The Watsons, and Sanditon*, ed. John Davie

—— *Persuasion*, ed. John Davie.

—— *Pride and Prejudice*, ed. James Kinsley.

—— *Sense and Sensibility*, ed. James Kinsley.

Beeton, Isabella, *Mrs Beeton's Book of Household Management*, ed. Nicola Humble.

Burney, Fanny, *Camilla*, ed. Edward A. Bloom and Lillian D. Bloom.

—— *Cecilia*, ed. Peter Sabor and Margaret Anne Doody.

—— *Evelina*, ed. Edward A. Bloom.

Edgeworth, Maria, *The Absentee*, ed. W. J. McCormack and Kim Walker.

—— *Belinda*, ed. Kathryn Kirkpatrick.

—— *Castle Rackrent*, ed. George Watson.

Ferrier, Susan, *Marriage*, ed. Herbert Foltinek and Kathryn Kirkpatrick.

Gaskell, Elizabeth, *The Life of Charlotte Brontë*, ed. Angus Easson.
Opie, Amelia, *Adeline Mowbray*, ed. Shelley King and John B. Pierce.
Scott, Sir Walter, *The Antiquary*, ed. Nicola Watson.
—— *Waverley*, ed. Claire Lamont.
Staël, Mme de, *Corinne*, trans. and ed. Sylvia Raphael.

A CHRONOLOGY OF THE AUSTEN FAMILY

1764 26 April, Marriage of the Revd George Austen and Cassandra Leigh.

1765 13 February, James Austen, JEAL's father and JA's eldest brother, born at **Deane**.

1766 26 August, George Austen the younger born at Deane.

1767 7 October, Edward Austen born at Deane.

1768 July/August, Austen family move to **Steventon**.

1771 8 June, Henry Austen born at Steventon.

1773 9 January, Cassandra Austen born at Steventon; 23 March, the Revd Austen becomes Rector of Deane as well as Steventon; Pupils are boarded at Steventon from now until 1796.

1774 23 April, Francis (Frank) Austen born at Steventon.

1775 16 December, JA born at Steventon.

1779 23 June, Charles Austen born at Steventon.

1781 Marriage of JA's cousin, Eliza Hancock, to Jean-François Capot de Feuillide, in France.

1783 Edward Austen adopted by Mr and Mrs Thomas Knight of Godmersham, Kent.

1785–6 JA and Cassandra attend the Abbey School, Reading.

1786 Eliza de Feuillide's son Hastings born.

1787 JA begins writing juvenilia.

1787–9 Amateur theatricals are performed at Steventon.

1789 Spring, the Lloyd family rent Deane parsonage.

1791 27 December, marriage of Edward Austen and Elizabeth Bridges.

1792 The Lloyds leave Deane for Ibthorpe; marriage of James Austen and Anne Mathew and their removal to Deane parsonage; (?) Winter, Cassandra engaged to the Revd Tom Fowle.

1793 23 January, Edward Austen's first child, Fanny, born; 15 April, James Austen's first child, Anna, born; 3 June, JA writes last item of juvenilia.

1794 M. de Feuillide guillotined in Paris; death of Edward Austen's adopted father Thomas Knight.

1795 JA probably writes 'Elinor and Marianne'; death of Anne Mathew Austen at Deane; Anna sent to live at Steventon; December, Tom Lefroy visits Ashe rectory.

1796 January, Tom Lefroy leaves Ashe for London; Tom Fowle sails for West Indies; October, JA begins 'First Impressions' (finished August 1797).

1797 Marriage of James Austen and Mary Lloyd; Anna returns to live at Deane; February, Tom Fowle dies of fever at San Domingo; 1 November, the Revd Austen unsuccessfully offers 'First Impressions' to Cadell; JA begins *Sense and Sensibility*; 31 December, marriage of Henry Austen and his cousin Eliza de Feuillide.

1798 JA begins writing 'Susan' (*Northanger Abbey*); 17 November, James's son James Edward (JEAL), JA's future biographer, is born at Deane.

1799 Mrs Leigh Perrot, JA's aunt, charged with theft and committed to Ilchester Gaol.

1800 Mrs Leigh Perrot tried at Taunton and acquitted; December, the Revd Austen decides to retire and move to Bath.

1801 Henry Austen sets up as banker and army agent in London; May, the Austens leave Steventon and settle in **Bath**; the family story of JA's seaside romance derives from holidays spent in the West Country between now and autumn 1804; Eliza de Feuillide Austen's son Hastings dies.

1802 2 December, Harris Bigg-Wither proposes to JA; JA revises 'Susan' (*Northanger Abbey*).

1803 JA sells 'Susan' to Crosby and Co.

1804–5 JA perhaps writing 'The Watsons' and 'Lady Susan'; 16 December 1804, JA's early friend Mrs Lefroy of Ashe killed in a riding accident.

1805 21 January, death of the Revd Austen in Bath; 16 April, death of Mrs Lloyd at Ibthorpe; Martha Lloyd joins the Austen household; 18 June, James Austen's youngest child Caroline born at Steventon.

1806 October, the Austens take lodgings in **Southampton** with Frank Austen and his new wife.

1807 March, the Austens move into house in Castle Square, Southampton.

1808 10 October, death of Edward Austen's wife, Elizabeth.

1809 5 April, JA attempts unsuccessfully to secure publication of 'Susan'; the Austens move to **Chawton Cottage**, owned by JA's brother Edward.

1810 *Sense and Sensibility* accepted for publication by Thomas Egerton.

1811 February, JA planning *Mansfield Park*; March, JA staying with Henry in London and correcting proofs of *Sense and Sensibility*; 30 October, *Sense and Sensibility* published; ?Winter, JA begins revising 'First Impressions' as *Pride and Prejudice*.

1812 Death of Mrs Thomas Knight; Edward Austen officially takes name of Knight; Autumn, JA sells copyright of *Pride and Prejudice* to Egerton.

1813 28 January, *Pride and Prejudice* published; 25 April, Eliza de Feuillide Austen dies; ?July, JA finishes *Mansfield Park*; Anna Austen engaged to Ben Lefroy; November, second editions of *Pride and Prejudice* and *Sense and Sensibility*.

1814 21 January, JA begins *Emma*; 9 May, *Mansfield Park* published by Egerton; 8 November, marriage of Anna Austen and Ben Lefroy.

1815 29 March, *Emma* finished; July, Mary Lloyd Austen and Caroline Austen stay at Chawton; 8 August, JA begins *Persuasion*; Anna and Ben Lefroy move to Wyards, near Chawton; October, JA in London nursing Henry who is ill; 13 November, JA visits the Prince Regent's Library at Carlton House; December, *Emma* published by John Murray.

1816 Spring, JA begins to feel unwell; Henry buys back MS of 'Susan', which JA revises (as 'Catharine') and intends to offer again for publication; 15 March, Henry's bank fails and he leaves London; 18 July, first draft of *Persuasion* finished; 6 August, *Persuasion* finally completed; second edition of *Mansfield Park* from Murray; December, Henry ordained and becomes curate of Chawton.

1817 27 January–18 March, JA at work on 'Sanditon'; 28 March, death of Mr Leigh Perrot, JA's uncle; 27 April, JA makes her will; 24 May, Cassandra takes JA to Winchester, where they lodge at 8 College Street; 18 July, JA dies in early morning; 24 July, JA buried in Winchester Cathedral; December, *Northanger Abbey* and *Persuasion* published together by Murray (dated 1818), with Henry's 'Biographical Notice of the Author'.

1819 James Austen, JA's eldest brother and father of Anna Lefroy, JEAL, and Caroline Austen, dies.

1820 Fanny Knight, eldest child of Edward Austen Knight of Godmersham, marries Sir Edward Knatchbull.

1827 Mrs Austen, JA's mother, dies.

1828 Frank Austen marries as his second wife Martha Lloyd.

1832–3 *Elizabeth Bennet; or, Pride and Prejudice*, and the other novels, published in America (Philadelphia).

1833 Bentley's collected edition of JA's novels (frequently reprinted until 1882, the Steventon Edition); Henry's revised 'Memoir' prefixed to *Sense and Sensibility* (1833).

1837 The Revd James Edward Austen takes name of Leigh.

1843 Mrs James Austen (Mary Lloyd) dies; Lady (Francis) Austen (Martha Lloyd) dies; 9 May, Cassandra Austen executes her will.

1845 22 March, Cassandra Austen dies and JA's manuscripts and letters are divided among the family.

1850 Henry Austen dies.

1852 Admiral Sir Francis Austen sends a letter of JA's to Eliza Susan Quincy of Boston, Mass.; Edward Austen Knight dies; Charles Austen dies.

1864 Anna Lefroy writes down her 'Recollections of Aunt Jane'.

1865 Sir Francis Austen dies, the last of JA's remaining siblings; *Recollections of the Vine Hunt* by JEAL.

1867 Caroline Austen writes *My Aunt Jane Austen: A Memoir* (1952).

1870 *Memoir* of JA by her nephew JEAL.

1871 Second edition of JEAL's *Memoir*, with 'Lady Susan', 'The Watsons', and the cancelled chapter of *Persuasion*.

1872 Brass Memorial Tablet placed in Winchester Cathedral by JEAL, from the proceeds of the *Memoir*.

1884 *Letters of Jane Austen*, edited by her great-nephew Lord Brabourne.

1906 *Jane Austen's Sailor Brothers*, by J. H. and E. C. Hubback, JA's great-nephew and great-great niece; first publication of her letters to Frank Austen.

1913 *Life and Letters of Jane Austen*, by W. and R. A. Austen-Leigh, JA's great-nephew and great-great nephew.

1920 *Personal Aspects of Jane Austen*, by Mary Augusta Austen-Leigh, JA's great-niece.

1940 The Jane Austen Society is founded.

1947 Chawton Cottage, JA's last home, is purchased by the Jane Austen Memorial Trust.

James Edward Austen-Leigh, a portrait added as a frontispiece to the *Memoir*, ed. R. W. Chapman (1926)

JAMES EDWARD AUSTEN-LEIGH

A MEMOIR OF JANE AUSTEN

(1871)

Jane Austen, steel-engraved portrait by Lizars from a likeness drawn by Mr Andrews of Maidenhead (after Cassandra Austen's watercolour sketch now in the National Portrait Gallery, London), used as a frontispiece to the first edition of the *Memoir* (1870)

PREFACE

THE Memoir of my Aunt, Jane Austen, has been received with more favour than I had ventured to expect. The notices taken of it in the periodical press, as well as letters addressed to me by many with whom I am not personally acquainted, show that an unabated interest is still taken in every particular that can be told about her. I am thus encouraged not only to offer a Second Edition of the Memoir, but also to enlarge it with some additional matter which I might have scrupled to intrude on the public if they had not thus seemed to call for it. In the present Edition, the narrative is somewhat enlarged, and a few more letters are added; with a short specimen of her childish stories. The cancelled chapter of 'Persuasion' is given, in compliance with wishes both publicly and privately expressed. A fragment of a story entitled 'The Watsons' is printed; and extracts are given from a novel which she had begun a few months before her death; but the chief addition is a short tale never before published, called 'Lady Susan.'° I regret that the little which I have been able to add could not appear in my First Edition; as much of it was either unknown to me, or not at my command, when I first published; and I hope that I may claim some indulgent allowance for the difficulty of recovering little facts and feelings which had been merged half a century deep in oblivion.

NOVEMBER 17, 1870.

CONTENTS

He knew of no one but himself who was inclined to the work. This is no uncommon motive. A man sees something to be done, knows of no one who will do it but himself, and so is driven to the enterprise.

HELPS' *Life of Columbus*, ch. i°

CHAPTER I

Introductory Remarks—Birth of Jane Austen—Her Family Connections—Their Influence on her Writings

MORE than half a century has passed away since I, the youngest of the mourners,[1] attended the funeral of my dear aunt Jane in Winchester Cathedral; and now, in my old age, I am asked whether my memory will serve to rescue from oblivion any events of her life or any traits of her character to satisfy the enquiries of a generation of readers who have been born since she died. Of events her life was singularly barren: few changes and no great crisis ever broke the smooth current of its course. Even her fame may be said to have been posthumous: it did not attain to any vigorous life till she had ceased to exist. Her talents did not introduce her to the notice of other writers, or connect her with the literary world, or in any degree pierce through the obscurity of her domestic retirement. I have therefore scarcely any materials for a detailed life of my aunt; but I have a distinct recollection of her person and character; and perhaps many may take an interest in a delineation, if any such can be drawn, of that prolific mind whence sprung the Dashwoods and Bennets, the Bertrams and Woodhouses, the Thorpes and Musgroves,° who have been admitted as familiar guests to the firesides of so many families, and are known there as individually and intimately as if they were living neighbours. Many may care to know whether the moral rectitude, the correct taste, and the warm affections with which she invested her ideal characters, were really existing in the native source whence those ideas flowed, and were actually exhibited by her in the various relations of life. I can indeed bear witness that there was scarcely a charm

[1] I went to represent my father, who was too unwell to attend himself, and thus I was the only one of my generation present. [JEAL's father was JA's eldest brother James, who although at his sister's bedside the day before she died was too ill to attend the funeral. He died on 13 December 1819.]

in her most delightful characters that was not a true reflection of her own sweet temper and loving heart. I was young when we lost her; but the impressions made on the young are deep, and though in the course of fifty years I have forgotten much, I have not forgotten that 'Aunt Jane' was the delight of all her nephews and nieces. We did not think of her as being clever, still less as being famous; but we valued her as one always kind, sympathising, and amusing. To all this I am a living witness, but whether I can sketch out such a faint outline of this excellence as shall be perceptible to others may be reasonably doubted. Aided, however, by a few survivors[1] who knew her, I will not refuse to make the attempt. I am the more inclined to undertake the task from a conviction that, however little I may have to tell, no one else is left who could tell so much of her.

Jane Austen was born on December 16, 1775, at the Parsonage House of Steventon in Hampshire. Her father, the Rev. George Austen, was of a family long established in the neighbourhood of Tenterden and Sevenoaks in Kent. I believe that early in the seventeenth century they were clothiers. Hasted, in his history of Kent,° says: 'The clothing business was exercised by persons who possessed most of the landed property in the Weald, insomuch that almost all the ancient families of these parts, now of large estates and genteel rank in life, and some of them ennobled by titles, are sprung from ancestors who have used this great staple manufacture, now almost unknown here.' In his list of these families Hasted places the Austens, and he adds that these clothiers 'were usually called the Gray Coats of Kent; and were a body so numerous and united that at county elections whoever had their vote and interest was almost certain of being elected.' The family still retains a badge of this origin; for their livery is of that

[1] My chief assistants have been my sisters, Mrs. B. Lefroy and Miss Austen, whose recollections of our aunt are, on some points, more vivid than my own. I have not only been indebted to their memory for facts, but have sometimes used their words. Indeed some passages towards the end of the work were entirely written by the latter.

I have also to thank some of my cousins, and especially the daughters of Admiral Charles Austen, for the use of letters and papers which had passed into their hands, without which this Memoir, scanty as it is, could not have been written.

[For the evolution of the *Memoir* and the assistance provided by JEAL's sisters and cousins, see Introduction.]

peculiar mixture of light blue and white called Kentish gray, which forms the facings of the Kentish militia.

Mr. George Austen° had lost both his parents before he was nine years old. He inherited no property from them; but was happy in having a kind uncle, Mr. Francis Austen, a successful lawyer at Tunbridge, the ancestor of the Austens of Kippington, who, though he had children of his own, yet made liberal provision for his orphan nephew. The boy received a good education at Tunbridge School, whence he obtained a scholarship, and subsequently a fellowship, at St. John's College, Oxford. In 1764 he came into possession of the two adjoining Rectories of Deane and Steventon in Hampshire; the former purchased for him by his generous uncle Francis, the latter given by his cousin Mr. Knight. This was no very gross case of plurality, according to the ideas of that time, for the two villages were little more than a mile apart, and their united populations scarcely amounted to three hundred. In the same year he married Cassandra,° youngest daughter of the Rev. Thomas Leigh, of the family of Leighs of Warwickshire, who, having been a fellow of All Souls, held the College living of Harpsden, near Henley-upon-Thames. Mr. Thomas Leigh was a younger brother of Dr. Theophilus Leigh, a personage well known at Oxford in his day, and his day was not a short one, for he lived to be ninety, and held the Mastership of Balliol College for above half a century. He was a man more famous for his sayings than his doings, overflowing with puns and witticisms and sharp retorts; but his most serious joke was his practical one of living much longer than had been expected or intended. He was a fellow of Corpus, and the story is that the Balliol men, unable to agree in electing one of their own number to the Mastership, chose him, partly under the idea that he was in weak health and likely soon to cause another vacancy. It was afterwards said that his long incumbency had been a judgement on the Society for having elected an *Out-College Man*.[1] I imagine that the

[1] There seems to have been some doubt as to the validity of this election; for Hearne says that it was referred to the Visitor, who confirmed it. (Hearne's *Diaries*, v. 2.) [The incident is recorded in *Reliquiae Hernianae, The Remains* of *Thomas Hearne, MA* (2nd edn., 3 vols., 1869), ii. 308–9.]

front of Balliol towards Broad Street which has recently been pulled down must have been built, or at least restored, while he was Master, for the Leigh arms were placed under the cornice at the corner nearest to Trinity gates. The beautiful building lately erected has destroyed this record, and thus 'monuments themselves memorials need.'°

His fame for witty and agreeable conversation extended beyond the bounds of the University. Mrs. Thrale, in a letter to Dr. Johnson, writes thus: 'Are you acquainted with Dr. Leigh,[1] the Master of Balliol College, and are you not delighted with his gaiety of manners and youthful vivacity, now that he is eighty-six years of age? I never heard a more perfect or excellent pun than his, when some one told him how, in a late dispute among the Privy Councillors, the Lord Chancellor struck the table with such violence that he split it. "No, no, no," replied the Master; "I can hardly persuade myself that he *split* the *table*, though I believe he *divided* the *Board*."'°

Some of his sayings of course survive in family tradition. He was once calling on a gentleman notorious for never opening a book, who took him into a room overlooking the Bath Road, which was then a great thoroughfare for travellers of every class, saying rather pompously, 'This, Doctor, I call my study.' The Doctor, glancing his eye round the room, in which no books were to be seen, replied, 'And very well named too, sir, for you know Pope tells us, "The proper *study* of mankind is *Man*."'° When my father went to Oxford he was honoured with an invitation to dine with this dignified cousin. Being a raw undergraduate, unaccustomed to the habits of the University, he was about to take off his gown, as if it were a great coat, when the old man, then considerably turned eighty, said, with a grim smile, 'Young man, you need not strip: we are not going to fight.' This humour remained in him so strongly to the last that he might almost have supplied Pope with another instance of 'the ruling passion strong in death,'° for only three days before he expired, being told that an old acquaintance was lately married, having recovered from a

[1] Mrs. Thrale writes Dr. *Lee*, but there can be no doubt of the identity of person.

long illness by eating eggs, and that the wits said that he had been egged on to matrimony, he immediately trumped the joke, saying, 'Then may the yoke sit easy on him.' I do not know from what common ancestor the Master of Balliol and his great-niece Jane Austen, with some others of the family, may have derived the keen sense of humour which they certainly possessed.

Mr. and Mrs. George Austen resided first at Deane, but removed in 1771 to Steventon,° which was their residence for about thirty years. They commenced their married life with the charge of a little child, a son of the celebrated Warren Hastings,° who had been committed to the care of Mr. Austen before his marriage, probably through the influence of his sister, Mrs. Hancock, whose husband at that time held some office under Hastings in India. Mr. Gleig, in his 'Life of Hastings,' says that his son George, the offspring of his first marriage, was sent to England in 1761 for his education, but that he had never been able to ascertain to whom this precious charge was entrusted, nor what became of him. I am able to state, from family tradition, that he died young, of what was then called putrid sore throat; and that Mrs. Austen had become so much attached to him that she always declared that his death had been as great a grief to her as if he had been a child of her own.

About this time, the grandfather of Mary Russell Mitford,° Dr. Russell, was Rector of the adjoining parish of Ashe; so that the parents of two popular female writers must have been intimately acquainted with each other.

As my subject carries me back about a hundred years, it will afford occasions for observing many changes gradually effected in the manners and habits of society, which I may think it worth while to mention. They may be little things, but time gives a certain importance even to trifles, as it imparts a peculiar flavour to wine. The most ordinary articles of domestic life are looked on with some interest, if they are brought to light after being long buried; and we feel a natural curiosity to know what was done and said by our forefathers, even though it may be nothing wiser or better than what we are daily doing or saying ourselves. Some of this generation may be little aware how many conveniences, now considered to be necessaries and matters of course, were unknown to their grandfathers and grandmothers. The lane between Deane and Steventon has long been as smooth as the best turnpike road; but when the family removed from the one residence to the other in 1771, it was a mere cart track, so cut up by deep ruts as to be impassable for a light carriage. Mrs. Austen, who was not then in strong health,° performed the short journey on a feather-bed, placed upon some soft articles of furniture in the waggon which held their household goods. In those days it was not unusual to set men to work with shovel and pickaxe to fill up ruts and holes in roads seldom used by carriages, on such special occasions as a funeral or a wedding. Ignorance and coarseness of language also were still lingering even upon higher levels of society than might have been expected to retain such mists. About this time, a neighbouring squire, a man of many acres, referred the following difficulty to Mr. Austen's decision: 'You know all about these sort of things. Do tell us. Is Paris in France, or France in Paris? for my wife has been disputing with me about it.' The same gentleman, narrating some conversation which he had heard between the rector and his wife, represented the latter as beginning her reply to her husband with a round oath; and when his daughter called him to task, reminding him that Mrs. Austen never swore, he replied, 'Now, Betty, why do you pull me up for nothing? that's neither here nor there; you know very well that's only *my way of telling the story*.'° Attention has lately been called by a celebrated writer to the inferiority of the clergy to the laity of England two centuries ago. The charge no doubt is true, if the rural clergy are to be compared with that higher section of country gentlemen who went into parliament, and mixed in London society, and took the lead in their several counties; but it might be found less true if they were to be compared, as in all fairness they ought to be, with that lower section with whom they usually associated. The smaller landed proprietors, who seldom went farther from home than their county town, from the squire with his thousand acres to the yeoman who cultivated his hereditary property of one or two hundred, then formed a numerous class—each the aristocrat of his own parish; and there was probably a greater difference in manners and refinement between this class and that immediately above them than could now be found between any two persons who rank as gentlemen. For in the progress of civilisation, though all orders may make some progress, yet it is most perceptible in the lower. It is a process of 'levelling up;' the rear rank 'dressing up,' as it were, close to the front rank. When Hamlet mentions, as something which he had 'for *three years taken* note of,' that 'the toe of the peasant comes so near the heel of the courtier,'° it was probably intended by Shakspeare as a satire on his own times; but it expressed a principle which is working at all times in which society makes any progress. I believe that a century ago the improvement in most country parishes began with the clergy; and that in those days a rector who chanced to be a gentleman and a scholar found himself superior to his chief parishioners in information and manners, and became a sort of centre of refinement and politeness.

Mr. Austen was a remarkably good-looking man, both in his youth and his old age. During his year of office at Oxford he had been called 'the handsome Proctor;'° and at Bath, when more than seventy years old, he attracted observation by his fine features and abundance of snow-white hair. Being a good scholar he was able to prepare two of his sons for the University, and to direct the studies of his other children, whether sons or daughters, as well as to increase his income by taking pupils.

In Mrs. Austen also was to be found the germ of much of the ability which was concentrated in Jane, but of which others of her children had a share. She united strong common sense with a lively imagination, and often expressed herself, both in writing and in conversation, with epigrammatic force and point. She lived, like many of her family, to an advanced age. During the last years of her life she endured continual pain, not only patiently but with characteristic cheerfulness. She once said to me, 'Ah, my dear, you find me just where you left me—on the sofa. I sometimes think that God Almighty must have forgotten me; but I dare say He will come for me in His own good time.' She died and was buried at Chawton, January 1827, aged eighty-eight.

*

Her own family were so much, and the rest of the world so little, to Jane Austen, that some brief mention of her brothers and sister is necessary in order to give any idea of the objects which principally occupied her thoughts and filled her heart, especially as some of them, from their characters or professions in life, may be supposed to have had more or less influence on her writings: though I feel some reluctance in bringing before public notice persons and circumstances essentially private.

Her eldest brother James, my own father, had, when a very young man, at St. John's College, Oxford, been the originator and chief supporter of a periodical paper called 'The Loiterer,'° written somewhat on the plan of the 'Spectator' and its successors, but nearly confined to subjects connected with the University. In after life he used to speak very slightingly of this early work, which he had the better right to do, as, whatever may have been the degree of their merits, the best papers had certainly been written by himself. He was well read in English literature, had a correct taste, and wrote readily and happily, both in prose and verse. He was more than ten years older than Jane, and had, I believe, a large share in directing her reading and forming her taste.

Her second brother, Edward,° had been a good deal separated from the rest of the family, as he was early adopted by his cousin, Mr. Knight, of Godmersham Park in Kent and Chawton House in Hampshire; and finally came into possession both of the property and the name. But though a good deal separated in childhood, they were much together in after life, and Jane gave a large share of her affections to him and his children. Mr. Knight was not only a very amiable man, kind and indulgent to all connected with him, but possessed also a spirit of fun and liveliness, which made him especially delightful to all young people.

Her third brother, Henry, had great conversational powers, and inherited from his father an eager and sanguine disposition. He was a very entertaining companion, but had perhaps less steadiness of purpose, certainly less success in life, than his brothers.° He became a clergyman when middle-aged; and an allusion to his sermons will be found in one of Jane's letters. At one time he resided in London, and was useful in transacting his sister's business with her publishers.

Her two youngest brothers, Francis and Charles, were sailors during that glorious period of the British navy which comprises the close of the last and the beginning of the present century, when it was impossible for an officer to be almost always afloat, as these brothers were, without seeing service which, in these days, would be considered distinguished. Accordingly, they were continually engaged in actions of more or less importance, and sometimes gained promotion by their success. Both rose to the rank of Admiral, and carried out their flags to distant stations.

Francis lived to attain the very summit of his profession, having died, in his ninety-third year, G.C.B.° and Senior Admiral of the Fleet, in 1865. He possessed great firmness of character, with a strong sense of duty, whether due from himself to others, or from others to himself. He was consequently a strict disciplinarian; but, as he was a very religious man, it was remarked of him (for in those days, at least, it was remarkable) that he maintained this discipline without ever uttering an oath or permitting one in his presence. One one occasion, when ashore in a seaside town, he was spoken of as '*the* officer who kneeled at church;' a custom which now happily would not be thought peculiar.

Charles was generally serving in frigates or sloops; blockading harbours, driving the ships of the enemy ashore, boarding gunboats, and frequently making small prizes.° At one time he was absent from England on such services for seven years together. In later life he commanded the Bellerophon, at the bombardment of St. Jean d'Acre in 1840. In 1850 he went out in the Hastings, in command of the East India and China station, but on the breaking out of the Burmese war he transferred his flag to a steam sloop, for the purpose of getting up the shallow waters of the Irrawaddy, on board of which he died of cholera in 1852, in the seventy-fourth year of his age. His sweet temper and affectionate disposition, in which he resembled his sister Jane, had secured to him an unusual portion of attachment, not only from his own family, but from all the officers and common sailors who served under him. One who was with him at his death has left this record of him: 'Our good Admiral won the hearts of all by his gentleness and kindness while he was struggling with disease, and endeavouring to do his duty as Commander-in-chief of the British naval forces in these waters. His death was a great grief to the whole fleet. I know that I cried bitterly when I found he was dead.' The Order in Council of the Governor-General of India, Lord Dalhousie, expresses 'admiration of the staunch high spirit which, notwithstanding his age and previous sufferings, had led the Admiral to take his part in the trying service which has closed his career.'

These two brothers have been dwelt on longer than the others because their honourable career accounts for Jane Austen's partiality for the Navy, as well as for the readiness and accuracy with which she wrote about it. She was always very careful not to meddle with matters which she did not thoroughly understand. She never touched upon politics, law, or medicine, subjects which some novel writers have ventured on rather too boldly, and have treated, perhaps, with more brilliancy than accuracy. But with ships and sailors she felt herself at home, or at least could always trust to a brotherly critic to keep her right. I believe that no flaw has ever been found in her seamanship either in 'Mansfield Park' or in 'Persuasion.'

But dearest of all to the heart of Jane was her sister Cassandra, about three years her senior. Their sisterly affection for each other could scarcely be exceeded.° Perhaps it began on Jane's side with the feeling of deference natural to a loving child towards a kind elder sister. Something of this feeling always remained; and even in the maturity of her powers, and in the enjoyment of increasing success, she would still speak of Cassandra as of one wiser and better than herself. In childhood, when the elder was sent to the school of a Mrs. Latournelle, in the Forbury at Reading,° the younger went with her, not because she was thought old enough to profit much by the instruction there imparted, but because she would have been miserable without her sister; her mother observing that 'if Cassandra were going to have her head cut off, Jane would insist on sharing her fate.' This attachment was never interrupted or weakened. They lived in the same home, and shared the same bed-room, till separated by death. They were not exactly alike. Cassandra's was the colder and calmer disposition; she was always prudent and well judging, but with less outward demonstration of feeling and less sunniness of temper than Jane possessed. It was remarked in her family that 'Cassandra had the *merit* of having her temper always under command, but that Jane had the *happiness* of a temper that never required to be commanded.' When 'Sense and Sensibility' came out, some persons, who knew the family slightly, surmised that the two elder Miss Dashwoods were intended by the author for her sister and herself; but this could not be the case. Cassandra's character might indeed represent the '*sense*' of Elinor, but Jane's had little in common with the '*sensibility*' of Marianne. The young woman who, before the age of twenty, could so clearly discern the failings of Marianne Dashwood, could hardly have been subject to them herself.

This was the small circle, continually enlarged, however, by the increasing families of four of her brothers, within which Jane Austen found her wholesome pleasures, duties, and interests, and beyond which she went very little into society during the last ten years of her life. There was so much that was agreeable and attractive in this family party that its members may be excused if they were inclined to live somewhat too exclusively within it. They might see in each other much to love and esteem, and something to admire. The family talk had abundance of spirit and vivacity, and was never troubled by disagreements even in little matters, for it was not their habit to dispute or argue with each other: above all, there was strong family affection and firm union, never to be broken but by death. It cannot be doubted that all this had its influence on the author in the construction of her stories, in which a family party usually supplies the narrow stage, while the interest is made to revolve round a few actors.

It will be seen also that though her circle of society was small, yet she found in her neighbourhood persons of good taste and cultivated minds. Her acquaintance, in fact, constituted the very class from which she took her imaginary characters, ranging from the member of parliament, or large landed proprietor, to the young curate or younger midshipman of equally good family; and I think that the influence of these early associations may be traced in her writings, especially in two particulars. First, that she is entirely free from the vulgarity, which is so offensive in some novels, of dwelling on the outward appendages of wealth or rank, as if they were things to which the writer was unaccustomed; and, secondly, that she deals as little with very low as with very high stations in life. She does not go lower than the Miss Steeles, Mrs. Elton, and John Thorpe, people of bad taste and underbred manners, such as are actually found sometimes mingling with better society. She has nothing resembling the Brangtons, or Mr. Dubster and his friend Tom Hicks, with whom Madame D'Arblay° loved to season her stories, and to produce striking contrasts to her well bred characters.

CHAPTER II

Description of Steventon—Life at Steventon—Changes of Habits and Customs in the last Century

As the first twenty-five years, more than half of the brief life of Jane Austen, were spent in the parsonage of Steventon, some description of that place ought to be given. Steventon is a small rural village upon the chalk hills of north Hants, situated in a winding valley about seven miles from Basingstoke. The South-Western railway crosses it by a short embankment, and, as it curves round, presents a good view of it on the left hand to those who are travelling down the line, about three miles before entering the tunnel under Popham Beacon. It may be known to some sportsmen, as lying in one of the best portions of the Vine Hunt.° It is certainly not a picturesque country; it presents no grand or extensive views; but the features are small rather than plain. The surface continually swells and sinks, but the hills are not bold, nor the valleys deep; and though it is sufficiently well clothed with woods and hedgerows, yet the poverty of the soil in most places prevents the timber from attaining a large size. Still it has its beauties. The lanes wind along in a natural curve, continually fringed with irregular borders of native turf, and lead to pleasant nooks and corners. One who knew and loved it well very happily expressed its quiet charms, when he wrote

> True taste is not fastidious, nor rejects,
> Because they may not come within the rule
> Of composition pure and picturesque,
> Unnumbered simple scenes which fill the leaves
> Of Nature's sketch book.°

Of this somewhat tame country, Steventon, from the fall of the ground, and the abundance of its timber, is certainly one of the prettiest spots; yet one cannot be surprised that, when Jane's mother, a little before her marriage, was shown the scenery of her

Wood engraving of Steventon Parsonage

future home, she should have thought it unattractive, compared with the broad river, the rich valley, and the noble hills which she had been accustomed to behold at her native home near Henley-upon-Thames.

The house itself stood in a shallow valley, surrounded by sloping meadows, well sprinkled with elm trees, at the end of a small village of cottages, each well provided with a garden, scattered about prettily on either side of the road. It was sufficiently commodious to hold pupils in addition to a growing family, and was in those times considered to be above the average of parsonages; but the rooms were finished with less elegance than would now be found in the most ordinary dwellings. No cornice marked the junction of wall and ceiling; while the beams which supported the upper floors projected into the rooms below in all their naked simplicity, covered only by a coat of paint or whitewash:° accordingly it has since been considered unworthy of being the Rectory house of a family living, and about forty-five years ago it was pulled down for the purpose of erecting a new house in a far better situation on the opposite side of the valley.

North of the house, the road from Deane to Popham Lane ran at a sufficient distance from the front to allow a carriage drive, through turf and trees. On the south side the ground rose gently, and was occupied by one of those old-fashioned gardens in which vegetables and flowers are combined, flanked and protected on the east by one of the thatched mud walls common in that country, and overshadowed by fine elms. Along the upper or southern side of this garden, ran a terrace of the finest turf, which must have been in the writer's thoughts when she described Catherine Morland's childish delight in 'rolling down the green slope at the back of the house.'°

But the chief beauty of Steventon consisted in its hedgerows. A hedgerow, in that country, does not mean a thin formal line of quickset, but an irregular border of copse-wood and timber, often wide enough to contain within it a winding footpath, or a rough cart track. Under its shelter the earliest primroses, anemones, and wild hyacinths were to be found; sometimes, the first bird's-nest; and, now and then, the unwelcome adder. Two such hedgerows radiated, as it were, from the parsonage garden. One, a continuation of the turf terrace, proceeded westward, forming the southern boundary of the home meadows; and was formed into a rustic shrubbery, with occasional seats, entitled 'The Wood Walk.' The other ran straight up the hill, under the name of 'The Church Walk,' because it led to the parish church, as well as to a fine old manor-house, of Henry VIII.'s time, occupied by a family named Digweed,° who have for more than a century rented it, together with the chief farm in the parish. The church itself—I speak of it as it then was, before the improvements made by the present rector—

A little spireless fane,
Just seen above the woody lane,°

might have appeared mean and uninteresting to an ordinary observer; but the adept in church architecture would have known that it must have stood there some seven centuries, and would have found beauty in the very narrow early English windows, as well as in the general proportions of its little chancel; while its solitary position, far from the hum of the village, and within sight of no habitation, except a glimpse of the gray manor-house through its circling screen of sycamores, has in it something solemn and appropriate to the last resting-place of the silent dead. Sweet violets, both purple and white, grow in abundance beneath its south wall. One may imagine for how many centuries the ancestors of those little flowers have occupied that undisturbed, sunny nook, and may think how few living families can boast of as ancient a tenure of their land. Large elms protrude their rough branches; old hawthorns shed their annual blossoms over the graves; and the hollow yew-tree must be at least coeval with the church.

But whatever may be the beauties or defects of the surrounding scenery, this was the residence of Jane Austen for twenty-five years. This was the cradle of her genius. These were the first objects which inspired her young heart with a sense of the beauties of nature. In strolls along those wood-walks, thick-coming fancies rose in her mind, and gradually assumed the forms in

Wood engraving of Steventon Manor House

which they came forth to the world. In that simple church she brought them all into subjection to the piety which ruled her in life, and supported her in death.

The home at Steventon must have been, for many years, a pleasant and prosperous one. The family was unbroken by death, and seldom visited by sorrow. Their situation had some peculiar advantages beyond those of ordinary rectories. Steventon was a family living. Mr. Knight, the patron, was also proprietor of nearly the whole parish. He never resided there, and consequently the rector and his children came to be regarded in the neighbourhood as a kind of representatives of the family.° They shared with the principal tenant the command of an excellent manor, and enjoyed, in this reflected way, some of the consideration usually awarded to landed proprietors. They were not rich, but, aided by Mr. Austen's powers of teaching,° they had enough to afford a good education to their sons and daughters, to mix in the best society of the neighbourhood, and to exercise a liberal hospitality to their own relations and friends. A carriage and a pair of horses were kept. This might imply a higher style of living in our days than it did in theirs. There were then no assessed taxes.° The carriage, once bought, entailed little further expense; and the horses probably, like Mr. Bennet's, were often employed on farm work.° Moreover, it should be remembered that a pair of horses in those days were almost necessary, if ladies were to move about at all; for neither the condition of the roads nor the style of carriage-building admitted of any comfortable vehicle being drawn by a single horse. When one looks at the few specimens still remaining of coach-building in the last century, it strikes one that the chief object of the builders must have been to combine the greatest possible weight with the least possible amount of accommodation.

The family lived in close intimacy with two cousins, Edward and Jane Cooper,° the children of Mrs. Austen's eldest sister, and Dr. Cooper, the vicar of Sonning, near Reading. The Coopers lived for some years at Bath, which seems to have been much frequented in those days by clergymen retiring from work. I believe that Cassandra and Jane sometimes visited them there, and that Jane thus acquired the intimate knowledge of the topography and customs of Bath, which enabled her to write 'Northanger Abbey' long before she resided there herself. After the death of their own parents, the two young Coopers paid long visits at Steventon. Edward Cooper did not live undistinguished. When an undergraduate at Oxford, he gained the prize for Latin hexameters on 'Hortus Anglicus' in 1791; and in later life he was known by a work on prophecy, called 'The Crisis,' and other religious publications, especially for several volumes of Sermons, much preached in many pulpits in my youth. Jane Cooper was married from her uncle's house at Steventon, to Captain, afterwards Sir Thomas Williams, under whom Charles Austen served in several ships. She was a dear friend of her namesake, but was fated to become a cause of great sorrow to her, for a few years after the marriage she was suddenly killed by an accident to her carriage.

There was another cousin closely associated with them at Steventon, who must have introduced greater variety into the family circle. This was the daughter of Mr. Austen's only sister, Mrs. Hancock. This cousin had been educated in Paris, and married to a Count de Feuillade,° of whom I know little more than that he perished by the guillotine during the French Revolution. Perhaps his chief offence was his rank; but it was said that the charge of 'incivism,' under which he suffered, rested on the fact of his having laid down some arable land into pasture—a sure sign of his intention to embarrass the Republican Government by producing a famine! His wife escaped through dangers and difficulties to England, was received for some time into her uncle's family, and finally married her cousin Henry Austen. During the short peace of Amiens, she and her second husband went to France, in the hope of recovering some of the Count's property, and there narrowly escaped being included amongst the *détenus*. Orders had been given by Buonaparte's government to detain all English travellers, but at the post-houses Mrs. Henry Austen gave the necessary orders herself, and her French was so perfect that she passed everywhere for a native, and her husband escaped under this protection.

She was a clever woman, and highly accomplished, after the French rather than the English mode; and in those days, when intercourse with the Continent was long interrupted by war, such an element in the society of a country parsonage must have been a rare acquisition. The sisters may have been more indebted to this cousin than to Mrs. La Tournelle's teaching for the considerable knowledge of French which they possessed. She also took the principal parts in the private theatricals in which the family several times indulged, having their summer theatre in the barn, and their winter one within the narrow limits of the dining-room, where the number of the audience must have been very limited. On these occasions, the prologues and epilogues were written by Jane's eldest brother, and some of them are very vigorous and amusing.° Jane was only twelve years old at the time of the earliest of these representations, and not more than fifteen when the last took place. She was, however, an early observer, and it may be reasonably supposed that some of the incidents and feelings which are so vividly painted in the Mansfield Park theatricals are due to her recollections of these entertainments.

Some time before they left Steventon, one great affliction came upon the family. Cassandra was engaged to be married to a young clergyman.° He had not sufficient private fortune to permit an immediate union; but the engagement was not likely to be a hopeless or a protracted one, for he had a prospect of early preferment from a nobleman with whom he was connected both by birth and by personal friendship. He accompanied this friend to the West Indies, as chaplain to his regiment, and there died of yellow fever, to the great concern of his friend and patron, who afterwards declared that, if he had known of the engagement, he would not have permitted him to go out to such a climate. This little domestic tragedy caused great and lasting grief to the principal sufferer, and could not but cast a gloom over the whole party. The sympathy of Jane was probably, from her age, and her peculiar attachment to her sister, the deepest of all.

Of Jane herself I know of no such definite tale of love to relate. Her reviewer in the 'Quarterly' of January 1821° observes, concerning the attachment of Fanny Price to Edmund Bertram: 'The silence in which this passion is cherished, the slender hopes and enjoyments by which it is fed, the restlessness and jealousy with which it fills a mind naturally active, contented, and unsuspicious, the manner in which it tinges every event, and every reflection, are painted with a vividness and a detail of which we can scarcely conceive any one but a female, and we should almost add, a female writing from recollection, capable.' This conjecture, however probable, was wide of the mark. The picture was drawn from the intuitive perceptions of genius, not from personal experience. In no circumstance of her life was there any similarity between herself and her heroine in 'Mansfield Park.' She did not indeed pass through life without being the object of warm affection. In her youth she had declined the addresses of a gentleman who had the recommendations of good character, and connections, and position in life, of everything, in fact, except the subtle power of touching her heart. There is, however, one passage of romance in her history with which I am imperfectly acquainted, and to which I am unable to assign name, or date, or place, though I have it on sufficient authority. Many years after her death, some circumstances induced her sister Cassandra to break through her habitual reticence, and to speak of it. She said that, while staying at some seaside place, they became acquainted with a gentleman, whose charm of person, mind, and manners was such that Cassandra thought him worthy to possess and likely to win her sister's love. When they parted, he expressed his intention of soon seeing them again; and Cassandra felt no doubt as to his motives. But they never again met. Within a short time they heard of his sudden death. I believe that, if Jane ever loved, it was this unnamed gentleman; but the acquaintance had been short, and I am unable to say whether her feelings were of such a nature as to affect her happiness.°

Any description that I might attempt of the family life at Steventon, which closed soon after I was born,° could be little better than a fancy-piece. There is no doubt that if we could look into the households of the clergy and the small gentry of that period, we should see some things which would seem strange to us, and should miss many more to which we are accustomed. Every hundred years, and especially a century like the last, marked by an extraordinary advance in wealth, luxury, and refinement of taste, as well as in the mechanical arts which embellish our houses, must produce a great change in their aspect. These changes are always at work; they are going on now, but so silently that we take no note of them. Men soon forget the small objects which they leave behind them as they drift down the stream of life. As Pope says—

> Nor does life's stream for observation stay;
> It hurries all too fast to mark their way.°

Important inventions, such as the applications of steam, gas, and electricity, may find their places in history; but not so the alterations, great as they may be, which have taken place in the appearance of our dining and drawing-rooms. Who can now record the degrees by which the custom prevalent in my youth of asking each other to take wine together at dinner became obsolete? Who will be able to fix, twenty years hence, the date when our dinners began to be carved and handed round by servants, instead of smoking before our eyes and noses on the table? To record such little matters would indeed be 'to chronicle small beer.'° But, in a slight memoir like this, I may be allowed to note some of those changes in social habits which give a colour to history, but which the historian has the greatest difficulty in recovering.

At that time the dinner-table presented a far less splendid appearance than it does now. It was appropriated to solid food, rather than to flowers, fruits, and decorations. Nor was there much glitter of plate upon it; for the early dinner hour rendered candlesticks unnecessary, and silver forks had not come into general use:° while the broad rounded end of the knives indicated the substitute generally used instead of them.[1]

[1] The celebrated Beau Brummel, who was so intimate with George IV. as to be able to quarrel with him, was born in 1771. It is reported that when he was questioned about his parents, he replied that it was long since he had heard of them, but that he imagined the worthy couple must have cut their own throats by that time, because when he last saw them they were eating peas with their knives. Yet Brummel's father had probably lived in good society; and was certainly able to put his son into a fashionable regiment, and to leave him 30,000*l*. (Raikes's *Memoirs*, vol. ii. p. 207.) Raikes believes that he had been Secretary to Lord North. Thackeray's idea that he had been a footman cannot stand against the authority of Raikes, who was intimate with the son.

The dinners too were more homely, though not less plentiful and savoury; and the bill of fare in one house would not be so like that in another as it is now, for family receipts were held in high estimation. A grandmother of culinary talent could bequeath to her descendant fame for some particular dish, and might influence the family dinner for many generations.

> Dos est magna parentium
> Virtus.°

One house would pride itself on its ham, another on its game-pie, and a third on its superior furmity, or tansey-pudding.° Beer and home-made wines, especially mead, were more largely consumed. Vegetables were less plentiful and less various. Potatoes were used, but not so abundantly as now; and there was an idea that they were to be eaten only with roast meat. They were novelties to a tenant's wife who was entertained at Steventon Parsonage, certainly less than a hundred years ago; and when Mrs. Austen advised her to plant them in her own garden, she replied, 'No, no; they are very well for you gentry, but they must be terribly *costly to rear*.'°

But a still greater difference would be found in the furniture of the rooms, which would appear to us lamentably scanty. There was a general deficiency of carpeting in sitting-rooms, bedrooms, and passages. A pianoforte, or rather a spinnet or harpsichord, was by no means a necessary appendage. It was to be found only where there was a decided taste for music, not so common then as now, or in such great houses as would probably contain a billiard-table. There would often be but one sofa in the house, and that a stiff, angular, uncomfortable article. There were no deep easy-chairs, nor other appliances for lounging; for to lie down, or even to lean back, was a luxury permitted only to old persons or invalids. It was said of a nobleman, a personal friend of George III. and a model gentleman of his day, that he would have made the tour of Europe without ever touching the back of his travelling carriage. But perhaps we should be most struck with the total absence of those elegant little articles which now embellish and encumber our drawing-room tables. We should miss the sliding bookcases and picture-stands, the letter-weighing machines and envelope cases, the periodicals and illustrated newspapers—above all, the countless swarm of photograph books which now threaten to swallow up all space. A small writing-desk, with a smaller work-box, or netting-case, was all that each young lady contributed to occupy the table; for the large family work-basket, though often produced in the parlour, lived in the closet.°

There must have been more dancing° throughout the country in those days than there is now: and it seems to have sprung up more spontaneously, as if it were a natural production, with less fastidiousness as to the quality of music, lights, and floor. Many country towns had a monthly ball throughout the winter, in some of which the same apartment served for dancing and tea-room. Dinner parties more frequently ended with an extempore dance on the carpet, to the music of a harpsichord in the house, or a fiddle from the village. This was always supposed to be for the entertainment of the young people, but many, who had little pretension to youth, were very ready to join in it. There can be no doubt that Jane herself enjoyed dancing, for she attributes this taste to her favourite heroines; in most of her works, a ball or a private dance is mentioned, and made of importance.

Many things connected with the ball-rooms of those days have now passed into oblivion. The barbarous law which confined the lady to one partner throughout the evening must indeed have been abolished before Jane went to balls. It must be observed, however, that this custom was in one respect advantageous to the gentleman, inasmuch as it rendered his duties more practicable. He was bound to call upon his partner the next morning, and it must have been convenient to have only one lady for whom he was obliged

> To gallop all the country over,
> The last night's partner to behold,
> And humbly hope she caught no cold.°

But the stately minuet still reigned supreme; and every regular ball commenced with it. It was a slow and solemn movement, expressive of grace and dignity, rather than of merriment. It abounded in formal bows and courtesies, with measured paces, forwards, backwards and sideways, and many complicated gyrations. It was executed by one lady and gentleman, amidst the admiration, or the criticism, of surrounding spectators. In its earlier and most palmy days, as when Sir Charles and Lady Grandison delighted the company by dancing it at their own wedding,° the gentleman wore a dress sword, and the lady was armed with a fan of nearly equal dimensions. Addison observes that 'women are armed with fans, as men with swords, and sometimes do more execution with them.' The graceful carriage of each weapon was considered a test of high breeding. The clownish man was in danger of being tripped up by his sword getting between his legs: the fan held clumsily looked more of a burden than an ornament; while in the hands of an adept it could be made to speak a language of its own.[1] It was not everyone who felt qualified to make this public exhibition, and I have been told that those ladies who intended to dance minuets, used to distinguish themselves from others by wearing a particular kind of lappet° on their head-dress. I have heard also of another curious proof of the respect in which this dance was held. Gloves immaculately clean were considered requisite for its due performance,° while gloves a little soiled were thought good enough for a country dance; and accordingly some prudent ladies provided themselves with two pairs for their several purposes. The minuet expired with the last century: but long after it had ceased to be danced publicly it was taught to boys and girls, in order to give them a graceful carriage.

Hornpipes, cotillons, and reels,° were occasionally danced; but the chief occupation of the evening was the interminable country dance, in which all could join. This dance presented a great show of enjoyment, but it was not without its peculiar troubles. The ladies and gentlemen were ranged apart from each other in

[1] See 'Spectator,' No. 102, on the Fan Exercise. Old gentlemen who had survived the fashion of wearing swords were known to regret the disuse of that custom, because it put an end to one way of distinguishing those who had, from those who had not, been used to good society. To wear the sword easily was an art which, like swimming and skating, required to be learned in youth. Children could practise it early with their toy swords adapted to their size.

opposite rows, so that the facilities for flirtation, or interesting intercourse, were not so great as might have been desired by both parties. Much heart-burning and discontent sometimes arose as to *who* should stand above *whom*, and especially as to who was entitled to the high privilege of calling and leading off the first dance: and no little indignation was felt at the lower end of the room when any of the leading couples retired prematurely from their duties, and did not condescend to dance up and down the whole set. We may rejoice that these causes of irritation no longer exist; and that if such feelings as jealousy, rivalry, and discontent ever touch celestial bosoms in the modern ball-room they must arise from different and more recondite sources.

I am tempted to add a little about the difference of personal habits. It may be asserted as a general truth, that less was left to the charge and discretion of servants, and more was done, or superintended, by the masters and mistresses. With regard to the mistresses, it is, I believe, generally understood, that at the time to which I refer, a hundred years ago, they took a personal part in the higher branches of cookery, as well as in the concoction of home-made wines,° and distilling of herbs for domestic medicines, which are nearly allied to the same art. Ladies did not disdain to spin the thread of which the household linen was woven. Some ladies liked to wash with their own hands their choice china after breakfast or tea. In one of my earliest child's books, a little girl, the daughter of a gentleman, is taught by her mother to make her own bed before leaving her chamber.° It was not so much that they had not servants to do all these things for them, as that they took an interest in such occupations. And it must be borne in mind how many sources of interest enjoyed by this generation were then closed, or very scantily opened to ladies. A very small minority of them cared much for literature or science. Music° was not a very common, and drawing was a still rarer, accomplishment; needle-work, in some form or other, was their chief sedentary employment.

But I doubt whether the rising generation are equally aware how much gentlemen also did for themselves in those times, and whether some things that I can mention will not be a surprise to them. Two homely proverbs were held in higher estimation in my early days than they are now—'The master's eye makes the horse fat;' and, 'If you would be well served, serve yourself.'° Some gentlemen took pleasure in being their own gardeners, performing all the scientific, and some of the manual, work themselves. Well-dressed young men of my acquaintance, who had their coat from a London tailor, would always brush their evening suit themselves, rather than entrust it to the carelessness of a rough servant, and to the risks of dirt and grease in the kitchen; for in those days servants' halls were not common in the houses of the clergy and the smaller country gentry. It was quite natural that Catherine Morland should have contrasted the magnificence of the offices at Northanger Abbey with the few shapeless pantries in her father's parsonage.° A young man who expected to have his things packed or unpacked for him by a servant, when he travelled, would have been thought exceptionally fine, or exceptionally lazy. When my uncle undertook to teach me to shoot, his first lesson was how to clean my own gun. It was thought meritorious on the evening of a hunting day, to turn out after dinner, lanthorn in hand, and visit the stable, to ascertain that the horse had been well cared for. This was of the more importance, because, previous to the introduction of clipping, about the year 1820, it was a difficult and tedious work to make a long-coated hunter dry and comfortable, and was often very imperfectly done. Of course, such things were not practised by those who had gamekeepers, and stud-grooms, and plenty of well-trained servants; but they were practised by many who were unequivocally gentlemen, and whose grandsons, occupying the same position in life, may perhaps be astonished at being told that '*such things were*.'

I have drawn pictures for which my own experience, or what I heard from others in my youth, have supplied the materials. Of course, they cannot be universally applicable. Such details varied in various circles, and were changed very gradually; nor can I pretend to tell how much of what I have said is descriptive of the family life at Steventon in Jane Austen's youth. I am sure that the ladies there had nothing to do with the mysteries of the stew-pot or the preserving-pan; but it is probable that their way of life differed a little from ours, and would have appeared to us more homely. It may be that useful articles, which would not now be produced in drawing-rooms, were hemmed, and marked, and darned in the old-fashioned parlour.° But all this concerned only the outer life; there was as much cultivation and refinement of mind as now, with probably more studied courtesy and ceremony of manner to visitors; whilst certainly in that family literary pursuits were not neglected.

I remember to have heard of only two little things different from modern customs. One was, that on hunting mornings the young men usually took their hasty breakfast in the kitchen. The early hour at which hounds then met may account for this; and probably the custom began, if it did not end, when they were boys; for they hunted at an early age, in a scrambling sort of way, upon any pony or donkey that they could procure, or, in default of such luxuries, on foot. I have been told° that Sir Francis Austen, when seven years old, bought on his own account, it must be supposed with his father's permission, a pony for a guinea and a half; and after riding him with great success for two seasons, sold him for a guinea more. One may wonder how the child could have so much money, and how the animal could have been obtained for so little. The same authority informs me that his first cloth suit was made from a scarlet habit, which, according to the fashion of the times, had been his mother's usual morning dress. If all this is true, the future admiral of the British Fleet must have cut a conspicuous figure in the hunting-field. The other peculiarity was that, when the roads were dirty, the sisters took long walks in pattens.° This defence against wet and dirt is now seldom seen. The few that remain are banished from good society, and employed only in menial work; but a hundred and fifty years ago they were celebrated in poetry, and considered so clever a contrivance that Gay, in his 'Trivia,' ascribes the invention to a god stimulated by his passion for a mortal damsel, and derives the name 'Patten' from 'Patty.'

> The patten now supports each frugal dame,
> Which from the blue-eyed Patty takes the name.°

But mortal damsels have long ago discarded the clumsy implement. First it dropped its iron ring and became a clog; afterwards it was fined down into the pliant galoshe—lighter to wear and more effectual to protect—a no less manifest instance of gradual improvement than Cowper indicates when he traces through eighty lines of poetry his 'accomplished sofa' back to the original three-legged stool.°

As an illustration of the purposes which a patten was intended to serve, I add the following epigram, written by Jane Austen's uncle, Mr. Leigh Perrot, on reading in a newspaper the marriage of Captain Foote to Miss Patten:—

Through the rough paths of life, with a patten your guard,
  May you safely and pleasantly jog;
May the knot never slip, nor the ring press too hard,
  Nor the *Foot* find the *Patten* a clog.°

At the time when Jane Austen lived at Steventon, a work was carried on in the neighbouring cottages which ought to be recorded, because it has long ceased to exist.

Up to the beginning of the present century, poor women found profitable employment in spinning flax or wool. This was a better occupation for them than straw plaiting, inasmuch as it was carried on at the family hearth, and did not admit of gadding and gossiping about the village. The implement used was a long narrow machine of wood, raised on legs, furnished at one end with a large wheel, and at the other with a spindle on which the flax or wool was loosely wrapped, connected together by a loop of string. One hand turned the wheel, while the other formed the thread. The outstretched arms, the advanced foot, the sway of the whole figure backwards and forwards, produced picturesque attitudes, and displayed whatever of grace or beauty the work-woman might possess.[1] Some ladies were fond of spinning, but they worked in a quieter manner, sitting at a neat little machine of varnished wood, like Tunbridge ware,° generally turned by the foot, with a basin of water at hand to supply the moisture

[1] Mrs. Gaskell, in her tale of 'Sylvia's Lovers,' declares that this hand-spinning rivalled harp-playing in its gracefulness. [*Sylvia's Lovers* (1863), Ch. 4.]

required for forming the thread, which the cottager took by a more direct and natural process from her own mouth. I remember two such elegant little wheels in our own family.

It may be observed that this hand-spinning is the most primitive of female accomplishments, and can be traced back to the earliest times. Ballad poetry and fairy tales are full of allusions to it. The term 'spinster' still testifies to its having been the ordinary employment of the English young woman. It was the labour assigned to the ejected nuns by the rough earl who said, 'Go spin, ye jades, go spin.'° It was the employment at which Roman matrons and Grecian princesses presided amongst their handmaids. Heathen mythology celebrated it in the three Fates° spinning and measuring out the thread of human life. Holy Scripture honours it in those 'wise-hearted women' who 'did spin with their hands, and brought that which they had spun' for the construction of the Tabernacle in the wilderness:° and an old English proverb carries it still farther back to the time 'when Adam delved and Eve span.'° But, at last, this time-honoured domestic manufacture is quite extinct amongst us—crushed by the power of steam, overborne by a countless host of spinning jennies,° and I can only just remember some of its last struggles for existence in the Steventon cottages.

CHAPTER III

Early Compositions—Friends at Ashe—A very old Letter—Lines on the Death of Mrs. Lefroy—Observations on Jane Austen's Letter-writing—Letters

I KNOW little of Jane Austen's childhood.° Her mother followed a custom, not unusual in those days, though it seems strange to us, of putting out her babies to be nursed in a cottage in the village.° The infant was daily visited by one or both of its parents, and frequently brought to them at the parsonage, but the cottage was its home, and must have remained so till it was old enough to run about and talk; for I know that one of them, in after life, used to speak of his foster mother as 'Movie,' the name by which he had called her in his infancy. It may be that the contrast between the parsonage house and the best class of cottages was not quite so extreme then as it would be now, that the one was somewhat less luxurious, and the other less squalid. It would certainly seem from the results that it was a wholesome and invigorating system, for the children were all strong and healthy. Jane was probably treated like the rest in this respect. In childhood every available opportunity of instruction was made use of. According to the ideas of the time, she was well educated, though not highly accomplished, and she certainly enjoyed that important element of mental training, associating at home with persons of cultivated intellect. It cannot be doubted that her early years were bright and happy, living, as she did, with indulgent parents, in a cheerful home, not without agreeable variety of society. To these sources of enjoyment must be added the first stirrings of talent within her, and the absorbing interest of original composition. It is impossible to say at how early an age she began to write. There are copy books extant containing tales some of which must have been composed while she was a young girl, as they had amounted to a considerable number by the time she was sixteen.° Her earliest stories are of a slight and flimsy texture, and are generally intended to be nonsensical, but the nonsense has much spirit in it. They are usually preceded by a dedication of mock solemnity to some one of her family. It would seem that the grandiloquent dedications prevalent in those days had not escaped her youthful penetration. Perhaps the most characteristic feature in these early productions is that, however puerile the matter, they are always composed in pure simple English, quite free from the over-ornamented style which might be expected from so young a writer. One of her juvenile effusions is given, as a specimen of the kind of transitory amusement which Jane was continually supplying to the family party.

THE MYSTERY.°

AN UNFINISHED COMEDY.

DEDICATION.

To the Rev. George Austen.

Sir,—I humbly solicit your patronage to the following Comedy, which, though an unfinished one, is, I flatter myself, as complete a *Mystery* as any of its kind.

I am, Sir, your most humble Servant,
The Author.

THE MYSTERY, A COMEDY.

DRAMATIS PERSONÆ.

Men.	*Women.*
Col. Elliott.	Fanny Elliott.
Old Humbug.	Mrs. Humbug
Young Humbug.	*and*
Sir Edward Spangle	Daphne.
and	
Corydon.	

ACT I.

SCENE I.—*A Garden.*

Enter CORYDON.

Corydon. But hush: I am interrupted. [*Exit* CORYDON.

Enter OLD HUMBUG *and his* SON, *talking.*

Old Hum. It is for that reason that I wish you to follow my advice. Are you convinced of its propriety?

Young Hum. I am, sir, and will certainly act in the manner you have pointed out to me.

Old Hum. Then let us return to the house. [*Exeunt.*

SCENE II.—*A parlour in* HUMBUG'S *house.* MRS. HUMBUG *and* FANNY *discovered at work.*

Mrs. Hum. You understand me, my love?

Fanny. Perfectly, ma'am: pray continue your narration.

Mrs. Hum. Alas! it is nearly concluded; for I have nothing more to say on the subject.

Fanny. Ah! here is Daphne.

Enter DAPHNE.

Daphne. My dear Mrs. Humbug, how d'ye do? Oh! Fanny, it is all over.

Fanny. Is it indeed!

Mrs. Hum. I'm very sorry to hear it.

Fanny. Then 'twas to no purpose that I——

Daphne. None upon earth.

Mrs. Hum. And what is to become of——?

Daphne. Oh! 'tis all settled. (*Whispers* MRS. HUMBUG.)

Fanny. And how is it determined?

Daphne. I'll tell you. (*Whispers* FANNY.)

Mrs. Hum. And is he to——?

Daphne. I'll tell you all I know of the matter. (*Whispers* MRS. HUMBUG *and* FANNY.)

Fanny. Well, now I know everything about it, I'll go away.

Mrs. Hum. }
Daphne } And so will I. [*Exeunt.*

SCENE III.—*The curtain rises, and discovers* SIR EDWARD SPANGLE *reclined in an elegant attitude on a sofa fast asleep.*

Enter COL. ELLIOTT.

Col. E. My daughter is not here, I see. There lies Sir Edward. Shall I tell him the secret? No, he'll certainly blab it. But he's asleep, and won't hear me;—so I'll e'en venture. (*Goes up to* SIR EDWARD, *whispers him, and exit.*)

END OF THE FIRST ACT.

FINIS.

Her own mature opinion of the desirableness of such an early habit of composition is given in the following words of a niece:°—

'As I grew older, my aunt would talk to me more seriously of my reading and my amusements. I had taken early to writing verses and stories, and I am sorry to think how I troubled her with reading them. She was very kind about it, and always had some praise to bestow, but at last she warned me against spending too much time upon them. She said—how well I recollect it!—that she knew writing stories was a great amusement, and *she* thought a harmless one, though many people, she was aware, thought otherwise; but that at my age it would be bad for me to be much taken up with my own compositions. Later still—it was after she had gone to Winchester—she sent me a message to this effect, that if I would take her advice I should cease writing till I was sixteen; that she had herself often wished she had read more, and written less in the corresponding years of her own life.' As this niece was only twelve years old at the time of her aunt's death, these words seem to imply that the juvenile tales to which I have referred had, some of them at least, been written in her childhood.

But between these childish effusions, and the composition of her living works, there intervened another stage of her progress, during which she produced some stories, not without merit, but which she never considered worthy of publication. During this preparatory period her mind seems to have been working in a very different direction from that into which it ultimately settled. Instead of presenting faithful copies of nature, these tales were generally burlesques, ridiculing the improbable events and exaggerated sentiments which she had met with in sundry silly romances. Something of this fancy is to be found in 'Northanger Abbey,' but she soon left it far behind in her subsequent course. It would seem as if she were first taking note of all the faults to be avoided, and curiously considering how she ought *not* to write before she attempted to put forth her strength in the right direction. The family have, rightly, I think, declined to let these early works be published.° Mr. Shortreed observed very pithily of Walter Scott's early rambles on the borders, 'He was makin' himsell a' the time; but he didna ken, may be, what he was about till years had passed. At first he thought of little, I dare say, but the queerness and the fun.'° And so, in a humbler way, Jane Austen was 'makin' hersell,' little thinking of future fame, but caring only for 'the queerness and the fun;' and it would be as unfair to expose this preliminary process to the world, as it would be to display all that goes on behind the curtain of the theatre before it is drawn up.

It was, however, at Steventon that the real foundations of her fame were laid. There some of her most successful writing was composed at such an early age as to make it surprising that so young a woman could have acquired the insight into character, and the nice observation of manners which they display. 'Pride and Prejudice,' which some consider the most brilliant of her novels, was the first finished, if not the first begun. She began it in October 1796, before she was twenty-one years old, and completed it in about ten months, in August 1797. The title then intended for it was 'First Impressions.' 'Sense and Sensibility' was begun, in its present form, immediately after the completion of the former, in November 1797; but something similar in story and character had been written earlier under the title of 'Elinor and Marianne;' and if, as is probable, a good deal of this earlier production was retained, it must form the earliest specimen of her writing that has been given to the world. 'Northanger Abbey,' though not prepared for the press till 1803, was certainly first composed in 1798.°

Amongst the most valuable neighbours of the Austens were Mr. and Mrs. Lefroy and their family.° He was rector of the adjoining parish of Ashe; she was sister to Sir Egerton Brydges, to whom we are indebted for the earliest notice of Jane Austen that exists. In his autobiography, speaking of his visits at Ashe, he writes thus: 'The nearest neighbours of the Lefroys were the Austens of Steventon. I remember Jane Austen, the novelist, as a little child. She was very intimate with Mrs. Lefroy, and much encouraged by her. Her mother was a Miss Leigh, whose paternal grandmother was sister to the first Duke of Chandos. Mr. Austen was of a Kentish family, of which several branches have been settled in the Weald of Kent, and some are still remaining there. When I knew Jane Austen, I never suspected that she was an authoress; but my eyes told me that she was fair and handsome, slight and elegant, but with cheeks a little too full.'° One may wish that Sir Egerton had dwelt rather longer on the subject of these memoirs, instead of being drawn away by his extreme love for genealogies to her great-grandmother and ancestors. That great-grandmother however lives in the family records as Mary Brydges,° a daughter of Lord Chandos, married in Westminster Abbey to Theophilus Leigh of Addlestrop in 1698. When a girl she had received a curious letter of advice and reproof, written by her mother from Constantinople. Mary, or 'Poll,' was remaining in England with her grandmother, Lady Bernard, who seems to have been wealthy and inclined to be too indulgent to her granddaughter. This letter is given. Any such authentic document, two hundred years old, dealing with domestic details, must possess some interest. This is remarkable, not only as a specimen of the homely language in which ladies of rank then expressed themselves, but from the sound sense which it contains. Forms of expression vary, but good sense and right principles are the same in the nineteenth that they were in the seventeenth century.

'My deares Poll,

'Y^{r} letters by Cousin Robbert Serle arrived here not before the 27th of Aprill, yett were they hartily wellcome to us, bringing ye joyful news which a great while we had longed for of my most dear Mother & all other relations & friends good health which I beseech God continue to you all, & as I observe in y^{rs} to y^{r} Sister Betty ye extraordinary kindness of (as I may truly say) the best Moth^{r} & Gnd Moth^{r} in the world in pinching herself to make you fine, so I cannot but admire her great good Housewifry in affording you so very plentifull an allowance, & yett to increase her Stock at the rate I find she hath done; & think I can never sufficiently mind you how very much it is y^{r} duty on all occasions to pay her y^{r} gratitude in all humble submission & obedience to all her commands soe long as you live. I must tell you 'tis to her bounty & care in ye greatest measure you are like to owe y^{r} well living in this world, & as you cannot but be very sensible you are an extraordinary charge to her so it behoves you to take particular heed th^{t} in ye whole course of y^{r} life, you render her a proportionable comfort, especially since 'tis ye best way you can ever hope to make her such amends as God requires of y^{r} hands. but Poll! it grieves me a little & y^{t} I am forced to take notice of & reprove you for some vaine expressions in y^{r} lett^{rs} to y^{r} Sister—you say concerning y^{r} allowance "you aime to bring y^{r} bread & cheese even"° in this I do not discommend you, for a foule shame indeed it would be should you out run the Constable° having soe liberall a provision made you for y^{r} maintenance—but ye reason you give for y^{r} resolution I cannot at all approve for you say "to spend more you can't" thats because you have it not to spend, otherwise it seems you would. So y^{t} 'tis y^{r} Grandmoth^{rs} discretion & not yours th^{t} keeps you from extravagancy, which plainly appears in ye close of y^{r} sentence, saying y^{t} you think it simple covetousness to save out of y^{rs} but 'tis my opinion if you lay all on y^{r} back 'tis ten tymes a greater sin & shame th^{n} to save some what out of soe large an allowance in y^{r} purse to help you at a dead lift.° Child, we all know our beginning, but who knows his end?° Y^{e} best use th^{t} can be made of fair weath^{r} is to provide against foule & 'tis great discretion & of noe small commendations for a young woman betymes to shew herself housewifly & frugal. Y^{r} Mother neither Maide nor wife ever yett bestowed forty pounds a yeare on herself & yett if you never fall und^{r} a worse reputation in ye world th^{n} she (I thank God for it) hath hitherto done, you need not repine at it, & you cannot be ignorant of ye difference th^{t} was between my fortune & what you are to expect. You ought likewise to consider th^{t} you have seven brothers & sisters & you are all one man's children & therefore it is very unreasonable that one should expect to be preferred in finery soe much above all ye rest for 'tis impossible you should soe much mistake y^{r} ffather's condition as to fancy he is able to allow every one of you forty pounds a yeare a piece, for such an allowance with the charge of their diett over and above will amount to at least five hundred pounds a yeare, a sum y^{r} poor ffather can ill spare, besides doe but be think y^{r}self what a ridiculous sight it will be when y^{r} grandmoth^{r} & you come to us to have noe less th^{n} seven waiting gentlewomen in one house, for what reason can you give why every one of y^{r} Sist^{rs} should not have every one of y^{m} a Maide as well as you, & though you may spare to pay y^{r} maide's wages out of y^{r} allowance yett you take no care of ye unnecessary charge you put y^{r} ffath^{r} to in y^{r} increase of his family, whereas if it were not a piece of pride to have ye name of keeping y^{r} maide she y^{t} waits on y^{r} good Grandmother might easily doe as formerly you know she hath done, all ye business you have for a maide unless as you grow old^{r} you grow a veryer Foole which God forbid!

'Poll, you live in a place where you see great plenty & splendour but let not ye allurements of earthly pleasures tempt you to forget or neglect ye duty of a good Christian in dressing y^{r} bett^{r} part which is y^{r} soule, as will best please God. I am not against y^{r} going decent & neate as becomes y^{r} ffathers daughter but to clothe y^{r}self rich & be running into every gaudy fashion can never become y^{r} circumstances & instead of doing you creditt & getting you a good prefer^{nt} it is ye readiest way you can take to fright all sober men from ever thinking of matching th^{m}selves with women that live above thy^{r} fortune, & if this be a wise way of spending money judge you! & besides, doe but reflect what an od sight it will be to a stranger that comes to our house to see y^{r} Grandmoth^{r} y^{r} Moth^{r} & all y^{r} Sisters in a plane dress & you only trick^{d} up like a bartlemew-babby°—you know what sort of people those are th^{t} can't faire well but they must cry rost meate° now what effect could you imagine y^{r} writing in such a high straine to y^{r} Sisters could have but eithe^{r} to provoke th^{m} to envy you or murmur against us. I must tell you neith^{r} of y^{r} Sisters have ever had twenty pounds a yeare allowance from us yett, & yett they^{r} dress hath not disparaged neith^{r} th^{m} nor us & without incurring ye censure of simple covetousness they will have some what to shew out of their saving that will doe th^{m} creditt & I expect y^{t} you th^{t} are theyr elder Sister sh^{d} rather sett th^{m} examples of ye like nature th^{n} tempt th^{m} from treading in ye steps of their good Grandmoth^{r} & poor Moth^{r}. This is not half what might be saide on this occasion but believing thee to be a very good natured dutyfull child I sh^{d} have thought it a great deal too much but y^{t} having in my coming hither past through many most desperate dangers I cannot forbear thinking & preparing myself for all events, & therefore not knowing how it may please God to dispose of us I conclude it my duty to God & thee my d^{r} child to lay this matter as home to thee as I could, assuring you my daily prayers are not nor shall not be wanting that God may give you grace always to remember to make a right use of this truly affectionate counsell of y^{r} poor Moth^{r}. & though I speak very plaine downright english to you yett I would not have you doubt but that I love you as hartily as any child I have & if you serve God and take good courses I promise you my kindness to you shall be according to y^{r} own hart's desire, for you may be certain I can aime at nothing in what I have now writ but y^{r} real good which to promote shall be ye study & care day & night

'Of my dear Poll
'thy truly affectionate Moth^{r}.
'ELIZA CHANDOS.

'Pera of Galata,° May ye 6th 1686.

'P.S.—Thy ffath^{r} & I send thee our blessing, & all thy broth^{rs} & sist^{rs} they^{r} service. Our harty & affectionate service to my broth^{r}

& sist^{r} Childe & all my dear cozens. When you see my Lady Worster & cozen Howlands pray present th^{m} my most humble service.'

This letter shows that the wealth acquired by trade was already manifesting itself in contrast with the straitened circumstances of some of the nobility. Mary Brydges's 'poor ffather,' in whose household economy was necessary, was the King of England's ambassador at Constantinople; the grandmother, who lived in 'great plenty and splendour,' was the widow of a Turkey merchant.° But then, as now, it would seem, rank had the power of attracting and absorbing wealth.

At Ashe also Jane became acquainted with a member of the Lefroy family, who was still living when I began these memoirs, a few months ago; the Right Hon. Thomas Lefroy, late Chief Justice of Ireland.° One must look back more than seventy years to reach the time when these two bright young persons were, for a short time, intimately acquainted with each other, and then separated on their several courses, never to meet again; both destined to attain some distinction in their different ways, one to survive the other for more than half a century, yet in his extreme old age to remember and speak, as he sometimes did, of his former companion, as one to be much admired, and not easily forgotten by those who had ever known her.

Mrs. Lefroy herself was a remarkable person. Her rare endowments of goodness, talents, graceful person, and engaging manners, were sufficient to secure her a prominent place in any society into which she was thrown; while her enthusiastic eagerness of disposition rendered her especially attractive to a clever and lively girl. She was killed by a fall from her horse on Jane's birthday, Dec. 16, 1804. The following lines to her memory were written by Jane four years afterwards, when she was thirty-three years old. They are given, not for their merits as poetry, but to show how deep and lasting was the impression made by the elder friend on the mind of the younger:—

To the Memory of Mrs. Lefroy°

1

The day returns again, my natal day;
  What mix'd emotions in my mind arise!
Beloved Friend; four years have passed away
  Since thou wert snatched for ever from our eyes.

2

The day commemorative of my birth,
  Bestowing life, and light, and hope to me,
Brings back the hour which was thy last on earth.
  O! bitter pang of torturing memory!

3

Angelic woman! past my power to praise
  In language meet thy talents, temper, mind,
Thy solid worth, thy captivating grace,
  Thou friend and ornament of human kind.

4

But come, fond Fancy, thou indulgent power;
  Hope is desponding, chill, severe, to thee:
Bless thou this little portion of an hour;
  Let me behold her as she used to be.

5

I see her here with all her smiles benign,
  Her looks of eager love, her accents sweet,
That voice and countenance almost divine,
  Expression, harmony, alike complete.

6

Listen! It is not sound alone, 'tis sense,
  'Tis genius, taste, and tenderness of soul:
'Tis genuine warmth of heart without pretence,
  And purity of mind that crowns the whole.

7

She speaks! 'Tis eloquence, that grace of tongue,
  So rare, so lovely, never misapplied
By her, to palliate vice, or deck a wrong:
  She speaks and argues but on virtue's side.

8

Hers is the energy of soul sincere;
  Her Christian spirit, ignorant to feign,
Seeks but to comfort, heal, enlighten, cheer,
  Confer a pleasure or prevent a pain.

9

Can aught enhance such goodness? yes, to me
  Her partial favour from my earliest years
Consummates all: ah! give me but to see
  Her smile of love! The vision disappears.

10

'Tis past and gone. We meet no more below.
  Short is the cheat of Fancy o'er the tomb.
Oh! might I hope to equal bliss to go,
  To meet thee, angel, in thy future home.

11

Fain would I feel an union with thy fate:
  Fain would I seek to draw an omen fair
From this connection in our earthly date.
  Indulge the harmless weakness. Reason, spare.

The loss of their first home is generally a great grief to young persons of strong feeling and lively imagination; and Jane was exceedingly unhappy when she was told that her father, now seventy years of age, had determined to resign his duties to his eldest son, who was to be his successor in the Rectory of Steventon, and to remove with his wife and daughters to Bath. Jane had been absent from home when this resolution was taken; and, as her father was always rapid both in forming his resolutions and in acting on them, she had little time to reconcile herself to the change.°

A wish has sometimes been expressed that some of Jane Austen's letters should be published. Some entire letters, and many extracts, will be given in this memoir; but the reader must be warned not to expect too much from them.° With regard to accuracy of language indeed every word of them might be printed without correction. The style is always clear, and generally animated, while a vein of humour continually gleams through the whole; but the materials may be thought inferior to the execution, for they treat only of the details of domestic life. There is in them no notice of politics or public events; scarcely any discussions on literature, or other subjects of general interest. They may be said to resemble the nest which some little bird builds of the materials nearest at hand, of the twigs and mosses supplied by the tree in which it is placed; curiously constructed out of the simplest matters.

Her letters have very seldom the date of the year, or the signature of her christian name at full length; but it has been easy to ascertain their dates, either from the post-mark, or from their contents.

The two following letters are the earliest that I have seen. They were both written in November 1800;° before the family removed from Steventon. Some of the same circumstances are referred to in both.

The first is to her sister Cassandra, who was then staying with their brother Edward at Godmersham Park, Kent:—

'Steventon, Saturday evening, Nov. 8th.°

'My dear Cassandra,

'I thank you for so speedy a return to my two last, and particularly thank you for your anecdote of Charlotte Graham and her cousin, Harriet Bailey,° which has very much amused both my mother and myself. If you can learn anything farther of that interesting affair, I hope you will mention it. I have two messages; let me get rid of them, and then my paper will be my own. Mary fully intended writing to you by Mr. Chute's frank,° and only happened entirely to forget it, but will write soon; and my father wishes Edward to send him a memorandum of the price of the hops. The tables are come, and give general contentment. I had not expected that they would so perfectly suit the fancy of us all three, or that we should so well agree in the disposition of them; but nothing except their own surface can have been smoother. The two ends put together form one constant table° for everything, and the centre piece stands exceedingly well under the glass, and holds a great deal most commodiously, without looking awkwardly. They are both covered with green baize, and send their best love. The Pembroke° has got its destination by the sideboard, and my mother has great delight in keeping her money and papers locked up. The little table which used to stand there has most conveniently taken itself off into the best bedroom; and we are now in want only of the chiffonniere,° which is neither finished nor come. So much for that subject; I now come to another, of a very different nature, as other subjects are very apt to be. Earle Harwood° has been again giving uneasiness to his family and talk to the neighbourhood; in the present instance, however, he is only unfortunate, and not in fault.

'About ten days ago, in cocking a pistol in the guard-room at Marcau,° he accidentally shot himself through the thigh. Two young Scotch surgeons in the island were polite enough to propose taking off the thigh at once, but to that he would not consent; and accordingly in his wounded state was put on board a cutter and conveyed to Haslar Hospital, at Gosport, where the bullet was extracted, and where he now is, I hope, in a fair way of doing well. The surgeon of the hospital wrote to the family on the occasion, and John Harwood went down to him immediately, attended by James,[1] whose object in going was to be the means of bringing back the earliest intelligence to Mr. and Mrs. Harwood, whose anxious sufferings, particularly those of the latter, have of course been dreadful. They went down on Tuesday, and James came back the next day, bringing such favourable accounts as greatly to lessen the distress of the family at Deane, though it will probably be a long while before Mrs. Harwood can be quite at ease. *One* most material comfort, however, they have; the assurance of its being really an accidental wound, which is not only positively declared by Earle himself, but is likewise testified by the particular direction of the bullet. Such a wound could not have been received in a duel. At present he is going on very well,

[1] James, the writer's eldest brother.

but the surgeon will not declare him to be in no danger.[1] Mr. Heathcote° met with a genteel little accident the other day in hunting. He got off to lead his horse over a hedge, or a house, or something, and his horse in his haste trod upon his leg, or rather ancle, I believe, and it is not certain whether the small bone is not broke. Martha has accepted Mary's invitation for Lord Portsmouth's ball.° He has not yet sent out his own invitations, but *that* does not signify; Martha comes, and a ball there is to be. I think it will be too early in her mother's absence for me to return with her.

'*Sunday Evening.*—We have had a dreadful storm of wind in the fore part of this day, which has done a great deal of mischief among our trees. I was sitting alone in the dining-room when an odd kind of crash startled me—in a moment afterwards it was repeated. I then went to the window, which I reached just in time to see the last of our two highly valued elms descend into the Sweep!!!!!° The other, which had fallen, I suppose, in the first crash, and which was the nearest to the pond, taking a more easterly direction, sunk among our screen of chestnuts and firs, knocking down one spruce-fir, beating off the head of another, and stripping the two corner chestnuts of several branches in its fall. This is not all. One large elm out of the two on the left-hand side as you enter what I call the elm walk, was likewise blown down; the maple° bearing the weathercock was broke in two, and what I regret more than all the rest is, that all the three elms which grew in Hall's meadow, and gave such ornament to it, are gone; two were blown down, and the other so much injured that it cannot stand. I am happy to add, however, that no greater evil than the loss of trees has been the consequence of the storm in this place, or in our immediate neighbourhood. We grieve, therefore, in some comfort.

'I am yours ever, 'J.A.'

The next letter, written four days later than the former, was addressed to Miss Lloyd,° an intimate friend, whose sister (my mother) was married to Jane's eldest brother:—

[1] The limb was saved.

'Steventon, Wednesday evening, Nov. 12th.

'MY DEAR MARTHA,

'I did not receive your note yesterday till after Charlotte had left Deane, or I would have sent my answer by her, instead of being the means, as I now must be, of lessening the elegance of your new dress for the Hurstbourne ball by the value of 3*d.* You are very good in wishing to see me at Ibthorp° so soon, and I am equally good in wishing to come to you. I believe our merit in that respect is much upon a par, our self-denial mutually strong. Having paid this tribute of praise to the virtue of both, I shall here have done with panegyric, and proceed to plain matter of fact. In about a fortnight's time I hope to be with you. I have two reasons for not being able to come before. I wish so to arrange my visit as to spend some days with you after your mother's return. In the 1st place, that I may have the pleasure of seeing her, and in the 2nd, that I may have a better chance of bringing you back with me. Your promise in my favour was not quite absolute, but if your will is not perverse, you and I will do all in our power to overcome your scruples of conscience. I hope we shall meet next week to talk all this over, till we have tired ourselves with the very idea of my visit before my visit begins. Our invitations for the 19th are arrived, and very curiously are they worded.[1] Mary mentioned to you yesterday poor Earle's unfortunate accident, I dare say. He does not seem to be going on very well. The two or three last posts have brought less and less favourable accounts of him. John Harwood has gone to Gosport again to-day. We have two families of friends now who are in a most anxious state; for though by a note from Catherine this morning there seems now to be a revival of hope at Manydown,° its continuance may be too reasonably

[1] The invitation, the ball dress, and some other things in this and the preceding letter refer to a ball annually given at Hurstbourne Park, on the anniversary of the Earl of Portsmouth's marriage with his first wife. He was the Lord Portsmouth whose eccentricities afterwards became notorious, and the invitations, as well as other arrangements about these balls, were of a peculiar character. [John Charles Wallop, Earl of Portsmouth (1767–1853). He was briefly a pupil of Revd George Austen in 1773. For further details, see *Letters*, 564.]

doubted. Mr. Heathcote,[1] however, who has broken the small bone of his leg, is so good as to be going on very well. It would be really too much to have three people to care for.

'You distress me cruelly by your request about books. I cannot think of any to bring with me, nor have I any idea of our wanting them. I come to you to be talked to, not to read or hear reading; I can do that at home; and indeed I am now laying in a stock of intelligence to pour out on you as my share of the conversation. I am reading Henry's History of England,° which I will repeat to you in any manner you may prefer, either in a loose, desultory,° unconnected stream, or dividing my recital, as the historian divides it himself, into seven parts:—The Civil and Military: Religion: Constitution: Learning and Learned Men: Arts and Sciences: Commerce, Coins, and Shipping: and Manners. So that for every evening in the week there will be a different subject. The Friday's lot—Commerce, Coins, and Shipping—you will find the least entertaining; but the next evening's portion will make amends. With such a provision on my part, if you will do yours by repeating the French Grammar, and Mrs. Stent[2] will now and then ejaculate some wonder about the cocks and hens, what can we want? Farewell for a short time. We all unite in best love, and I am your very affectionate

'J.A.'

The two next letters must have been written early in 1801, after the removal from Steventon had been decided on, but before it had taken place. They refer to the two brothers who were at sea, and give some idea of a kind of anxieties and uncertainties to which sisters are seldom subject in these days of peace, steamers, and electric telegraphs. At that time ships were often windbound or becalmed, or driven wide of their destination; and sometimes they had orders to alter their course for some secret service; not to mention the chance of conflict with a vessel of superior

[1] The father of Sir William Heathcote, of Hursley, who was married to a daughter of Mr. Bigg Wither, of Manydown, and lived in the neighbourhood.

[2] A very dull old lady, then residing with Mrs. Lloyd. [Mary Stent, died 24 December 1812, described in Caroline Austen's *Reminiscences*, 7.]

power—no improbable occurrence before the battle of Trafalgar.° Information about relatives on board men-of-war was scarce and scanty, and often picked up by hearsay or chance means; and every scrap of intelligence was proportionably valuable:—

'My dear Cassandra,°

'I should not have thought it necessary to write to you so soon, but for the arrival of a letter from Charles to myself. It was written last Saturday from off the Start, and conveyed to Popham Lane by Captain Boyle, on his way to Midgham. He came from Lisbon in the "Endymion." I will copy Charles's account of his conjectures about Frank: "He has not seen my brother lately, nor does he expect to find him arrived, as he met Captain Inglis at Rhodes, going up to take command of the 'Petrel,' as he was coming down; but supposes he will arrive in less than a fortnight from this time, in some ship which is expected to reach England about that time with dispatches from Sir Ralph Abercrombie."° The event must show what sort of a conjuror Captain Boyle is. The "Endymion" has not been plagued with any more prizes. Charles spent three pleasant days in Lisbon.

'They were very well satisfied with their royal passenger,[1] whom they found jolly and affable,° who talks of Lady Augusta as his wife, and seems much attached to her.

'When this letter was written, the "Endymion" was becalmed, but Charles hoped to reach Portsmouth by Monday or Tuesday. He received my letter, communicating our plans, before he left England; was much surprised, of course, but is quite reconciled to them, and means to come to Steventon once more while Steventon is ours.'°

From a letter written later in the same year:—°

'Charles has received 30*l*. for his share of the privateer,° and expects 10*l*. more; but of what avail is to take prizes if he lays out the produce in presents to his sisters? He has been buying gold chains and topaze crosses for us.° He must be well scolded. The

[1] The Duke of Sussex, son of George III., married, without royal consent, to the Lady Augusta Murray.

"Endymion" has already received orders for taking troops to Egypt, which I should not like at all if I did not trust to Charles being removed from her somehow or other before she sails. He knows nothing of his own destination, he says, but desires me to write directly, as the "Endymion" will probably sail in three or four days. He will receive my yesterday's letter, and I shall write again by this post to thank and reproach him. We shall be unbearably fine.'

CHAPTER IV

Removal from Steventon—Residences at Bath and at Southampton—Settling at Chawton

THE family removed to Bath in the spring of 1801, where they resided first at No. 4 Sydney Terrace, and afterwards in Green Park Buildings.° I do not know whether they were at all attracted to Bath by the circumstance that Mrs. Austen's only brother, Mr. Leigh Perrot,° spent part of every year there. The name of Perrot, together with a small estate at Northleigh° in Oxfordshire, had been bequeathed to him by a great uncle. I must devote a few sentences to this very old and now extinct branch of the Perrot family; for one of the last survivors, Jane Perrot, married to a Walker, was Jane Austen's great grandmother, from whom she derived her Christian name. The Perrots were settled in Pembrokeshire at least as early as the thirteenth century. They were probably some of the settlers whom the policy of our Plantagenet kings placed in that county, which thence acquired the name of 'England beyond Wales,' for the double purpose of keeping open a communication with Ireland from Milford Haven, and of overawing the Welsh. One of the family seems to have carried out this latter purpose very vigorously; for it is recorded of him that he slew *twenty-six men* of Kemaes, a district of Wales, and *one wolf*. The manner in which the two kinds of game are classed together, and the disproportion of numbers, are remarkable; but probably at that time the wolves had been so closely killed down, that *lupicide* was become a more rare and distinguished exploit than *homicide*. The last of this family died about 1778, and their property was divided between Leighs and Musgraves, the larger portion going to the latter. Mr. Leigh Perrot pulled down the mansion, and sold the estate to the Duke of Marlborough, and the name of these Perrots is now to be found only on some monuments in the church of Northleigh.

Mr. Leigh Perrot was also one of several cousins to whom a life interest in the Stoneleigh property in Warwickshire was left, after the extinction of the earlier Leigh peerage, but he compromised his claim to the succession in his lifetime. He married a niece of Sir Montague Cholmeley° of Lincolnshire. He was a man of considerable natural power, with much of the wit of his uncle, the Master of Balliol,° and wrote clever epigrams and riddles, some of which, though without his name, found their way into print; but he lived a very retired life, dividing his time between Bath and his place in Berkshire called Scarlets. Jane's letters from Bath make frequent mention of this uncle and aunt.

The unfinished story, now published under the title of 'The Watsons,' must have been written during the author's residence in Bath.° In the autumn of 1804 she spent some weeks at Lyme, and became acquainted with the Cobb, which she afterwards made memorable for the fall of Louisa Musgrove.° In February 1805, her father died at Bath, and was buried at Walcot Church. The widow and daughters went into lodgings for a few months, and then removed to Southampton.° The only records that I can find about her during those four years° are the three following letters to her sister; one from Lyme, the others from Bath. They shew that she went a good deal into society, in a quiet way, chiefly with ladies; and that her eyes were always open to minute traits of character in those with whom she associated:—

Extract from a letter from Jane Austen to her Sister°

'Lyme, Friday, Sept. 14 (1804).

'MY DEAR CASSANDRA,—I take the first sheet of fine striped paper to thank you for your letter from Weymouth, and express my hopes of your being at Ibthorp before this time. I expect to hear that you reached it yesterday evening, being able to get as far as Blandford on Wednesday. Your account of Weymouth contains nothing which strikes me so forcibly as there being no ice in the town. For every other vexation I was in some measure prepared, and particularly for your disappointment in not seeing the Royal Family° go on board on Tuesday, having already heard from Mr. Crawford that he had seen you in the very act of being too late.

But for there being no ice, what could prepare me! You found my letter at Andover, I hope, yesterday, and have now for many hours been satisfied that your kind anxiety on my behalf was as much thrown away as kind anxiety usually is. I continue quite well; in proof of which I have bathed again this morning. It was absolutely necessary that I should have the little fever and indisposition which I had: it has been all the fashion this week in Lyme. We are quite settled in our lodgings by this time, as you may suppose, and everything goes on in the usual order. The servants behave very well, and make no difficulties, though nothing certainly can exceed the inconvenience of the offices,° except the general dirtiness of the house and furniture, and all its inhabitants. I endeavour, as far as I can, to supply your place, and be useful, and keep things in order. I detect dirt in the water decanters, as fast as I can, and keep everything as it was under your administration. . . . The ball last night was pleasant, but not full for Thursday. My father staid contentedly till half-past nine (we went a little after eight), and then walked home with James and a lanthorn, though I believe the lanthorn was not lit, as the moon was up; but sometimes this lanthorn may be a great convenience to him. My mother and I staid about an hour later. Nobody asked me the two first dances; the two next I danced with Mr. Crawford, and had I chosen to stay longer might have danced with Mr. Granville, Mrs. Granville's son, whom my dear friend Miss A. introduced to me, or with a new odd-looking man who had been eyeing me for some time, and at last, without any introduction, asked me if I meant to dance again. I think he must be Irish by his ease, and because I imagine him to belong to the hon[bl] B.'s, who are son, and son's wife of an Irish viscount, bold queer-looking people, just fit to be quality at Lyme. I called yesterday morning (ought it not in strict propriety to be termed yester-morning?) on Miss A. and was introduced to her father and mother. Like other young ladies she is considerably genteeler than her parents. Mrs. A. sat darning a pair of stockings the whole of my visit. But do not mention° this at home, lest a warning should act as an example. We afterwards walked together for an hour on the Cobb; she is very converseable in a common way; I do not perceive wit or genius, but she has sense and some degree of taste, and her manners are very engaging. She seems to like people rather too easily.

'Your's affect^{ly},
'J. A.'

Letter from Jane Austen to her sister Cassandra° at Ibthorp, alluding to the sudden death of Mrs. Lloyd at that place:—

'25 Gay Street (Bath), Monday,
'April 8, 1805.

'MY DEAR CASSANDRA,—Here is a day for you. Did Bath or Ibthorp ever see such an 8th of April? It is March and April together; the glare of the one and the warmth of the other. We do nothing but walk about. As far as your means will admit, I hope you profit by such weather too. I dare say you are already the better for change of place. We were out again last night. Miss Irvine invited us, when I met her in the Crescent, to drink tea with them, but I rather declined it, having no idea that my mother would be disposed for another evening visit there so soon; but when I gave her the message, I found her very well inclined to go; and accordingly, on leaving Chapel, we walked to Lansdown. This morning we have been to see Miss Chamberlaine look hot on horseback. Seven years and four months ago we went to the same riding-house to see Miss Lefroy's performance![1]° What a different set are we now moving in! But seven years, I suppose, are enough to change every pore of one's skin and every feeling of one's mind. We did not walk long in the Crescent yesterday. It was hot and not crowded enough; so we went into the field, and passed close by S. T. and Miss S.[2] again. I have not yet seen her face, but neither her dress nor air have anything of the dash or; stylishness which the Browns talked of; quite the contrary; indeed, her dress is not even smart, and her appearance very

[1] Here is evidence that Jane Austen was acquainted with Bath before it became her residence in 1801. See pp. 26–7 [and my note at p. 26° 'Edward and Jane Cooper'].

[2] A gentleman and lady lately engaged to be married [The original reads 'Stephen Terry & Miss Seymer'.]

quiet. Miss Irvine says she is never speaking a word. Poor wretch; I am afraid she is *en pénitence*. Here has been that excellent Mrs. Coulthart calling, while my mother was out, and I was believed to be so. I always respected her, as a good-hearted friendly woman. And the Browns have been here; I find their affidavits° on the table. The "Ambuscade" reached Gibraltar on the 9th of March, and found all well; so say the papers. We have had no letters from anybody, but we expect to hear from Edward tomorrow, and from you soon afterwards. How happy they are at Godmersham now! I shall be very glad of a letter from Ibthorp, that I may know how you all are, but particularly yourself. This is nice weather for Mrs. J. Austen's going to Speen, and I hope she will have a pleasant visit there. I expect a prodigious account of the christening dinner; perhaps it brought you at last into the company of Miss Dundas again.

'*Tuesday.*—I received your letter last night, and wish it may be soon followed by another to say that all is over; but I cannot help thinking that nature will struggle again, and produce a revival. Poor woman! May her end be peaceful and easy as the exit we have witnessed!° And I dare say it will. If there is no revival, suffering must be all over; even the consciousness of existence, I suppose, was gone when you wrote. The nonsense I have been writing in this and in my last letter seems out of place at such a time, but I will not mind it; it will do you no harm, and nobody else will be attacked by it. I am heartily glad that you can speak so comfortably of your own health and looks, though I can scarcely comprehend the latter being really approved. Could travelling fifty miles produce such an immediate change? You were looking very poorly here, and everybody seemed sensible of it. Is there a charm in a hack postchaise?° But if there were, Mrs. Craven's carriage might have undone it all. I am much obliged to you for the time and trouble you have bestowed on Mary's cap, and am glad it pleases her; but it will prove a useless gift at present, I suppose. Will not she leave Ibthorp on her mother's death? As a companion you are all that Martha can be supposed to want, and in that light, under these circumstances, your visit will indeed have been well timed.

'*Thursday*.—I was not able to go on yesterday; all my wit and leisure were bestowed on letters to Charles and Henry. To the former I wrote in consequence of my mother's having seen in the papers that the "Urania" was waiting at Portsmouth for the convoy for Halifax. This is nice, as it is only three weeks ago that you wrote by the "Camilla." I wrote to Henry because I had a letter from him in which he desired to hear from me very soon. His to me was most affectionate and kind, as well as entertaining; there is no merit to him in *that*; he cannot help being amusing. He offers to meet us on the sea coast, if the plan of which Edward gave him some hint takes place. Will not this be making the execution of such a plan more desirable and delightful than ever? He talks of the rambles we took together last summer° with pleasing affection.

'Yours ever,

'J. A.'

From the same to the same°

'Gay St. Sunday Evening,

'April 21 (1805).

'My dear Cassandra,—I am much obliged to you for writing to me again so soon; your letter yesterday was quite an unexpected pleasure. Poor Mrs. Stent!° it has been her lot to be always in the way; but we must be merciful, for perhaps in time we may come to be Mrs. Stents ourselves, unequal to anything, and unwelcome to everybody. . . . My morning engagement was with the Cookes, and our party consisted of George and Mary, a Mr. L., Miss B.,° who had been with us at the concert, and the youngest Miss W. Not Julia; we have done with her; she is very ill; but Mary. Mary W.'s turn is actually come to be grown up, and have a fine complexion, and wear great square muslin shawls. I have not expressly enumerated myself among the party, but there I was, and my cousin George was very kind, and talked sense to me every now and then, in the intervals of his more animated fooleries with Miss B., who is very young, and rather handsome, and whose gracious manners, ready wit, and solid remarks, put me somewhat in mind of my old acquaintance L. L. There was a monstrous deal of stupid quizzing and common-place nonsense talked, but scarcely any wit; all that bordered on it or on sense came from my cousin George, whom altogether I like very well. Mr. B. seems nothing more than a tall young man. My evening engagement and walk was with Miss A.,° who had called on me the day before, and gently upbraided me in her turn with a change of manners to her since she had been in Bath, or at least of late. Unlucky me! that my notice should be of such consequence, and my manners so bad! She was so well disposed, and so reasonable, that I soon forgave her, and made this engagement with her in proof of it. She is really an agreeable girl, so I think I may like her; and her great want of a companion at home, which may well make any tolerable acquaintance important to her, gives her another claim on my attention. I shall endeavour as much as possible to keep my intimacies in their proper place, and prevent their clashing. Among so many friends, it will be well if I do not get into a scrape; and now here is Miss Blashford come. I should have gone distracted if the Bullers had staid. . . . When I tell you I have been° visiting a countess this morning, you will immediately, with great justice, but no truth, guess it to be Lady Roden.° No: it is Lady Leven, the mother of Lord Balgonie. On receiving a message from Lord and Lady Leven through the Mackays, declaring their intention of waiting on us, we thought it right to go to them. I hope we have not done too much, but the friends and admirers of Charles must be attended to. They seem very reasonable, good sort of people, very civil, and full of his praise.[1] We were shewn at first into an empty drawing-room, and presently in came his lordship, not knowing who we were, to apologise for the servant's mistake, and to say himself what was untrue,° that Lady Leven was not within. He is a tall gentlemanlike looking man, with spectacles, and rather deaf. After sitting with him ten minutes we walked away; but Lady Leven coming out of the dining parlour as we passed the door, we were obliged to attend her back to it, and pay our visit over again. She is a stout woman,

[1] It seems that Charles Austen, then first lieutenant of the 'Endymion,' had had an opportunity of shewing attention and kindness to some of Lord Leven's family.

with a very handsome face. By this means we had the pleasure of hearing Charles's praises twice over. They think themselves excessively obliged to him, and estimate him so highly as to wish Lord Balgonie, when he is quite recovered, to go out to him. There is a pretty little Lady Marianne of the party, to be shaken hands with, and asked if she remembered Mr. Austen. . . .

'I shall write to Charles by the next packet, unless you tell me in the meantime of your intending to do it.

'Believe me, if you chuse,
'Y^r aff^te Sister.'

Jane did not estimate too highly the 'Cousin George' mentioned in the foregoing letter; who might easily have been superior in sense and wit to the rest of the party. He was the Rev. George Leigh Cooke,° long known and respected at Oxford, where he held important offices, and had the privilege of helping to form the minds of men more eminent than himself. As Tutor in Corpus Christi College, he became instructor to some of the most distinguished undergraduates of that time: amongst others to Dr. Arnold, the Rev. John Keble, and Sir John Coleridge. The latter has mentioned him in terms of affectionate regard, both in his Memoir of Keble, and in a letter which appears in Dean Stanley's 'Life of Arnold.' Mr. Cooke was also an impressive preacher of earnest awakening sermons. I remember to have heard it observed by some of my undergraduate friends that, after all, there was more good to be got from George Cooke's plain sermons than from much of the more laboured oratory of the University pulpit. He was frequently Examiner in the schools, and occupied the chair of the Sedleian Professor of Natural Philosophy, from 1810 to 1853.

Before the end of 1805, the little family party removed to Southampton.° They resided in a commodious old-fashioned house in a corner of Castle Square.

I have no letters of my aunt, nor any other record of her, during her four years' residence at Southampton;° and though I now began to know, and, what was the same thing, to love her myself, yet my observations were only those of a young boy, and were not capable of penetrating her character, or estimating her powers. I have, however, a lively recollection of some local circumstances at Southampton, and as they refer chiefly to things which have been long ago swept away, I will record them.° My grandmother's house had a pleasant garden, bounded on one side by the old city walls; the top of this wall was sufficiently wide to afford a pleasant walk, with an extensive view, easily accessible to ladies by steps. This must have been a part of the identical walls which witnessed the embarkation of Henry V. before the battle of Agincourt, and the detection of the conspiracy of Cambridge, Scroop, and Grey, which Shakspeare has made so picturesque; when, according to the chorus in Henry V., the citizens saw

> The well-appointed King at Hampton Pier
> Embark his royalty.°

Among the records of the town of Southampton, they have a minute and authentic account, drawn up at that time, of the encampment of Henry V. near the town, before his embarkment for France. It is remarkable that the place where the army was encamped, then a low level plain, is now entirely covered by the sea, and is called Westport.[1] At that time Castle Square was occupied by a fantastic edifice, too large for the space in which it stood, though too small to accord well with its castellated style, erected by the second Marquis of Lansdowne, half-brother to the well-known statesman, who succeeded him in the title.° The Marchioness had a light phaeton,° drawn by six, and sometimes by eight little ponies, each pair decreasing in size, and becoming lighter in colour, through all the grades of dark brown, light brown, bay, and chestnut, as it was placed farther away from the carriage. The two leading pairs were managed by two boyish postilions, the two pairs nearest to the carriage were driven in hand. It was a delight to me to look down from the window and see this fairy equipage put together; for the premises of this castle

[1] See Wharton's note to Johnson and Steevens' Shakspeare. [*The Plays* of *William Shakespeare* (2nd edn, 10 vols., London, 1778). The reference is to Thomas Warton (1728–90) (not Wharton).]

were so contracted that the whole process went on in the little space that remained of the open square. Like other fairy works, however, it all proved evanescent. Not only carriage and ponies, but castle itself, soon vanished away, 'like the baseless fabric of a vision.'° On the death of the Marquis in 1809, the castle was pulled down. Few probably remember its existence; and any one who might visit the place now would wonder how it ever could have stood there.

In 1809° Mr. Knight was able to offer his mother the choice of two houses on his property; one near his usual residence at Godmersham Park in Kent; the other near Chawton House, his occasional residence in Hampshire. The latter was chosen; and in that year the mother and daughters, together with Miss Lloyd,° a near connection who lived with them, settled themselves at Chawton Cottage.

Chawton may be called the *second*, as well as the *last* home of Jane Austen; for during the temporary residences of the party at Bath and Southampton she was only a sojourner in a strange land,° but here she found a real home amongst her own people. It so happened that during her residence at Chawton circumstances brought several of her brothers and their families within easy distance of the house. Chawton must also be considered the place most closely connected with her career as a writer; for there it was that, in the maturity of her mind, she either wrote or rearranged, and prepared for publication the books by which she has become known to the world. This was the home where, after a few years, while still in the prime of life, she began to droop and wither away, and which she left only in the last stage of her illness, yielding to the persuasion of friends hoping against hope.

This house stood in the village of Chawton, about a mile from Alton, on the right hand side, just where the road to Winchester branches off from that to Gosport. It was so close to the road that the front door opened upon it; while a very narrow enclosure, paled in on each side, protected the building from danger of collision with any runaway vehicle. I believe it had been originally built for an inn, for which purpose it was certainly well situated. Afterwards it had been occupied by Mr. Knight's steward; but by

Wood engraving of Chawton Church

some additions to the house, and some judicious planting and skreening, it was made a pleasant and commodious abode. Mr. Knight was experienced and adroit at such arrangements, and this was a labour of love to him. A good-sized entrance and two sitting-rooms made the length of the house, all intended originally to look upon the road, but the large drawing-room window was blocked up and turned into a book-case, and another opened at the side which gave to view only turf and trees, as a high wooden fence and hornbeam hedge shut out the Winchester road, which skirted the whole length of the little domain. Trees were planted each side to form a shrubbery walk, carried round the enclosure, which gave a sufficient space for ladies' exercise. There was a pleasant irregular mixture of hedgerow, and gravel walk, and orchard, and long grass for mowing, arising from two or three little enclosures having been thrown together. The house itself was quite as good as the generality of parsonage-houses then were, and much in the same style; and was capable of receiving other members of the family as frequent visitors. It was sufficiently well furnished; everything inside and out was kept in good repair, and it was altogether a comfortable and ladylike establishment, though the means which supported it were not large.°

I give this description because some interest is generally taken in the residence of a popular writer. Cowper's unattractive house in the street of Olney has been pointed out to visitors, and has even attained the honour of an engraving in Southey's edition of his works:° but I cannot recommend any admirer of Jane Austen to undertake a pilgrimage to this spot. The building indeed still stands,° but it has lost all that gave it its character. After the death of Mrs. Cassandra Austen, in 1845, it was divided into tenements for labourers, and the grounds reverted to ordinary uses.

CHAPTER V

Description of Jane Austen's person, character, and tastes°

As my memoir has now reached the period when I saw a great deal of my aunt, and was old enough to understand something of her value, I will here attempt a description of her person, mind, and habits. In person she was very attractive; her figure was rather tall and slender, her step light and firm, and her whole appearance expressive of health and animation. In complexion she was a clear brunette with a rich colour; she had full round cheeks, with mouth and nose small and well formed, bright hazel eyes, and brown hair forming natural curls close round her face. If not so regularly handsome as her sister, yet her countenance had a peculiar charm of its own to the eyes of most beholders. At the time of which I am now writing, she never was seen, either morning or evening, without a cap; I believe that she and her sister were generally thought to have taken to the garb of middle age earlier than their years or their looks required; and that, though remarkably neat in their dress as in all their ways, they were scarcely sufficiently regardful of the fashionable, or the becoming.

She was not highly accomplished according to the present standard. Her sister drew well, and it is from a drawing of hers that the likeness prefixed to this volume has been taken.° Jane herself was fond of music, and had a sweet voice, both in singing and in conversation; in her youth she had received some instruction on the pianoforte; and at Chawton she practised daily, chiefly before breakfast. I believe she did so partly that she might not disturb the rest of the party who were less fond of music. In the evening she would sometimes sing, to her own accompaniment, some simple old songs, the words and airs of which, now never heard, still linger in my memory.°

She read French with facility, and knew something of Italian.°

In those days German was no more thought of than Hindostanee, as part of a lady's education. In history she followed the old guides—Goldsmith, Hume, and Robertson.° Critical enquiry into the usually received statements of the old historians was scarcely begun. The history of the early kings of Rome had not yet been dissolved into legend. Historic characters lay before the reader's eyes in broad light or shade, not much broken up by details. The virtues of King Henry VIII. were yet undiscovered, nor had much light been thrown on the inconsistencies of Queen Elizabeth; the one was held to be an unmitigated tyrant, and an embodied Blue Beard; the other a perfect model of wisdom and policy. Jane, when a girl, had strong political opinions, especially about the affairs of the sixteenth and seventeenth centuries. She was a vehement defender of Charles I. and his grandmother Mary;° but I think it was rather from an impulse of feeling than from any enquiry into the evidences by which they must be condemned or acquitted. As she grew up, the politics of the day occupied very little of her attention, but she probably shared the feeling of moderate Toryism which prevailed in her family. She was well acquainted with the old periodicals from the 'Spectator' downwards.° Her knowledge of Richardson's works was such as no one is likely again to acquire, now that the multitude and the merits of our light literature have called off the attention of readers from that great master. Every circumstance narrated in Sir Charles Grandison, all that was ever said or done in the cedar parlour, was familiar to her; and the wedding days of Lady L. and Lady G. were as well remembered as if they had been living friends.° Amongst her favourite writers, Johnson in prose, Crabbe in verse, and Cowper in both, stood high.° It is well that the native good taste of herself and of those with whom she lived, saved her from the snare into which a sister novelist° had fallen, of imitating the grandiloquent style of Johnson. She thoroughly enjoyed Crabbe; perhaps on account of a certain resemblance to herself in minute and highly finished detail; and would sometimes say, in jest, that, if she ever married at all, she could fancy being Mrs. Crabbe;° looking on the author quite as an abstract idea, and ignorant and regardless what manner of man he might be. Scott's poetry gave her great pleasure; she did not live to make much acquaintance with his novels. Only three of them were published before her death; but it will be seen by the following extract from one of her letters, that she was quite prepared to admit the merits of 'Waverley';° and it is remarkable that, living, as she did, far apart from the gossip of the literary world, she should even then have spoken so confidently of his being the author of it:—

'Walter Scott has no business to write novels;° especially good ones. It is not fair. He has fame and profit enough as a poet, and ought not to be taking the bread out of other people's mouths. I do not mean to like "Waverley," if I can help it, but I fear I must. I am quite determined, however, not to be pleased with Mrs.——'s,° should I ever meet with it, which I hope I may not. I think I can be stout against anything written by her. I have made up my mind to like no novels really, but Miss Edgeworth's, E.'s, and my own.'°

It was not, however, what she *knew*, but what she *was*, that distinguished her from others. I cannot better describe the fascination which she exercised over children than by quoting the words of two of her nieces. One says:—°

'As a very little girl I was always creeping up to aunt Jane, and following her whenever I could, in the house and out of it. I might not have remembered this but for the recollection of my mother's telling me privately, that I must not be troublesome to my aunt. Her first charm to children was great sweetness of manner. She seemed to love you, and you loved her in return. This, as well as I can now recollect, was what I felt in my early days, before I was old enough to be amused by her cleverness. But soon came the delight of her playful talk. She could make everything amusing to a child. Then, as I got older, when cousins came to share the entertainment, she would tell us the most delightful stories, chiefly of Fairyland, and her fairies had all characters of their own. The tale was invented, I am sure, at the moment, and was continued for two or three days, if occasion served.'

Again: 'When staying at Chawton, with two of her other nieces,° we often had amusements in which my aunt was very helpful. She was the one to whom we always looked for help. She would furnish us with what we wanted from her wardrobe; and she would be the entertaining visitor in our make-believe house. She amused us in various ways. Once, I remember, in giving a conversation as between myself and my two cousins, supposing we were all grown up, the day after a ball.'

Very similar is the testimony of another niece:°—'Aunt Jane was the general favourite with children; her ways with them being so playful, and her long circumstantial stories so delightful. These were continued from time to time, and were begged for on all possible and impossible occasions; woven, as she proceeded, out of nothing but her own happy talent for invention. Ah! if but one of them could be recovered! And again, as I grew older, when the original seventeen years between our ages seemed to shrink to seven, or to nothing, it comes back to me now how strangely I missed her. It had become so much a habit with me to put by things in my mind with a reference to her, and to say to myself, I shall keep this for aunt Jane.'

A nephew of hers° used to observe that his visits to Chawton, after the death of his aunt Jane, were always a disappointment to him. From old associations he could not help expecting to be particularly happy in that house; and never till he got there could he realise to himself how all its peculiar charm was gone. It was not only that the chief light in the house was quenched, but that the loss of it had cast a shade over the spirits of the survivors. Enough has been said to show her love for children, and her wonderful power of entertaining them; but her friends of all ages felt her enlivening influence. Her unusually quick sense of the ridiculous led her to play with all the common-places of everyday life, whether as regarded persons or things; but she never played with its serious duties or responsibilities, nor did she ever turn individuals into ridicule. With all her neighbours in the village she was on friendly, though not on intimate, terms. She took a kindly interest in all their proceedings, and liked to hear about them. They often served for her amusement; but it was her own nonsense that gave zest to the gossip. She was as far as possible from being censorious or satirical. She never abused them or *quizzed*° them—*that* was the word of the day; an ugly word, now obsolete; and the ugly practice which it expressed is much less prevalent now than it was then. The laugh which she occasionally raised was by imagining for her neighbours, as she was equally ready to imagine for her friends or herself, impossible contingencies, or by relating in prose or verse some trifling anecdote coloured to her own fancy, or in writing a fictitious history of what they were supposed to have said or done, which could deceive nobody.

The following specimens may be given of the liveliness of mind which imparted an agreeable flavour both to her correspondence and her conversation:—

On reading in the Newspapers the Marriage of Mr. Gell to Miss Gill, of Eastbourne.°

At Eastbourne Mr. Gell, From being perfectly well,
Became dreadfully ill, For love of Miss Gill.
So he said, with some sighs, I'm the slave of your *iis*;
Oh, restore, if you please, By accepting my *ees*.

On the Marriage of a Middle-aged Flirt with a Mr. Wake, whom, it was supposed, she would scarcely have accepted in her youth.°

Maria, good-humoured, and handsome, and tall,
For a husband was at her last stake;
And having in vain danced at many a ball,
Is now happy to *jump at a Wake*.

'We were all at the play last night to see Miss O'Neil in Isabella.° I do not think she was quite equal to my expectation. I fancy I want something more than can be. Acting seldom satisfies me. I took two pockethandkerchiefs, but had very little occasion for either. She is an elegant creature, however, and hugs Mr. Young delightfully.'

'So, Miss B. is actually married, but I have never seen it in the papers; and one may as well be single if the wedding is not to be in print.'°

Once, too, she took it into her head to write the following mock panegyric on a young friend, who really was clever and handsome:—

1

In measured verse I'll now rehearse°
The charms of lovely Anna:
And, first, her mind is unconfined
Like any vast savannah.

2

Ontario's lake may fitly speak
Her fancy's ample bound:
Its circuit may, on strict survey,
Five hundred miles be found.

3

Her wit descends on foes and friends
Like famed Niagara's Fall;
And travellers gaze in wild amaze,
And listen, one and all.

4

Her judgment sound, thick, black, profound,
Like transatlantic groves,
Dispenses aid, and friendly shade
To all that in it roves.

5

If thus her mind to be defined
America exhausts,
And all that's grand in that great land
In similes it costs—

6

Oh how can I her person try
To image and portray?
How paint the face, the form how trace
In which those virtues lay?

7

Another world must be unfurled,
Another language known,
Ere tongue or sound can publish round
Her charms of flesh and bone.

I believe that all this nonsense was nearly extempore, and that the fancy of drawing the images from America arose at the moment from the obvious rhyme which presented itself in the first stanza.

The following extracts are from letters addressed to a niece who was at that time amusing herself by attempting a novel,° probably never finished, certainly never published, and of which I know nothing but what these extracts tell. They show the good-natured sympathy and encouragement which the aunt, then herself occupied in writing 'Emma,' could give to the less matured powers of the niece. They bring out incidentally some of her opinions concerning compositions of that kind:—

Extracts

'Chawton, Aug. 10, 1814.°

'Your aunt C. does not like desultory novels, and is rather fearful that yours will be too much so; that there will be too frequent a change from one set of people to another, and that circumstances will be sometimes introduced, of apparent consequence, which will lead to nothing. It will not be so great an objection to me. I allow much more latitude than she does, and think nature and spirit cover many sins of a wandering story. And people in general do not care much about it, for your comfort. . . .'

'Sept. 9.°

'You are now collecting your people delightfully, getting them exactly into such a spot as is the delight of my life. Three or four families in a country village is the very thing to work on; and I hope you will write a great deal more, and make full use of them while they are so very favourably arranged.'

'Sept. 28.°

'Devereux Forrester being ruined by his vanity is very good: but I wish you would not let him plunge into a "vortex of dissipation." I do not object to the thing, but I cannot bear the expression: it is such thorough novel slang; and so old that I dare say Adam met with it in the first novel that he opened.'

'Hans Place (Nov. 1814).°

'I have been very far from finding your book an evil, I assure you. I read it immediately, and with great pleasure. Indeed, I do think you get on very fast. I wish other people of my acquaintance could compose as rapidly. Julian's history was quite a surprise to me. You had not very long known it yourself, I suspect; but I have no objection to make to the circumstance; it is very well told, and his having been in love with the aunt gives Cecilia an additional interest with him. I like the idea; a very proper compliment to an aunt! I rather imagine, indeed, that nieces are seldom chosen but in compliment to some aunt or other. I dare say your husband° was in love with me once, and would never have thought of you if he had not supposed me dead of a scarlet fever.'

Jane Austen was successful in everything that she attempted with her fingers. None of us could throw spilikins in so perfect a circle, or take them off with so steady a hand. Her performances with cup and ball° were marvellous. The one used at Chawton was an easy one, and she has been known to catch it on the point above an hundred times in succession, till her hand was weary. She sometimes found a resource in that simple game, when unable, from weakness in her eyes, to read or write long together. A specimen of her clear strong handwriting is here given.° Happy would the compositors for the press be if they had always so legible a manuscript to work from. But the writing was not the only part of her letters which showed superior handiwork. In those days there was an art in folding and sealing. No adhesive envelopes made all easy. Some people's letters always looked loose and untidy; but her paper was sure to take the right folds, and her sealing-wax to drop into the right place. Her needlework both plain and ornamental was excellent, and might almost have put a sewing machine to shame. She was considered especially great in satin stitch.° She spent much time in these occupations, and some of her merriest talk was over clothes which she and her

On reading in the Newspaper, the Marriage of "Mr. Gell of Eastbourne to Miss Gill."

Of Eastbourne Mr Gell
From being perfectly well
Became dreadfully ill
For the love of Miss Gill

So he said with some sighs
"I'm the slave of your eyes.
Oh! restore if you please
By accepting my ease."

J. A.

Lithographic facsimile of an autograph manuscript of the verses on Mr Gell and Miss Gill, now in the Pump Room, Bath companions were making, sometimes for themselves, and sometimes for the poor. There still remains a curious specimen of her needlework made for a sister-in-law, my mother. In a very small bag is deposited a little rolled up housewife,° furnished with minikin needles and fine thread. In the housewife is a tiny pocket, and in the pocket is enclosed a slip of paper, on which, written as with a crow quill, are these lines:—

This little bag, I hope, will prove
  To be not vainly made;
For should you thread and needles want,
  It will afford you aid.

And, as we are about to part,
  'T will serve another end:
For, when you look upon this bag,
  You'll recollect your friend.

It is the kind of article that some benevolent fairy might be supposed to give as a reward to a diligent little girl. The whole is of flowered silk, and having been never used and carefully preserved, it is as fresh and bright as when it was first made seventy years ago; and shows that the same hand which painted so exquisitely with the pen could work as delicately with the needle.

I have collected some of the bright qualities which shone, as it were, on the surface of Jane Austen's character, and attracted most notice; but underneath them there lay the strong foundations of sound sense and judgment, rectitude of principle, and delicacy of feeling, qualifying her equally to advise, assist, or amuse. She was, in fact, as ready to comfort the unhappy, or to nurse the sick, as she was to laugh and jest with the light-hearted. Two of her nieces were grown up, and one of them was married,° before she was taken away from them. As their minds became more matured, they were admitted into closer intimacy with her, and learned more of her graver thoughts; they know what a sympathising friend and judicious adviser they found her to be in many little difficulties and doubts of early womanhood.

I do not venture to speak of her religious principles:° that is a subject on which she herself was more inclined to *think* and *act* than to *talk*, and I shall imitate her reserve; satisfied to have shown how much of Christian love and humility abounded in her heart, without presuming to lay bare the roots whence those graces grew. Some little insight, however, into these deeper recesses of the heart must be given, when we come to speak of her death.

CHAPTER VI

Habits of Composition resumed after a long interval—First publication—The interest taken by the Author in the success of her Works

It may seem extraordinary that Jane Austen should have written so little° during the years that elapsed between leaving Steventon and settling at Chawton; especially when this cessation from work is contrasted with her literary activity both before and after that period. It might rather have been expected that fresh scenes and new acquaintance would have called forth her powers; while the quiet life which the family led both at Bath and Southampton must have afforded abundant leisure for composition; but so it was that nothing which I know of, certainly nothing which the public have seen, was completed° in either of those places. I can only state the fact, without assigning any cause for it; but as soon as she was fixed in her second home, she resumed the habits of composition which had been formed in her first, and continued them to the end of her life. The first year of her residence at Chawton seems to have been devoted to revising and preparing for the press 'Sense and Sensibility,' and 'Pride and Prejudice'; but between February 1811 and August 1816,° she began and completed 'Mansfield Park,' 'Emma,' and 'Persuasion,' so that the last five years of her life produced the same number of novels with those which had been written in her early youth. How she was able to effect all this is surprising, for she had no separate study to retire to, and most of the work must have been done in the general sitting-room, subject to all kinds of casual interruptions. She was careful that her occupation should not be suspected by servants, or visitors, or any persons beyond her own family party. She wrote upon small sheets of paper which could easily be put away, or covered with a piece of blotting paper. There was, between the front door and the offices, a swing door which creaked when it was opened; but she objected to having this little inconvenience remedied, because it gave her notice when anyone was coming.° She was not, however, troubled with companions like her own Mrs. Allen in 'Northanger Abbey,' whose 'vacancy of mind and incapacity for thinking were such that, as she never talked a great deal, so she could never be entirely silent; and therefore, while she sat at work, if she lost her needle, or broke her thread, or saw a speck of dirt on her gown, she must observe it, whether there were any one at leisure to answer her or not.'° In that well occupied female party there must have been many precious hours of silence during which the pen was busy at the little mahogany writing-desk,[1] while Fanny Price, or Emma Woodhouse, or Anne Elliott was growing into beauty and interest. I have no doubt that I, and my sisters and cousins, in our visits to Chawton, frequently disturbed this mystic process, without having any idea of the mischief that we were doing; certainly we never should have guessed it by any signs of impatience or irritability in the writer.

As so much had been previously prepared, when once she began to publish, her works came out in quick succession. 'Sense and Sensibility' was published in 1811, 'Pride and Prejudice' at the beginning of 1813, 'Mansfield Park' in 1814, 'Emma' early in 1816; 'Northanger Abbey' and 'Persuasion' did not appear till after her death, in 1818. It will be shown farther on why 'Northanger Abbey,' though amongst the first written, was one of the last published. Her first three novels were published by Egerton, her last three by Murray. The profits of the four which had been printed before her death had not at that time amounted to seven hundred pounds.°

I have no record of the publication of 'Sense and Sensibility,'° nor of the author's feelings at this her first appearance before the public; but the following extracts from three letters to her sister give a lively picture of the interest with which she watched the reception of 'Pride and Prejudice,' and show the carefulness with

[1] This mahogany desk, which has done good service to the public, is now in the possession of my sister, Miss Austen. [The desk may be that purchased by JA's father in 1794 (*Fam. Rec.*, 83). It was bequeathed by Cassandra to her niece Caroline and descended in the Austen-Leigh family. It can now be seen in the British Library.]

which she corrected her compositions, and rejected much that had been written:—

'Chawton, Friday, January 29 (1813).°

'I hope you received my little parcel by J. Bond on Wednesday evening, my dear Cassandra, and that you will be ready to hear from me again on Sunday, for I feel that I must write to you to-day. I want to tell you that I have got my own darling child from London. On Wednesday I received one copy sent down by Falkener,° with three lines from Henry to say that he had given another to Charles and sent a third by the coach to Godmersham. . . . The advertisement is in our paper to-day for the first time: 18*s*. He shall ask 1*l*. 1*s*. for my two next, and 1*l*. 8*s*. for my stupidest of all.° Miss B. dined with us on the very day of the book's coming, and in the evening we fairly set at it, and read half the first vol. to her, prefacing that, having intelligence from Henry that such a work would soon appear, we had desired him to send it whenever it came out, and I believe it passed with her unsuspected. She was amused, poor soul! *That* she could not help, you know, with two such people to lead the way, but she really does seem to admire Elizabeth. I must confess that I think her as delightful a creature as ever appeared in print, and how I shall be able to tolerate those who do not like *her* at least I do not know. There are a few typical errors;° and a "said he," or a "said she," would sometimes make the dialogue more immediately clear; but "I do not write for such dull elves"° as have not a great deal of ingenuity themselves. The second volume is shorter than I could wish, but the difference is not so much in reality as in look, there being a larger proportion of narrative in that part. I have lop't and crop't so successfully, however, that I imagine it must be rather shorter than "Sense and Sensibility" altogether. Now I will try and write of something else.'

'Chawton, Thursday, February 4 (1813).°

'My dear Cassandra,—Your letter was truly welcome, and I am much obliged to you for all your praise;° it came at a right time, for I had had some fits of disgust. Our second evening's reading to Miss B. had not pleased me so well, but I believe something must be attributed to my mother's too rapid way of getting on: though she perfectly understands the characters herself, she cannot speak as they ought. Upon the whole, however, I am quite vain enough and well satisfied enough. The work is rather too light, and bright, and sparkling; it wants shade; it wants to be stretched out here and there with a long chapter of sense, if it could be had; if not, of solemn specious nonsense, about something unconnected with the story; an essay on writing, a critique on Walter Scott, or the history of Buonaparté, or something that would form a contrast, and bring the reader with increased delight to the playfulness and epigrammatism of the general style. . . . The greatest blunder in the printing that I have met with is in page 220, v. 3, where two speeches are made into one. There might as well be no suppers at Longbourn; but I suppose it was the remains of Mrs. Bennett's old Meryton habits.'

The following letter seems to have been written soon after the last two: in February 1813:—°

'This will be a quick return for yours, my dear Cassandra; I doubt its having much else to recommend it; but there is no saying; it may turn out to be a very long and delightful letter. I am exceedingly pleased that you can say what you do, after having gone through the whole work, and Fanny's° praise is very gratifying. My hopes were tolerably strong of *her*, but nothing like a certainty. Her liking Darcy and Elizabeth is enough. She might hate all the others, if she would. I have her opinion under her own hand this morning, but your transcript of it, which I read first, was not, and is not, the less acceptable. To *me* it is of course all praise, but the more exact truth which she sends *you* is good enough. . . . Our party on Wednesday was not unagreeable, though we wanted a master of the house less anxious and fidgety, and more conversible. Upon Mrs. ——'s mentioning that she had sent the rejected addresses° to Mrs. H., I began talking to her a little about them, and expressed my hope of their having amused her. Her answer was, "Oh dear yes, very much, very droll indeed, the opening of the house, and the striking up of the fiddles!"

What she meant, poor woman, who shall say? I sought no farther. As soon as a whist party was formed, and a round table threatened, I made my mother an excuse and came away, leaving just as many for *their* round table as there were at Mrs. Grant's.[1] I wish they might be as agreeable a set. My mother is very well, and finds great amusement in glove-knitting, and at present wants no other work. We quite run over with books. She has got Sir John Carr's "Travels in Spain," and I am reading a Society octavo, an "Essay on the Military Police and Institutions of the British Empire," by Capt. Pasley of the Engineers,° a book which I protested against at first, but which upon trial I find delightfully written and highly entertaining. I am as much in love with the author as I ever was with Clarkson or Buchanan, or even the two Mr. Smiths of the city.° The first soldier I ever sighed for; but he does write with extraordinary force and spirit. Yesterday, moreover, brought us "Mrs. Grant's Letters,"° with Mr. White's compliments; but I have disposed of them, compliments and all, to Miss P., and amongst so many readers or retainers of books as we have in Chawton, I dare say there will be no difficulty in getting rid of them for another fortnight, if necessary. I have disposed of Mrs. Grant for the second fortnight to Mrs. ——. It can make no difference to *her* which of the twenty-six fortnights in the year the 3 vols. lie on her table.° I have been applied to for information as to the oath taken in former times of Bell, Book, and Candle, but have none to give. Perhaps you may be able to learn something of its origin where you now are.° Ladies who read those enormous great stupid thick quarto volumes which one always sees in the breakfast parlour there must be acquainted with everything in the world. I detest a quarto.° Capt. Pasley's book is too good for their society. They will not understand a man who condenses his thoughts into an octavo. I have learned from Sir J. Carr that there is no Government House at Gibraltar. I must alter it to the Commissioner's'.°

The following letter° belongs to the same year, but treats of a

[1] At this time, February 1813, 'Mansfield Park' was nearly finished. [The reference is to the 'round game' in *MP*, Ch. 25.]

different subject. It describes a journey from Chawton to London, in her brother's curricle,° and shows how much could be seen and enjoyed in course of a long summer's day by leisurely travelling amongst scenery which the traveller in an express train now rushes through in little more than an hour, but scarcely sees at all:—

'Sloane Street, Thursday, May 20 (1813).°

'MY DEAR CASSANDRA,

'Before I say anything else, I claim a paper full of halfpence on the drawing-room mantel-piece; I put them there myself, and forgot to bring them with me. I cannot say that I have yet been in any distress for money, but I chuse to have my due, as well as the Devil. How lucky we were in our weather yesterday! This wet morning makes one more sensible of it. We had no rain of any consequence. The head of the curricle was put half up three or four times, but our share of the showers was very trifling, though they seemed to be heavy all round us, when we were on the Hog's-back,° and I fancied it might then be raining so hard at Chawton as to make you feel for us much more than we deserved. Three hours and a quarter took us to Guildford, where we staid barely two hours, and had only just time enough for all we had to do there; that is, eating a long and comfortable breakfast, watching the carriages, paying Mr. Harrington, and taking a little stroll afterwards. From some views which that stroll gave us, I think most highly of the situation of Guildford. We wanted all our brothers and sisters to be standing with us in the bowling-green, and looking towards Horsham. I was very lucky in my gloves—got them at the first shop I went to, though I went into it rather because it was near than because it looked at all like a glove shop, and gave only four shillings for them; after which everybody at Chawton will be hoping and predicting that they cannot be good for anything, and their worth certainly remains to be proved; but I think they look very well. We left Guildford at twenty minutes before twelve (I hope somebody cares for these minutiæ), and were at Esher in about two hours more. I was very much pleased with the country in general. Between Guildford and Ripley I thought it particularly pretty, also about Painshill; and from a Mr. Spicer's grounds at Esher, which we walked into before dinner, the views were beautiful. I cannot say what we did *not* see, but I should think there could not be a wood, or a meadow, or palace, or remarkable spot in England that was not spread out before us on one side or other. Claremont is going to be sold: a Mr. Ellis has it now. It is a house that seems never to have prospered. After dinner we walked forward to be overtaken at the coachman's time, and before he did overtake us we were very near Kingston. I fancy it was about half-past six when we reached this house—a twelve hours' business, and the horses did not appear more than reasonably tired. I was very tired too, and glad to get to bed early, but am quite well to-day. I am very snug in the front drawing-room all to myself, and would not say "thank you" for any company but you. The quietness of it does me good. I have contrived to pay my two visits, though the weather made me a great while about it, and left me only a few minutes to sit with Charlotte Craven.[1] She looks very well, and her hair is done up with an elegance to do credit to any education. Her manners are as unaffected and pleasing as ever. She had heard from her mother to-day. Mrs. Craven spends another fortnight at Chilton. I saw nobody but Charlotte, which pleased me best. I was shewn upstairs into a drawing-room, where she came to me, and the appearance of the room, so totally unschool-like, amused me very much; it was full of modern elegancies.°

'Yours very affec$^{tly.}$, 'J. A.'

The next letter, written in the following year, contains an account of another journey to London, with her brother Henry, and reading with him the manuscript of 'Mansfield Park':—

'Henrietta Street, Wednesday, March 2 (1814).°

'My dear Cassandra,

'You were wrong in thinking of us at Guildford last night: we

[1] The present Lady Pollen, of Redenham, near Andover, then at a school in London.

were at Cobham. On reaching G. we found that John and the horses were gone on. We therefore did no more than we had done at Farnham—sit in the carriage while fresh horses were put in, and proceeded directly to Cobham, which we reached by seven, and about eight were sitting down to a very nice roast fowl, &c. We had altogether a very good journey, and everything at Cobham was comfortable. I could not pay Mr. Harrington! That was the only alas! of the business. I shall therefore return his bill, and my mother's 2*l*., that you may try your luck. We did not begin reading till Bentley Green. Henry's approbation is hitherto even equal to my wishes. He says it is different° from the other two, but does not appear to think it at all inferior. He has only married Mrs. R. I am afraid he has gone through the most entertaining part. He took to Lady B. and Mrs. N. most kindly, and gives great praise to the drawing of the characters. He understands them all, likes Fanny, and, I think, foresees how it will all be. I finished the "Heroine"° last night, and was very much amused by it. I wonder James did not like it better. It diverted me exceedingly. We went to bed at ten. I was very tired, but slept to a miracle, and am lovely to-day, and at present Henry seems to have no complaint. We left Cobham at half-past eight, stopped to bait and breakfast at Kingston, and were in this house considerably before two. Nice smiling Mr. Barlowe met us at the door and, in reply to enquiries after news, said that peace was generally expected.° I have taken possession of my bedroom, unpacked my bandbox, sent Miss P.'s two letters to the two-penny post,° been visited by M[d.] B.,° and am now writing by myself at the new table in the front room. It is snowing. We had some snowstorms yesterday, and a smart frost at night, which gave us a hard road from Cobham to Kingston; but as it was then getting dirty and heavy, Henry had a pair of leaders put on to the bottom of Sloane St. His own horses, therefore, cannot have had hard work. I watched for *veils* as we drove through the streets, and had the pleasure of seeing several upon vulgar heads. And now, how do you all do?—you in particular, after the worry of yesterday and the day before. I hope Martha had a pleasant visit again, and that you and my mother could eat your beef-pudding. Depend upon my thinking of the chimney-sweeper as soon as I wake to-morrow. Places are secured at Drury Lane for Saturday, but so great is the rage for seeing Kean° that only a third and fourth row could be got; as it is in a front box, however, I hope we shall do pretty well—Shylock, a good play for Fanny—she cannot be much affected, I think. Mrs. Perigord has just been here. She tells me that we owe her master for the silk-dyeing. My poor old muslin has never been dyed yet. It has been promised to be done several times. What wicked people dyers are. They begin with dipping their own souls in scarlet sin. It is evening. We have drank tea, and I have torn through the third vol. of the "Heroine." I do not think it falls off. It is a delightful burlesque, particularly on the Radcliffe style. Henry is going on with "Mansfield Park." He admires H. Crawford: I mean properly, as a clever, pleasant man. I tell you all the good I can, as I know how much you will enjoy it. We hear that Mr. Kean is more admired than ever. There are no good places to be got in Drury Lane for the next fortnight, but Henry means to secure some for Saturday fortnight, when you are reckoned upon. Give my love to little Cass. I hope she found my bed comfortable last night.° I have seen nobody in London yet with such a long chin as Dr. Syntax, nor anybody quite so large as Gogmagolicus.°

'Yours aff^tly.,

'J. AUSTEN.'

CHAPTER VII

Seclusion from the literary world—Notice from the Prince Regent—Correspondence with Mr. Clarke—Suggestions to alter her style of writing

Jane Austen lived in entire seclusion from the literary world: neither by correspondence, nor by personal intercourse was she known to any contemporary authors. It is probable that she never was in company with any person whose talents or whose celebrity equalled her own; so that her powers never could have been sharpened by collision with superior intellects, nor her imagination aided by their casual suggestions. Whatever she produced was a genuine home-made article. Even during the last two or three years of her life, when her works were rising in the estimation of the public, they did not enlarge the circle of her acquaintance. Few of her readers knew even her name, and none knew more of her than her name. I doubt whether it would be possible to mention any other author of note, whose personal obscurity was so complete. I can think of none like her, but of many to contrast with her in that respect. Fanny Burney, afterwards Madame D'Arblay,° was at an early age petted by Dr. Johnson, and introduced to the wits and scholars of the day at the tables of Mrs. Thrale and Sir Joshua Reynolds. Anna Seward,° in her self-constituted shrine at Lichfield, would have been miserable, had she not trusted that the eyes of all lovers of poetry were devoutly fixed on her. Joanna Baillie and Maria Edgeworth° were indeed far from courting publicity; they loved the privacy of their own families, one with her brother and sister in their Hampstead villa, the other in her more distant retreat in Ireland; but fame pursued them, and they were the favourite correspondents of Sir Walter Scott. Crabbe, who was usually buried in a country parish, yet sometimes visited London, and dined at Holland House, and was received as a fellow-poet by Campbell, Moore, and Rogers;° and on one memorable occasion he was Scott's guest at Edinburgh, and gazed with wondering eyes on the incongruous pageantry with which George IV. was entertained in that city.° Even those great writers who hid themselves amongst lakes and mountains associated with each other; and though little seen by the world were so much in its thoughts that a new term, 'Lakers,'° was coined to designate them. The chief part of Charlotte Brontë's life° was spent in a wild solitude compared with which Steventon and Chawton might be considered to be in the gay world; and yet she attained to personal distinction which never fell to Jane's lot. When she visited her kind publisher in London, literary men and women were invited purposely to meet her: Thackeray bestowed upon her the honour of his notice; and once in Willis's Rooms,[1] she had to walk shy and trembling through an avenue of lords and ladies, drawn up for the purpose of gazing at the author of 'Jane Eyre.' Miss Mitford,° too, lived quietly in 'Our Village,' devoting her time and talents to the benefit of a father scarcely worthy of her; but she did not live there unknown. Her tragedies gave her a name in London. She numbered Milman and Talfourd° amongst her correspondents; and her works were a passport to the society of many who would not otherwise have sought her. Hundreds admired Miss Mitford on account of her writings for one who ever connected the idea of Miss Austen with the press. A few years ago, a gentleman visiting Winchester Cathedral desired to be shown Miss Austen's grave. The verger, as he pointed it out, asked, 'Pray, sir, can you tell me whether there was anything particular about that lady; so many people want to know where she was buried?'° During her life the ignorance of the verger was shared by most people; few knew that 'there was anything particular about that lady.'

It was not till towards the close of her life, when the last of the works that she saw published was in the press, that she received the only mark of distinction ever bestowed upon her; and that was remarkable for the high quarter whence it emanated rather than for any actual increase of fame that it conferred. It happened thus. In the autumn of 1815 she nursed her brother Henry through a dangerous fever and slow convalescence at his house in

[1] See Mrs. Gaskell's 'Life of Miss Brontë,' vol. ii. p. 215.

Hans Place. He was attended by one of the Prince Regent's physicians.° All attempts to keep her name secret had at this time ceased, and though it had never appeared on a title-page, all who cared to know might easily learn it: and the friendly physician was aware that his patient's nurse was the author of 'Pride and Prejudice.' Accordingly he informed her one day that the Prince was a great admirer of her novels; that he read them often, and kept a set in every one of his residences; that he himself therefore had thought it right to inform his Royal Highness that Miss Austen was staying in London, and that the Prince had desired Mr. Clarke, the librarian of Carlton House,° to wait upon her. The next day Mr. Clarke made his appearance, and invited her to Carlton House, saying that he had the Prince's instructions to show her the library and other apartments, and to pay her every possible attention. The invitation was of course accepted, and during the visit to Carlton House Mr. Clarke declared himself commissioned to say that if Miss Austen had any other novel forthcoming she was at liberty to dedicate it to the Prince. Accordingly such a dedication was immediately prefixed to 'Emma,' which was at that time in the press.°

Mr. Clarke was the brother of Dr. Clarke, the traveller and mineralogist, whose life has been written by Bishop Otter.° Jane found in him not only a very courteous gentleman, but also a warm admirer of her talents; though it will be seen by his letters that he did not clearly apprehend the limits of her powers, or the proper field for their exercise. The following correspondence took place between them.

Feeling some apprehension lest she should make a mistake in acting on the verbal permission which she had received from the Prince, Jane addressed the following letter to Mr. Clarke:—

'Nov. 15, 1815.°

'Sir,—I must take the liberty of asking you a question. Among the many flattering attentions which I received from you at Carlton House on Monday last was the information of my being at liberty to dedicate any future work to His Royal Highness the Prince Regent, without the necessity of any solicitation on my part. Such, at least, I believed to be your words; but as I am very anxious to be quite certain of what was intended, I entreat you to have the goodness to inform me how such a permission is to be understood, and whether it is incumbent on me to show my sense of the honour by inscribing the work now in the press to His Royal Highness; I should be equally concerned to appear either presumptuous or ungrateful.'

The following gracious answer was returned by Mr. Clarke, together with a suggestion which must have been received with some surprise:—

'Carlton House, Nov. 16, 1815.°

'DEAR MADAM,—It is certainly not *incumbent* on you to dedicate your work now in the press to His Royal Highness; but if you wish to do the Regent that honour either now or at any future period I am happy to send you that permission, which need not require any more trouble or solicitation on your part.

'Your late works, Madam, and in particular "Mansfield Park," reflect the highest honour on your genius and your principles. In every new work your mind seems to increase its energy and power of discrimination. The Regent has read and admired all your publications.

'Accept my best thanks for the pleasure your volumes have given me. In the perusal of them I felt a great inclination to write and say so. And I also, dear Madam, wished to be allowed to ask you to delineate in some future work the habits of life, and character, and enthusiasm of a clergyman, who should pass his time between the metropolis and the country, who should be something like Beattie's Minstrel—

Silent when glad, affectionate tho' shy,
 And in his looks was most demurely sad;
And now he laughed aloud, yet none knew why.°

Neither Goldsmith, nor La Fontaine in his "Tableau de Famille,"° have in my mind quite delineated an English clergyman, at least of the present day, fond of and entirely engaged in literature, no man's enemy but his own.° Pray, dear Madam, think of these things.

'Believe me at all times with sincerity and respect,
your faithful and obliged servant,
'J. S. CLARKE, Librarian.'

The following letter, written in reply, will show how unequal the author of 'Pride and Prejudice' felt herself to delineating an enthusiastic clergyman of the present day, who should resemble Beattie's Minstrel:—

'Dec. 11.°

'DEAR SIR,—My "Emma" is now so near publication that I feel it right to assure you of my not having forgotten your kind recommendation of an early copy for Carlton House, and that I have Mr. Murray's promise of its being sent to His Royal Highness, under cover to you, three days previous to the work being really out. I must make use of this opportunity to thank you, dear Sir, for the very high praise you bestow on my other novels. I am too vain to wish to convince you that you have praised them beyond their merits. My greatest anxiety at present is that this fourth work should not disgrace what was good in the others. But on this point I will do myself the justice to declare that, whatever may be my wishes for its success, I am strongly haunted with the idea that to those readers who have preferred "Pride and Prejudice" it will appear inferior in wit, and to those who have preferred "Mansfield Park" inferior in good sense. Such as it is, however, I hope you will do me the favour of accepting a copy. Mr. Murray will have directions for sending one. I am quite honoured by your thinking me capable of drawing such a clergyman as you gave the sketch of in your note of Nov. 16th. But I assure you I am *not*. The comic part of the character I might be equal to, but not the good, the enthusiastic, the literary. Such a man's conversation must at times be on subjects of science and philosophy, of which I know nothing; or at least be occasionally abundant in quotations and allusions which a woman who, like me, knows only her own mother tongue, and has read little in that, would be totally without the power of giving. A classical education, or at any rate a very extensive acquaintance with English literature, ancient and modern, appears to me quite indispensable for the person who would do any justice to your clergyman; and I think I may boast myself to be, with all possible vanity, the most unlearned and uninformed female who ever dared to be an authoress.

'Believe me, dear Sir,
'Your obliged and faithful hum[bl] Ser[t].
'JANE AUSTEN.'[1]

Mr. Clarke, however, was not to be discouraged from proposing another subject. He had recently been appointed chaplain and private English secretary to Prince Leopold, who was then about to be united to the Princess Charlotte;° and when he again wrote to express the gracious thanks of the Prince Regent for the copy of 'Emma' which had been presented, he suggests that 'an historical romance illustrative of the august House of Cobourg would just now be very interesting,'° and might very properly be dedicated to Prince Leopold. This was much as if Sir William Ross° had been set to paint a great battle-piece; and it is amusing to see with what grave civility she declined a proposal which must have struck her as ludicrous, in the following letter:—

'MY DEAR SIR,—I am honoured° by the Prince's thanks and very much obliged to yourself for the kind manner in which you mention the work. I have also to acknowledge a former letter forwarded to me from Hans Place. I assure you I felt very grateful for the friendly tenor of it, and hope my silence will have been considered, as it was truly meant, to proceed only from an unwillingness to tax your time with idle thanks. Under every interesting circumstance which your own talents and literary labours have placed you in, or the favour of the Regent bestowed, you have my best wishes. Your recent appointments I hope are a

[1] It was her pleasure to boast of greater ignorance than she had any just claim to. She knew more than her mother tongue, for she knew a good deal of French and a little of Italian. [See pp. 70–1 above.]

step to something still better. In my opinion, the service of a court can hardly be too well paid, for immense must be the sacrifice of time and feeling required by it.

'You are very kind in your hints as to the sort of composition which might recommend me at present, and I am fully sensible that an historical romance, founded on the House of Saxe Cobourg, might be much more to the purpose of profit or popularity than such pictures of domestic life in country villages as I deal in. But I could no more write a romance than an epic poem. I could not sit seriously down to write a serious romance under any other motive than to save my life; and if it were indispensable for me to keep it up and never relax into laughing at myself or at other people, I am sure I should be hung before I had finished the first chapter. No, I must keep to my own style and go on in my own way; and though I may never succeed again in that, I am convinced that I should totally fail in any other.

'I remain, my dear Sir,
'Your very much obliged, and sincere friend,
'J. AUSTEN.

'Chawton, near Alton, April 1, 1816.'

Mr. Clarke should have recollected the warning of the wise man, 'Force not the course of the river.' If you divert it from the channel in which nature taught it to flow, and force it into one arbitrarily cut by yourself, you will lose its grace and beauty.

But when his free course is not hindered,
He makes sweet music with the enamelled stones,
Giving a gentle kiss to every sedge
He overtaketh in his pilgrimage:
And so by many winding nooks he strays
With willing sport.°

All writers of fiction, who have genius strong enough to work out a course of their own, resist every attempt to interfere with its direction. No two writers could be more unlike each other than Jane Austen and Charlotte Brontë; so much so that the latter was unable to understand why the former was admired, and confessed that she herself 'should hardly like to live with her ladies and gentlemen, in their elegant but confined houses;'° but each writer equally resisted interference with her own natural style of composition. Miss Brontë, in reply to a friendly critic, who had warned her against being too melodramatic, and had ventured to propose Miss Austen's works to her as a study, writes thus:—

'Whenever I *do* write another book, I think I will have nothing of what you call "melodrama." I *think* so, but I am not sure. I *think*, too, I will endeavour to follow the counsel which shines out of Miss Austen's "mild eyes," to finish more, and be more subdued; but neither am I sure of that. When authors write best, or, at least, when they write most fluently, an influence seems to waken in them which becomes their master—which will have its way—putting out of view all behests but its own, dictating certain words, and insisting on their being used, whether vehement or measured in their nature, new moulding characters, giving unthought of turns to incidents, rejecting carefully elaborated old ideas, and suddenly creating and adopting new ones. Is it not so? And should we try to counteract this influence? Can we indeed counteract it?'[1]

The playful raillery with which the one parries an attack on her liberty, and the vehement eloquence of the other in pleading the same cause and maintaining the independence of genius, are very characteristic of the minds of the respective writers.

The suggestions which Jane received as to the sort of story that she ought to write were, however, an amusement to her, though they were not likely to prove useful; and she has left amongst her papers one entitled, 'Plan of a novel according to hints from various quarters.'° The names of some of those advisers° are written on the margin of the manuscript opposite to their respective suggestions.

'Heroine to be the daughter of a clergyman, who after having lived much in the world had retired from it, and settled on a curacy with a very small fortune of his own. The most excellent

[1] Mrs. Gaskell's 'Life of Miss Brontë,' vol. ii. p. 53.

man that can be imagined, perfect in character, temper, and manner, without the smallest drawback or peculiarity to prevent his being the most delightful companion to his daughter from one year's end to the other. Heroine faultless in character, beautiful in person, and possessing every possible accomplishment. Book to open with father and daughter conversing in long speeches, elegant language, and a tone of high serious sentiment. The father induced, at his daughter's earnest request, to relate to her the past events of his life. Narrative to reach through the greater part of the first volume; as besides all the circumstances of his attachment to her mother, and their marriage, it will comprehend his going to sea as chaplain to a distinguished naval character about the court;° and his going afterwards to court himself, which involved him in many interesting situations, concluding with his opinion of the benefits of tithes° being done away with. . . . From this outset the story will proceed, and contain a striking variety of adventures. Father an exemplary parish priest, and devoted to literature; but heroine and father never above a fortnight in one place: he being driven from his curacy by the vile arts of some totally unprincipled and heartless young man, desperately in love with the heroine, and pursuing her with unrelenting passion. No sooner settled in one country of Europe, than they are compelled to quit it, and retire to another, always making new acquaintance, and always obliged to leave them. This will of course exhibit a wide variety of character. The scene will be for ever shifting from one set of people to another, but there will be no mixture, all the good will be unexceptionable in every respect. There will be no foibles or weaknesses but with the wicked, who will be completely depraved and infamous, hardly a resemblance of humanity left in them. Early in her career, the heroine must meet with the hero: all perfection, of course, and only prevented from paying his addresses to her by some excess of refinement. Wherever she goes, somebody falls in love with her, and she receives repeated offers of marriage, which she refers wholly to her father, exceedingly angry that *he* should not be the first applied to. Often carried away by the anti-hero, but rescued either by her father or the hero. Often reduced to support herself and her father by her talents, and work for her bread;° continually cheated, and defrauded of her hire; worn down to a skeleton, and now and then starved to death. At last, hunted out of civilised society, denied the poor shelter of the humblest cottage, they are compelled to retreat into Kamtschatka,° where the poor father quite worn down, finding his end approaching, throws himself on the ground, and after four or five hours of tender advice and parental admonition to his miserable child, expires in a fine burst of literary enthusiasm, intermingled with invectives against the holders of tithes. Heroine inconsolable for some time, but afterwards crawls back towards her former country, having at least twenty narrow escapes of falling into the hands of anti-hero; and at last, in the very nick of time, turning a corner to avoid him, runs into the arms of the hero himself, who, having just shaken off the scruples which fettered him before, was at the very moment setting off in pursuit of her. The tenderest and completest *éclaircissement* takes place, and they are happily united. Throughout the whole work heroine to be in the most elegant society, and living in high style.'°

Since the first publication of this memoir, Mr. Murray of Albemarle Street° has very kindly sent to me copies of the following letters, which his father received from Jane Austen, when engaged in the publication of 'Emma.' The increasing cordiality of the letters shows that the author felt that her interests were duly cared for, and was glad to find herself in the hands of a publisher whom she could consider as a friend.

Her brother had addressed to Mr. Murray a strong complaint of the tardiness of a printer:—

'23 Hans Place, Thursday, November 23 (1815).°

'Sir,—My brother's note last Monday has been so fruitless, that I am afraid there can be but little chance of my writing to any good effect; but yet I am so very much disappointed and vexed by the delays of the printers, that I cannot help begging to know whether there is no hope of their being quickened. Instead of the work being ready by the end of the present month, it will hardly, at the rate we now proceed, be finished by the end of the next; and as I expect to leave London early in December, it is of consequence that no more time should be lost. Is it likely that the printers will be influenced to greater dispatch and punctuality by knowing that the work is to be dedicated, by permission, to the Prince Regent? If you can make that circumstance operate, I shall be very glad. My brother returns "Waterloo"° with many thanks for the loan of it. We have heard much of Scott's account of Paris.[1] If it be not incompatible with other arrangements, would you favour us with it, supposing you have any set already opened? You may depend upon its being in careful hands.

'I remain, Sir, your ob[t.] humble Se[t.]

'J. AUSTEN.'

'Hans Place, December 11 (1815).°

DEAR SIR,—As I find that "Emma" is advertised for publication as early as Saturday next, I think it best to lose no time in settling all that remains to be settled on the subject, and adopt this method as involving the smallest tax on your time.

'In the first place, I beg you to understand that I leave the terms on which the trade should be supplied with the work entirely to your judgment, entreating you to be guided in every such arrangement by your own experience of what is most likely to clear off the edition rapidly. I shall be satisfied with whatever you feel to be best. The title-page must be "Emma, dedicated by permission to H.R.H. the Prince Regent." And it is my particular wish that one set should be completed and sent to H.R.H. two or three days before the work is generally public. It should be sent under cover to the Rev. J. S. Clarke, Librarian, Carlton House. I shall subjoin a list of those persons to whom I must trouble you to forward also a set each, when the work is out; all unbound,° with "From the Authoress" in the first page.

'I return you, with very many thanks, the books you have so obligingly supplied me with. I am very sensible, I assure you, of

[1] This must have been 'Paul's Letters to his Kinsfolk' [published by Murray in 1815].

the attention you have paid to my convenience and amusement. I return also "Mansfield Park," as ready for a second edition, I believe, as I can make it. I am in Hans Place till the 16th. From that day inclusive, my direction will be Chawton, Alton, Hants.

'I remain, dear Sir,
'Y^r faithful humb. Servt.
'J. AUSTEN.

'I wish you would have the goodness to send a line by the bearer, stating *the day* on which the set will be ready for the Prince Regent.'

'Hans Place, December 11 (1815).°

'DEAR SIR,—I am much obliged by yours, and very happy to feel everything arranged to our mutual satisfaction. As to my direction about the title-page, it was arising from my ignorance only, and from my having never noticed the proper place for a dedication.° I thank you for putting me right. Any deviation from what is usually done in such cases is the last thing I should wish for. I feel happy in having a friend to save me from the ill effect of my own blunder.

'Yours, dear Sir, &c.
'J. AUSTEN.'

'Chawton, April 1, 1816.°

'DEAR SIR,—I return you the "Quarterly Review" with many thanks. The Authoress of "Emma" has no reason, I think, to complain of her treatment in it, except in the total omission of "Mansfield Park." I cannot but be sorry that so clever a man as the Reviewer of "Emma"° should consider it as unworthy of being noticed. You will be pleased to hear that I have received the Prince's thanks for the *handsome* copy I sent him of "Emma." Whatever he may think of *my* share of the work, yours seems to have been quite right.

'In consequence of the late event in Henrietta Street,° I must request that if you should at any time have anything to communicate by letter, you will be so good as to write by the post, directing to me (Miss J. Austen), Chawton, near Alton; and that for anything of a larger bulk, you will add to the same direction, by *Collier's Southampton coach*.

'I remain, dear Sir,
'Yours very faithfully,
'J. AUSTEN.'

About the same time the following letters passed between the Countess of Morley° and the writer of 'Emma.' I do not know whether they were personally acquainted with each other, nor in what this interchange of civilities originated:—

The Countess of Morley to Miss J. Austen

'Saltram, December 27 (1815).

'MADAM,—I have been most anxiously waiting for an introduction to "Emma," and am infinitely obliged to you for your kind recollection of me, which will procure me the pleasure of her acquaintance some days sooner than I should otherwise have had it. I am already become intimate with the Woodhouse family, and feel that they will not amuse and interest me less than the Bennetts, Bertrams, Norrises,° and all their admirable predecessors. I can give them no higher praise.

'I am, Madam, your much obliged
'F. MORLEY.'

Miss J. Austen to the Countess of Morley

'MADAM,—Accept my thanks for the honour of your note, and for your kind disposition in favour of "Emma." In my present state of doubt as to her reception in the world, it is particularly gratifying to me to receive so early an assurance of your Ladyship's approbation. It encourages me to depend on the same share of general good opinion which "Emma's" predecessors have experienced, and to believe that I have not yet, as almost every writer of fancy does sooner or later, overwritten myself.

'I am, Madam,

'Your obliged and faithful Serv[t.]

'J. AUSTEN.

'December 31, 1815.'

CHAPTER VIII

Slow growth of her fame—Ill success of first attempts at publication—Two Reviews of her works contrasted

SELDOM has any literary reputation been of such slow growth as that of Jane Austen. Readers of the present day know the rank that is generally assigned to her. They have been told by Archbishop Whately, in his review of her works, and by Lord Macaulay, in his review of Madame D'Arblay's,° the reason why the highest place is to be awarded to Jane Austen, as a truthful drawer of character, and why she is to be classed with those who have approached nearest, in that respect, to the great master Shakspeare. They see her safely placed, by such authorities, in her niche, not indeed amongst the highest orders of genius, but in one confessedly her own, in our British temple of literary fame; and it may be difficult to make them believe how coldly her works were at first received, and how few readers had any appreciation of their peculiar merits. Sometimes a friend or neighbour, who chanced to know of our connection with the author, would condescend to speak with moderate approbation of 'Sense and Sensibility,' or 'Pride and Prejudice'; but if they had known that we, in our secret thoughts, classed her with Madame D'Arblay or Miss Edgeworth, or even with some other novel writers of the day whose names are now scarcely remembered, they would have considered it an amusing instance of family conceit. To the multitude her works appeared tame and commonplace,[1] poor in colouring, and sadly deficient in incident and interest. It is true that we

[1] A greater genius than my aunt shared with her the imputation of being *commonplace*. Lockhart, speaking of the low estimation in which Scott's conversational powers were held in the literary and scientific society of Edinburgh, says: 'I think the epithet most in vogue concerning it was "commonplace."' He adds, however, that one of the most eminent of that society was of a different opinion, 'who, when some glib youth chanced to echo in his hearing the consolatory tenet of local mediocrity, answered quietly, "I have the misfortune to think differently from you—in my humble opinion Walter Scott's *sense* is a still more wonderful thing than his genius."'—Lockhart's *Life of Scott*, vol. iv. chap. v.

were sometimes cheered by hearing that a different verdict had been pronounced by more competent judges: we were told how some great statesman or distinguished poet held these works in high estimation; we had the satisfaction of believing that they were most admired by the best judges, and comforted ourselves with Horace's 'satis est Equitem mihi plaudere.'° So much was this the case, that one of the ablest men of my acquaintance[1] said, in that kind of jest which has much earnest in it, that he had established it in his own mind, as a new test of ability, whether people *could* or *could not* appreciate Miss Austen's merits.

But though such golden opinions were now and then gathered in, yet the wide field of public taste yielded no adequate return either in praise or profit. Her reward was not to be the quick return of the cornfield, but the slow growth of the tree which is to endure to another generation. Her first attempts at publication were very discouraging. In November, 1797, her father wrote the following letter to Mr. Cadell:—°

'Sir,—I have in my possession a manuscript novel, comprising 3 vols., about the length of Miss Burney's "Evelina." As I am well aware of what consequence it is that a work of this sort sh^d make its first appearance under a respectable name, I apply to you. I shall be much obliged therefore if you will inform me whether you choose to be concerned in it, what will be the expense of publishing it at the author's risk, and what you will venture to advance for the property of it,° if on perusal it is approved of. Should you give any encouragement, I will send you the work.

'I am, Sir, your humble Servant,
'GEORGE AUSTEN.'

'Steventon, near Overton, Hants,
'1st Nov. 1797.'

This proposal was declined by return of post! The work thus summarily rejected must have been 'Pride and Prejudice.'

The fate of 'Northanger Abbey' was still more humiliating. It was sold, in 1803, to a publisher in Bath,° for ten pounds, but it

[1] The late Mr. R. H. Cheney.

found so little favour in his eyes, that he chose to abide by his first loss rather than risk farther expense by publishing such a work. It seems to have lain for many years unnoticed in his drawers; somewhat as the first chapters of 'Waverley' lurked forgotten amongst the old fishing-tackle in Scott's cabinet.° Tilneys, Thorpes, and Morlands consigned apparently to eternal oblivion! But when four novels of steadily increasing success had given the writer some confidence in herself, she wished to recover the copyright of this early work. One of her brothers° undertook the negotiation. He found the purchaser very willing to receive back his money, and to resign all claim to the copyright. When the bargain was concluded and the money paid, but not till then, the negotiator had the satisfaction of informing him that the work which had been so lightly esteemed was by the author of 'Pride and Prejudice.' I do not think that she was herself much mortified by the want of early success. She wrote for her own amusement. Money, though acceptable, was not necessary for the moderate expenses of her quiet home. Above all, she was blessed with a cheerful contented disposition, and an humble mind; and so lowly did she esteem her own claims, that when she received 150*l.* from the sale of 'Sense and Sensibility,' she considered it a prodigious recompense for that which had cost her nothing.° It cannot be supposed, however, that she was altogether insensible to the superiority of her own workmanship over that of some contemporaries who were then enjoying a brief popularity. Indeed a few touches in the following extracts from two of her letters° show that she was as quicksighted to absurdities in composition as to those in living persons.

'Mr. C.'s opinion is gone down in my list;° but as my paper relates only to "Mansfield Park," I may fortunately excuse myself from entering Mr. D's. I will redeem my credit with him by writing a close imitation of "Self-Control,"° as soon as I can. I will improve upon it. My heroine shall not only be wafted down an American river in a boat by herself. She shall cross the Atlantic in the same way; and never stop till she reaches Gravesend.'

'We have got "Rosanne" in our Society,° and find it much as you describe it; very good and clever, but tedious. Mrs. Hawkins' great excellence is on serious subjects. There are some very delightful conversations and reflections on religion: but on lighter topics I think she falls into many absurdities; and, as to love, her heroine has very comical feelings. There are a thousand improbabilities in the story. Do you remember the two Miss Ormsdens introduced just at last? Very flat and unnatural. Mad$^{elle.}$ Cossart is rather my passion.'

Two notices of her works appeared in the 'Quarterly Review.'° One in October 1815, and another, more than three years after her death, in January 1821. The latter article is known to have been from the pen of Whately, afterwards Archbishop of Dublin.[1] They differ much from each other in the degree of praise which they award, and I think also it may be said, in the ability with which they are written. The first bestows some approval, but the other expresses the warmest admiration. One can scarcely be satisfied with the critical acumen of the former writer, who, in treating of 'Sense and Sensibility,' takes no notice whatever of the vigour with which many of the characters are drawn, but declares that 'the interest and *merit* of the piece depends *altogether* upon the behaviour of the elder sister!' Nor is he fair when, in 'Pride and Prejudice,' he represents Elizabeth's change of sentiments towards Darcy as caused by the sight of his house and grounds. But the chief discrepancy between the two reviewers is to be found in their appreciation of the commonplace and silly characters to be found in these novels. On this point the difference almost amounts to a contradiction, such as one sometimes sees drawn up in parallel columns, when it is desired to convict some writer or some statesman of inconsistency. The Reviewer, in 1815, says: 'The faults of these works arise from the minute detail which the author's plan comprehends. Characters of folly or sim-

[1] Lockhart had supposed that this article had been written by Scott, because it exactly accorded with the opinions which Scott had often been heard to express, but he learned afterwards that it had been written by Whately; and Lockhart, who became the Editor of the Quarterly, must have had the means of knowing the truth. (See Lockhart's *Life of Sir Walter Scott*, vol. v. p. 158.) I remember that, at the time when the review came out, it was reported in Oxford that Whately had written the article at the request of the lady whom he afterwards married. [JEAL does not appear to know that Scott wrote the earlier of the two reviews.]

plicity, such as those of old Woodhouse and Miss Bates, are ridiculous when first presented, but if too often brought forward, or too long dwelt on, their prosing is apt to become as tiresome in fiction as in real society.'° The Reviewer, in 1821, on the contrary, singles out the fools as especial instances of the writer's abilities, and declares that in this respect she shows a regard to character hardly exceeded by Shakspeare himself. These are his words: 'Like him (Shakespeare) she shows as admirable a discrimination in the character of fools as of people of sense; a merit which is far from common. To invent indeed a conversation full of wisdom or of wit requires that the writer should himself possess ability; but the converse does not hold good, it is no fool that can describe fools well; and many who have succeeded pretty well in painting superior characters have failed in giving individuality to those weaker ones which it is necessary to introduce in order to give a faithful representation of real life: they exhibit to us mere folly in the abstract, forgetting that to the eye of the skilful naturalist the insects on a leaf present as wide differences as exist between the lion and the elephant. Slender, and Shallow, and Aguecheek, as Shakspeare has painted them, though equally fools, resemble one another no more than Richard, and Macbeth, and Julius Cæsar; and Miss Austen's[1] Mrs. Bennet, Mr. Rushworth, and Miss Bates are no more alike than her Darcy, Knightley, and Edmund Bertram. Some have complained indeed of finding her fools too much like nature, and consequently tiresome. There is no disputing about tastes; all we can say is, that such critics must (whatever deference they may outwardly pay to received opinions) find the "Merry Wives of Windsor" and "Twelfth Night" very tiresome; and that those who look with pleasure at Wilkie's pictures,° or those of the Dutch school, must admit that excellence of imitation may confer attraction on that which would be insipid or disagreeable in the reality. Her minuteness of detail has also been found fault with; but even where it produces, at the time, a degree of tediousness, we know not whether that can justly be reckoned a blemish, which is absolutely essential to a very high excellence.

[1] In transcribing this passage I have taken the liberty so far to correct it as to spell her name properly with an 'e.'

Now it is absolutely impossible, without this, to produce that thorough acquaintance with the characters which is necessary to make the reader heartily interested in them. Let any one cut out from the "Iliad" or from Shakspeare's plays everything (we are far from saying that either might not lose some parts with advantage, but let him reject everything) which is absolutely devoid of importance and interest *in itself*; and he will find that what is left will have lost more than half its charms. We are convinced that some writers have diminished the effect of their works by being scrupulous to admit nothing into them which had not some absolute and independent merit. They have acted like those who strip off the leaves of a fruit tree, as being of themselves good for nothing, with the view of securing more nourishment to the fruit, which in fact cannot attain its full maturity and flavour without them.'°

The world, I think, has endorsed the opinion of the later writer; but it would not be fair to set down the discrepancy between the two entirely to the discredit of the former. The fact is that, in the course of the intervening five years, these works had been read and reread by many leaders in the literary world. The public taste was forming itself all this time, and 'grew by what it fed on.' These novels belong to a class which gain rather than lose by frequent perusals, and it is probable that each Reviewer represented fairly enough the prevailing opinions of readers in the year when each wrote.

Since that time, the testimonies in favour of Jane Austen's works have been continual and almost unanimous. They are frequently referred to as models; nor have they lost their first distinction of being especially acceptable to minds of the highest order. I shall indulge myself by collecting into the next chapter instances of the homage paid to her by such persons.

CHAPTER IX

Opinions expressed by eminent persons—Opinions of others of less eminence—Opinion of American readers

INTO this list of the admirers of my Aunt's works, I admit those only whose eminence will be universally acknowledged. No doubt the number might have been increased.

Southey, in a letter to Sir Egerton Brydges,° says: 'You mention Miss Austen. Her novels are more true to nature, and have, for my sympathies, passages of finer feeling than any others of this age. She was a person of whom I have heard so well and think so highly, that I regret not having had an opportunity of testifying to her the respect which I felt for her.'

It may be observed that Southey had probably heard from his own family connections of the charm of her private character. A friend of hers, the daughter of Mr. Bigge Wither, of Manydown Park near Basingstoke, was married to Southey's uncle, the Rev. Herbert Hill,° who had been useful to his nephew in many ways, and especially in supplying him with the means of attaining his extensive knowledge of Spanish and Portuguese literature. Mr. Hill had been Chaplain to the British Factory at Lisbon, where Southey visited him and had the use of a library in those languages which his uncle had collected. Southey himself continually mentions his uncle Hill in terms of respect and gratitude.

S. T. Coleridge° would sometimes burst out into high encomiums of Miss Austen's novels as being, 'in their way, perfectly genuine and individual productions.'

I remember Miss Mitford's° saying to me: 'I would almost cut off one of my hands, if it would enable me to write like your aunt with the other.'

The biographer of Sir J. Mackintosh° says: 'Something recalled to his mind the traits of character which are so delicately touched in Miss Austen's novels . . . He said that there was genius in sketching out that new kind of novel . . . He was vexed for the credit of the "Edinburgh Review" that it had left her unnoticed.[1] . . . The "Quarterly" had done her more justice . . . It was impossible for a foreigner to understand fully the merit of her works. Madame de Staël,° to whom he had recommended one of her novels, found no interest in it; and in her note to him in reply said it was "vulgaire": and yet, he said, nothing could be more true than what he wrote in answer: "There is no book which that word would so little suit." . . . Every village could furnish matter for a novel to Miss Austen. She did not need the common materials for a novel, strong emotions, or strong incidents."[2]

It was not, however, quite impossible for a foreigner to appreciate these works; for Mons. Guizot° writes thus: 'I am a great novel reader, but I seldom read German or French novels. The characters are too artificial. My delight is to read English novels, particularly those written by women. "C'est toute une école de morale." Miss Austen, Miss Ferrier, &c., form a school which in the excellence and profusion of its productions resembles the cloud of dramatic poets of the great Athenian age.'

In the 'Keepsake' of 1825° the following lines appeared, written by Lord Morpeth, afterwards seventh Earl of Carlisle, and Lord-Lieutenant of Ireland, accompanying an illustration of a lady reading a novel.

> Beats thy quick pulse o'er Inchbald's thrilling leaf,
> Brunton's high moral, Opie's deep wrought grief?
> Has the mild chaperon claimed thy yielding heart,
> Carroll's dark page, Trevelyan's gentle art?
> Or is it thou, all perfect Austen? Here
> Let one poor wreath adorn thy early bier,
> That scarce allowed thy modest youth to claim
> Its living portion of thy certain fame!
> Oh! Mrs. Bennet! Mrs. Norris too!
> While memory survives we'll dream of you.
> And Mr. Woodhouse, whose abstemious lip
> Must thin, but not too thin, his gruel sip.

[1] Incidentally she had received high praise in Lord Macaulay's Review of Madame D'Arblay's Works in the 'Edinburgh.' [*Edinburgh Review*, 76 (Jan. 1843), 561–2.]

[2] *Life of Sir J. Mackintosh*, vol. ii, p. 472. [R. J. Mackintosh, *Memoirs of the Life of the Right Honourable Sir James Mackintosh* (2 vols., 1835).]

Miss Bates, our idol, though the village bore;
And Mrs. Elton, ardent to explore.
While the clear style flows on without pretence,
With unstained purity, and unmatched sense:
Or, if a sister e'er approached the throne,
She called the rich 'inheritance' her own.

The admiration felt by Lord Macaulay° would probably have taken a very practical form, if his life had been prolonged. I have the authority of his sister, Lady Trevelyan, for stating that he had intended to undertake the task upon which I have ventured. He purposed to write a memoir of Miss Austen, with criticisms on her works, to prefix it to a new edition of her novels, and from the proceeds of the sale to erect a monument to her memory in Winchester Cathedral. Oh! that such an idea had been realised! That portion of the plan in which Lord Macaulay's success would have been most certain might have been almost sufficient for his object. A memoir written by him would have been a monument.

I am kindly permitted by Sir Henry Holland° to give the following quotation from his printed but unpublished recollections of his past life:—

'I have the picture still before me of Lord Holland lying on his bed, when attacked with gout, his admirable sister, Miss Fox, beside him reading aloud, as she always did on these occasions, some one of Miss Austen's novels, of which he was never wearied. I well recollect the time when these charming novels, almost unique in their style of humour, burst suddenly on the world. It was sad that their writer did not live to witness the growth of her fame.'

My brother-in-law, Sir Denis Le Marchant,° has supplied me with the following anecdotes from his own recollections:—

'When I was a student at Trinity College, Cambridge, Mr. Whewell,° then a Fellow and afterwards Master of the College, often spoke to me with admiration of Miss Austen's novels. On one occasion I said that I had found "Persuasion" rather dull. He quite fired up in defence of it, insisting that it was the most beautiful of her works. This accomplished philosopher was deeply versed in works of fiction. I recollect his writing to me from Caernarvon, where he had the charge of some pupils, that he was weary of *his* stay, for he had read the circulating library twice through.

'During a visit I paid to Lord Lansdowne,° at Bowood, in 1846, one of Miss Austen's novels became the subject of conversation and of praise, especially from Lord Lansdowne, who observed that one of the circumstances of his life which he looked back upon with vexation was that Miss Austen should once have been living some weeks in his neighbourhood without his knowing it.

'I have heard Sydney Smith,° more than once, dwell with eloquence on the merits of Miss Austen's novels. He told me he should have enjoyed giving her the pleasure of reading her praises in the "Edinburgh Review." "Fanny Price" was one of his prime favourites.'

I close this list of testimonies, this long 'Catena Patrum,'° with the remarkable words of Sir Walter Scott, taken from his diary for March 14, 1826:[1] 'Read again, for the third time at least, Miss Austen's finely written° novel of "Pride and Prejudice." That young lady had a talent for describing the involvements and feelings and characters of ordinary life, which is to me the most wonderful I ever met with. The big Bow-Wow strain I can do myself like any now going; but the exquisite touch which renders ordinary common-place things and characters interesting from the truth of the description and the sentiment is denied to me. What a pity such a gifted creature died so early!' The well-worn condition of Scott's own copy of these works attests that they were much read in his family. When I visited Abbotsford, a few years after Scott's death, I was permitted, as an unusual favour, to take one of these volumes in my hands. One cannot suppress the wish that she had lived to know what such men thought of her powers, and how gladly they would have cultivated a personal acquaintance with her. I do not think that it would at all have impaired the modest simplicity of her character; or that we should have lost our own dear 'Aunt Jane' in the blaze of literary fame.

[1] Lockhart's *Life of Scott*, vol. vi. chap. vii.

It may be amusing to contrast with these testimonies from the great, the opinions expressed by other readers of more ordinary intellect. The author herself has left a list of criticisms° which it had been her amusement to collect, through means of her friends. This list contains much of warm-hearted sympathising praise, interspersed with some opinions which may be considered surprising.

One lady could say nothing better of 'Mansfield Park,' than that it was 'a mere novel.'

Another owned that she thought 'Sense and Sensibility' and 'Pride and Prejudice' downright nonsense; but expected to like 'Mansfield Park' better, and having finished the first volume, hoped that she had got through the worst.

Another did not like 'Mansfield Park.' Nothing interesting in the characters. Language poor.

One gentleman read the first and last chapters of 'Emma,' but did not look at the rest, because he had been told that it was not interesting.

The opinions of another gentleman about 'Emma' were so bad that they could not be reported to the author.

'Quot homines, tot sententiæ.'°

Thirty-five years after her death there came also a voice of praise from across the Atlantic. In 1852 the following letter was received by her brother Sir Francis Austen:—

'Boston, Massachusetts, U.S.A.
6th Jan. 1852.

'Since high critical authority has pronounced the delineations of character in the works of Jane Austen second only to those of Shakspeare, transatlantic admiration appears superfluous; yet it may not be uninteresting to her family to receive an assurance that the influence of her genius is extensively recognised in the American Republic, even by the highest judicial authorities. The late Mr. Chief Justice Marshall, of the supreme Court of the United States, and his associate Mr. Justice Story, highly estimated and admired Miss Austen, and to them we owe our introduction to her society. For many years her talents have brightened our daily path, and her name and those of her characters are familiar to us as "household words." We have long wished to express to some of her family the sentiments of gratitude and affection she has inspired, and request more information relative to her life than is given in the brief memoir prefixed to her works.

'Having accidentally heard that a brother of Jane Austen held a high rank in the British Navy, we have obtained his address from our friend Admiral Wormley, now resident in Boston, and we trust this expression of our feeling will be received by her relations with the kindness and urbanity characteristic of Admirals of *her creation*. Sir Francis Austen, or one of his family, would confer a great favour by complying with our request. The autograph of his sister, or a few lines in her handwriting, would be placed among our chief treasures.

'The family who delight in the companionship of Jane Austen, and who present this petition, are of English origin. Their ancestor held a high rank among the first emigrants to New England, and his name and character have been ably represented by his descendants in various public stations of trust and responsibility to the present time in the colony and state of Massachusetts. A letter addressed to Miss Quincey, care of the Honble Josiah Quincey, Boston, Massachusetts, would reach its destination.'

Sir Francis Austen returned a suitable reply to this application; and sent a long letter of his sister's,° which, no doubt, still occupies the place of honour promised by the Quincey family.

CHAPTER X

Observations on the Novels

It is not the object of these memoirs to attempt a criticism on Jane Austen's novels. Those particulars only have been noticed which could be illustrated by the circumstances of her own life; but I now desire to offer a few observations on them, and especially on one point, on which my age renders me a competent witness—the fidelity with which they represent the opinions and manners of the class of society in which the author lived early in this century. They do this the more faithfully on account of the very deficiency with which they have been sometimes charged—namely, that they make no attempt to raise the standard of human life, but merely represent it as it was. They certainly were not written to support any theory or inculcate any particular moral, except indeed the great moral which is to be equally gathered from an observation of the course of actual life—namely, the superiority of high over low principles, and of greatness over littleness of mind. These writings are like photographs, in which no feature is softened; no ideal expression is introduced, all is the unadorned reflection of the natural object; and the value of such a faithful likeness must increase as time gradually works more and more changes in the face of society itself. A remarkable instance of this is to be found in her portraiture of the clergy. She was the daughter and the sister of clergymen, who certainly were not low specimens of their order: and she has chosen three of her heroes from that profession; but no one in these days can think that either Edmund Bertram or Henry Tilney had adequate ideas of the duties of a parish minister. Such, however, were the opinions and practice then prevalent among respectable and conscientious clergymen before their minds had been stirred, first by the Evangelical, and afterwards by the High Church movement which this century has witnessed. The country may be congratulated which, on looking back to such a fixed landmark, can find that it has been advancing instead of receding from it.

The long interval that elapsed between the completion of 'Northanger Abbey' in 1798,° and the commencement of 'Mansfield Park' in 1811, may sufficiently account for any difference of style which may be perceived between her three earlier and her three later productions. If the former showed quite as much originality and genius, they may perhaps be thought to have less of the faultless finish and high polish which distinguish the latter. The characters of the John Dashwoods, Mr. Collins, and the Thorpes stand out from the canvas with a vigour and originality which cannot be surpassed; but I think that in her last three works are to be found a greater refinement of taste, a more nice sense of propriety, and a deeper insight into the delicate anatomy of the human heart, marking the difference between the brilliant girl and the mature woman. Far from being one of those who have over-written themselves, it may be affirmed that her fame would have stood on a narrower and less firm basis, if she had not lived to resume her pen at Chawton.

Some persons have surmised that she took her characters from individuals with whom she had been acquainted. They were so life-like that it was assumed that they must once have lived, and have been transferred bodily, as it were, into her pages. But surely such a supposition betrays an ignorance of the high prerogative of genius to create out of its own resources imaginary characters, who shall be true to nature and consistent in themselves. Perhaps, however, the distinction between keeping true to nature and servilely copying any one specimen of it is not always clearly apprehended. It is indeed true, both of the writer and of the painter, that he can use only such lineaments as exist, and as he has observed to exist, in living objects; otherwise he would produce monsters instead of human beings; but in both it is the office of high art to mould these features into new combinations, and to place them in the attitudes, and impart to them the expressions which may suit the purposes of the artist; so that they are nature, but not exactly the same nature which had come before his eyes; just as honey can be obtained only from the natural flowers which the bee has sucked; yet it is not a reproduction of the odour or flavour of any particular flower, but becomes something different when it has gone through the process of transformation which that little insect is able to effect. Hence, in the case of painters, arises the superiority of original compositions over portrait painting. Reynolds was exercising a higher faculty when he designed Comedy and Tragedy contending for Garrick, than when he merely took a likeness of that actor.° The same difference exists in writings between the original conceptions of Shakspeare and some other creative geniuses, and such full-length likenesses of individual persons, 'The Talking Gentleman' for instance, as are admirably drawn by Miss Mitford.° Jane Austen's powers, whatever may be the degree in which she possessed them, were certainly of that higher order. She did not copy individuals, but she invested her own creations with individuality of character. A reviewer in the 'Quarterly'° speaks of an acquaintance who, ever since the publication of 'Pride and Prejudice,' had been called by his friends Mr. Bennet, but the author did not know him. Her own relations never recognised any individual in her characters; and I can call to mind several of her acquaintance whose peculiarities were very tempting and easy to be caricatured of whom there are no traces in her pages. She herself, when questioned on the subject by a friend,° expressed a dread of what she called such an 'invasion of social proprieties.' She said that she thought it quite fair to note peculiarities and weaknesses, but that it was her desire to create, not to reproduce; 'besides,' she added, 'I am too proud of my gentlemen to admit that they were only Mr. A. or Colonel B.' She did not, however, suppose that her imaginary characters were of a higher order than are to be found in nature; for she said, when speaking of two of her great favourites, Edmund Bertram and Mr. Knightley: 'They are very far from being what I know English gentlemen often are.'

She certainly took a kind of parental interest in the beings whom she had created, and did not dismiss them from her thoughts when she had finished her last chapter. We have seen, in one of her letters, her personal affection for Darcy and Elizabeth;° and when sending a copy of 'Emma' to a friend whose daughter had been lately born, she wrote thus: 'I trust you will be as glad to see my "Emma," as I shall be to see your Jemima.'° She was very fond of Emma, but did not reckon on her being a general favourite; for, when commencing that work, she said, 'I am going to take a heroine whom no one but myself will much like.'° She would, if asked, tell us many little particulars about the subsequent career of some of her people.° In this traditionary way we learned that Miss Steele never succeeded in catching the Doctor; that Kitty Bennet was satisfactorily married to a clergyman near Pemberley, while Mary obtained nothing higher than one of her uncle Philip's clerks, and was content to be considered a star in the society of Meriton; that the 'considerable sum' given by Mrs. Norris to William Price was one pound; that Mr. Woodhouse survived his daughter's marriage, and kept her and Mr. Knightley from settling at Donwell, about two years; and that the letters placed by Frank Churchill before Jane Fairfax, which she swept away unread, contained the word 'pardon.' Of the good people in 'Northanger Abbey' and 'Persuasion' we know nothing more than what is written: for before those works were published their author had been taken away from us, and all such amusing communications had ceased for ever.

CHAPTER XI

Declining health of Jane Austen—Elasticity of her spirits—Her resignation and humility—Her death

EARLY in the year 1816 some family troubles° disturbed the usually tranquil course of Jane Austen's life; and it is probable that the inward malady, which was to prove ultimately fatal, was already felt by her; for some distant friends,[1] whom she visited in the spring of that year, thought that her health was somewhat impaired, and observed that she went about her old haunts, and recalled old recollections connected with them in a particular manner, as if she did not expect ever to see them again. It is not surprising that, under these circumstances, some of her letters were of a graver tone than had been customary with her, and expressed resignation rather than cheerfulness. In reference to these troubles in a letter to her brother Charles,° after mentioning that she had been laid up with an attack of bilious fever, she says: 'I live up stairs for the present and am coddled. I am the only one of the party who has been so silly, but a weak body must excuse weak nerves.' And again, to another correspondent:° 'But I am getting too near complaint; it has been the appointment of God, however secondary causes may have operated.' But the elasticity of her spirits soon recovered their tone. It was in the latter half of that year that she addressed the two following lively letters to a nephew, one while he was at Winchester School, the other soon after he had left it:—

'Chawton, July 9, 1816.

'MY DEAR E.°—Many thanks. A thank for every line, and as many to Mr. W. Digweed for coming. We have been wanting very much to hear of your mother,° and are happy to find she continues

[1] The Fowles, of Kintbury, in Berkshire. [Eliza Lloyd, elder sister of Martha and Mary, had married her cousin Fulwar Craven Fowle, a former pupil of JA's father at Steventon and brother of Cassandra's dead fiancé Tom Fowle.]

to mend, but her illness must have been a very serious one indeed. When she is really recovered, she ought to try change of air, and come over to us. Tell your father that I am very much obliged to him for his share of your letter, and most sincerely join in the hope of her being eventually much the better for her present discipline. She has the comfort moreover of being confined in such weather as gives one little temptation to be out. It is really too bad, and has been too bad for a long time, much worse than any one *can* bear, and I begin to think it will never be fine again. This is a *finesse*° of mine, for I have often observed that if one writes about the weather, it is generally completely changed before the letter is read. I wish it may prove so now, and that when Mr. W. Digweed reaches Steventon to-morrow, he may find you have had a long series of hot dry weather. We are a small party at present, only grandmamma, Mary Jane,° and myself. Yalden's coach cleared off the rest yesterday.° I am glad you recollected to mention your being come home.[1] My heart began to sink within me when I had got so far through your letter without its being mentioned. I was dreadfully afraid that you might be detained at Winchester by severe illness, confined to your bed perhaps, and quite unable to hold a pen, and only dating from Steventon in order, with a mistaken sort of tenderness, to deceive me. But now I have no doubt of your being at home. I am sure you would not say it so seriously unless it actually were so. We saw a countless number of post-chaises full of boys pass by yesterday morning[2]—full of future heroes, legislators, fools, and villains. You have never thanked me for my last letter, which went by the cheese. I cannot bear not to be thanked. You will not pay us a visit yet of course; we must not think of it. Your mother must get well first, and you must go to Oxford and *not* be elected;° after that a little change of scene may be good for you, and your physicians I hope will order you to the sea, or to a house by the side of a very

[1] It seems that her young correspondent, after dating from his home, had been so superfluous as to state in his letter that he was returned home, and thus to have drawn on himself this banter.

[2] The road by which many Winchester boys returned home ran close to Chawton Cottage.

considerable pond.[1] Oh! it rains again. It beats against the window. Mary Jane and I have been wet through once already to-day; we set off in the donkey-carriage for Farringdon, as I wanted to see the improvement° Mr. Woolls is making, but we were obliged to turn back before we got there, but not soon enough to avoid a pelter all the way home. We met Mr. Woolls. I talked of its being bad weather for the hay, and he returned me the comfort of its being much worse for the wheat. We hear that Mrs. S. does not quit Tangier:° why and wherefore? Do you know that our Browning is gone? You must prepare for a William when you come, a good-looking lad, civil and quiet, and seeming likely to do. Good bye. I am sure Mr. W.D.[2] will be astonished at my writing so much, for the paper is so thin that he will be able to count the lines if not to read them.

'Yours affec^ly^,
'JANE AUSTEN.'

In the next letter will be found her description of her own style of composition, which has already appeared in the notice prefixed to 'Northanger Abbey' and 'Persuasion':—

'Chawton, Monday, Dec. 16th (1816).

'MY DEAR E.,°—One reason for my writing to you now is, that I may have the pleasure of directing to you Esqre. I give you joy of having left Winchester. Now you may own how miserable you were there; now it will gradually all come out, your crimes and your miseries—how often you went up by the Mail to London and threw away fifty guineas at a tavern, and how often you were on the point of hanging yourself, restrained only, as some ill-natured aspersion upon poor old Winton has it, by the want of a tree within some miles of the city. Charles Knight° and his companions passed through Chawton about 9 this morning; later than it used to be. Uncle Henry and I had a glimpse of his handsome

[1] There was, though it exists no longer, a pond close to Chawton Cottage, at the junction of the Winchester and Gosport roads.

[2] Mr. Digweed, who conveyed the letters to and from Chawton, was the gentleman named in page 24,° as renting the old manor-house and the large farm at Steventon.

face, looking all health and good humour. I wonder when you will come and see us. I know what I rather speculate upon, but shall say nothing. We think uncle Henry in excellent looks. Look at him this moment, and think so too, if you have not done it before; and we have the great comfort of seeing decided improvement in uncle Charles, both as to health, spirits, and appearance. And they are each of them so agreeable in their different way, and harmonise so well, that their visit is thorough enjoyment. Uncle Henry writes very superior sermons.° You and I must try to get hold of one or two, and put them into our novels: it would be a fine help to a volume; and we could make our heroine read it aloud on a Sunday evening, just as well as Isabella Wardour, in the "Antiquary," is made to read the "History of the Hartz Demon" in the ruins of St. Ruth, though I believe, on recollection, Lovell is the reader.° By the bye, my dear E., I am quite concerned for the loss your mother mentions in her letter. Two chapters and a half° to be missing is monstrous! It is well that *I* have not been at Steventon lately, and therefore cannot be suspected of purloining them: two strong twigs and a half towards a nest of my own would have been something. I do not think, however, that any theft of that sort would be really very useful to me. What should I do with your strong, manly, vigorous sketches,° full of variety and glow? How could I possibly join them on to the little bit (two inches wide) of ivory on which I work with so fine a brush, as produces little effect after much labour?

'You will hear from uncle Henry how well Anna is.° She seems perfectly recovered. Ben was here on Saturday, to ask uncle Charles and me to dine with them, as to-morrow, but I was forced to decline it, the walk is beyond my strength (though I am otherwise very well), and this is not a season for donkey-carriages; and as we do not like to spare uncle Charles, he has declined it too. *Tuesday*. Ah, ha! Mr. E. I doubt your seeing uncle Henry at Steventon to-day. The weather will prevent your expecting him, I think. Tell your father, with aunt Cass's love and mine, that the pickled cucumbers are extremely good, and tell him also—"tell him what you will."° No, don't tell him what you will, but tell him that grandmamma begs him to make Joseph Hall° pay his rent, if he can.

'You must not be tired of reading the word *uncle*, for I have not done with it. Uncle Charles thanks your mother for her letter; it was a great pleasure to him to know that the parcel was received and gave so much satisfaction, and he begs her to be so good as to give three shillings for him to Dame Staples,° which shall be allowed for in the payment of her debt here.

'Adieu, Amiable! I hope Caroline behaves well to you.

'Yours affec^{ly},

'J. AUSTEN.'

I cannot tell how soon she was aware of the serious nature of her malady. By God's mercy it was not attended with much suffering; so that she was able to tell her friends as in the foregoing letter, and perhaps sometimes to persuade herself that, excepting want of strength, she was 'otherwise very well;' but the progress of the disease became more and more manifest as the year advanced. The usual walk was at first shortened, and then discontinued; and air was sought in a donkey-carriage. Gradually, too, her habits of activity within the house ceased, and she was obliged to lie down much. The sitting-room contained only one sofa, which was frequently occupied by her mother, who was more than seventy years old. Jane would never use it, even in her mother's absence; but she contrived a sort of couch for herself with two or three chairs, and was pleased to say that this arrangement was more comfortable to her than a real sofa. Her reasons for this might have been left to be guessed, but for the importunities of a little niece,° which obliged her to explain that if she herself had shown any inclination to use the sofa, her mother might have scrupled being on it so much as was good for her.

It is certain, however, that the mind did not share in this decay of the bodily strength. 'Persuasion' was not finished before the middle of August in that year; and the manner in which it was then completed affords proof that neither the critical nor the creative powers of the author were at all impaired. The book had been brought to an end in July;° and the re-engagement of the hero and heroine effected in a totally different manner in a scene laid at Admiral Croft's lodgings. But her performance did not satisfy her. She thought it tame and flat, and was desirous of producing something better. This weighed upon her mind, the more so probably on account of the weak state of her health; so that one night she retired to rest in very low spirits. But such depression was little in accordance with her nature, and was soon shaken off. The next morning she awoke to more cheerful views and brighter inspirations: the sense of power revived; and imagination resumed its course. She cancelled the condemned chapter, and wrote two others, entirely different, in its stead.° The result is that we possess the visit of the Musgrove party to Bath; the crowded and animated scenes at the White Hart Hotel; and the charming conversation between Capt. Harville and Anne Elliot, overheard by Capt. Wentworth, by which the two faithful lovers were at last led to understand each other's feelings. The tenth and eleventh chapters of 'Persuasion' then, rather than the actual winding-up of the story, contain the latest of her printed compositions, her last contribution to the entertainment of the public. Perhaps it may be thought that she has seldom written anything more brilliant; and that, independent of the original manner in which the *dénouement* is brought about, the pictures of Charles Musgrove's goodnatured boyishness and of his wife's jealous selfishness would have been incomplete without these finishing strokes. The cancelled chapter exists in manuscript. It is certainly inferior to the two which were substituted for it: but it was such as some writers and some readers might have been contented with; and it contained touches which scarcely any other hand could have given, the suppression of which may be almost a matter of regret.[1]

The following letter° was addressed to her friend Miss Bigg, then staying at Streatham with her sister, the wife of the Reverend Herbert Hill, uncle of Robert Southey.° It appears to have been written three days before she began her last work,° which will

[1] This cancelled chapter is now printed, in compliance with the requests addressed to me from several quarters. [Not included here.]

be noticed in another chapter; and shows that she was not at that time aware of the serious nature of her malady:—

'Chawton, January 24, 1817.

'MY DEAR ALETHEA,°—I think it time there should be a little writing between us, though I believe the epistolary debt is on *your* side, and I hope this will find all the Streatham party well, neither carried away by the flood, nor rheumatic through the damps. Such mild weather is, you know, delightful to *us*, and though we have a great many ponds, and a fine running stream through the meadows on the other side of the road, it is nothing but what beautifies us and does to talk of. *I* have certainly gained strength through the winter and am not far from being well; and I think I understand my own case now so much better than I did, as to be able by care to keep off any serious return of illness. I am convinced° that *bile* is at the bottom of all I have suffered, which makes it easy to know how to treat myself. You will be glad to hear thus much of me, I am sure. We have just had a few days' visit from Edward, who brought us a good account of his father,° and the very circumstance of his coming at all, of his father's being able to spare him, is itself a good account. He grows still, and still improves in appearance, at least in the estimation of his aunts, who love him better and better, as they see the sweet temper and warm affections of the boy confirmed in the young man: I tried hard to persuade him that he must have some message for William,[1] but in vain. . . . This is not a time of year for donkey-carriages, and our donkeys are necessarily having so long a run of luxurious idleness that I suppose we shall find they have forgotten much of their education when we use them again. We do not use two at once however; don't imagine such excesses . . . Our own new clergyman[2] is expected here very soon, perhaps in time to assist Mr. Papillon on Sunday. I shall be very glad when the first hearing is over. It will be a nervous hour for our pew, though we hear that he acquits himself with as much ease and collectedness,

[1] Miss Bigg's nephew, the present Sir William Heathcote, of Hursley. [JEAL's boyhood friend, who probably lent the letter for use in Ed. 2 of the *Memoir*.]

[2] Her brother Henry, who had been ordained late in life.

as if he had been used to it all his life. We have no chance we know of seeing you between Streatham and Winchester:° you go the other road and are engaged to two or three houses; if there should be any change, however, you know how welcome you would be. . . . We have been reading the "Poet's Pilgrimage to Waterloo,"° and generally with much approbation. Nothing will please all the world, you know; but parts of it suit me better than much that he has written before. The opening—*the proem* I believe he calls it—is very beautiful. Poor man! one cannot but grieve for the loss of the son so fondly described. Has he at all recovered it? What do Mr. and Mrs. Hill know about his present state?

'Yours aff[ly],

'J. AUSTEN.

'The real object of this letter is to ask you for a receipt, but I thought it genteel not to let it appear early. We remember some excellent orange wine at Manydown, made from Seville oranges, entirely or chiefly. I should be very much obliged to you for the receipt, if you can command it within a few weeks.'

On the day before, January 23rd, she had written to her niece° in the same hopeful tone: 'I feel myself getting stronger than I was, and can so perfectly walk *to* Alton, *or* back again without fatigue, that I hope to be able to do *both* when summer comes.'

Alas! summer came to her only on her deathbed. March 17th is the last date to be found in the manuscript on which she was engaged; and as the watch of the drowned man indicates the time of his death, so does this final date seem to fix the period when her mind could no longer pursue its accustomed course.

And here I cannot do better than quote the words of the niece° to whose private records of her aunt's life and character I have been so often indebted:—'I do not know how early the alarming symptoms of her malady came on. It was in the following March that I had the first idea of her being seriously ill. It had been settled that about the end of that month, or the beginning of April, I should spend a few days at Chawton, in the absence of my father and mother, who were just then engaged with Mrs. Leigh

Perrot in arranging her late husband's affairs;° but Aunt Jane became too ill to have me in the house, and so I went instead to my sister Mrs. Lefroy at Wyards'. The next day we walked over to Chawton to make enquiries after our aunt. She was then keeping her room, but said she would see us, and we went up to her. She was in her dressing gown, and was sitting quite like an invalid in an arm-chair, but she got up and kindly greeted us, and then, pointing to seats which had been arranged for us by the fire, she said, "There is a chair for the married lady, and a little stool for you, Caroline."[1] It is strange, but those trifling words were the last of hers that I can remember, for I retain no recollection of what was said by anyone in the conversation that ensued. I was struck by the alteration in herself. She was very pale, her voice was weak and low, and there was about her a general appearance of debility and suffering; but I have been told that she never had much acute pain. She was not equal to the exertion of talking to us, and our visit to the sick room was a very short one, Aunt Cassandra soon taking us away. I do not suppose we stayed a quarter of an hour; and I never saw Aunt Jane again.'

In May 1817 she was persuaded to remove to Winchester, for the sake of medical advice from Mr. Lyford.° The Lyfords have, for some generations, maintained a high character in Winchester for medical skill, and the Mr. Lyford of that day was a man of more than provincial reputation, in whom great London practitioners expressed confidence. Mr. Lyford spoke encouragingly. It was not, of course, his business to extinguish hope in his patient, but I believe that he had, from the first, very little expectation of a permanent cure. All that was gained by the removal from home was the satisfaction of having done the best that could be done, together with such alleviations of suffering as superior medical skill could afford.

Jane and her sister Cassandra took lodgings in College Street.° They had two kind friends living in the Close, Mrs. Heathcote and Miss Bigg, the mother and aunt of the present Sir Wm. Heathcote of Hursley, between whose family and ours a close

[1] The writer was at that time under twelve years old.

friendship has existed for several generations. These friends did all that they could to promote the comfort of the sisters, during that sad sojourn in Winchester, both by their society, and by supplying those little conveniences in which a lodging-house was likely to be deficient. It was shortly after settling in these lodgings that she wrote to a nephew the following characteristic letter, no longer, alas! in her former strong, clear hand.

'Mrs. David's, College St., Winton,
Tuesday, May 27th.

'There is no better way, my dearest E.,° of thanking you for your affectionate concern for me during my illness than by telling you myself, as soon as possible, that I continue to get better. I will not boast of my handwriting; neither that nor my face have yet recovered their proper beauty, but in other respects I gain strength very fast. I am now out of bed from 9 in the morning to 10 at night: upon the sofa, it is true, but I eat my meals with aunt Cassandra in a rational way, and can employ myself, and walk from one room to another. Mr. Lyford says he will cure me, and if he fails, I shall draw up a memorial and lay it before the Dean and Chapter, and have no doubt of redress from that pious, learned, and disinterested body. Our lodgings are very comfortable. We have a neat little drawing-room with a bow window overlooking Dr. Gabell's garden.[1] Thanks to the kindness of your father and mother in sending me their carriage, my journey hither on Saturday was performed with very little fatigue, and had it been a fine day, I think I should have felt none; but it distressed me to see uncle Henry and Wm. Knight, who kindly attended us on horseback, riding in the rain almost the whole way. We expect a visit from them to-morrow, and hope they will stay the night; and on Thursday, which is a confirmation and a holiday, we are to get Charles° out to breakfast. We have had but one visit from *him*, poor fellow, as he is in sick-room, but he hopes to be out to-night. We see Mrs. Heathcote every day, and William° is to call upon us soon. God bless you, my dear E. If ever you are ill, may you be as

[1] It was the corner house in College Street, at the entrance to Commoners. [Henry Dyson Gabell, headmaster of Winchester College, 1810–23.]

tenderly nursed as I have been. May the same blessed alleviations of anxious, sympathising friends be yours: and may you possess, as I dare say you will, the greatest blessing of all in the consciousness of not being unworthy of their love. *I* could not feel this.

'Your very affec[te] Aunt,

'J. A.'

The following extract from a letter which has been before printed,° written soon after the former, breathes the same spirit of humility and thankfulness:—

'I will only say further that my dearest sister, my tender, watchful, indefatigable nurse, has not been made ill by her exertions. As to what I owe her, and the anxious affection of all my beloved family on this occasion, I can only cry over it, and pray God to bless them more and more.'

Throughout her illness she was nursed by her sister, often assisted by her sister-in-law, my mother.° Both were with her when she died. Two of her brothers, who were clergymen,° lived near enough to Winchester to be in frequent attendance, and to administer the services suitable for a Christian's death-bed. While she used the language of hope to her correspondents, she was fully aware of her danger, though not appalled by it. It is true that there was much to attach her to life. She was happy in her family; she was just beginning to feel confidence in her own success; and, no doubt, the exercise of her great talents was an enjoyment in itself. We may well believe that she would gladly have lived longer; but she was enabled without dismay or complaint to prepare for death. She was a humble, believing Christian. Her life had been passed in the performance of home duties, and the cultivation of domestic affections, without any self-seeking or craving after applause. She had always sought, as it were by instinct, to promote the happiness of all who came within her influence, and doubtless she had her reward in the peace of mind which was granted her in her last days. Her sweetness of temper never failed. She was ever considerate and grateful to those who attended on her. At times, when she felt rather better, her playfulness of spirit revived, and she amused them even in their sadness.° Once, when she thought herself near her end, she said what she imagined might be her last words to those around her, and particularly thanked her sister-in-law for being with her, saying: 'You have always been a kind sister to me, Mary.'° When the end at last came, she sank rapidly, and on being asked by her attendants whether there was anything that she wanted, her reply was, '*Nothing but death.*' These were her last words. In quietness and peace she breathed her last on the morning of July 18, 1817.

On the 24th of that month she was buried in Winchester Cathedral, near the centre of the north aisle, almost opposite to the beautiful chantry tomb of William of Wykeham. A large slab of black marble in the pavement marks the place. Her own family only attended the funeral. Her sister returned to her desolated home, there to devote herself, for ten years, to the care of her aged mother; and to live much on the memory of her lost sister, till called many years later to rejoin her. Her brothers went back sorrowing to their several homes. They were very fond and very proud of her. They were attached to her by her talents, her virtues, and her engaging manners; and each loved afterwards to fancy a resemblance in some niece or daughter of his own to the dear sister Jane, whose perfect equal they yet never expected to see.

POSTSCRIPT

When first I was asked to put together a memoir of my aunt, I saw reasons for declining the attempt. It was not only that, having passed the three score years and ten usually allotted to man's strength, and being unaccustomed to write for publication, I might well distrust my ability to complete the work, but that I also knew the extreme scantiness of the materials out of which it must be constructed. The grave closed over my aunt fifty-two years ago; and during that long period no idea of writing her life had been entertained by any of her family. Her nearest relatives, far from making provision for such a purpose, had actually destroyed many of the letters and papers by which it might have been facilitated.° They were influenced, I believe, partly by an extreme dislike to publishing private details, and partly by never having assumed that the world would take so strong and abiding an interest in her works as to claim her name as public property. It was therefore necessary for me to draw upon recollections rather than on written documents for my materials; while the subject itself supplied me with nothing striking or prominent with which to arrest the attention of the reader. It has been said that the happiest individuals, like nations during their happiest periods, have no history.° In the case of my aunt, it was not only that her course of life was unvaried, but that her own disposition was remarkably calm and even. There was in her nothing eccentric or angular; no ruggedness of temper; no singularity of manner; none of the morbid sensibility or exaggeration of feeling, which not unfrequently accompanies great talents, to be worked up into a picture. Hers was a mind well balanced on a basis of good sense, sweetened by an affectionate heart, and regulated by fixed principles; so that she was to be distinguished from many other amiable and sensible women only by that peculiar genius which shines out clearly enough in her works, but of which a biographer can make little use. The motive which at last induced me to make the attempt is exactly expressed in the passage prefixed to these pages.° I thought that I saw something to be done: knew of no one who could do it but myself, and so was driven to the enterprise. I am glad that I have been able to finish my work. As a family record it can scarcely fail to be interesting to those relatives who must ever set a high value on their connection with Jane Austen, and to them I especially dedicate it; but as I have been asked to do so, I also submit it to the censure of the public, with all its faults both of deficiency and redundancy. I know that its value in their eyes must depend, not on any merits of its own, but on the degree of estimation in which my aunt's works may still be held; and indeed I shall esteem it one of the strongest testimonies ever borne to her talents, if for her sake an interest can be taken in so poor a sketch as I have been able to draw.

BRAY VICARAGE:
Sept. 7, 1869.

Postscript printed at the end of the first edition; omitted from the second.

Since these pages were in type, I have read with astonishment the strange misrepresentation of my aunt's manners given by Miss Mitford in a letter which appears in her lately-published Life, vol. i. p. 305.° Miss Mitford does not profess to have known Jane Austen herself, but to report what had been told her by her mother. Having stated that her mother '*before her marriage*' was well acquainted with Jane Austen and her family, she writes thus:—'Mamma says that she was *then* the prettiest, silliest, most affected, husband-hunting butterfly she ever remembers.' The editor of Miss Mitford's Life very properly observes in a note how different this description is from 'every other account of Jane Austen from whatever quarter.' Certainly it is so totally at variance with the modest simplicity of character which I have attributed to my aunt, that if it could be supposed to have a semblance of truth, it must be equally injurious to her memory and to my trustworthiness as her biographer. Fortunately I am not driven to put my authority in competition with that of Miss Mitford, nor to ask which ought to be considered the better witness in this case; because I am able to prove by a reference to dates that Miss Mitford must have been under a mistake, and that her mother could not possibly have known what she was supposed to have reported; inasmuch as Jane Austen, at the time referred to, was a little girl.

Mrs. Mitford was the daughter of Dr. Russell, Rector of Ashe, a parish adjoining Steventon, so that the families of Austen and Russell must at that time have been known to each other. But the date assigned by Miss Mitford for the termination of the acquaintance is the time of her mother's marriage. This took place in October 1785, when Jane, who had been born in December 1775, was not quite ten years old. In point of fact, however, Miss Russell's opportunities of observing Jane Austen must have come to an end still earlier: for upon Dr. Russell's death, in January 1783, his widow and daughter removed from the neighbourhood, so that all intercourse between the families ceased when Jane was little more than seven years old.

All persons who undertake to narrate from hearsay things which are supposed to have taken place before they were born are liable to error, and are apt to call in imagination to the aid of memory: and hence it arises that many a fancy piece has been substituted for genuine history.

I do not care to correct the inaccurate account of Jane Austen's manners in after life: because Miss Mitford candidly expresses a doubt whether she had not been misinformed on that point.

Nov. 17, 1869.

HENRY AUSTEN

'BIOGRAPHICAL NOTICE OF THE AUTHOR' (1818)

Henry Austen, miniature, *c.*1820

THE following pages are the production of a pen which has already contributed in no small degree to the entertainment of the public. And when the public, which has not been insensible to the merits of 'Sense and Sensibility,' 'Pride and Prejudice,' 'Mansfield Park,' and 'Emma,' shall be informed that the hand which guided that pen is now mouldering in the grave, perhaps a brief account of Jane Austen will be read with a kindlier sentiment than simple curiosity.

Short and easy will be the task of the mere biographer. A life of usefulness, literature, and religion, was not by any means a life of event. To those who lament their irreparable loss, it is consolatory to think that, as she never deserved disapprobation, so, in the circle of her family and friends, she never met reproof; that her wishes were not only reasonable, but gratified; and that to the little disappointments incidental to human life was never added, even for a moment, an abatement of good-will from any who knew her.

Jane Austen was born on the 16th of December, 1775, at Steventon, in the county of Hants. Her father was Rector of that parish upwards of forty years. There he resided, in the conscientious and unassisted discharge of his ministerial duties, until he was turned of seventy years. Then he retired with his wife, our authoress, and her sister, to Bath, for the remainder of his life, a period of about four years. Being not only a profound scholar, but possessing a most exquisite taste in every species of literature, it is not wonderful that his daughter Jane should, at a very early age, have become sensible to the charms of style, and enthusiastic in the cultivation of her own language. On the death of her father she removed, with her mother and sister, for a short time, to Southampton, and finally, in 1809, to the pleasant village of Chawton, in the same county. From this place she sent into the world those novels, which by many have been placed on the same shelf as the works of a D'Arblay and an Edgeworth.° Some of these novels had been the gradual performances of her previous life. For though in composition she was equally rapid and correct, yet an invincible distrust of her own judgement induced her to withhold her works from the public, till time and many perusals had satisfied her that the charm of recent composition was dissolved. The natural constitution, the regular habits, the quiet and happy occupations of our authoress, seemed to promise a long succession of amusement to the public, and a gradual increase of reputation to herself. But the symptoms of a decay, deep and incurable, began to shew themselves in the commencement of 1816. Her decline was at first deceitfully slow; and until the spring of this present year, those who knew their happiness to be involved in her existence could not endure to despair. But in the month of May, 1817, it was found advisable that she should be removed to Winchester for the benefit of constant medical aid, which none even then dared to hope would be permanently beneficial. She supported, during two months, all the varying pain, irksomeness, and tedium, attendant on decaying nature, with more than resignation, with a truly elastic cheerfulness. She retained her faculties, her memory, her fancy, her temper, and her affections, warm, clear, and unimpaired, to the last. Neither her love of God, nor of her fellow creatures flagged for a moment. She made a point of receiving the sacrament before excessive bodily weakness might have rendered her perception unequal to her wishes. She wrote whilst she could hold a pen, and with a pencil when a pen was become too laborious. The day preceding her death she composed some stanzas replete with fancy and vigour.° Her last voluntary speech conveyed thanks to her medical attendant; and to the final question asked of her, purporting to know her wants, she replied, 'I want nothing but death.'

She expired shortly after, on Friday the 18th of July, 1817, in the arms of her sister, who, as well as the relator of these events, feels too surely that they shall never look upon her like again.

Jane Austen was buried on the 24th of July, 1817, in the cathedral church of Winchester, which, in the whole catalogue of its mighty dead, does not contain the ashes of a brighter genius or a sincerer Christian.

Of personal attractions she possessed a considerable share. Her stature was that of true elegance. It could not have been increased without exceeding the middle height. Her carriage and deportment were quiet, yet graceful. Her features were separately good. Their assemblage produced an unrivalled expression of that cheerfulness, sensibility, and benevolence, which were her real characteristics. Her complexion was of the finest texture. It might with truth be said, that her eloquent blood spoke through her modest cheek.° Her voice was extremely sweet. She delivered herself with fluency and precision. Indeed she was formed for elegant and rational society, excelling in conversation as much as in composition. In the present age it is hazardous to mention accomplishments. Our authoress would, probably, have been inferior to few in such acquirements, had she not been so superior to most in higher things. She had not only an excellent taste for drawing, but, in her earlier days, evinced great power of hand in the management of the pencil. Her own musical attainments she held very cheap. Twenty years ago they would have been thought more of, and twenty years hence many a parent will expect their daughters to be applauded for meaner performances. She was fond of dancing, and excelled in it. It remains now to add a few observations on that which her friends deemed more important, on those endowments which sweetened every hour of their lives.

If there be an opinion current in the world, that perfect placidity of temper is not reconcileable to the most lively imagination, and the keenest relish for wit, such an opinion will be rejected for ever by those who have had the happiness of knowing the authoress of the following works. Though the frailties, foibles, and follies of others could not escape her immediate detection, yet even on their vices did she never trust herself to comment with unkindness. The affectation of candour is not uncommon; but she had no affectation. Faultless herself, as nearly as human nature can be, she always sought, in the faults of others, something to excuse, to forgive or forget. Where extenuation was impossible, she had a sure refuge in silence. She never uttered either a hasty, a silly, or a severe expression. In short, her temper was as polished as her wit. Nor were her manners inferior to her temper. They were of the happiest kind. No one could be often in her company without feeling a strong desire of obtaining her friendship, and cherishing a hope of having obtained it. She was tranquil without reserve or stiffness; and communicative without intrusion or self-sufficiency. She became an authoress entirely from taste and inclination. Neither the hope of fame nor profit mixed with her early motives. Most of her works, as before observed, were composed many years previous to their publication. It was with extreme difficulty that her friends, whose partiality she suspected whilst she honoured their judgement, could prevail on her to publish her first work. Nay, so persuaded was she that its sale would not repay the expense of publication, that she actually made a reserve from her very moderate income to meet the expected loss. She could scarcely believe what she termed her great good fortune when 'Sense and Sensibility' produced a clear profit of about £150. Few so gifted were so truly unpretending. She regarded the above sum as a prodigious recompense for that which had cost her nothing. Her readers, perhaps, will wonder that such a work produced so little at a time when some authors have received more guineas than they have written lines. The works of our authoress, however, may live as long as those which have burst on the world with more éclat. But the public has not been unjust; and our authoress was far from thinking it so. Most gratifying to her was the applause which from time to time reached her ears from those who were competent to discriminate. Still, in spite of such applause, so much did she shrink from notoriety, that no accumulation of fame would have induced her, had she lived, to affix her name to any productions of her pen. In the bosom of her own family she talked of them freely, thankful for praise, open to remark, and submissive to criticism. But in public she turned away from any allusion to the character of an authoress. She read aloud with very great taste and effect. Her own works, probably, were never heard to so much advantage as from her own mouth; for she partook largely in all the best gifts of the comic muse. She was a warm and judicious admirer of landscape, both in nature and on canvass. At a very early age she was enamoured of Gilpin on the

Picturesque;° and she seldom changed her opinions either on books or men.

Her reading was very extensive in history and belles lettres; and her memory extremely tenacious. Her favourite moral writers were Johnson in prose, and Cowper in verse. It is difficult to say at what age she was not intimately acquainted with the merits and defects of the best essays and novels in the English language. Richardson's power of creating, and preserving the consistency of his characters, as particularly exemplified in 'Sir Charles Grandison,' gratified the natural discrimination of her mind, whilst her taste secured her from the errors of his prolix style and tedious narrative. She did not rank any work of Fielding quite so high.° Without the slightest affectation she recoiled from every thing gross. Neither nature, wit, nor humour, could make her amends for so very low a scale of morals.

Her power of inventing characters seems to have been intuitive, and almost unlimited. She drew from nature; but, whatever may have been surmised to the contrary, never from individuals.

The style of her familiar correspondence was in all respects the same as that of her novels. Every thing came finished from her pen; for on all subjects she had ideas as clear as her expressions were well chosen. It is not hazarding too much to say that she never dispatched a note or letter unworthy of publication.

One trait only remains to be touched on. It makes all others unimportant. She was thoroughly religious and devout; fearful of giving offence to God, and incapable of feeling it towards any fellow creature. On serious subjects she was well-instructed, both by reading and meditation, and her opinions accorded strictly with those of our Established Church.

London, Dec. 13, 1817.

POSTSCRIPT

SINCE concluding the above remarks, the writer of them has been put in possession of some extracts from the private correspondence of the authoress. They are few and short; but are submitted to the public without apology, as being more truly descriptive of her temper, taste, feelings, and principles than any thing which the pen of a biographer can produce.

The first extract is a playful defence of herself from a mock charge of having pilfered the manuscripts of a young relation.

'What should I do, my dearest E.° with your manly, vigorous sketches, so full of life and spirit? How could I possibly join them on to a little bit of ivory, two inches wide, on which I work with a brush so fine as to produce little effect after much labour?'

The remaining extracts are from various parts of a letter written a few weeks before her death.°

'My attendant is encouraging, and talks of making me quite well. I live chiefly on the sofa, but am allowed to walk from one room to the other. I have been out once in a sedan-chair, and am to repeat it, and be promoted to a wheel-chair as the weather serves. On this subject I will only say further that my dearest sister, my tender, watchful, indefatigable nurse, has not been made ill by her exertions. As to what I owe to her, and to the anxious affection of all my beloved family on this occasion, I can only cry over it, and pray to God to bless them more and more.'

She next touches with just and gentle animadversion on a subject of domestic disappointment. Of this the particulars do not concern the public. Yet in justice to her characteristic sweetness and resignation, the concluding observation of our authoress thereon must not be suppressed.

'But I am getting too near complaint. It has been the appointment of God, however secondary causes may have operated.'

The following and final extract will prove the facility with which she could correct every impatient thought, and turn from complaint to cheerfulness.

'You will find Captain —— a very respectable, well-meaning man, without much manner, his wife and sister all good humour and obligingness, and I hope (since the fashion allows it) with rather longer petticoats than last year.'

London, Dec. 20, 1817.

HENRY AUSTEN

'MEMOIR OF MISS AUSTEN' (1833)

JANE AUSTEN was born on the 16th of December, 1775, at Steventon, in the county of Hants. Her father was rector of that parish upwards of forty years. There he resided in the conscientious and unassisted discharge of his ministerial duties until he was turned of seventy years. Then he retired with his wife, our authoress, and her sister, to Bath, for the remainder of his life, a period of about four years. Being not only a profound scholar, but possessing a most exquisite taste in every species of literature, it is not wonderful that his daughter Jane should, at a very early age, have become sensible to the charms of style, and enthusiastic in the cultivation of her own language. On the death of her father, she removed, with her mother and sister, for a short time, to Southampton; and finally, in 1809, to the pleasant village of Chawton in the same county. From this place she sent her novels into the world. Some of them had been the gradual performances of her previous life; for though in composition she was equally rapid and correct, yet an invincible distrust of her own judgment induced her to withhold her works from the public, till time and many perusals had satisfied her that the charm of recent composition was dissolved. The natural constitution, the regular habits, the quiet and happy occupations of our authoress, seemed to promise a long succession of amusement to the public, and a gradual increase of reputation to herself. But the symptoms of a decay, deep and incurable, began to show themselves in the commencement of 1816. Her decline was at first deceitfully slow; but in the month of May, 1817, it was found advisable that she should be removed to Winchester for the benefit of constant medical aid, which none, even then, dared to hope would be permanently beneficial. She supported, during two months, all the varying pain, irksomeness, and tedium, attendant on decaying nature, with more than resignation—with a truly elastic cheerfulness. She retained her faculties, her memory, her fancy, her temper, and her affections, warm, clear, and unimpaired, to the last. Her last voluntary speech conveyed thanks to her medical attendant; and to the final question asked of her, purporting to know her wants, she replied, 'I want nothing but death.' She expired shortly after, on Friday, the 18th of July, 1817, in the arms of her sister; and was buried, on the 24th of the same month, in the cathedral church of Winchester.

Of personal attractions she possessed a considerable share; her stature rather exceeded the middle height; her carriage and deportment were quiet, but graceful; her features were separately good; their assemblage produced an unrivalled expression of that cheerfulness, sensibility, and benevolence, which were her real characteristics; her complexion was of the finest texture—it might with truth be said, that her eloquent blood spoke through her modest cheek; her voice was sweet; she delivered herself with fluency and precision; indeed, she was formed for elegant and rational society, excelling in conversation as much as in composition. In the present age it is hazardous to mention accomplishments; our authoress would probably have been inferior to few in such acquirements, had she not been so superior to most, in higher things.

It remains to make a few observations on that which her friends deemed more important, on those endowments which sweetened every hour of their lives. If there be an opinion current in the world that a perfectly amiable temper is not reconcilable to a lively imagination, and a keen relish for wit, such an opinion will be rejected for ever by those who had the happiness of knowing the authoress of the following work. Though the frailties, foibles, and follies of others, could not escape her immediate detection, yet even on their vices did she never trust herself to comment with unkindness. The affectation of candour is not uncommon, but she had no affectation. Faultless herself, as nearly as human nature can be, she always sought, in the faults of others, something to excuse, to forgive, or forget. Where extenuation was impossible, she had a sure refuge in silence. She never uttered either a hasty, a silly, or a severe expression. In short, her temper was as polished as her wit; and no one could be often in her company without feeling a strong desire of obtaining her friendship, and cherishing a hope of having obtained it. She became an authoress entirely from taste and inclination. Neither the hope of fame nor profit mixed with her early motives. It was with extreme difficulty that her friends, whose partiality she suspected, whilst she honoured their judgment, could persuade her to publish her first work. Nay, so persuaded was she that the sale would not repay the expense of publication, that she actually made a reserve from her moderate income to meet the expected loss. She could scarcely believe what she termed her great good fortune, when 'Sense and Sensibility' produced a clear profit of about 150*l*. Few so gifted were so truly unpretending. She regarded the above sum as a prodigious recompense for that which had cost her nothing. Her readers, perhaps, will wonder that such a work produced so little, at a time when some authors have received more guineas than they have written lines. But the public has not been unjust; and our authoress was far from thinking it so. Most gratifying to her was the applause which from time to time reached her ears from those who were competent to discriminate. When 'Pride and Prejudice' made its appearance, a gentleman, celebrated for his literary attainments, advised a friend of the authoress to read it, adding, with more point than gallantry, 'I should like to know who is the author, for it is much too clever to have been written by a woman.' Still, in spite of such applause, so much did she shrink from notoriety, that no increase of fame would have induced her, had she lived, to affix her name to any productions of her pen. In the bosom of her family she talked of them freely; thankful for praise, open to remark, and submissive to criticism. But in public she turned away from any allusion to the character of an authoress. In proof of this, the following circumstance, otherwise unimportant, is stated. Miss Austen was on a visit in London soon after the publication of 'Mansfield Park': a nobleman, personally unknown to her, but who had good reasons for considering her to be the authoress of that work, was desirous of her joining a literary circle at his house. He communicated his wish in the politest manner, through a mutual friend, adding, what his Lordship doubtless thought would be an irresistible inducement, that the celebrated Madame de Staël would be of the party.° Miss Austen immediately declined the invitation. To her truly delicate mind such a display would have given pain instead of pleasure.

Her power of inventing characters seems to have been intuitive, and almost unlimited. She drew from nature; but, whatever may have been surmised to the contrary, never from individuals. The style of her familiar correspondence was in all respects the same as that of her novels. Every thing came finished from her pen; for on all subjects she had ideas as clear as her expressions were well chosen. It is not too much to say that she never despatched a note or letter unworthy of publication. The following few short extracts from her private correspondence are submitted to the public without apology, as being more truly descriptive of her temper, taste, and feelings, than any thing which the pen of a biographer can produce. The first is a playful defence of herself from a mock charge of having pilfered the manuscripts of a young relation. 'What should I do, my dearest E., with your manly, vigorous sketches, so full of life and spirit? How could I possibly join them on to a little bit of ivory, two inches wide, on which I work with a brush so fine, as to produce little effect after much labour?' The remaining extracts are from a letter written a few weeks before her death. 'My medical attendant is encouraging, and talks of making me quite well. I live chiefly on the sofa, but am allowed to walk from one room to the other. I have been out once in a sedan chair, and am to repeat it, and be promoted to a wheel-chair as the weather serves. On this subject I will only say farther, that my dearest sister, my tender, watchful, indefatigible nurse, has not been made ill by her exertions. As to what I owe to her, and to the anxious affection of all my beloved family on this occasion, I can only cry over it, and pray to God to bless them more and more.' She next touches with just and gentle animadversion on a subject of domestic disappointment. Of this, the particulars do not concern the public. Yet, in justice to her characteristic sweetness and resignation, the concluding observation of our authoress thereon must not be suppressed. 'But I am getting too near complaint. It has been the appointment of God, however secondary causes may have operated.'

The above brief biographical sketch has been, in substance, already published with Miss Austen's posthumous novels. It is a matter of deep regret to the writer, that materials for a more detailed account of so talented a woman cannot be obtained; therefore, as a tribute due to her memory, he subjoins the following extracts from a critical journal of the highest reputation:—

'Unlike that of many writers, Miss Austen's fame has grown fastest since she died:° there was no éclat about her first appearance: the public took time to make up its mind; and she, not having staked her hopes of happiness on success or failure, was content to wait for the decision of her claims. Those claims have long been established beyond a question; but the merit of *first* recognising them belongs less to reviewers than to general readers. So retired, so unmarked by literary notoriety, was the life Miss Austen led, that if any likeness was ever taken of her, none has ever been engraved.[1] With regard to her genius, we must adventure a few remarks. She herself compares her productions to a little bit of ivory, two inches wide, worked upon with a brush so fine, that little effect is produced after much labour. It is so: her portraits are perfect likenesses, admirably finished, many of them gems, but it is all miniature painting; and, satisfied with being inimitable in one line, she never essayed canvass and oils; never tried her hand at a majestic daub. Her "two inches of ivory" just describes her preparations for a tale of three volumes. A village—two families connected together—three or four interlopers, out of whom are to spring a little tracasserie;—and by means of village or country town visiting and gossiping a real plot shall thicken, and its "rear of darkness" never be scattered till six pages off *finis*. The plots are simple in construction, and yet intricate in development;—the main characters, those that the reader feels sure are to love, marry, and make mischief, are introduced in the

[1] No likeness ever was taken of Miss Austen; which the editor much laments, as he is thereby precluded from the gratification of prefixing her portrait to this edition. [The editor means that no likeness was taken by a professional.]

first or second chapter; the work is all done by half a dozen people; no person, scene, or sentence, is ever introduced needless to the matter in hand:—no catastrophes, or discoveries, or surprises of a grand nature, are allowed—neither children nor fortunes are lost or found by accident—the mind is never taken off the level surface of life—the reader breakfasts, dines, walks, and gossips, with the various worthies, till a process of transmutation takes place in him, and he absolutely fancies himself one of the company. Yet the winding up of the plot involves a surprise: a few incidents are entangled at the beginning in the most simple and natural manner, and till the close one never feels quite sure how they are to be disentangled. Disentangled, however, they are, and that in a most satisfactory manner. The secret is, Miss Austen was a thorough mistress in the knowledge of human character; how it is acted upon by education and circumstance; and how, when once formed, it shows itself through every hour of every day, and in every speech to every person. Her conversations would be tiresome but for this; and her personages, the fellows to whom may be met in the streets, or drank tea with at half an hour's notice, would excite no interest; but in Miss Austen's hands we see into their hearts and hopes, their motives, their struggles within themselves; and a sympathy is induced, which, if extended to daily life, and the world at large, would make the reader a more amiable person; and we must think it that reader's own fault who does not close her pages with more charity in his heart towards unpretending, if prosing, worth; with a higher estimation of simple kindness, and sincere good-will; with a quickened sense of the duty of bearing and forbearing, in domestic intercourse, and of the pleasure of adding to the little comforts even of persons who are neither wits nor beauties,—who, in a word, does not feel more disposed to be benevolent. In the last posthumous tale ("Persuasion") there is a strain of a higher mood; there is still the exquisite delineation of common life, such life as we hear, and see, and make part of, with the addition of a finer, more poetic, yet equally real tone of thought and actions in the principals. If Miss Austen was sparing in her introduction of nobler characters, it was because they are scattered sparingly in life. Her death has made a chasm in our light literature,—the domestic novel, with its home-born incidents, its "familiar matter of to-day," its slight array of names, and great cognisance of people and things, its confinement to country life, and total oblivion of costume, manners, the great world, and "the mirror of fashion." Every species of composition is, when good, to be admired in its way; but the revival of the domestic novel would make a pleasant interlude to the showy, sketchy novels of high life.

'Miss Austen has the merit (in our judgment most essential) of being evidently a Christian writer:° a merit which is much enhanced, both on the score of good taste and of practical utility, by her religion being not at all obtrusive. She might defy the most fastidious critic to call any of her novels (as Cœlebs° was designated) a dramatic sermon. The subject is rather alluded to, and that incidentally, than studiously brought forward and dwelt upon. In fact, she is more sparing of it than would be thought desirable by some persons; perhaps even by herself, had she consulted merely her own sentiments; but she probably introduced it as far as she thought would be generally profitable; for when the purpose of inculcating a religious principle is made too palpably prominent, many readers, if they do not throw aside the book with disgust, are apt to fortify themselves with that respectful kind of apathy with which they undergo a regular sermon, and prepare themselves as they do to swallow a dose of medicine, endeavouring to get it down in large gulps, without tasting it more than is necessary.'

Perhaps these volumes may be perused by some readers who will feel a solicitude respecting the authoress, extending beyond the perishable qualities of temper, manners, taste, and talents.—We can assure all such (and the being able so to do gratifies us more than the loudest voice of human praise) that Jane Austen's hopes of immortality were built upon the Rock of ages. That she deeply felt, and devoutly acknowledged, the insignificance of all worldly attainments, and the worthlessness of all human services, in the eyes of her heavenly Father. That she had no other hope of mercy, pardon, and peace, but through the merits and sufferings of her Redeemer.

October 5. 1832.

The Editor of 'The Standard Novels' feels happy in being able to state, that arrangements have been made for including several other of the works of Miss Austen in this collection. Miss Austen is the founder of a school of novelists; and her followers are not confined to her own sex, but comprise in their number some male writers of considerable merit. The authoress of 'Sense and Sensibility' had for her contemporaries several female novelists, whose works attained instant popularity—Madame D'Arblay, Miss Edgeworth, Mrs. Opie, Miss Porter,° and others, most of whose novels preceded hers in order of time: but, notwithstanding the temptation which nearly all writers are under (especially at the commencement of their vocation) to imitate that which has commanded distinguished success, Miss Austen at once freed herself from such influence, and, with combined boldness and modesty, struck into a path of her own, of which she remains, to this day, the undisputed mistress. The truth, spirit, ease, and refined humour of her conversations have rarely been equalled. She is, emphatically, the novelist of home. One of the most remarkable traits of her genius may be found in the power by which, without in the slightest degree violating the truth of portraiture, she is able to make the veriest every-day person a character of great interest. This is, indeed, turning lead into gold; but it would be difficult to detect the secret of the process. [An editorial paragraph issued from Bentley's office and not strictly part of Henry Austen's 'Memoir'.]

ANNA LEFROY

'RECOLLECTIONS OF AUNT JANE' (1864)

Anna Lefroy as a young woman

Southern Hill Reading
Dec[r] 1864

My dear Edward

You have asked me to put on paper my recollections of Aunt Jane, & to do so would be, both on your account & her's a labour of love if I had but a sufficiency of material.

I am sorry to say that my reminiscences are few; surprisingly so, considering how much I saw of her in childhood, & how much intercourse we had in later years. I look back to the first period but find little that I can grasp of any substance, or certainty: it seems now all so shadowy! I recollect the frequent visits of my two Aunts, & how they walked in wintry weather through the sloppy lane between Steventon & Dean in pattens, usually worn at that time even by Gentlewomen. I remember too their bonnets: because though precisely alike in colour, shape & material, I made it a pleasure to guess, & I believe always guessed right, which bonnet & which Aunt belonged to each other—Children do not think of Aunts, or perhaps of any grown up people as young; yet at the time to which I now refer my Aunts must have been very young women—even a little later, when I might be 9 or 10 y[rs]. old I thought it so very odd, to hear Grandpapa speak of them as 'the Girls'. 'Where are the Girls?' 'Are the Girls gone out?'

At the time of my birth Aunt Jane was not much over 17—She was thus entered in the family Bible in her Father's hand writing. A very good clear hand he wrote, by the by. 'Jane Austen born 16 Dec[r]. 1775. Privately baptised 17 Dec[r]. 1775. Rec[d]. into the Church 5 Ap[l]. 1776 Sponsors Rev[d]. M[r]. Cooke, Rector of Bookham Surry, M[rs]. Jane Austen of Sevenoaks Kent, Father's Uncle's Wife, M[rs]. Musgrave of Chinnor, Oxon.'

Aunt Jane was the general favorite with children; her ways with them being so playful, & her long circumstantial stories so delightful! These were continued from time to time, & begged for of course at all possible or impossible occasions; woven, as she proceeded out of nothing, but her own happy talent for invention. Ah! if but one of them could be now recovered!

Other things have been even more completely obliterated—

I have been told that one of her earliest Novels (Pride & Prejudice) was read aloud (in M.S. of course) in the Parsonage at Dean, whilst I was in the room, & not expected to listen—Listen however I did, with so much interest, & with so much talk afterwards about 'Jane & Elizabeth' that it was resolved, for prudence sake, to read no more of the story aloud in my hearing. This was related to me years afterwards, when the Novel had been published; & it was supposed that the names might recall to my recollection that early impression. Such however did not prove to be the case. Something you may expect me to say of our Aunt's personal appearance, though in the latter years of her life it must be as well remembered by you as by me. The Figure tall & slight, but not drooping; well balanced, as was proved by her quick firm step. Her complexion of that rather rare sort which seems the peculiar property of *light brunettes* A mottled skin, not fair, but perfectly clear & healthy in hue; the fine naturally curling hair, neither light nor dark; the bright hazel eyes to match, & the rather small but well shaped nose. One hardly understands how with all these advantages she could yet fail of being a decidedly handsome woman.

I have intimated that of the two Sisters Aunt Jane was generally the favorite with children, but with the young people of Godmersham it was not so. They liked her indeed as a playfellow, & as a teller of stories, but they were not really fond of her. I believe that their Mother was not; at least that she very much preferred the elder Sister. A little talent went a long way with the Goodneston Bridgeses° of that period; & *much* must have gone a long way too far. This preference lasted for a good while, nor do I think that there ever was any abatement in the love of that family for Aunt Cassandra. Time however brought, as it always does bring, new impressions or modifications of the old ones. Owing to particular circumstances there grew up during the latter years of Aunt Jane's life a great & affectionate intimacy between herself &

the eldest of her nieces; & I suppose there a [*sic*] few now living who can more fully appreciate the talent or revere the memory of Aunt Jane than Lady Knatchbull. This has brought me to the period of my own greatest share of intimacy; the two years before my marriage, & the two or three years after, when we lived, as you know almost close to Chawton when the original 17 years between us seemed to shrink to 7—or to nothing. It comes back to me now how strangely I missed her; it had become so much a habit with me to put by things in my mind with a reference to her and to say to myself, 'I shall keep this for Aunt Jane.' It was my great amusement during one summer visit at Chawton to procure Novels from a circulating Library at Alton, & after running them over to relate the stories to Aunt Jane. I may say it was her amusement also, as she sat busily stitching away at a work of charity, in which I fear that I took myself no more useful part. Greatly we both enjoyed it, one piece of absurdity leading to another, till Aunt Cassan[dr][a] fatigued with her own share of laughter w[d]. exclaim 'How *can* you both be so foolish?' & beg us to leave off—One of these Novels, written by a M[rs]. Hunter of Norwich,° was an exceedingly lengthy affair; there was no harm in the book, except that in a most unaccountable manner the same story about the same people, most of whom I think had died before the real story began was repeated 3 or 4 times over. A copy of the note written a few weeks afterwards,° in reply to one from 'M[rs]. Hunter' will give you some idea of the state of the case.

'Miss Jane Austen begs her best thanks may be conveyed to M[rs]. Hunter of Norwich for the Threadpapers which she has been so kind as to send her by M[r]. Austen, & which will be always very valuable on account of the spirited sketches (made it is supposed by Nicholson or Glover°) of the most interesting spots, Tarefield Hall, the Mill, & above all the Tomb of Howard's wife, of the faithful representation of which Miss Jane Austen is undoubtedly a good judge having spent so many summers at Tarefield Abbey the delighted guest of the worthy M[rs]. Wilson. Miss Jane Austen's tears have flowed over each sweet sketch in such a way as would do M[rs]. Hunter's heart good to see; if M[rs]. Hunter could understand all Miss Austen's interest in the subject she would certainly have the kindness to publish at least 4 vols more about the Flint family, & especially would give many fresh particulars on that part of it which M[rs]. H. has hitherto handled too briefly; viz, the history of Mary Flint's marriage with Howard.

Miss Austen cannot close this small epitome of the miniature abridgement of her thanks & admiration without expressing her sincere hope that M[rs]. Hunter is provided at Norwich with a more safe conveyance to London than Alton can now boast, as the Car of Falkenstein° which was the pride of that Town was overturned within the last 10 days.'

The Car of Falkenstein, Collier's, but at that time called Falkner's Coach, relates to some earlier nonsense.

Her unusually quick sense of the ridiculous inclined her to play with the trifling commonplaces of every day life, whether as regarded people or things; but she never played with it's serious duties or responsibilities—when grave she was *very* grave; I am not sure but that Aunt Cassandra's disposition was the most equally cheerful of the two. Their affection for each other was extreme; it passed the common love of sisters; and it had been so from childhood. My Grandmother talking to me once [of] by gone times, & of that particular time when my Aunts were placed at the Reading Abbey School, said that Jane was too young to make her going to school at all necessary, but it was her own doing; she *would* go with Cassandra; 'if Cassandra's head had been going to be cut off Jane would have her's cut off too'—

They must however have been separated some times as Cassandra in her childhood was a good deal with D[r]. & M[rs]. Cooper at Bath°—She once described to me her return to Steventon one fine summer evening. The Coopers had sent or conveyed her a good part of the journey, but my Grandfather had to go, I think as far as Andover to meet her—He might have conveyed himself by Coach, but he brought his Daughter home in a Hack chaise; & almost home they were when they met Jane & Charles, the two little ones of the family, who had got as far as New down to meet the chaise, & have the pleasure of riding home in it; but who first spied the chaise tradition does not say, whether such happiness

Anna Lefroy in later life, 1845

were the lawful property of Jane or Charles will never be exactly understood.

I have come to the end of my traditional lore, as well as of my personal recollections, & I am sorry that both should be so meagre & unsatisfactory; but if this attempt should incline others to do the same, even if no more, the contributions when put together may furnish a memorial of some value. You must have it in your own power to write something; & Caroline, though her recollections cannot go so far back even as your's, is, I know acquainted with some particulars of interest in the life of our Aunt; they relate to circumstances of which I never had any knowledge, but were communicated to her by the best of then living Authorities, Aunt Cassandra—There may be other sources of information, if we could get at them—Letters may have been preserved, & this is the more probable as Aunt Jane's talent for letter writing was so much valued & thought so delightful amongst her own family circle.

Such gleanings however are not likely to fall to our share, & we must content ourselves, I fear, with our own reminiscences.

Believe me d[r]. Edw[d]

y[r]. affect: Sister

J. A. E. Lefroy

CAROLINE AUSTEN

MY AUNT JANE AUSTEN: A MEMOIR

(1867)

Caroline Austen as a child

A MEMOIR of Miss Jane Austen has often been asked for, and strangers have declared themselves willing and desirous to undertake the task of writing it—and have wondered that the family should have refused to supply the necessary materials. But tho' none of her nearest relatives desired that the details of a very private and rather uneventful life should be laid before the world yet I think they would not willingly have had her memory die—and it *will* die and be lost, if no effort is made to preserve it—The grass grave in the village churchyard sinks down in a few years to the common level, and its place is no more to be found and so, to keep the remembrance of the departed a little longer in the world which they have left, we lay a stone over their graves, and inscribe upon it their name and age, and perhaps some few words of their virtues and of our own sorrow—and tho' the stone moulders and tho' the letters fade away, yet do they outlast the interest of *what* they record—We remember our dead always—but when *we* shall have joined them their memory may be said to have perished out of the earth, for no distinct idea of them remains behind, and the next generation soon forget that they ever existed—

For most of us therefore the memorial on the perishing tombstone is enough—and *more* than enough—it will tell its tale longer than anyone will care to read it—But not so for all—Every country has had its great men, whose lives have been and are still read—with unceasing interest; and so, in *some* families there has been *one* distinguished by talent or goodness, and known far beyond the home circle, whose memory ought to be preserved through more than a single generation—Such a one was my Aunt—Jane Austen—

Since her death, the public voice has placed her in the first rank of the Novellists of her day—given her, I may say, the first place amongst them—and it seems but right that *some* record should remain with *us* of her life and character; and that *she* herself should not be forgotten by her nearest descendants, whilst her writings still *live*, and are still spreading her fame wherever the English books are read.—Her last long surviving Brother° has recently died at the age of 91 ['1865' is in margin]—The generation who knew her is passing away—but those who are succeeding us must feel an interest in the personal character of their Great Aunt, who has made the family name in some small degree, illustrious—For *them* therefore, and for my own gratification I will try to call back my recollections of what she *was*, and what manner of life she led—It is not much that I have to tell—for I mean to relate only what I *saw* and what I *thought* myself—I was just twelve years old when she died—therefore, I knew her only with a child's knowledge—

My first very distinct remembrance of her is in her own home at Chawton—The house belonged to her second Brother, Mr. Knight (of Godmersham & Chawton) and was by him made a comfortable residence for his Mother and sisters—The family party *there* were, my Grandmother, Mrs. Austen—my two Aunts, her daughters—and a third Aunt of *mine*—Miss Lloyd, who had made her home with *them* before I can remember, and who remained their inmate as long as Mrs. Austen lived—

The dwelling place of a favourite Author always possesses a certain interest for those who love the books that issued from it—Tho' some of my Aunt's Novels were imagined and written, in her very early days—*some* certainly at Steventon yet it was from Chawton that after being rearranged and prepared for publication they were sent out into the world—and it is with Chawton therefore, that her name as an Author, must be identified—The house which she inhabited was in itself, not much more deserving of notice than Cowper's dwelling place at Olney°—and yet more than 30 years after his death, *that* was pointed out to us, as a *something* that strangers passing through the little town, *must* wish to see—Now, as the remembrance of Chawton Cottage, for so in later years it came to be called, is still pleasant to *me*—I will assume that those who never knew it, may like to have laid before them, a description of their Aunt's home—the *last* that she dwelt in—

where, in the maturity of her mind, she completed the works that have given her an *English* name—where after a few years, whilst still in the prime of life, she began to droop and wither away—the home from whence she removed only in the last stage of her illness, by the persuasion of her friends, hoping against hope—and to which her sister before long had to return alone—

My Grand Father, Mr. Austen, held for many years, the adjoining Livings of Deane and Steventon—but gave up his duties to his eldest son, and settled at Bath, a very few years before his own death—For a while, his Widow and daughters remained at Bath—then they removed to Southampton—and finally settled in the village of Chawton—

Mr. Knight had been able to offer his Mother the choice of two houses—one in Kent near to Godmersham—and the other at Chawton—and she and her daughters eventually decided on the Hampshire residence.

I have been told I know not how truly, that it *had* been originally a roadside Inn—and it was well placed for such a purpose—just where the road from Winchester comes into the London and Gosport line—The fork between the two being partly occupied by a large shallow pond—which pond I beleive has long since become dry ground—

The front door opened on the road,° a very narrow enclosure of each side, protected the house from the possible shock of any runaway vehicle—A good sized entrance, and two parlours, called dining and drawing room, made the *length* of the house; all intended originally to look on the road—but the large drawing room window was blocked-up and turned into a bookcase when Mrs. Austen took possession and another was opened at the side, which gave to view only turf and trees—A high wooden fence shut out the road (the Winchester road it was) all the length of the little domain, and trees were planted inside to form a shrubbery walk—which carried round the enclosure, gave a very sufficient space for exercise—you did not feel cramped for room; and there was a pleasant irregular mixture of hedgerow, and grass, and gravel walk and long grass for mowing, and orchard—which I imagine arose from two or three little enclosures having been thrown together, and arranged as best might be, for ladies' occupation—There was besides a good kitchen garden, large court and many out-buildings, not much occupied—and all this affluence of space was very delightful to children, and I have no doubt added considerably to the pleasure of a visit—

Everything *in*doors and *out* was well kept—the house was well furnished, and it was altogether a comfortable and ladylike establishment, tho' I beleive the means which supported it, were but small—

The house was quite as good as the generality of Parsonage houses *then*—and much in the same old style—the ceilings low and roughly finished—*some* bedrooms very small—*none* very large but in number sufficient to accomodate the inmates, and several guests—

The dining room could not be made to look anywhere *but* on the road—and *there* my Grandmother often sat for an hour or two in the morning, with her work or her writing—cheered by its sunny aspect, and by the stirring scene it afforded her.

I beleive the close vicinity of the road was really no more an evil to *her* than it was to her grandchildren. Collyer's daily coach with six horses was a sight to see! and most delightful was it to a child to have the awful stillness of night so frequently broken by the noise of passing carriages, which seemed sometimes, even to shake the bed—

The village of Chawton has, of course, long since been tranquilised—it is no more a great thoroughfare, and *other* and *many* changes have past over it—and if any of its visitants should fail to recognise from my description, the house by the pond—I must beg them not hastily to accuse me of having exaggerated its former pleasantness.

Twenty years ago, on being then left vacant by Aunt Cassandra's death, it was divided into habitations for the poor, and made to accomodate several families—so I was *told*—for I have never seen it since and I beleive trees have been cut down, and all that could be termed pleasure ground has reverted again to more ordinary purposes—

My visits to Chawton were frequent—I cannot tell *when* they began—they were very pleasant to me—and Aunt Jane was the great charm—As a very little girl, I was always creeping up to her, and following her whenever I *could*, *in* the house and out of it—I might not have remembered *this*, but for the recollection of my Mother's telling me privately, I must not be troublesome to my Aunt—

Her charm to children was great sweetness of manner—she seemed to love you, and you loved her naturally in return—*This* as well as I can now recollect and *analyse*, was what I felt in my earliest days, before I was old enough to be amused by her cleverness—But soon came the delight of her playful talk—*Every*thing she could make amusing to a child—Then, as I got older, and when cousins came to share the entertainment, she would tell us the most delightful stories chiefly of Fairyland, and her Fairies had all characters of their own—The tale was invented, I am sure, at the moment, and was sometimes continued for 2 or 3 days, if occasion served—

As to my Aunt's personal appearance, her's was the first face that I can remember thinking pretty, not that I *used* that word to myself, but I know I looked at her with admiration—Her face was rather *round* than long—she had a *bright*, but not a *pink* colour—a clear brown complexion and very good hazle eyes—She was not, I beleive, an absolute beauty, but before she left Steventon she was established as a very pretty girl, in the opinion of most of her neighbours—as I learnt afterwards from some of those who still remained—Her hair, a darkish brown, curled naturally—it was in short curls round her face (for *then* ringlets were *not*.) She always wore a cap—Such was the custom with ladies who were not quite young—at least of a morning but I never saw her without one, to the best of my remembrance, either morning or evening.

I beleive my two Aunts were not accounted very good dressers, and were thought to have taken to the garb of middle age unnecessarily soon—but they were particularly neat, and they held all untidy ways in great disesteem. Of the *two*, Aunt Jane was by far my favourite—I did not *dislike* Aunt Cassandra—but if my visit had at any time chanced to fall out during *her* absence, I don't think I should have missed her—whereas, *not* to have found Aunt Jane at Chawton, *would* have been a blank indeed!

As I grew older, I met with young companions at my Grandmother's—Of Capt. Charles Austen's motherless girls, *one* the eldest, Cassy—lived there chiefly, for a time—under the especial tutorage of Aunt Cassandra; and then Chawton House was for a while inhabited by Capt. Frank Austen; and *he* had many children°—I beleive we were all of us, according to our different ages and natures, very fond of our Aunt Jane—and that we ever retained a strong impression of the pleasantness of Chawton life—One of my cousins,° now long since dead, after he was grown up, used occasionally to go and see Aunt Cass[a.]—*then* left sole inmate of the old house—and he told me once, that his visits were always a disappointment to him—for that he could not help expecting to feel particularly happy at Chawton and never till he got there, could he fully realise to himself how all its peculiar pleasures were gone—

In the time of my childhood, it was a cheerful house—my Uncles, one or another, frequently coming for a few days; and they were all pleasant in their own family—I have thought since, after having seen more of other households, *wonderfully*, as the *family* talk had much of spirit and vivacity, and it was never troubled by disagreements as it was not their habit to argue with each other—There always was perfect harmony amongst the brothers and sisters, and over my Grandmother's door might have been inscribed the text, 'Behold how good—and joyful a thing it is, brethren, to dwell together in unity.'° There was firm family union, never broken but by death—tho' the time came when that union could not have been preserved if natural affection had not been by a spirit of forbearance and generosity°—

Aunt Jane began her day with music—for which I conclude she had a natural taste; as she thus kept it up—tho' she had no one to teach; was never induced (as I have heard) to play in company; and none of her family cared much for it. I suppose, that she might not trouble *them*, she chose her practising time before breakfast—when she could have the room to herself—She practised regularly every morning—She played very pretty tunes, *I* thought—and I liked to stand by her and listen to them; but the music, (for I knew the books well in after years) would now be thought disgracefully easy—Much that she played from was manuscript, copied out by herself—and so neatly and correctly, that it was as easy to read as print—

At 9 o'clock she made breakfast—*that* was *her* part of the household work—The tea and sugar stores were under *her* charge—*and* the wine—Aunt Cassandra did all the rest—for my Grandmother had suffered herself to be superseded by her daughters *before* I can remember; and soon *after*, she ceased even to sit at the head of the table—

I don't beleive Aunt Jane observed any particular method in parcelling out her day but I think she generally sat in the drawing room till luncheon: when visitors were there, chiefly at work°—She was fond of work—and she was a great adept at overcast and satin stitch—the peculiar delight of that day—General handiness and neatness were amongst her characteristics—*She* could throw the spilikens for us, better than anyone else, and she was wonderfully successful at cup and ball—She found a resource sometimes in that simple game, when she suffered from weak eyes and could not work or read for long together—

Her handwriting remains to bear testimony to its own excellence; and every note and letter of hers, was finished off *handsomely*—There was an art *then* in folding and sealing—no adhesive envelopes made all easy—some people's letters looked always loose and untidy—but *her* paper was sure to take the right folds, and *her* sealing wax to drop in the proper place—

After luncheon, my Aunts generally walked out—sometimes they went to Alton for shopping—Often, one or the other of them, to the Great House—as it was then called—when a brother was inhabiting it, to make a visit—or if the house were standing empty they liked to stroll about the grounds—sometimes to Chawton Park—a noble beech wood, just within a walk—but sometimes, but that was rarely, to call on a neighbour—They had no carriage, and their visitings did not extend far—there were a few famil**i**ties [*sic*] living in the village—but no great intimacy was kept up with any of them—they were upon *friendly* but rather *distant* terms, with all—Yet I am sure my Aunt Jane had a regard for her neighbours and felt a kindly interest in their proceedings. She liked immensely to hear all about them. They sometimes served for her amusement, but it was her own nonsense that gave zest to the gossip—She never turned *them* into ridicule—She was as far as possible from being either censorious or satirical—she never abused them or *quizzed*° them—*That* was the word of the day—an ugly word, now obsolete—and the ugly practise which it bespoke, is far less prevalent *now*, under *any* name, than it was *then*. The laugh she occasionally raised was by imagining for her neighbours impossible contingencies—by relating in prose or verse some trifling incident coloured to her own fancy, or in writing a history of what they had said or done, that *could* deceive nobody—As an instance I would give her description of the pursuits of Miss Mills and Miss Yates—two young ladies of whom she knew next to nothing—they were only on a visit to a near neighbour but their names tempted her into rhyme—and so *on* she went—This was before *my* time. Mrs. Lefroy knows the lines better than *I* do—I beleive she has a copy and I shall not attempt to quote them imperfectly here. To about the same date perhaps may be referred (at least it was equally before *my* time) a few chapters which I overheard of a mock heroic story, written between herself and one of her nieces,° and I doubt *not*, at *her* instigation—If I remember rightly, it had no other foundation than their having seen a neighbour passing on the coach, without having previously known that he was going to leave home—(*This* I have since been told was written entirely by the Niece only under her encouragement).

I did not often see my Aunt with a book in her hand, but I beleive she was fond of reading and that she *had* read and *did* read a good deal. I doubt whether she cared very much for poetry in *general*; but she was a great admirer of Crabbe, and consequently she took a keen interest in finding out *who* he was—Other contemporary writers were well-known, but *his* origen having been obscure, his name did not announce *itself*—however by diligent enquiry she was ere long able to inform the rest of the family that he held the Living of Trowbridge, and had recently married a second time—

A very warm admirer of my Aunt's writing but a stranger in England, lately made the observation that it would be most interesting to know what had been Miss Austen's opinions on the great public events of her time—a period as she rightly observed, of the greatest interest—for my Aunt must have been a young woman, able to *think*, at the time of the French Revolution & the long disastrous chapter then begun, was closed by the battle of Waterloo, two years before her death—anyone *might* naturally desire to know what part such a mind as her's had taken in the great strifes of war and policy which so disquieted Europe for more than 20 years—and yet, it was a question that had never before presented itself to me—and tho' I have *now* retraced my steps on *this* track, I have found absolutely nothing!—

The general politics of the family were Tory—rather taken for granted I suppose, than discussed, as even my Uncles seldom talked about it—and in vain do I try to recall any word or expression of Aunt Jane's that had reference to public events—*Some* bias of course she *must* have had—but I can only *guess* to which quarter it inclined—Of her historical opinions I *am* able to record *thus* much—that she was a most loyal adherent of Charles the 1st, and that she always encouraged my youthful beleif in Mary Stuart's perfect innocence of all the crimes with which History has charged her memory—°

My Aunt must have spent much time in writing—her desk lived in the drawing room. I often saw her writing letters on it, and I beleive she wrote much of her Novels in the same way—sitting with her family, when they were quite alone; but *I* never saw any manuscript of *that* sort, in progress—She wrote very fully to her Brothers when they were at sea, and she corresponded with many others of her family—

There is nothing in those letters which *I* have seen that would be acceptable to the public—They were very well expressed, and they must have been very interesting to those who received them—but they detailed chiefly home and family events: and she seldom committed herself *even* to an *opinion*—so that to strangers they could be *no* transcript of her mind—they would not feel that they knew her any the better for having read them—

They were rather *over*-cautious, for excellence—Her letters to Aunt Cassandra (for they were *sometimes* separated) were, I dare say,° open and confidential—My Aunt looked them over and burnt the greater part, (as she told me), 2 or 3 years before her own death—She left, or *gave* some as legacies to the Nieces—but of those that *I* have seen, several had portions cut out—Aunt Jane was so good as frequently to write to *me*; and in addressing a child, she was perfect—

When staying at Chawton, if my two cousins, Mary Jane and Cassy were there, we often had amusements in which my Aunt was very helpful—*She* was the one to whom we always looked for help—She would furnish us with what we wanted from her wardrobe, and *she* would often be the entertaining visitor in our make beleive house—She amused us in various ways—*once* I remember in giving a conversation as between myself and my two cousins, supposed to be grown up, the day after a Ball.

As I grew older, she would talk to me more seriously of my reading, and of my amusements—I had taken early to writing verses and stories, and I am sorry to think *how* I troubled her with reading them. She was very kind about it, and always had some praise to bestow but at last she warned me against spending too much time upon them—She said—how well I recollect it! that she *knew* writing stories was a great amusement, and *she* thought a harmless one—tho' many people, she was aware, thought otherwise—but that at *my* age it would be bad for me to be much taken up with my own compositions—Later still—it was after she got to Winchester, she sent me a message to this effect—That if I would take her advice, I should cease writing° till I was 16, and that she had herself often wished she had *read* more, and written *less*, in the corresponding years of her own life.

She was considered to read aloud remarkably well. I did not often hear her but *once* I knew her take up a volume of Evelina° and read a few pages of Mr. Smith and the Brangtons and I thought it was like a play. She had a very good *speaking* voice—This was the opinion of her contemporaries—and though I did not *then* think of it as a perfection, or ever hear it observed upon, yet its tones have never been forgotten—I can recall them even now—and I *know* they *were* very pleasant.

I have spoken of the family union that prevailed amongst my Grandmother's children—Aunt Jane was a very affectionate sister to all her Brothers—One of them in particular was her especial pride and delight:° but of all her family, the nearest and dearest throughout her whole life was, undoubtedly her sister—her *only* sister. Aunt Cassandra was the older by 3 or 4 years, and the habit of looking up to her begun in childhood, seemed always to continue—When I was a little girl, she would frequently say to me, if opportunity offered, that Aunt Cassandra could teach everything much better than *she* could—Aunt Cass[a.] *knew* more—Aunt Cass[a.] could tell me better whatever I wanted to know—all which, I ever received in respectful silence—Perhaps she thought *my* mind wanted a turn in *that* direction, but I truly beleive she did always *really* think of her sister, as the superior to herself. The most perfect affection and confidence ever subsisted between them—and great and lasting was the sorrow of the survivor when the final separation was made—

My Aunt's life at Chawton, as far as *I* ever knew, was an easy and pleasant one—it had little variety in it, and I am not aware of any particular trials, till her own health began to fail—She stayed from home occasionally—almost entirely with the families of her different Brothers—In the Autumn of 1815 she was in London, with my Uncle, Mr. Henry Austen, then living in Hans Place—and a widower—

During her visit, he was seized with low fever and became so ill that his life was despaired of, and Aunt Cassandra and my Father were summoned to the house—*there*, for a day or two, they hourly expected his death—but a favourable turn came, and he began to recover—My Father then went home. Aunt Cass[a.] stayed on nearly a month, and Aunt Jane remained some weeks longer, to nurse the Convalescent—

It was during this stay in London, that a little gleam of Court favor shone upon her. She had at first published her Novels with a great desire of remaining *herself* unknown—but it was found impossible to preserve a secret that so many of the family knew and by this time, she had given up the attempt—and her name had been made public enough—tho' it was never inserted in the title page—

Two of the great Physicians° of the day had attended my Uncle during his illness—I am not, at this distance of time, sufficiently sure *which* they were, as to give their names, but *one* of them had very intimate access to the Prince Regent, and continuing his visits during my Uncle's recovery, he told my Aunt one day, that the Prince was a great admirer of her Novels: that he often read them, and had a set in each of his residences—That *he*, the physician had told his Royal Highness that Miss Austen was now in London, and that by the Prince's desire, Mr. Clarke, the Librarian of Carlton House, would speedily wait upon her—

Mr. Clarke came, and endorsed all previous compliments, and invited my Aunt to see Carlton House, saying the Prince had charged him to show her the Library there, adding many civilities as to the pleasure his R.H. had received from her Novels—Three had *then* been published—The invitation could not be declined—and my Aunt went, at an appointed time, to Carlton House—

She saw the Library, and I beleive some other apartments, but the particulars of her visit, if I ever heard them, I have now forgotten—only *this*, I *do* well recollect—that in the course of it, Mr. Clarke, speaking again of the Regent's admiration of her writing, declared himself charged to say, that if Miss Austen had any other Novel forthcoming, she was quite at liberty to dedicate it to the Prince.

My Aunt made all proper acknowledgments at the moment, but had no intention of accepting the honor offered—until she was avised [*sic*] by some of her friends that she must consider the permission as a command—

Emma was then in the Publisher's hands—so a few lines of dedication were affixed to the 1st volume, and following still the instructions of the well informed she sent a Copy, handsomely bound, to Carlton House—and I *suppose* it was duly acknowledged by Mr. Clarke—

My Aunt soon after her visit to *him*, returned home, where the little adventure was talked of for a while with some interest, and afforded some amusement°—In the following Spring, Mr. Henry Austen ceased to reside in London, and my Aunt was never brought so near the precints of the Court again—nor did she ever try to recall herself to the recollection of Physician, Librarian or Prince, and so ended this little burst of Royal Patronage.

I beleive Aunt Jane's health began to fail some time before we knew she was really ill—but she became avowedly less equal to exercise. In a letter to me she says:°

'I have taken one ride on the donkey and I like it very much, and you must try to get me quiet mild days that I may be able to go out pretty constantly—a great deal of wind does not suit me, as I have still a tendency to rhumatism. In short, I am but a poor Honey at present—I will be better when you can come and see us.'—

A donkey carriage had been set up for my Grandmother's accomodation—but I think *she* seldom used it, and Aunt Jane found it a help to herself in getting to Alton—where, for a time, Capt. Austen had a house, after removing from his Brother's place at Chawton.—

In my later visits to Chawton Cottage, I remember Aunt Jane used often to lie down after dinner—My Grandmother herself was frequently on the sofa—sometimes in the afternoon, sometimes in the evening, at no fixed period of the day,—She had not bad health for her age, and she worked often for hours in the garden, and naturally wanted rest afterwards—There was only one sofa in the room—and Aunt Jane laid upon 3 chairs which she arranged for herself—I think she had a pillow, but it never looked comfortable—She called it *her* sofa, and even when the *other* was unoccupied, *she* never took it—It seemed understood that she preferred the chairs—

I wondered and wondered—for the *real* sofa was frequently vacant, and *still* she laid in this comfortless manner—I often asked her how she *could* like the chairs best—and I suppose I worried her into telling me the reason of her choice—which was, that if *she* ever used the sofa, Grandmama would be leaving it for *her*, and would not lie down, as she did now, whenever she felt inclined—

In May, 1816 my two Aunts went for a few weeks to Cheltenham—I am able to ascertain the date of *this*, and some similar occurrences, by a reference to old pocket books in my possession°—It was a journey in those days, to go from Hampshire into Gloucestershire and their first stage was to Steventon—They stayed° one whole day, and left my Cousin Cassy to remain with us during their absence—

They made also a short stay at Mr. Fowle's at Kintbury°—I beleive *that* was, as they returned—Mrs. Dexter, then Mary Jane Fowle, told me afterwards, that Aunt Jane went over the old places, and recalled old recollections associated with them, in a very particular manner—looked at them, my cousin thought, as if she never expected to see them again—The Kintbury family, during that visit, received an impression that her health was failing—altho' they did *not* know of any particular malady.

The year 1817, the last of my Aunt's life, began it seems under good auspices.

I copy from a letter of her's to myself dated Jany. 23rd–1817°—the only letter I have which *does* bear the date of the year—

'I feel myself getting stronger than I was—and can so perfectly well walk *to* Alton, *or* back again, without the slightest fatigue that I hope to be able to do *both*, when summer comes—'

I do not know *when* the alarming symptoms of her malady came on—It was in the following March that *I* had the first idea of her being seriously ill—It had been settled that about the end of that month, or the beginning of April, I should spend a few days at Chawton, in the absence of my Father and Mother, who were just then engaged with Mrs. Leigh Perrot in arranging her late husband's affairs—it was shortly after Mr. Leigh Perrot's death°—but Aunt Jane became too ill to have me in the house, and so I went instead to my sister, Mrs. Lefroy, at Wyards—The next day we walked over to Chawton to make enquiries after our Aunt—She was keeping her room but said she would see us, and we went up to her—She was in her dressing gown and was sitting quite like an invalide in an arm chair—but she got up, and kindly greeted us—and then pointing to seats which had been arranged for us by the fire, she said, 'There's a chair for the married lady, and a little stool for *you*, Caroline.'—It is strange, but those trifling words are the last of her's that I can remember—for I retain *no* recollection *at* all of what was said by any one in the conversation that of course ensued—

I was struck by the alteration in herself—She was very pale—her voice was weak and low and there was about her, a general appearance of debility and suffering; but I have been told that she never *had* much actual pain—

She was not equal to the exertion of talking to us, and our visit to the sick room was a very short one—Aunt Cassandra soon taking us away—I do not suppose we stayed a quarter of an hour; and *I* never saw Aunt Jane again—

I think she must have been particularly ill *that* day, and that in some degree she afterwards rallied—*I* soon went home again—but I beleive Mrs. Lefroy saw her more than once afterwards before she went to Winchester—

It was sometime in the following May, that she removed thither—Better medical advice was needed, than Alton could supply—Not I beleive with much hope that any skill could effect a cure but from the natural desire of her family to place her in the best hands—Mr. Lyford was thought to be very clever so much so, as to be generally summoned far beyond his own practise—to give his opinion in cases of serious illness—

In the earlier stages of her malady, my Aunt had had the advice, in London, of one of the eminent physicians of the day°—

Aunt Cassandra, of course, accompanied her sister and they had lodgings in College Street—Their great friends Mrs. Heathcote and Miss Bigg, then living in The Close, had made all the arrangements for them, and did all they could to promote their comfort during that melancholy sojourn in Winchester.

Mr. Lyford could give no hope of recovery—He told my Mother that the duration of the illness must be very uncertain—it *might* be lingering or it might, with equal probability come to a sudden close—and that he feared the *last* period, whenever it arrived, would be one of severe suffering—but *this* was mercifully ordered otherwise—My mother, after a little time, had joined her sisters-in-law—to make it more cheerful for them, and also to

Caroline Austen as an old lady

take a share in the necessary attendance—From *her*, therefore, I learned, that my Aunt's resignation and composure of spirit were such, as those who knew her well, would have hoped for and expected—She was a humble and beleiving Christian; her life had passed in the cheerful performance of all home duties, and with *no* aiming at applause, she had sought, as if by instinct to promote the happiness of all those who came within her influence—doubtless she had her reward, in the peace of mind which was granted to her in her last days—

She was quite aware of her own danger—it was no delusive hope that kept up her spirits—and there was everything to attach her to life—Tho' she had passed by the hopes and enjoyments of youth, yet its sorrows also were left behind—and Autumn is sometimes so calm and fair that it consoles us for the departure of Spring and Summer—and *thus* it might have been with *her*—She was happy in her family and in her home; and no doubt the exercise of her great talent, was a happiness also in itself—and she was just learning to feel confidence in her own success—In no human mind was there less of vanity than in her's—yet she could not *but* be pleased and gratified as her works, by slow degrees made their way in the world, with constantly increasing favour—

She had *no* cause to be weary of life, and there was much to make it very pleasant to her—We may be sure she would fain have lived on—yet she was enabled, without complaint, and without dismay, to prepare for death—She had for some time known that it *might* be approaching her; and *now* she saw it with certainty, to be very near at hand.

The religious services most suitable to her state were ministered to her, during this, the last stage of her illness—sometimes by a Brother—Two of them were Clergymen and at Winchester she was within easy distance of both—

Her sweetness of temper never failed her; she was considerate and grateful to those who attended on her, and at times, when feeling rather better, her playfulness of spirit prevailed, and she amused them even in their sadness—A Brother frequently went over for a few hours, or a day or two—

Suddenly she became much worse—Mr. Lyford thought the

end was near at hand, and she beleived *herself* to be dying—and under this conviction she said all that she *wished* to say to those around her—

In taking then, as she thought, a last leave of my Mother, she thanked her for being there, and said, 'You have always been a kind sister to me, Mary.'—Contrary to every expectation, the immediate danger passed away; she became comfortable again, and seemed really better—

My Mother then came home—but not for long as she was shortly summoned back—This was from no increase of my Aunt's illness, but because the Nurse could not be trusted for *her* share of the night attendance, having been more than once found asleep—so to relieve her from that part of her charge, Aunt Cassandra and my Mother and my Aunt's maid took the nights between them.

Aunt Jane continued very cheerful and comfortable, and there began to be a *hope* of, at least, a *respite* from death—

But soon, and suddenly, as it were, a great change came on—*not* apparently, attended with much suffering—she sank rapidly—Mr. Lyford—when he saw her, could give no further hope, and she must have felt her own state—for when he asked her if there was anything she wanted, she replied, 'Nothing but death.' Those were her last words—

They watched by her through the night, and in quietness and peace she breathed her last on the morning of the 18th of July, 1817—

I need scarcely say she was dearly loved by her family—Her Brothers were very proud of her—Her literary fame, at the close of her life, was only just spreading—but they were proud of her talents, which *they* even then estimated highly—proud of her home virtues, of her cheerful spirit—of her pleasant looks—and *each* loved afterwards to *fancy* a resemblance, in some daughter of his own, to the dear 'Aunt Jane', whose perfect equal they *yet* never expected to see—

March 1867—Written out,
At Frog Firle—Sussex.

APPENDIX

I have not recorded erasures or page breaks, but I have retained irregularities of orthography and punctuation. Later or superscript insertions into the manuscripts are signalled by the following convention:^ ^.

1. *Copy of part of a letter from Anna Lefroy to JEAL (NPG, RWC/HH,° fo. 1).*

Southern Hill,
Reading.
April 16th [1869?]

. . . I believe that a music Master attended at Steventon, who also gave lessons at Ashe: but am not *certain*. Any way, nobody could think more humbly of Aunt Jane's music than she did herself; so much so as at one time to resolve on giving it up. The Pianoforte was parted with on the removal from Steventon, and during the whole time of her residence at Bath she had none. In course of time she felt the loss of the amusement, or for some other reason repented of her own decision; for, when settled at Chawton she bought a Pianoforte, and practised upon it diligently—This, as I understood at the time, she found necessary in order to recover that facility of fingering, which no doubt she had once possessed.

. . . Both our Aunts read French easily, and understood it well grammatically, and both had some knowledge of Italian. I can answer for a double set of Veneroni Grammars° &c. How much they taught themselves I cannot say, but in these matters I think it probable they had very valuable assistance from their cousin, Uncle Henry's first wife, who was an extremely accomplished woman, not only for that day, but for any day.

2. Copy of a letter from Anna Lefroy to JEAL (NPG, RWC/HH, fos. 2–3).

Southern Hill,
Reading.
May 20th [1869?]

My dear Edward

Lady Le Marchant° remembered your message & I will lose no time in sending the copy you wish for. The lines on Mrs. Lefroy's death you shall have ˆalsoˆ if, when you have read, you desire to have them—but perhaps you may think them too long. The original of Poll's letters is in the possession of Mrs. George Austen°—it was given to her at Portsdown. Cassandra Austen in a second letter to Fanny° says, 'At Aunt Cassandra's death there were several scraps marked by her (of her Sister's compositions) to be given to different relations, & amongst others some to Lady Knatchbull—' (of course Lady Susan is here referred to) '& some to my Uncle Frank—*one* at least I know, or think probably he must have had—but I suppose his Daughter might object to giving it up.' Perhaps Cassandra has 'Sanditon' in her head, because a copy of that taken by stealth during Aunt C's life was undoubtedly at Portsdown, where it had no business to be.

If it could be managed without much inconvenience I should extremely like to see such papers as you have received [Anna wrote rec[d]] from Cassandra—It was the recollection of *one* on her lists that encouraged me to think there must be a deposit in that quarter—for that one *must* be somewhere, & probably more with it—the Herbert Austens° are gone from home, & so I have not been able to give your message ˆof thanksˆ but by a hasty note from Herbert written just before he left it appears that no letters to Uncle Henry have been kept.

The occasional correspondence between the Sisters when apart from each other would as a matter of course be destroyed by the Survivor—I can fancy what the indignation of Aunt Cass[a]. would have been at the mere idea of its' [*sic*] being read and commented upon by any of us, nephews and nieces, little or great—and indeed I I [*sic*] think myself she was right, in that as in most other things . . .

3. *Copy of a letter from Caroline Austen to JEAL (NPG, RWC/HH, fos. 4–7).*

April 1st. [1869?]

My dear Edward

I have lost no time in getting ready all the helps I have to offer for our Aunt's 'Life'—I wish they were more. Memory is treacherous, but I cannot be mistaken in saying that Sense and Sensibility was *first* written in letters—& *so* read to her family. Northanger Abbey, under a different name I beleive, was the *first* actually prepared for publication & was sold for (I think 20£) to a publisher—who declared that he had lost the copy—refused to have the loss supplied, and was contented to remain minus his 20£. Afterwards the copyright was purchased back again and it was left, as you know ready for publication at the time of her death—I enclose a copy of Mr. Austen's letter to Cadell°—I do not know *which* novel he would have sent—The letter does not do much credit to the tact or courtesy of our good Grandfather for Cadell was a great man in his day, and it is not surprising that he should have refused the *favor* so offered from an *unknown*—but the circumstance may be worth noting, especially as we have so few incidents to produce. At a sale of Cadell's papers &c Tom Lefroy picked up the original letter—and Jemima copied it for me—

My Aunt was very sorry to leave her native home, as I have heard my Mother relate—My Aunts had been away a little while, and were met in the Hall ^on their return^ by their Mother who told them it was all settled, and they were going to live at Bath. My Mother who was present.[*sic*] said my Aunt Jane was greatly distressed—All things were done in a hurry by Mr. Austen & of course this is *not* a *fact* to be written and printed—but you have authority for saying she *did* mind it—if you think it worth while—

As to the 'stuffing' of the projected volume, I have already said that I expect *little* from letters—but some of her light nonsensical verses *might* take—such as 'In measured verse I now rehearse, The charms of lovely Anna', & perhaps some few rimes or charades—& I have thought that the story, I beleive in your possession, all nonsense, *might* be used. I don't mean Kitty's Bower, but the other—of the gentleman who wanders forth and is put in possession of a stranger's house, and married to his daughter Maria.° I have always thought it remarkable that the early workings of her mind should have been in burlesque, and comic exaggeration, setting at nought all rules of probable or possible—when of all her finished and later writings, the exact contrary is the characteristic. The story I mean is clever nonsense but one knows not how it might be taken by the public, tho' *some*thing must *ever* be risked. What I should deprecate is publishing any of the 'betweenities' when the nonsense was passing away, and before her wonderful talent had found it's proper channel. Lady Knatchbull has a whole short story they were wishing years ago to make public—but were discouraged by others—& I hope the desire has passed away.

I think I need not warn *you* against raking up that old story of the still living 'Chief Justice'°—That there was *something* in it, is true—but nothing out of the common way—(as *I* beleive.) Nothing to call ill usage, & no very serious sorrow endured. The *York* Lefroys got up a very strong version of it all, & spread their own notions in the family—but they were for years very angry with their Kinsman, & rather delighted in a proof as *they* thought, of his early heartlessness. I have *my* story from my Mother, who was near at the time—It was a disappointment, but Mrs. Lefroy sent the gentleman off at the end of a *very* few weeks, that no more mischief might be done. If *his* love had continued a few more years, he *might* have sought her out again—as he was *then* making enough to marry on—but who can wonder that he did *not*? He was settled in Ireland, and he married an Irish lady—who certainly *had* the convenience of *money*—there was *no* engagement, & never *had* been.

I am very glad dear Edward that you have applied your-self to the settlement of this vexed question between the Austens and the Public. I am sure you will do justice to what there *is*—but I feel it must be a difficult task to dig up the *materials*, so carefully have they been buried out of our sight by the past generat[ion] As this is a letter of business. I will add nothing else.

Ever yr. aff. Sister
Car Austen.

4. *Copy of a letter from Caroline Austen to JEAL (NPG, RWC/HH, fos. 8–10).*

Wednesday Evg. [1869?]

My dear Edward

I have looked out the pocket book of 1817.° There are these entries—[‘] July 17th Jane Austen was taken for death, about ½ past 5 in the evening.

18th. Jane breathed her last at ½ past 4 in the morning—only Cassandra and I were with her. Henry came’—

The next day I see you and my Father came to Winchester, and *he* stayed there 2 nights.

On the 23d. Mr. Knight & Captn. Austen came late at night. On the 24th. ‘Edward came early in the morning. Jane was buried in Winchester Cathedral. We all returned home.’ On the 25th. you and my Father went to Chawton for one night. The *attendants* at the Funeral, you see, are not named—but I am *sure* they were only the Brothers, and that *you* went in your Father's place—he himself & others, feeling that in the sad state of his *own* health and nerves, the trial would be too much for him. *He* therefore stayed at home. Capt. Charles Austen is not named amongst those who came to Winchester & I make sure he must *then* have been at sea—or he would certainly have been amongst the mourners.

I am very glad you are getting on so fast with your task for this proves I hope, that you find it no *very great* trouble—

My own wish would be, that not any allusion should be made to the Manydown story°—or at *least* that the reference should be so vague, as to give *no* clue to the place or the person. Mr. Wither's children are still living & in the neighbourhood—probably they never yet heard the tale—but some of then [*sic*] are readers, & they would be sure to fall in with the Memoir. A few people remain thereabouts who know the tradition—The Knights certainly, and perhaps the Portals; it lies very harmless *now*, as good as dead, but the enquiry of *who* the gentleman might have been would probably bring it to life again, & so the story would go the round of the neighbourhood. Now I should not like the Withers to think that the Austen's had been so proud of her suitor, as to have handed down his name to all succeeding generations—I should not mind *telling* any body, at this distance of time—but printing and publishing seem to me very different from *talking* about the past—

During the few years my Grandfather lived at Bath, he went in the summer with his wife and daughters to *some* sea-side. They were in Devonshire, & in Wales—& in Devonshire an acquaintance was made with some very charming man—I never heard Aunt Cass. speak of anyone else with such admiration—she had no doubt that a mutual attachment was in progress between him and her sister. They parted—but he made it plain that he should seek them out again—& shortly afterwards he died!—My Aunt told me this in the late years of her own life—& it was quite new to me then—but all this, being nameless and dateless, cannot I know serve any purpose of your's—and it brings no contradiction to your theory that she ^Aunt Jane^ never *had* any attachment that overclouded her happiness, for long. *This* had not gone far enough, to leave misery behind.

Mr. Wither's *offer* was made after the family had left Steventon—tho' I suppose his *love* had grown in previous years of intimacy. My Aunts were on a visit to Steventon at the time. Aunt Jane I suppose was then about seven & twenty—If the circumstance *is* alluded to could you not make the matter less traceable by intimating that they had *then* left the neighbourhood?

5. *Letters to Anna Lefroy, 1819–69 and undated (HRO, MS 23M93°/84/1). From a letter of 8 July 1869 from JEAL then on a research trip to Steventon, in preparation for the* Memoir.

July 8
1869

Dear Anna

I accomplished my visit to Steventon, where I was kindly received, & found much to interest me. There is certainly no entry of the burial of young Hastings° either at Deane or Steventon; & the beautiful accuracy with which our Grandfather kept his register prevents the possibility of his having *omitted* to make an entry of such interest to him. I can only suppose that the child died else where (possibly having been sent some where for his health) or that by the desire of his family he was buried else-where.

The chief discovery that I made is that we were all mistaken in supposing that our Grandfather was not Rector of Steventon, as well as of Deane, from 1764, the year of his marriage. The Steventon Register *proves conclusively* that he was. He signs himself '*Geo: Austen, Rector*,' at the bottom of every page from 1764 to 1800. The entries for 1801 and 1802 are signed by '*James Austen Curate*.' After that date the entries are made in my father's hand, but no farther signature occurs.

All traces of former things are even more obliterated than I had expected. Even the terrace has been levelled, & its site is to be distinguished only by the finer turf on that place.

They have discovered & opened an old well, which must have been in our Grandfathers old garden, between the house & the terrace. Did you know of any such? One Lime planted by our father° near that part has become a magnificent tree. *The* Lime on the top of the other Hill looks healthy, but from its position must always be a one sided affair. Several of the trees in the East plantation are become good timber. The view from the parsonage windows is as pretty as good falls of ground & abundance of trees can make it; all that is seen is grass. W Knight° is very careful of the trees, though time gradually thins them. The great Elm close to his house is gone. Part of it nearly fell on the building, & it was necessary to remove the rest for fear of worse mischief. He has an abundance of well kept walks through hedgerows, all about his fields.

6. *Letters to James Edward Austen-Leigh (HRO, MS 23M93/86/3). Caroline Austen to JEAL, undated apart from 'Saturday', but annotated in a different hand at the end 'July 1871' (23M93/86/3b item 73°).*

Saturday

My dear Edward

I received yesterday from Anna, y^r^. despatch to *her*, & I dare say you wish to have the copies returned of L^d^. Stanhope's letter, & *your's* to him—I am rather sorry that L^d^. S. should be raising a hue & cry after those 'lines, replete with vigour & fancy'—to which unluckily Uncle Henry alluded more than half a Century ago°—Nobody felt any curiosity about them *then*—but see what it is to have a growing posthumous reputation! we cannot keep any thing to ourselves *now*, it seems.—I quite approve of y^r^. letter to Lord S.—I suppose it will bring a rejoinder—Tho' there are no reasons *ethical* or orthodox against the publication of these stanzas, there are reasons of taste—I never thought there was much point in them—they were good enough for a passing thought, but if she had lived she would probably soon have torn them up—however there is a much stronger objection to their being inserted in any memoir, than a want of literary merit—If put in at *all* they must have been introduced as the latest working of her mind—*They* are dated July 15th—her death followed on the 18th ['8' written over '7']—*Till* a few hours before she died, she had been feeling much better, & there was hope of amendment at least, if not of recovery—she amused herself by following a harmless fancy suggested by what was passing near her—but the joke about the dead Saint, & Winchester races, all jumbled up together, would read badly as amongst the few details given, of the closing scene—If I were to meet with it in any other biography, it would jar at once on my feelings, & I should think the insertion *then* & there of such light words, a sad incongruity—& so I doubt not would L^{d}. Stanhope if he *had* found them in the volume—I am pleased that Lady Susan should have his valuable approbation—& perhaps the more pleased because I have never felt quite sure how it would be taken by the public—I feared it might be thought too much of a monotone—but there must certainly be an interest in its complete contrast to those tales by which she became famous—I think the admission of these letters, with the slow travelling to London & her stay at her Brother's house, a very great gain°—as they give for a short period, *that* which is so much wanted—her proceedings—narrated by herself—I am glad that Charlotte Craven° gets her little meed of praise—I think that all persons who can be naturally named, contribute towards making a book of general interest—that is, after the lapse of 50 years—& if there is nothing stated to their disadvantage—

I suppose I may take the liberty of copying your letter that to M^{r}. Bentley from Lord Stanhope

7. *Copy of part of a letter from Catherine Hubback° to JEAL (NPG, RWC/HH, fos. 11–12).*

March 1st. 1870.

My dear Edward

. . . I gathered from the letters that it was in a momentary fit of self-delusion that she ˆAunt Janeˆ accepted Mr. Withers proposal,° and that when it was all settled eventually, and the negative decisively given she was much relieved—I think the affair vexed her a good deal—but I am sure she had no attachment to him. If ever she *was* in love, it was with Dr. Blackall° (I think that was the name) whom they met at some watering place, shortly before they settled at Chawton—There is no doubt she admired him extremely, and perhaps regretted parting, but she always said her books were her children, and supplied her sufficient interest for happiness; and some of her letters, triumphing over the married women of her acquaintance, & rejoicing in her own freedom from care were most amusing.

March 14th. 1870.

. . . I do not think Dr. Blackall died until long afterwards. If I do not mistake there were two brothers, one of whom was called Mr. Edwd. B—& I never heard what became of him—The other, the Dr.—Aunt Cassandra met with again long afterwards when she made an excursion to the Wye in company with Uncle Charles, two of his daughters & my sister Cassandra—My cousin Cassie Austen the only survivor of that party could I have no doubt tell where and how they met him—I only remember that my Aunt found him stout, red-faced and middle-aged—very different from their youthful hero—It must have been in '32'—or thereabouts, and I believe he died soon afterwards . . .

8. *Copy of a letter, undated, from Caroline Austen to JEAL, written after the publication of the first edition of the* Memoir *on 16 December 1869 (NPG, RWC/HH, fos. 16–17).*

My dear Edward

I should have sent you my thanks for your kind present by *that* day's post—only I waited till I should have read the book, & *so* be able to assure you, as I now *can*, that I am very much pleased with it & I congratulate you on having succeeded so well in arranging your scanty and miscellaneous materials, and connecting them from your *own* resources, so as to form an interesting narrative—*Such*, I hope and expect it will prove to general readers, who I think will only *wish* that it could have been longer. I have not read steadily as yet, quite to the end, but I see you have been very merciful to Mr. Clarke° in omitting the most ridiculous parts of his letter—

The portrait° is better than I expected—as considering its early date, and that it has lately passed through the hands of painter and engraver—I did not reckon upon finding *any* likeness—but there is a *look* which I recognise as *hers*—and though the general resemblance is *not* strong, yet as it represents a pleasant countenance it is *so* far a truth—& I am not dissatisfied with it.

I remain, my dear Edward, your very affecte. sister,

Car. Austen.

9. *Copy of a letter from Caroline Austen to JEAL, written, from its inclusion of the extract from F. W. Fowle's letter, after the publication of the first edition of the* Memoir, *perhaps when JEAL was collecting materials for the second edition (NPG, RWC/HH, fos. 18–19).*

My Aunt Miss Jane Austen had nearly left off singing, by the time I can recollect much about her performances—but *some* songs of hers I do remember—One was—
Her groves of green myrtle,° let foreign lands reckon,
Where bright beaming summer exalts their [. . .]
Far dearer to me are the Braes of [. . .]
With the wind stealing over the long yellow broom

——

My memory fails at the last word of the 3d. line—and one or two in the 4th. are a guess. The Song, as she sang it, was in M.S. I never saw it in print—
Another, already mentioned, was entitled Oh! no my Love no! or The Wife's [Farewell] I beleive from the Farce of Age to-morrow[.] I had a printed copy of this once, myself ages ago—
But the song that I heard her sing oftenest, was a little French ditty in her M.S. book[.] The 2 first lines were
[']Que j'aime à voir les Hirondelles
Volent ma fenêtre tous les jours'—
As a child, this was my favourite—& was what I asked for the oftenest. As M. Jacot is interested in my Aunt's musical powers, he may like to read an extract from a letter written by our cousin, tho' not *her* nephew, in answer to some enquiries of mine last year, as to his reminiscences of one whom he had known very well, after he was himself grown up—the Rev. F. W. Fowle° of Amesbury, Wilts—
[There follows an extract from Fowle's letter copied from the longer extract preserved in Caroline's hand in the Austen-Leigh archive, HRO, MS 23M93/66/2, for which see below.]

10. *Letters to Caroline Austen, 1815–75 (HRO, MS 23M93/66/2). A copy in Caroline's hand of an extract from a letter sent by the Revd F. W. Fowle, dated Jan. 9 1870, acknowledging receipt of the* Memoir. *It reads:*

Extract from a letter received from the Rev^{d}. F. W. Fowle of Amesbury acknowledging a Copy of The Memoir of Jane Austen

'I have read it with the greatest interest—nothing has so vividly brought back to me the vision of my early days & of all the dear friends whom in the interim I have lost—I was better acquainted with Steventon Parsonage & its talented inmates, or those who had been it's inmates, until the turmoil of life had scattered them, than probably you think for'

Then follow his recollections of each individual of the family till he comes down to the subject of The Memoir—& he thus continues. 'Your "dear Aunt Jane" I can testify to as being the attractive animated delightful person her biographer has represented her. I well remember her singing—& "The yellow haired Laddie" made an impression ^up^on me, which more than half a century has had no power to efface—Boscho / or some such name / (Bochsa?) a celebrated Italian harpist whom I heard at Salisbury once introduced in a ^beautiful^ medley of English & Scotch tunes, *that* touching air—& Jane Austen, whom I had come to know at last as a distinguished Authoress, rose up before me!—The last time I ever saw her, was at Steventon when she was on a visit to your Mother—I think Mrs Craven was there—She was a very sweet reader—She had finished the 1st Canto of Marmion,° & I was reading the 2nd—when Mr W. Digweed was announced. It was like the interruption of some pleasing dream the illusions of which suddenly vanish—Strange to say it was the last moment of my knowing any thing of "Jane Austen" excepting from recollections'—

Dated. Amesbury Jan^{y}—9th 1870

11. *Copy of part of a letter from G. D. Boyle, Vicar of Kidderminster, to JEAL (NPG, RWC/HH, fos. 26–9°).*

Summerhill,
Kidderminster.
Oct. 7. 1869
finished Oct. 16

Dear Sir

. . . I saw in the literary announcements of the autumn that you were engaged on a life of the incomparable novelist, Jane Austen; and I am tempted to tell you what I sincerely wish was better worth your attention.

I was on intimate terms with a lady who died a few years ago, Mrs. Barrett, whose maiden name was Turner or Edwards. It seems odd that I should have a difficulty about her name, but the fact is that her mother was twice married, and her daughters (by two husbands) had all been married before they were known to my wife or her family. Mrs. Barrett was no ordinary woman. She had read widely and wisely, and preserved that most rare of gifts, the power of entering fully into the tastes, ^and especially the intellectual tastes,^ of a younger generation than her own. She had enjoyed the friendship of some remarkable people; but I think I was more interested in hearing her recollections of the author of 'Persuasion' than in any other of the reminiscences she recalled. Most unfortunately for the purposes of your biography she had lost, through the carelessness of a friend, a series of letters from Miss Austen of great interest. I often entreated her to write down her recollections, but although she possessed in no ordinary degree the power of writing interesting and remarkable letters, the recollections of a time of happiness long past by were, she said, too overpowering.

There are, however, two or three matters I remember of interest. The artistic method of Miss Austen's character painting has been a subject of constant remark since the time when Lord Macaulay's epoz on Madame D'Arblay appeared in the Edinburgh Review. Her friend remembers well that, on one occasion, soon after the inimitable Mr. Collins had made his appearance in literature, an old friend attacked her on the score of having pourtrayed an individual; in recurring to the subject afterwards she expressed a very great dread of what she called 'such an invasion of social proprieties.' She said she thought it fair to note peculiarities, weaknesses, and even special phrases, but it was her desire to create not to reproduce, and at the same time said 'I am much too proud of my own gentlemen ever to admit that they are merely Mr. A or Major C.'

Mrs. Barrett declared that to a perfect modesty of character she united a real judgement of her own powers, and that on the appearance of a good review (I almost think it was one by Archbishop Whately in the Quarterly, at one time printed among Sir W. Scott's miscellanies) she said, 'Well! that *is* pleasant! Those are the very characters I took most pains with, and the writer has found me out.'

To a question 'which of your characters do you like best'? she once answered, 'Edmund Bertram and Mr. Knightley; but they are very far from being what I know English gentlemen often are.'

The change of ideas as to clerical duty may be discovered in a fact mentioned by the same lady, that Miss Austen was once attacked by an Irish dignitary, who preferred a residence at Bath to his own proper sphere, 'for being over particular about Clergymen residing on their cures.' This was, of course, in allusion to the conversation of Bertram & Crawford in Mansfield Park. There is one fragment more which I would willingly linger on and expand,—the tribute of my old friend to the real and true spring of a religion which was always present though never obtruded. Miss Austen, she used to say, had on all the subjects of enduring religious feeling the deepest and strongest convictions, but a contact with loud and noisy exponents of the then popular religious phase made her reticent almost to a fault. She had to suffer something in the way of reproach from those who believed she might have used her genius to greater effect; but her old friend used to say, 'I think I see her now defending what she thought was the real province of a delineator of life and manners, and declaring her belief that example and not "direct preaching" was all that a novelist could afford properly to exhibit.'—Mrs. Barrett used to add, 'Anne Elliott was herself; her enthusiasm for the navy, and her perfect unselfishness reflect her completely.'

I wish I had more to write. I often approached the subject, but 4 years have passed away since Mrs. Barrett died.

. . . . Very truly yours
G. D. Boyle
(Vicar of Kidderminster.)

12. *Extract from 'Family History by Fanny C. Lefroy' (HRO, MS 23M93/85/2°).*

In a note to my Father [Ben Lefroy] announcing her death Sir Francis Austen writes. 'I do not know if you have heard how very unfavourable the accounts which were brought from Winchester yesterday by my brother were. If not you and Anna will be the more shocked to hear that all is over. My dear sister was seized at five yesterday evening with extreme faintness and on Mr. Lyfords arriving soon after he pronounced her to be dying. She breathed her last at half past four this morning and went off without a struggle. My mother bears the shock as well as can be expected, and we have the satisfaction of hearing that Mrs. J. Austen and Cassandra are well.'

None of her nieces mourned her more deeply than did our mother. I might go further, and say not any one of them so much. She wrote immediately to her Grandmother offering to go to her. I copy the reply.

'I thank you sincerely for all your kind expressions and your offer. I am certainly in a good deal of affliction, but trust God will support me. I was not prepared for the blow for though it in a manner hung over us, I had reason to think it at a distance, and was not quite without hope that she might in part recover. After a four months illness she may be said to have died suddenly. Mr. Lyford supposed a large blood vessel had given way. I hope her sufferings were not severe—they were not long. I had a letter from Cassandra this morning. She is in great affliction but bears it like a Christian. Dear Jane is to be buried in the Cathedral, I believe on Thursday. In which case Cassandra will come home as soon as it is over. Miss Lloyd does not go.—Your father, M[r] Knight who is now here, your Uncle Henry (who is now at Winchester giving the necessary directions) and your Uncle Frank will attend. How fortunate for Cassandra that your mama was with her. She says she is all kindness and affection.'

Our Great Grandmother was 77 when she lost this beloved daughter. To her the separation could not be long, but Aunt Cassandra's loss in her sister was great indeed and most truly a loss never to be repaired. They were everything to each other. They seemed to lead a life to themselves, within the general family life, which was shared only by each other. I will not say their true but their full feelings and opinions were known only to themselves. They alone fully understood what each had suffered and felt and thought. Yet they had such a gift of reticence that the secrets of their respective friends were never betrayed to each other. They were thoroughly trustworthy and the young niece who brought her troubles to Aunt Jane for advice and sympathy knew she could depend absolutely on her silence even to her sister. A strict fidelity which is I think somewhat rare between any two so closely united.

EXPLANATORY NOTES

ABBREVIATIONS

JA	Jane Austen
JEAL	James Edward Austen-Leigh, her nephew
HRO, MS 23M93	Hampshire Record Office, Winchester, the Austen-Leigh Papers
NPG, RWC/HH	National Portrait Gallery, London, a file of correspondence between R. W. Chapman and Henry Hake, 1932–48
Memoir Ed.1	James Edward Austen-Leigh, *A Memoir of Jane Austen, by her nephew* (1870)
Memoir Ed.2	James Edward Austen-Leigh, *A Memoir of Jane Austen, by her nephew, to which is added Lady Susan and fragments of two other unfinished tales by Miss Austen* (2nd edn., 1871)
Memoir (1926)	James Edward Austen-Leigh, *Memoir of Jane Austen, by her nephew*, ed. R. W. Chapman (1926)
Austen Papers	*Austen Papers 1704–1856*, ed. R. A. Austen-Leigh (1942)
Fam. Rec.	William Austen-Leigh and Richard Arthur Austen-Leigh, *Jane Austen: A Family Record*, revised and enlarged by Deirdre Le Faye (1989)
Gilson	David Gilson, *A Bibliography of Jane Austen* (1982, revised 1997)
Letters	*Jane Austen's Letters*, ed. Deirdre Le Faye (3rd edn., 1995)
Life & Letters	William Austen-Leigh and Richard Arthur Austen-Leigh, *Jane Austen, Her Life and Letters, A Family Record* (1913)
MAJA	Caroline Austen, *My Aunt Jane Austen: A Memoir* (written 1867; first published 1952; included here in a revised edition from the manuscript)
Minor Works	*Minor Works, The Works of Jane Austen*, vol. 6, ed. R. W. Chapman (1954; revised B. C. Southam, 1969)
RAJ	Anna Lefroy, 'Recollections of Aunt Jane' (written 1864; first published 1988; included here in a revised edition from the manuscript, HRO, MS 23M93/97/4/104)
Reminiscences	*Reminiscences of Caroline Austen*, ed. Deirdre Le Faye (written 1870s; first published 1986)
Sailor Brothers	J. H. and Edith C. Hubback, *Jane Austen's Sailor Brothers: Being the Adventures of Sir Francis Austen, G.C.B., Admiral of the Fleet, and Rear-Admiral Charles Austen* (1906)

Tucker	George Holbert Tucker, *A History of Jane Austen's Family* (1983; revised 1998)
S&S	*Sense and Sensibility* (1811)
P&P	*Pride and Prejudice* (1813)
MP	*Mansfield Park* (1814)
E	*Emma* (1816)
NA	*Northanger Abbey* (1818)
P	*Persuasion* (1818)

References to the *Jane Austen Society Reports* are to articles as they are paginated in the collected volumes, where these exist: 1949–65; 1966–75; 1976–85; and 1986–95.

J. E. AUSTEN-LEIGH, *A Memoir of Jane Austen*

The text of the *Memoir* printed here follows the second, expanded edition of 1871, with minor misprints and errors corrected. I have, however, made certain changes. I have omitted the bulk of the manuscript writings which JEAL appended to this enlarged edition—the cancelled chapter of *Persuasion*, *Lady Susan*, and the unfinished novels *The Watsons* and *Sanditon* (the last mainly paraphrased by JEAL); and I have restored some features of the first edition text of 1870—namely, the set of five illustrations and the second postscript, dated 17 November 1869. In this, I follow the example of R. W. Chapman who edited the 1871 *Memoir* for the Clarendon Press in 1926. Chapman retained the cancelled chapter of *Persuasion* but omitted the other manuscript writings. He also restored the illustrations and second postscript and supplied running titles for each of the chapters, drawn from JEAL's own chapter head notes. I have adopted these, together with the frontispiece portrait of JEAL added to the 1926 edition. In other respects this is a reprint of the 1871 *Memoir*, collated against the 1870 edition for misprints and to record the substantial changes made between the two editions. The most important of these textual changes and expansions are signalled and described in the notes which follow. It is worth mentioning that neither JEAL nor his assistants in the *Memoir* were overly concerned to reproduce accurately the documents which they transcribed or quoted. Among the Austen family, there was much passing around of copies and much making of further copies of JA's letters and unpublished writings, and I alert the reader in the notes which follow to the more significant differences between JEAL's texts and the earlier, often autograph, copies published more recently. Such changes are particularly marked in his treatment of JA's letters, where not only was JEAL not concerned to follow scrupulously the original text (or perhaps he was not supplied with a wholly accurate copy), but he had a tendency to correct or improve grammar and sentence structure. In addition, as a near family member, he was sensitive to the substance of his material, and occasionally he omits or alters details which might still, in 1871, have caused offence to the living or cast JA or others in an unfavourable light. Wherever possible, I refer the reader to *Jane Austen's Letters*, ed. Deirdre Le Faye (3rd edn., 1995) for the most accurate text.

The following emendations have been made to the text:

p. 29, l. 34: if we look] if we could look [1870]
p. 52, l. 8: the chiffonniere, is] the chiffonniere, which is
p. 75, l. 8: on strict survey] on strict survey, [1870]
p. 82, l. 22: till,] till
p. 91, l. 15: worth] worthy [1870]
p. 112, l. 3: dear style] clear style
p. 123, l. 33: Ah, ah!] Ah, ha! [1870]

3 *called 'Lady Susan'*: the cancelled chapter of *P* etc. are not included in this edition.

8 *epigraph*: Sir Arthur Helps, *The Life of Columbus, the Discoverer of America* (1869), 9–10, slightly misquoted, from a description of Prince Henry of Portugal, the promoter of the discovery of America.

9 *the Dashwoods . . . and Musgroves*: families who appear in the six completed novels on which JA's nineteenth-century reputation rested. JEAL lists them in the order of the novels' first publication: the Dashwoods in *S&S* (1811); the Bennets in *P&P* (1813); the Bertrams in *MP* (1814); the Woodhouses in *E* (1816); the Thorpes in *NA*; and the Musgroves in *P* (published posthumously with *NA* in 1818).

10 *Hasted, in his History of Kent*: Edward Hasted, *The History and Topographical Survey of the County of Kent*, 2 (1782), 387–88; 3 (1790), 48.

11 *Mr. George Austen*: JA's father, the Revd George Austen (1731–1805), son of William Austen (1701–37) and ward of William's long-lived elder brother Francis (1698–1791). George Austen entered St John's College, Oxford, in 1747 at the age of 16, held a fellowship there from 1751 to 1760, and was ordained a clergyman in the Church of England in 1754. Of his two surviving sisters, the elder Philadelphia (1730–92) played a significant role in the Austen family during JA's early life, while Uncle Francis's second wife was one of her godmothers. JEAL's information about George Austen's clerical livings is not quite accurate. He became rector of Steventon, Hampshire, in 1761 but of the neighbouring parish of Deane only in 1773. To confuse matters, however, the newly-wed George and Cassandra Austen moved into the more comfortable parsonage at Deane in 1764 and only transferred to Steventon after some improvements, probably in 1768. This is clearly the source of JEAL's mistake, for he seems naturally enough to have assumed that his grandfather was rector of Deane when he lived there in 1764. On a trip to Steventon to collect materials for his *Memoir*, he writes to his half-sister Anna: 'The chief discovery that I made is that we were all mistaken in supposing that our Grandfather was not Rector of Steventon, as well as of Deane, from 1764, the year of his marriage. The Steventon Register *proves conclusively*

that he was. He signs himself "*Geo: Austen, Rector*", at the bottom of every page from 1764 to 1800' (HRO, MS 23M93/84/1, letter to Anna Lefroy, 8 July 1869). Himself a clergyman, JEAL is understandably anxious to acquit his grandfather of the contentious charge of pluralism (that is, of holding several livings at once). Though the practice might be justified, as implied here, by the poor financial returns of a single living and the closeness and smallness of the two parishes, pluralism often led to the neglect of responsibilities when a clergyman did not live in his parish. George Austen seems to have taken the matter sufficiently seriously to seek approval from the Archbishop of Canterbury in 1773 (*Fam. Rec.*, 6, 11, 23; Tucker, 29–31).

Cassandra: Cassandra Leigh (1739–1827), JA's mother. For the Leigh family, their Oxford connections, and their colourful but distant aristocratic pretensions, see Tucker, 53–65.

12 *'monuments ... memorials need'*: George Crabbe, *The Borough* (1810), Letter 2, 'The Church', l. 110.

Mrs. Thrale ... 'divided the Board': Theophilus Leigh (1693–1785), JA's great-uncle, was Master of Balliol College, Oxford, from 1726 to 1785. He is described by Hester Lynch Salusbury, Mrs Thrale, later Mrs Piozzi (1741–1821), diarist, memoirist, and travel writer, in her *Letters to and from the Late Samuel Johnson LL.D* (2 vols., 1788), ii. 245; here slightly misquoted by JEAL.

Pope ... 'study of mankind is Man': Alexander Pope, *An Essay on Man* (1733), Epistle 2, l. 2.

'the ruling passion ... death': Pope, Epistle 1, *To Cobham* (1734), l. 263 ('Shall feel your ruling passion strong in death').

13 *in 1771 to Steventon*: in 1768, see note to p. 11 above.

the celebrated Warren Hastings: plenty of speculation hangs around the relationship between Warren Hastings (1732–1818), the future Governor-General of Bengal (1773–85), and the Austen family. Taking his cue from the other main source of family authorized biography, *Life & Letters*, R. W. Chapman finds it 'very doubtful' that Hastings would have committed his son, only 3 years old when sent to England in 1761, to the charge of George Austen, a young bachelor. He therefore concurs with the later generation of Austen-Leighs in assuming a confusion with Hastings de Feuillide, another sickly and short-lived child, the son of George Austen's niece Eliza, 'who undoubtedly did stay at Steventon and did die young' (*Memoir* (1926), 215). But earlier family memory has it that Hastings's small son (also named George) died in the Austens' care in autumn 1764 and that Mrs Austen was deeply upset by his death. JEAL was clearly hoping to find confirmation on his 1869 visit to Steventon, but was disappointed, writing to Anna Lefroy: 'There is certainly no entry of the burial of young Hastings either at Deane or Steventon; & the beautiful accuracy with which our Grandfather kept his register prevents the possibility of his having *omitted* to make an entry of such interest to him. I can only suppose that the child died elsewhere (possibly having been sent somewhere for his health) or that by the desire of his family he was buried elsewhere' (HRO, MS 23M93/84/1). George Austen's elder sister Philadelphia had gone out to India in 1752 in search of a husband and there married Tysoe Saul Hancock, a surgeon and associate of Hastings. Hastings became a close family friend of the Hancocks and stood godfather to their daughter Elizabeth, for whom he subsequently made generous financial provision. It would be a natural reciprocal gesture for Philadelphia to recommend little George Hastings to her brother's charge in England. Further speculations by Austen scholars, that Warren Hastings may have known Mrs Cassandra Austen through a childhood link with her cousins, the Adlestrop Leighs, or the conjecture of a boyhood association between George Austen and Hastings, remain just that, speculation, with no substantial proof (see *Fam. Rec.*, 15; and Maggie Lane, *Jane Austen's Family through Five Generations* (1984), 39). However, the record becomes more tangled, with suggestions that Mrs Hancock's daughter Eliza, George Austen's niece, was her love-child by Hastings and not by her husband. Tucker (39–41) treats the family scandal (if such it was) cautiously, while David Nokes (*Jane Austen: A Life* (1997), 31–3, 48–50) is far more sensationalist and, though without proof, unequivocal. Certainly Hastings's interest in the welfare of the Hancock women, mother and daughter, remained strong, and his association with the Austens survived little George Hastings's death. But Deirdre Le Faye, whose biography of Eliza is forthcoming, has found no evidence at all to confirm Hastings's paternity or the scandal. JA's brother Henry, who became cousin Eliza's second husband in 1797, wrote to congratulate Hastings on his acquittal for impeachment in 1795 and maintained an occasional and obsequious correspondence with him thereafter. Hastings also used his influence with the Admiralty in Frank Austen's favour in 1794. (*Austen Papers*, 153–4, 176–8, 226–7; Keith Feiling, *Warren Hastings* (1966), 39–40; Robin Vick, 'The Hancocks', *Jane Austen Society Report* (1999), 19–23. JEAL refers to G. R. Gleig, *Memoirs of the Life of Warren Hastings* (1841).)

Mary Russell Mitford: (1787–1855), letter-writer, poet, dramatist, but best known for her popular sketches of village life, collected in *Our Village* (5 vols., 1824–32). Her grandfather, the Revd Dr Richard Russell, was rector of Ashe until 1783, at which time the Revd George Lefroy and his wife Anne, who was to become JA's great friend, took up residence there. At several points in the *Memoir* JEAL makes comparisons between JA and Mary Mitford, as near contemporaries and observers of Hampshire village society. The likely connections between their two families provided the source for an obviously malicious (but not necessarily false) representation of JA in *The Life of Mary Russell Mitford*, ed. A. G. L'Estrange (3 vols., 1870), to which JEAL alludes in Ed.1 of the *Memoir*, though he suppresses the reference in Ed.2 and later editions. See p. 133 below.

14 *in 1771 . . . not then in strong health*: the move to Steventon took place in 1768 (see note to p. 11 above.) Most likely Mrs Austen was again pregnant. If so, the baby miscarried. The Austens first three children, all sons, were born in three successive years, 1765–7; so a further pregnancy in 1768 is not unlikely. On the other hand, 1771, though not the year the family moved to Steventon, did see the birth of their fourth child, Henry. JEAL could be confusing and compressing these events.

Ignorance and coarseness . . . '. . . telling the story': in *Fam. Rec.*, 14, the ignorant squire is named as John Harwood (1719–87) of Deane House, and is further described as the reputed original of Squire Western in Fielding's novel *Tom Jones* (1749). But the real point of this and other similar family anecdotes is to stress the intellectual superiority of the Austens over their immediate neighbours, though their social standing was more uncertain.

15 *'the toe of the peasant . . . courtier'*: Shakespeare, *Hamlet*, v. i. 136–7.

'the handsome Proctor': George Austen was 'Junior Proctor for the academic year 1759–60' (*Fam. Rec.*, 4). Proctors are annual appointments from the academic community at Oxford and Cambridge, chosen to enforce university regulations.

16 *a periodical paper called 'The Loiterer'*: a humorous weekly paper jointly founded and largely written by James and Henry Austen, with help from undergraduate friends. Like their father, both James and Henry were students at St John's College, Oxford, though their association with the college was as 'Founder's kin', through their mother Cassandra Leigh Austen. The paper ran for sixty issues, from 31 January 1789 to 20 March 1790, when James left Oxford, and was issued commercially, though its circulation was small, through booksellers in Oxford, Birmingham, Bath, Reading, and London. Its model was Joseph Addison and Richard Steele's *Spectator*, whose first series ran daily from March 1711 to December 1712. But later examples of its enduring format—a continuing, partly simulated and partly genuine interaction between readers and writers, a kind of conversation in print—can be found in the two popular periodicals conducted by Henry Mackenzie, *The Mirror* (1779–80) and *The Lounger* (1785–7). A more immediate precedent, and one nearer to home, was the forty-eight numbers of the *Olla Podrida*, edited by Thomas Monro of Magdalen College, Oxford, and published in book form in 1788. The *Olla Podrida* is mentioned in issue 9 of *The Loiterer* as among 'the entertaining papers of our most celebrated periodical writers'; and it is among several college and schoolboy journals appearing in the late 1780s and early 1790s. It has been suggested that *The Loiterer* may contain JA's first published piece, a letter to the editor signed by 'Sophia Sentiment', in issue 9 (28 March 1789), in which the writer complains of the absence of stories to interest women, 'about love and

honour, and all that', from the first eight numbers of the periodical. JA was at this time 13 years old. But there is no extant family tradition of her authorship of the letter, and its style is very different from that of her juvenilia. As Claire Tomalin astutely observes: 'The trouble with attributing this to her is that the letter is not an encouragement to *The Loiterer* to address women readers so much as a mockery of women's poor taste in literature. "Sophia Sentiment" is more likely to have been a transvestite, Henry or James.' (See A. Walton Litz, '*The Loiterer*: A Reflection of Jane Austen's Early Environment', *Review of English Studies*, NS 12: 47 (1961), 251–61; Sir Zachary Cope, 'Who Was Sophia Sentiment? Was She Jane Austen?' *Book Collector*, 15 (1966), 143–51; John Gore, 'Sophia Sentiment: Jane Austen?' *Jane Austen Society Reports*, 2 (1966–75), 9–12; Deirdre Le Faye, 'Jane Austen and William Hayley', *Notes and Queries*, 232 (1987), 25–6; Claire Tomalin, *Jane Austen: A Life* (1997), 63. For a recent reassessment of the influence of the young James and Henry Austen's journalism on JA's early literary experiments, see Li-Ping Geng, '*The Loiterer* and Jane Austen's Literary Identity', *Eighteenth-Century Fiction*, 13 (2001), 579–92.)

Her second brother, Edward: R. W. Chapman, *Memoir* (1926), remained silent on this piece of family concealment. Edward was, in fact, the third brother, born in October 1767 (d. 1852) and adopted in 1783, at the age of 16, by his father's distant cousin Thomas Knight II (1735–94) of Godmersham, who was childless. From him he eventually inherited estates at Steventon and Chawton in Hampshire and Godmersham in Kent, taking the name of Knight officially in 1812. The second brother was George, born in 1766, epileptic from childhood and possibly deaf and dumb and mentally handicapped. He is mentioned by his anxious parents in two surviving letters from 1770 (*Austen Papers*, 23, 27), and in 1788 there appear to be fears that the sickly young son of Mr Austen's niece, Eliza Hancock (now de Feuillide), may have the same congenital defects (*Austen Papers*, 130). But Mrs Austen's younger brother Thomas was also mentally handicapped, and he and George may have been boarded out together. Whatever the precise facts, George Austen never lived in his family, is not mentioned in JA's letters, and is rarely glimpsed in other parts of the surviving family record. But he outlived his elder brother James (1765–1819) and his younger sister Jane, not dying until 1838. He was provided for by the family, and we find in 1827 Edward Knight making over to George's use the whole of his own inheritance from their mother (*Austen Papers*, 334). (W. A. W. Jarvis, 'Some Information about Jane Austen's Clerical Connections', *Jane Austen Society Report* (1976), 14–15; and Tucker, 115–17.)

Henry . . . less success in life, than his brothers: another piece of discreet family censorship on JEAL's part. He avoids mentioning the details of Henry Austen's (1771–1850) colourful and varied career: that, after soldiering in the Oxfordshire Militia, he set himself up in London as an

Army Agent, which led him into starting his own London bank, as well as several associated country banking partnerships. He went bankrupt in March 1816, with significant financial consequences for his brothers and his sister Jane. Immediately thereafter, he reverted to a boyhood plan and was ordained a clergyman the following December, becoming curate of Chawton. With the occasional fashionable clerical appointment, he remained a clergyman for the rest of his life and died in 1850. Henry acted informally as JA's literary agent, and it is from his various smart London addresses that her letters show her conducting some of her dealings with publishers and printers. He was also the first to make public biographical information about JA, in his 'Biographical Notice of the Author' (included in this collection), prefixed to the posthumously published *NA* and *P* (1818). According to family tradition (*Life & Letters*, 48), he was JA's favourite brother. JA mentions that 'Uncle Henry writes very superior Sermons' in a letter to JEAL, 16 December 1816 (*Letters*, 323).

17 *Francis . . . G.C.B.*: Knight Grand Cross of the Bath. The details of Francis (Frank) (1774–1865) and Charles Austen's (1779–1852) distinguished naval careers can be found in William R. O'Byrne, *A Naval Biographical Dictionary* (1849; rev. edn., 1859–61). This can be further supplemented by *Sailor Brothers*. Another family production (its authors, John Henry Hubback and his daughter Edith, were Frank Austen's grandson and great-granddaughter), this book provides unique anecdotes about Frank and Charles from family papers and oral tradition, and includes the story that Frank was '*the* officer who knelt at church' (p. 17). It was in *Sailor Brothers* that JA's five surviving letters to Frank were published for the first time, presumably the letters that cousin Fanny Sophia told JEAL he might see but not print. Tucker, 165–90, conveniently collects together in briefer space much of what is known. As the surviving letters make clear, JA wove into her novels details from her brothers' naval experiences—notably the names of their ships in *MP*—and may have borrowed aspects of their characters for William Price in *MP* and for Captain Harville in *P*, who Frank much later described as bearing 'a strong resemblance' to himself (*Letters*, 217, 91; *Austen Papers*, 303).

prizes: the money realized by the capture of an enemy ship (or cargo) as a prize of war and shared out among a ship's officers. Depending on rank, substantial prize money could be won. Captain Wentworth in *P*, ch. 24, has made in the course of the war with France 'five-and-twenty thousand pounds' in salary and prizes.

18 *sister Cassandra . . . scarcely be exceeded*: the closeness of the relationship between JA and Cassandra (1773–1845) has been the subject of much speculation by modern biographers, ranging through good sense, bizarre curiosity, and wild surmise. It is described by various family members as a deep and mutually sustaining emotional bond. It is also clear that it was

decisively influential on the selective preservation of JA's writings after her death and on the shape and content of the oral record as it passed down to nieces and nephews. For more consideration of Cassandra's legacy, see the Introduction (pp. xxviii–xxxi). In this paragraph JEAL's major source of supplementary information is his half-sister Anna, whose long letter of December 1864 recording her 'recollections of Aunt Jane' is included in this collection (as *RAJ*). In this letter is to be found the story, told to her by her grandmother, of Jane wishing to share Cassandra's fate even if it meant having her head cut off. It is Anna's daughter Fanny Caroline Lefroy who records in old age and from her mother's recounting that Jane and Cassandra 'were everything to each other. They seemed to lead a life to themselves, within the general family life, which was shared only by each other' (Fanny C. Lefroy, 'Family History', HRO, MS 23M93/85/2, written *c.*1880–5, unpaginated).

Mrs. Latournelle . . . at Reading: behind the impressive name of Mrs, or Madame, La Tournelle, she was plain Sarah Hackitt (Hackett), though still something of a colourful character, with almost Dickensian touches to her appearance: when JA encountered her she was a woman in her sixties with a cork leg (*Gentleman's Magazine* for 1797, p. 983; and F. J. Harvey Darton (ed.), *The Life and Times of Mrs Sherwood, 1775–1851* (1910), 123–34). Cassandra and JA attended Mrs La Tournelle's Ladies Boarding School in the Abbey House, Reading, a private school for the daughters of the clergy and minor gentry, in 1785–6; they had previously been sent away together to be boarded by Mrs Ann Cawley, a family connection, in Oxford and Southampton in 1783, when JA was only 7. JEAL does not record this. (See T. A. B. Corley, 'Jane Austen's Schooldays', *Jane Austen Society Report* (1996), 10–20.)

20 *the Miss Steeles . . . Madame D'Arblay*: the vulgar Miss Steeles, Anne (Nancy) and Lucy, are to be found in *S&S*, where they are thus summed up on their earliest appearance: 'This specimen of the Miss Steeles was enough. The vulgar freedom and folly of the eldest left her no recommendation, and as Elinor was not blinded by the beauty, or the shrewd look of the youngest, to her want of real elegance and artlessness, she left the house without any wish of knowing them better' (ch. 21). Mrs Elton is to be found in *E*, and John Thorpe in *NA*. Madame D'Arblay is more commonly referred to by her unmarried name of Fanny or Frances Burney (1752–1840). One of her contemporary novelists most admired by JA, Burney has from the first provided a point of critical comparison, as, for example, in Henry Austen's 'Biographical Notice' of 1818. The ill-bred Brangtons are to be found in Burney's first novel *Evelina* (1778); Mr Dubster and Tom Hicks appear in *Camilla* (1796). Critics now regard such characters as among the liveliest aspects of Burney's social scene.

21 *It may be known . . . Vine Hunt*: a sentence JEAL added in Ed.2. Himself a keen huntsman, it was, according to his daughter's later account, his writing for private circulation his *Recollections of the Early Days of*

the Vine Hunt (1865) which encouraged him to undertake the more ambitious task of a memoir of his aunt Jane (Mary Augusta Austen-Leigh, *James Edward Austen-Leigh* [*JEAL*], *A Memoir* (1911), 261).

21 *One who knew and loved it well . . . Of Nature's sketch book*: JEAL's father, James Austen, rector of Steventon from 1805 until his death in 1819. The verses are from 'Lines written in the Autumn of 1817 after a recovery from sickness', a 455-line poem to be found in an unpaginated leather-bound volume of James Austen's occasional writings, copied out by JEAL, probably in the mid-1830s (HRO, MS 23M93/60/3/2). In the version in this volume, line 2 of the quoted lines reads, 'Although they may not come within the rule'. Working from another manuscript collection of James Austen's verses (HRO, MS 23M93/60/3/1), but missing the Autumn 1817 poem, R. W. Chapman offered an ingenious but incorrect attribution of these lines (*Memoir* (1926), 215–16).

23 *but the rooms . . . or whitewash*: one of several expansions of the text between Ed.1 and Ed.2, by which JEAL deepens the impression of a bygone world to which JA now belongs. Since JEAL's father James Austen moved into Steventon rectory with his young family in 1801, on his own father's retirement to Bath, this also became JEAL's childhood home, and in what follows he is drawing as much on his own early memories as establishing what JA's might have been.

Catharine Morland's . . . '. . . back of the house': in *NA*, ch. 1. In printed editions of the novel, the name is spelt Catherine. In a letter to Anna Lefroy, dated 8 July 1869, JEAL describes the disappointment of his recent visit to Steventon, a research trip to collect information and soak up the atmosphere: 'All traces of former things are even more obliterated than I had expected. Even the terrace has been levelled, & its site is to be distinguished only by the finer turf on that place' (HRO, MS 23M93/84/1). The old rectory had been demolished in 1824 and replaced by a more elegant new rectory on the opposite hill. Anna's sketch facing this passage in Chapter 2, is drawn from a rather hazy memory of how things were.

24 *a family named Digweed*: the Digweeds had been tenants of the Steventon manor house and estate since at least the early eighteenth century, renting it from the Knights of Godmersham. In JA's time the manor house was inhabited by Hugh Digweed, his wife Ruth, and their four surviving sons—John, Harry, James, and William—who were much of an age with the Austen children (*Fam. Rec.*, 14, 46). On Mr Knight's death in 1794, his heir JA's brother Edward (Knight from 1812) inherited the Steventon estate.

The church . . . above the woody lane: the church of St Nicholas, stone-built and dating from the thirteenth century (Emma Austen-Leigh, *Jane Austen and Steventon* (1937), 6). In 1869 the 'present rector' was JEAL's cousin the Revd William Knight, with whom he spent a night while collecting materials for the *Memoir* (Mary Augusta Austen-Leigh, *JEAL*,

A Memoir, 263). The fragment of verse is again James Austen's, from a poem 'To Edward On planting a lime tree on the terrace in the meadow before the house. January 1813', to be found in the same volume as the verses quoted above, where it reads 'the little spireless Fane, | Just seen above the woody lane' (HRO, MS 23M93/60/3/2). The Edward of the poem is James's son, James Edward, the writer of the *Memoir*, known as Edward in the family.

26 *Mr. Knight . . . representatives of the family*: JA's father was a distant cousin of Thomas Knight, and the connection was strengthened by his adoption of the Austens' third son Edward (see note to p. 16 above). While the Digweeds rented the larger part of the Steventon estate from Mr Knight, George Austen had use of a 200-acre farm as a further source of income (*Fam. Rec.*, 14).

Mr. Austen's powers of teaching: from 1773 George Austen supplemented his clerical income and the needs of his ever growing family by taking as boarders in the rectory private paying pupils from good families. The success of the scheme may have led to overcrowding at Steventon and caused the need to send Cassandra and Jane away to school, if only temporarily (*Fam. Rec.*, 23, 39; Tucker, 31–2). In his 'Biographical Notice' of his sister, Henry Austen recalled how their father was 'not only a profound scholar, but possessing a most exquisite taste in every species of literature' (see p. 137 in the present collection).

then no assessed taxes: beginning in 1784, with fixed taxes on such items as horses, hackney coaches, windows, and candles, the prime minister, William Pitt, managed a highly lucrative taxation policy. In a letter of 24 January 1813 JA writes to Cassandra of a journey she took with a Mrs Clement and her husband 'in their Tax-cart', an open cart used mainly for work purposes, on which was charged only a reduced duty (*Letters*, 198).

employed on farm work: the reference is to a passage in *P&P*, ch. 7, where Mrs Bennet discusses with her daughter Jane whether the horses are available for private pleasure (to draw the coach) or for work on the farm. In the fictional case, the comparative economic restriction that the inability to keep dedicated coach horses suggests serves to further Mrs Bennet's matchmaking schemes. The passage anticipates Mary Crawford's failure to appreciate the difference between city and country living and that horses are needed for harvesting when she wants her harp transported (*MP*, ch. 6).

Edward and Jane Cooper: the children of Jane Leigh Cooper, Mrs Austen's sister, and the Revd Dr Edward Cooper. Mrs Jane Cooper died in October 1783 from the typhus fever infecting Mrs Cawley's Southampton household in which JA, Cassandra, and their Cooper cousin Jane were then boarding. JA, too, was severely ill with it. Of the two cousins, Edward (1770–1833) wrote dull sermons, which are mentioned unenthusiastically in JA's letters to Cassandra on 17–18 January 1809 and again on 8–9 September 1816, where she writes: 'We do not much like

M[r] Cooper's new Sermons:—they are fuller of Regeneration & Conversion than ever—with the addition of his zeal in the cause of the Bible Society' (*Letters*, 322). His sister Jane (1771–98) maintained throughout her short life the intimacy with JA and Cassandra established in their schooldays. She is mentioned as joining in the Austen family theatricals at Christmas 1788–9 (*Austen Papers*, 138, in a letter of Eliza de Feuillide), when she may have spoken the 'epilogue' to *The Sultan*, written by James Austen for 'Miss C . . . in the character of Roxalana' (HRO, MS 23M93/60/3/2), and she is the dedicatee of JA's spoof sentimental novel 'Henry and Eliza' in the collection of juvenile writings known as *Volume the First* (see note to p. 39). After the death of her father in August 1792, she was married from her aunt and uncle's at Steventon a few months later, in December. For her own early death in a carriage accident, see *Fam. Rec.*, 98. The conjecture that JA may have acquired an early acquaintance with Bath on visits there to the Coopers is probably derived from Anna Lefroy's memory that 'Cassandra in her childhood was a good deal with D[r]. & M[rs]. Cooper at Bath' (see p. 160 in this collection). Cassandra and Jane Cooper were of course nearer in age to each other and more likely companions in childhood. Following Mrs Cooper's death, the family left Bath in 1784, at which time JA was 8 and hardly likely to be storing topographical impressions for a future novel. Her first recorded visit there is in November 1797, to the Leigh Perrots, though earlier visits may well have occurred (*Fam. Rec.*, 95). JA did not live permanently in Bath until her father retired there in 1801.

27 *Count de Feuillade*: Jean-François Capot de Feuillide (not Feuillade) was a captain in the French army and probably not a count. He married JA's cousin Eliza Hancock in 1781; their son, Hastings, was born in 1786 and, sickly for most of his short life, died in 1801. The 'Comte' was guillotined in February 1794, having attempted to bribe an official to favour the Marquise de Marboeuf, then on trial. It was the Marquise who was accused of trying to produce famine by laying down arable land to pasture. According to family tradition, Eliza was with her husband in France until his arrest, barely escaping with her life. Henry Austen married his cousin Eliza de Feuillide on 31 December 1797. JEAL's *Memoir* appears to be the only record for the family tradition that Henry and Eliza subsequently visited France during the Peace of Amiens (1802–3), hoping to recover her French property, and that they fled in what sounds like a frightening repetition of past events. Eliza, lively, fashionable, and irreverent, was one of JA's most colourful connections and a significant influence on her teenage years; the spoof epistolary novel 'Love and Freindship', dated at the end as finished on 'June 13th 1790', is dedicated 'To Madame la Comtesse de Feuillide'. Eliza died in 1813 (*Fam. Rec.*, 34–7, 72–3, 123).

28 *prologues and epilogues . . . vigorous and amusing*: the volume of James Austen's occasional writings, copied out by JEAL (HRO, MS 23M93/

60/3/2), contains specimens of James's prologues and epilogues dating back to the 1780s, with notes of the members of the family who took the relevant roles in family theatricals. Another cousin, the sensible Philadelphia Walter, writes of the performances expected to take place at Steventon over Christmas 1787: 'My uncle's barn is fitting up quite like a theatre, & all the young folks are to take their part.' She describes Eliza de Feuillide, whom she is seeing again after a gap of ten years: 'The Countess has many amiable qualities . . . Her dissipated life she was brought up to—therefore it cannot be wondered at . . . ' Philadelphia, who kept her letters from her exotic, Frenchified cousin, is our main source of information on Eliza. The Christmas theatricals being planned in 1787 included Hannah Cowley's *Which Is the Man?* (1783) and David Garrick's *Bon Ton* (1775), and Eliza clearly fancied herself in the leading female roles (*Austen Papers*, 125–8). According to James Austen's additional verses for that year, the play eventually performed, with Eliza playing the heroine, was Susannah Centlivre's *The Wonder! A Woman Keeps a Secret!* (1714).

Cassandra . . . a young clergyman: this was Tom Fowle (1765–97), Mr Austen's former pupil at Steventon rectory and therefore a childhood friend. He accompanied his kinsman Lord Craven to the West Indies and died of yellow fever off St Domingo in February 1797. He was buried at sea. Cassandra and he may have become engaged around the time that he officiated at the marriage of Jane Cooper and Captain Thomas Williams in December 1792. On his death he left Cassandra £1,000, which invested would have helped to give her a very limited independence. Some details can be found in letters written in May and July 1797 from Eliza de Feuillide to Philadelphia Walter (*Austen Papers*, 159, 161).

Her reviewer . . . January 1821: Richard Whately (1787–1863), later Archbishop of Dublin, in an unsigned review of *NA* and *P* in the *Quarterly Review*, 24 (January 1821), 352–76. The passage quoted here occurs at pp. 366–7. JEAL returns to this important early critical assessment of JA's work in Chapter 8 of the *Memoir*.

29 *In her youth . . . to affect her happiness*: this is one of the significant revisions to the text of the *Memoir* made between Ed.1 and Ed.2. Ed.1 reads at this point: 'She did not indeed pass through life without being the object of strong affection, and it is probable that she met with some whom she found attractive; but her taste was not easily satisfied, nor her heart to be lightly won. I have no reason to think that she ever felt any attachment by which the happiness of her life was at all affected.' There the paragraph ends, and JEAL moves at once to his description of domestic life and home comforts at Steventon almost a century before. The details of two romantic episodes, still insubstantial, and quite deliberately so ('one passage of romance . . . imperfectly acquainted . . . unable to assign name, or date, or place, though . . . on sufficient authority'), which he included in Ed.2, he owed to his sister Caroline Austen.

Both can be dated to the turbulent period 1801–4, soon after the family move from Steventon to Bath, when JA was 25–29 years old. The first episode can be fixed precisely, in December 1802, and refers to the proposal by Harris Bigg-Wither, the younger brother of JA and Cassandra's old friends Catherine and Alethea Bigg, of Manydown Park. JA apparently accepted the offer but immediately had a change of heart and rejected him. Writing to JEAL with details of this and the second, far shadowier, seaside romance, Caroline observed: 'My own wish would be, that not any allusion should be made to the Manydown story—or at *least* that the reference should be so vague, as to give *no* clue to the place or the person.' Bigg-Wither is not named until Constance Hill does so in her *Jane Austen: Her Homes and Her Friends* (1902; 1904 edn., 240). The second episode, the seaside romance, is possibly earlier, and refers to a chance meeting when JA was on holiday in Sidmouth, Devon, in the summer of 1801; again it is from Caroline Austen's account. She got it from the elderly Cassandra, and in the various family versions it becomes steadily more inconsistent. Caroline writes of it to JEAL: 'My Aunt told me this in the last years of her own life—& it was quite new to me then—but all this, being nameless and dateless, cannot I know serve any purpose of your's—and it brings no contradiction to your theory that she ^Aunt Jane^ never *had* any attachment that overclouded her happiness, for long.' (See Caroline Austen's letter to JEAL, included in the Appendix to this collection from transcribed extracts, NPG, RWC/HH, fos. 8–10; *Life & Letters*, 84–94; and *Fam. Rec.* 121–2, 250–1.)

29 *soon after I was born*: JEAL was born at Deane on 17 November 1798. His father James Austen moved his family into Steventon rectory in May 1801, at which time the Austens went to Bath.

30 *Pope . . . 'to mark their way'*: slightly misquoting Pope, Epistle 1, *To Cobham*, ll. 31–2.

'to chronicle small beer': to make something trifling appear important. Cf. Shakespeare, *Othello*, II. i. 160 ('To suckle fools, and chronicle small beer').

the dinner-table . . . general use: for the splendid appearance, notionally desirable for the mid-Victorian dinner-table, see the table plans in *Mrs Beeton's Book of Household Management* (1861). It was usual in the eighteenth century to have dinner, the main meal of the day, in the mid-afternoon. But from the end of the century mealtimes slowly changed, with the emergence of luncheon and an increasingly late dinner hour among the fashion-conscious. In the grand surroundings of Godmersham Park, her brother Edward Knight's Kent estate, JA dines at a comfortable family time of half past four; and on special occasions as late as half past six. But at Steventon in 1798 dinner is at 'half after Three', with the knowledge that they are finished before Cassandra, then staying at Godmersham, has even begun (*Letters*, 251, 244, and 27). In *P&P* the smart Bingleys dine at half past six (ch. 8), while Tom Musgrave, in *The*

Watsons, hopes to impress by the extreme lateness of his dinner hour—'For whether he dined at eight or nine . . . was a matter of very little consequence.' The barely genteel Watsons, however, are discovered dining inelegantly early, at three.

31 *Dos est . . . Virtus*: Adam von Bremen, an eleventh-century theologian, in his *Gesta Hammaburgensis Ecclesiae Pontificum* ('German Church History'), of which an edition was published in Hanover in 1846. It should read 'Dos est magna parentum Virtus' ('excellence is the great legacy of parents').

furmity, or tansey-pudding: furmity or frumenty, a dish of wheat boiled in milk with spices and sugar; tansy-pudding, traditionally eaten at Easter, flavoured with the bitter herb tansy. Mrs Austen thanks her sister-in-law Mrs Walter for her 'receipt for potato cakes' on 12 December 1773 (*Austen Papers*, 30). In a letter to Cassandra, then staying at Godmersham Park, JA jokes of her own good housekeeping, which she defines as pleasing 'my own appetite', mentioning her favourite dishes—'ragout veal' and 'haricot mutton' (17 November 1798, *Letters*, 20). At Chawton, after 1809, Martha Lloyd shared the housekeeping with Cassandra, and her manuscript recipe book from that time survives. See Maggie Black and Deirdre Le Faye, *The Jane Austen Cookbook* (1995).

'*. . . costly to rear*': when in her seventies and living at Chawton Cottage, Mrs Austen, according to family tradition, still kept the kitchen garden and dug her own potatoes: 'I have heard my mother [Anna Lefroy] say that when at work she wore a green round frock like a day labourer' (Fanny Caroline Lefroy, 'Family History', in *Fam. Rec.*, 158).

32 *A small writing-desk . . . in the closet*: in the Lefroy Manuscript, the Austen family history that Anna Lefroy embarked on in the 1850s but left uncompleted, is included a description from her own childhood memories, perhaps refocused in later conversations with her aunt Cassandra, of the two modest rooms and their cheap furniture—a dressing room and smaller bedroom—which JA and Cassandra shared at Steventon in the 1790s. Its defensive tone, though not its detail, is echoed by JEAL: ' . . . one of the Bed chambers, that over the Dining room, was plainly fitted up, & converted into a sort of Drawing room . . . This room, the Dressing room, as they were pleased to call it, communicated with one of smaller size where my two Aunts slept; I remember the common-looking carpet with its chocolate ground that covered the floor, and some portions of the furniture. A painted press, with shelves above for books, that stood with its back to the wall next the Bedroom, & opposite the fireplace; my Aunt Jane's Pianoforte—& above all, on a table between the windows, above which hung a looking-glass, 2 Tonbridge-ware work boxes of oval shape, fitted up with ivory barrels containing reels for silk, yard measures, etc. I thought them beautiful, & so perhaps in their day, & their degree, they were. But the charm of the room, with its scanty furniture and cheaply papered walls, must have been, for those old

enough to understand it, the flow of native homebred wit, with all the fun & nonsense of a clever family who had but little intercourse with the outer world' (Lefroy MS, quoted in *Fam. Rec.*, 69).

There must have been more dancing: this marks the beginning of a long section, added to Ed.2, explaining late eighteenth-century manners and customs. The inserted passage ends six pages later at: 'nor can I pretend to tell how much of what I have said is descriptive of the family life at Steventon in Jane Austen's youth.' In his 'Biographical Notice' of 1818, Henry Austen writes of his sister: 'She was fond of dancing, and excelled in it.'

To gallop . . . caught no cold: the lines are probably by Walter Scott. They occur in slightly different form in his novel *The Antiquary* (1816), ch. 11: 'When courtiers gallop'd o'er four counties | The ball's fair partner to behold, | And humbly hope she caught no cold.'

33 *Sir Charles and Lady Grandison . . . at their own wedding*: a reference to Samuel Richardson's *The History of Sir Charles Grandison* (1753–4), vol. vi, letter 53.

lappet: a kind of flap.

Gloves immaculately clean . . . performance: in Fanny Burney's novel *Camilla*, book 2, ch. 2, the vulgar Mr Dubster is prevented from dancing with Camilla, much to her relief, because he has lost one of his gloves. The name of 'Miss J. Austen, Steventon' is printed in the list of subscribers to *Camilla*; and JA refers to the novel in an early letter to Cassandra (*Letters*, 6).

Hornpipes, cotillons, and reels: all lively country dances. Where hornpipes would be of English origin and reels Scottish or Irish, the cotillon would have been a modified version of a French peasant dance, its name deriving from the French word for 'petticoat'. See *Letters*, 330, where JA writes to her niece Fanny Knight: 'Much obliged for the *Quadrilles*, which I am grown to think pretty enough, though of course they are very inferior to the Cotillons of my own day.'

34 *the concoction of home-made wines*: JA writes in her letters of 'brewing Spruce Beer again' (a drink made from sugar and the green tops of the Spruce, a variety of fir-tree); and she asks her friend Alethea Bigg for the recipe for 'orange Wine' (*Letters*, 156 and 328). Extracts from the letter to Alethea Bigg (no. 150) are included by JEAL in ch. 11 of the *Memoir*.

a little girl . . . leaving her chamber: middle-class children's books of the 1780s and 1790s regularly taught the value of practical self-sufficiency, of self-denial, and the rejection of excessive idleness and luxury. JEAL is probably remembering R. L. and Maria Edgeworth's *Early Lessons* (1801), where Lucy must make her bed before she is allowed breakfast.

Music: according to Caroline Austen's memories: 'Aunt Jane began her day with music—for which I conclude she had a natural taste; as she thus kept it up—tho' she had no one to teach; was never induced (as I have heard) to play in company; and none of her family cared much for it' (see p. 170).

35 *'The master's eye . . . serve yourself'*: both self-explanatory sayings, implying the advantages of self-reliance.

Catherine Morland . . . her father's parsonage: the reference is to *NA*, ch. 23, where Catherine, the heroine, is being shown the kitchen and domestic offices of Northanger Abbey, all of them to her dismay modernized and with no trace of medieval privation. The narrator observes: 'The purposes for which a few shapeless pantries and a comfortless scullery were deemed sufficient at Fullerton [her father's parsonage], were here carried on in appropriate divisions, commodious and roomy.'

36 *useful articles . . . in the old-fashioned parlour*: in a letter from Steventon to Cassandra (1 November 1800) JA appears to be sewing shirts to send out by the half-dozen, as they are finished, to their brother Charles who is waiting to set sail (*Letters*, 53). But see also JA's letter complaining of the ungenteel behaviour of a Mrs A[rmstrong], who 'sat darning a pair of stockings the whole of my visit' (quoted in Ch. 4 below). One senses already a generational self-consciousness about the display of such homely activities as she advises Cassandra 'I do not mention this at home, lest a warning should act as an example' (*Letters*, 94).

I have been told: the source of the story of little Frank (known in the family as 'Fly') Austen's pony and his scarlet suit, made in fact from his mother's wedding-dress, may be JEAL's half-sister Anna Lefroy, who got other childhood tales from Frank himself, now Sir Francis, in 1855 (see *Fam. Rec.*, 44–5 and 260, n. 34). These details are not included in Ed.1., which omits the section: 'The early hour . . . conspicuous figure in the hunting-field.'

pattens: wooden soles, and mounted on iron rings, for raising the normal footwear out of the mud. The source for this detail is Anna Lefroy. See p. 157.

Gay . . . Patty takes the name: John Gay, *Trivia* (1716), book 1, ll. 281–2.

37 *Cowper . . . three-legged stool*: a reference to one of JA's favourite poets, William Cowper (1731–1800). In Book 1 of his long poem *The Task* (1785), he fancifully traces the evolution of the sofa from the stool: 'Thus first necessity invented stools, | Convenience next suggested elbow-chairs, | And luxury th' accomplish'd SOFA last' (ll. 86–8).

Mr. Leigh Perrot . . . the Patten a clog: James Leigh (1735–1817), Mrs Austen's brother, added Perrot to his name in 1751 in order to inherit the estate of his maternal great-uncle Thomas Perrot. Some of JA's books were probably gifts from this uncle (David Gilson, 'Jane Austen's Books', *Book Collector*, 23 (1974), 27–39). He also stood surety for Henry Austen when he was appointed Receiver-General for Oxfordshire, losing £10,000 on Henry's bankruptcy in 1816. Punning epigrams seem to have been a speciality in the Leigh and Austen families, and JEAL records two of JA's in Chapter 5 of this *Memoir*. A manuscript in JA's hand of a poem ascribed to James Leigh Perrot, now in the Pierpont Morgan Library, New York, reads: 'Thro' the rough ways of Life, with a patten your Guard, | May you safely and pleasantly jog; | May the ring never break, nor the Knot press too hard, | Nor the Foot find the Patten a Clog' (*Jane Austen: Letters and Manuscripts in the Pierpont Morgan Library* (1975), 26). B. C. Southam includes this epigram among JA's own verses (*Minor Works*, 452), but he does not explain his decision. We may wonder why the piece did survive among papers attributed to JA. The marriage of Captain Edward James Foote, known to the Austens, and Miss Mary Patton occurred in 1803.

37 *Tunbridge ware*: wooden articles, with a characteristic mosaic decoration made from inlaid wood, manufactured in and about Tunbridge Wells. Cf. *E*, ch. 40: 'Within abundance of silver paper was a pretty little Tunbridge-ware box, which Harriet opened.'

38 *the rough earl . . . '. . . go spin'*: attributed to William Herbert, Earl of Pembroke (*c.*1501–70). It is quoted by Walter Scott, in his journal for 9 February 1826, included in the biography written by his son-in-law, J. G. Lockhart, *Memoirs of the Life of Sir Walter Scott, Bart* (2nd edn., 1839), viii. 223, to which JEAL refers below, at p. 43.

the three Fates: in classical and northern myth, the goddesses who determine the course of human life.

Holy Scripture . . . in the wilderness: Exodus, 35: 25.

'when Adam delved and Eve span': fourteenth-century proverb.

spinning jennies: early steam-powered machines for spinning a number of threads at once, already in use in the 1770s.

39 *I know little of Jane Austen's childhood*: this opening section, as far as 'associating at home with persons of cultivated intellect', was added in Ed.2.

putting out her babies . . . in the village: this account of Mrs Austen's system of child-rearing was added in Ed.2. Her practice seems to have been to breast-feed each baby for a few months and then to hand the child over to a woman in the village for the next year or longer, certainly until he or she was able to walk. This is what she describes in letters to her sister-in-law Susannah Walter: 'My little boy is come home from nurse, and a fine stout little fellow he is, and can run anywhere, so now I have all four at home, and some time in January I expect a fifth.' The date is November 1772; so the little boy must be Henry, born in June 1771. Of the fifth child, Cassandra, she writes in June 1773, five months after the birth, 'I suckled my little girl thro' the first quarter; she has been weaned and settled at a good woman's at Deane just eight weeks; she is very healthy and lively, and puts on her short petticoats to-day' (*Austen Papers*, 28 and 29). With a steadily increasing family of children, the parsonage to run, and her husband's boarding pupils to care for, Mrs Austen may have found this the most efficient plan, and perhaps one that assured the babies a degree of attention she could not provide. It sounds from the account she gives of Cassandra that she used, at least in this instance, a dry nurse, in which case Mrs Austen's babies were weaned very young. In the course of the eighteenth century there was mounting pressure on middle-class women to set a good example to their sex and rank by breast-feeding rather than farming their children out. The argument was posed as a matter of hygiene and sound medical advice, but also contained a strong moral imperative. There was the added warning in some advice manuals that to hand over one's baby to the care of another might endanger the natural bond of affection between mother and child ('That those Mothers who do, as it were, discharge their Children from them, and thus dispose of them, do at least weaken, if not dissolve the Bond of Love and Tenderness which Nature ties between them', *The Ladies Dispensatory: or, Every Woman her own Physician* (1740)). Some modern biographers have attempted to explain what they sense as JA's emotional defensiveness in terms of this early severance (e.g. 'the emotional distance between child and mother is obvious throughout her life', Tomalin, *Jane Austen*, 6). Such theories tend to have a late twentieth-century feel to them. It is worth noting, on the other side of the argument, that the practice of farming out was not uncommon at the time, that the Austen babies seemed to thrive on it, and that they were not banished totally out of sight but were apparently visited daily by their parents. Deirdre Le Faye has suggested that a couple called John and Elizabeth Littleworth may have been regular foster-parents to the Austen children. The extended Littleworth family remained in service to the Austens for several generations, but there is no hard evidence for their fostering (see 'The Austens and the Littleworths', *Jane Austen Society Report* (1987), 64–70).

40 *copy books extant . . . by the time she was sixteen*: in Ed.1 this sentence reads: 'There is extant an old copy-book containing several tales, some of which seem to have been composed while she was quite a girl.' The description of JA's early writings is much briefer in Ed.1, and no specimen example is given. The 'copy books' to which JEAL refers can be assumed to be the three transcript volumes of juvenilia, 'Volume the First', 'Volume the Second', and 'Volume the Third', begun as early as 1787 and continued to 1793. JA herself gave them their imposing titles. By the terms of Cassandra's will (she died in 1845 and had inherited all JAs manuscripts), 'Volume the First' went to Charles Austen, 'Volume the Second' to Frank, and 'Volume the Third' to James Edward (JEAL). In the interval between Ed.1 and Ed.2 of the *Memoir*, JEAL may have gained more first-hand knowledge of these copy-books and their contents. B. C. Southam has assumed that JEAL did not see 'Volume the First' but worked instead from copied extracts from which he chose to include in Ed.2 'The Mystery' ('The Manuscript of Jane Austen's *Volume the First*', *The Library*, 5th series, 17 (1962), 231–7 (at p. 231). But

this is by no means the implication of what he writes. His detached style of reference—'There are copy books extant . . . '—and restricted quotation is more likely a reflection of his strong desire to protect JA's reputation as a writer of mature and sober novels of realism, which might suffer with the wide publication of early pieces that he felt sure were meant for family eyes only. Charles's eldest daughter, Cassy Esten, was helpful, we know, with material for the *Memoir*; so there is no reason to suppose that she did not allow JEAL sight of 'Volume the First', since her father's death in her possession. An interesting question is why he did not include extracts from his own inherited manuscript, 'Volume the Third'.

The Mystery: here printed for the first time from *Volume the First*. Dedicated to JA's father, it may have been written for a family theatrical as early as 1788; and if so it is certainly one of the earliest pieces to have survived. The inspiration for its two scenes of whispering was possibly Sheridan's burlesque play *The Critic* (1779), II, i. For Sheridan's impact on the juvenilia, see John McAleer, 'What a Biographer Can Learn about Jane Austen from Her Juvenilia', in J. David Grey (ed.), *Jane Austen's Beginnings: The Juvenilia and Lady Susan* (1989), 15.

42 *following words of a niece*: Caroline Austen. JEAL is here quoting, with only slight discrepancies, from his sister's recollections, in *MAJA*, included in this collection (see p. 174). The passage is not included in Ed.1.

43 *The family . . . declined to let these early works be published*: as it stands in Ed.2, this sentence is puzzling. It is a reference to what Caroline Austen, in a letter of 1 April [1869?] to JEAL, then collecting materials for the *Memoir*, called the 'betweenities', making it clear that she specifically has in mind *Lady Susan*, the original manuscript of which was now in Fanny, Lady Knatchbull's possession. At this stage, she suggests her brother might print 'Evelyn' from *Volume the Third*, in his keeping since Aunt Cassandra's death, and she continues: 'What I should deprecate is publishing any of the "betweenities" when the nonsense was passing away, and before her wonderful talent had found its proper channel. Lady Knatchbull has a whole short story they were wishing years ago to make public—but were discouraged by others – & I hope the desire has passed away' (from the transcript, NPG, RWC/HH, fos. 4–7), included in the Appendix to this edition). But JEAL was not prepared to risk exposing the surreal nonsense of 'Evelyn', and Ed.1 of his *Memoir* contained only a small selection of JA's tame occasional verses (the lines 'To the Memory of Mrs. Lefroy', two humorous epigrams, and the verses to 'Lovely Anna'). It was in the enlarged Ed.2, printed here, that he included, along with more of JA's letters, a tiny sample of the juvenilia ('The Mystery'), the cancelled chapter of *P*, a summary of *Sanditon* (the autograph manuscripts of both now in Anna Lefroy's possession), *The Watsons* (so-named by JEAL and now owned by his sister Caroline), and *Lady Susan*, not from Lady Knatchbull's original but from a copy. Why the earlier strong

family decision against publishing *Lady Susan* was revoked is not clear, though a reasonable guess would be that JEAL was attempting to forestall a rival publishing plan from within the family. But in the light of this change of heart, the paragraph (largely unaltered since Ed.1), and especially this sentence, reads oddly and should have been emended.

'He was makin' himsell . . . and the fun': Robert Shortreed accompanied Scott on his early ballad-collecting expeditions into the Scottish Borders. These ballads, Shortreed suggests, became the groundwork for much of Scott's later writing. The quotation is taken from Lockhart's, *Life of Scott* (1839), i. 266.

44 *'Pride and Prejudice' . . . first composed in 1798*: JEAL's dating and other information about the early drafts of *P&P*, *S&S*, and *NA* accords with Cassandra Austen's brief memorandum of composition, which may have been drawn up soon after JA's death, perhaps for Henry when he was preparing his 'Biographical Notice' towards the end of 1817, though if that is so, he seems not to have used it. It does, however, appear to have been consulted by JEAL. There is only one slight discrepancy: Cassandra records 'North-hanger Abby [*sic*] was written about the years 98 & 99'. An illustration of the manuscript of Cassandra's notes (now in the Pierpont Morgan Library, New York) is included in *Minor Works*, plate facing p. 242.

Mr. and Mrs. Lefroy and their family: the Revd I. P. George Lefroy was rector of Ashe from 1783. He had married Anne Brydges (1748/9–1804) in 1778, and it is she, not her husband, who is the important figure in JA's life. 'Madam Lefroy', as she was known locally, became the great friend and intellectual inspiration of the young JA, is mentioned often in her early letters, is named in the spoof 'History of England' (*Volume the Second*), as one of the advocates for Mary Queen of Scots, and played a part in ending the early flirtation with her nephew Tom Lefroy (see note to p. 48 below). She was a distant cousin of JA's mother through their common Brydges ancestry, and by her brother's account 'had an exquisite taste for poetry . . . and she composed easy verses herself with great facility' (Egerton Brydges, *The Autobiography, Times, Opinions, and Contemporaries of Sir Egerton Brydges* (2 vols., 1834), i. 5). These verses were published as *Carmina Domestica*, ed. C. E. Lefroy (1812). Later in this chapter JEAL includes JA's poem 'To the Memory of Mrs. Lefroy', written in 1808 on the fourth anniversary of her sudden death in a riding accident. The Austens and Lefroys were subsequently linked by marriage when James Austen's elder daughter Anna (JEAL's half-sister) married in 1814 Anne Lefroy's youngest son Benjamin.

Sir Egerton Brydges . . . ' . . . cheeks a little too full': Samuel Egerton Brydges (1762–1837), the younger brother of Mrs Anne Lefroy (see note above), was an antiquarian bibliographer and genealogist with an excruciatingly pretentious and florid prose style. JA describes his novel *Arthur Fitz-Albini* (1798) in uncomplimentary terms in a letter to

Cassandra, 25 November 1798 (*Letters*, 22). His account of JA is not the earliest published notice, as Henry Austen's pieces included here show; it appears in his *Autobiography* (1834), ii. 41.

Mary Brydges: JA's mother, the former Cassandra Leigh, shared with Anne Brydges Lefroy a common ancestor in Mary Brydges, who married Theophilus Leigh (*c.*1643–1725) as his second wife in November 1689, making her JA's great-grandmother. Mary Brydges was a daughter of James Brydges, eighth Lord of Chandos and ambassador at Constantinople, and Eliza Chandos, who wrote the 'curious letter of advice and reproof' included here. With the injection of mercantile wealth from Eliza's family, in the next generation their son, Mary's brother, was able to live in great magnificence. He became the first Duke of Chandos and was Handel's patron. It was in compliment to the first Duke's wife Cassandra that this unusual name entered the Leigh family and was continued by generations of Austens. Writing to her brother as he was collecting materials for the *Memoir* Anna Lefroy drew his attention to 'the original of Poll's letters . . . in the possession of Mrs. George Austen—it was given to her at Portsdown' (NPG, RWC/HH, fo. 2). The letter must have been a cherished heirloom, handed down through the Leigh and Austen families. Portsdown Lodge, near Portsmouth, became the home of Frank Austen, and Mrs George Austen would be the wife of Frank's son George. JEAL's inclusion of this letter to JA's great-grandmother can only be explained as symptomatic of that social anxiety which surfaces in the *Memoir* at various points and was itself a major feature of JA's novels. Writing of her fictional society, David Spring has adopted Alan Everitt's useful term 'pseudo-gentry' to describe the group comprising trade, the professions, rentiers, and clergymen whose concerns propel her novels. It is a group whose membership in reality can be extended to the diversely positioned Austens themselves. The 'pseudo-gentry' are characteristically insecure—in some cases upwardly mobile and with growing incomes and social prestige, and in others in straitened circumstances; but in either case aspiring to the lifestyle of the traditional rural gentry. The Chandos letter not only serves to remind the reader of JA's distant aristocratic pretensions, but internally it registers the periodic readjustment of relations between rank and trade. JA was not without her own snobbish streak, while her brother Henry was downright opportunistic. (See Agnes Leigh, 'An Old Family History', *National Review*, 49 (1907), 277–86; D. J. Greene, 'Jane Austen and the Peerage', *PMLA*, 68 (1953), 1017–31; and David Spring, 'Interpreters of Jane Austen's Social World: Literary Critics and Historians', in Janet Todd (ed.), *Jane Austen: New Perspectives*, (1983), 53–72, esp. 61–3.)

45 *bring y^r bread & cheese even'*: live within your means.

out run the Constable: fall into debt.

a dead lift: an extremity, a hopeless situation.

know our beginning . . . who knows his end: cf. Psalm 39: 4.

47 *bartlemew-babby*: a Bartholomew doll—someone gaudily dressed, so named after the fair traditionally held around 24 August (Feast of St Bartholomew) at West Smithfield, London.

cry rost meate: publish one's good luck foolishly.

Pera of Galata: south of Constantinople; in the seventeenth and eighteenth centuries this district was home to most European diplomats to Turkey.

48 *a Turkey merchant*: one trading with the Near East generally and dealing in luxury items. The late seventeenth and early eighteenth centuries saw their heyday, when fabulous fortunes could be made.

Right Hon. Thomas Lefroy . . . Ireland: (1776–1869), mentioned by name in JA's earliest extant letters, where she records for Cassandra their brief romance over the Christmas holidays of 1795–6 when she was just 20. By 15 January 1796 she is writing: 'At length the Day is come on which I am to flirt my last with Tom Lefroy, & when you receive this it will be over—My tears flow as I write, at the melancholy idea' (*Letters*, 4). Almost three years later, in November 1798, she has news of him, reluctantly provided by his aunt, her friend Mrs Anne Lefroy, that 'he was gone back to London in his way to Ireland, where he is called to the Bar and means to practise' (*Letters*, 19). Tom Lefroy practised as a barrister in Dublin, married in 1799, had nine children, and became Lord Chief Justice of Ireland in 1852. These letters, by that time in the possession of Fanny, Lady Knatchbull, were not known to JEAL when he made reference to the incident in the *Memoir*; but the story was not forgotten in family tradition. Both Caroline Austen and Anna Lefroy shared versions of it with their brother. As usual, Caroline pressed for discretion if not total silence: 'I think I need not warn *you* against raking up that old story', which she admits to having from their mother Mary Lloyd Austen. Anna, on the other hand, writing to JEAL's wife, is far less discreet and, having married into the Lefroy family, has a different perspective on events. Before the *Memoir* was published Tom Lefroy had died, and in August 1870 his nephew T. E. P. Lefroy (who had married Anna Jemima, Anna Lefroy's eldest daughter) wrote to JEAL communicating his uncle's late admission 'that he was in love with her' but that 'it was a boyish love'. T. E. P. Lefroy continued: 'As this occurred in a friendly, & private conversation, I feel some doubt whether I ought to make it public.' In the event, JEAL confined himself to the extremely guarded paragraph printed here. (See the transcript of Caroline Austen's letter, 1 April [1869?], NPG, RWC/HH, fos. 4–7, printed in the Appendix; also, Le Faye, 'Tom Lefroy and Jane Austen', *Jane Austen Society Report* (1985), 336–8, for Anna Lefroy's version; and R. W. Chapman, *Jane Austen: Facts and Problems* (1948), 58, for extracts from T. E. P. Lefroy's communication to JEAL.)

49 *To the Memory of Mrs. Lefroy*: for details of Mrs Anne Lefroy, see note to p. 44 above. An account of the accident which killed her can be found in

Reminiscences of Caroline Austen, ed. Deirdre Le Faye (1986), 6–7. Caroline compiled these reminiscences in the early 1870s, after the publication of her brother's *Memoir*. She got her account of the accident, which occurred in 1804, the year before she was born, from her mother Mary Lloyd Austen. JA's poem, composed in 1808, to commemorate what she describes in stanza 11 as 'this connection in our earthly date' (the fact that her friend died on JA's birthday), was the first of her works to be published after the six novels. It was included in Sir John Henry Lefroy's *Notes and Documents relating to the Family of Loffroy . . . by a cadet* (1868), 117–18. The manuscript (apparently in JA's hand) of the version held by the Lefroy family is now in Winchester Cathedral Library (Gilson, M124 and M1343). This version has thirteen stanzas, two more than JEAL prints in the *Memoir*. For the fuller version, see *Catharine and Other Writings*, ed. Margaret Anne Doody and Douglas Murray (1993), 238–40. The version printed by R. W. Chapman in *Minor Works*, 440–2, derives from that in the *Memoir* rather than from one of the manuscripts, and prints the two missing stanzas as an appendix rather than inserting them in their appropriate place, as stanzas 4 and 5. According to David Gilson, 'Jane Austen's Verses', *Book Collector*, 33 (1984), 25–8, there are four known manuscripts.

50 *reconcile herself to the change*: biographers have speculated much about this incident in JA's life and how it affected her. JEAL's informant was Caroline Austen, who got the details from their mother, Mary Lloyd Austen, who 'was present' when the news of the move to Bath was broken to Jane in November 1800. Caroline wrote to her brother: 'My Mother who was present said my Aunt Jane was greatly distressed' (transcript of Caroline's letter, 1 April [1869?], NPG, RWC/HH, fos. 4–7, included in the Appendix). Another family account, deriving from Fanny Caroline Lefroy, Anna Lefroy's daughter, tells how JA 'fainted away' when told of the imminent departure. It is this version which is recorded in the authorized family biography of the next generation (*Life & Letters*, 155–6), where the authors add, on no discernible grounds, that Cassandra's destruction of her sister's letters for the period 30 November 1800 to 3 January 1801 'was a proof of their emotional interest'. See the Introduction for further consideration of this episode.

not to expect too much from them: this is Caroline Austen's view as expressed in correspondence with her brother as well as in her own memoir, *MAJA*: 'There is nothing in those letters which *I* have seen that would be acceptable to the public . . . they detailed chiefly home and family events' (p. 173, in this collection). Their half-sister Anna Lefroy writes vaguely, 'Letters may have been preserved' (*RAJ*, 162 also printed here). The *Memoir* makes use (much expanded in Ed.2) of the letters that these three, James Austen's children, had from their aunt to themselves. It draws on the further letters which Caroline inherited after Cassandra's death in 1845 and on those inherited in turn by Charles Austen's eldest daughter Cassy Esten. JEAL does not seem to have had access to the bulk of his aunt's letters to Cassandra, though he knew from Caroline of their existence and dissemination as legacies. The largest cache, in Fanny, Lady Knatchbull's possession, was not available for inspection during the writing of the *Memoir* and was only published after her death by her son, as *Letters of Jane Austen*, ed. Edward, Lord Brabourne (2 vols., 1884). Hence JEAL's statement at p. 65—'I have no letters of my aunt, nor any other record of her, during her four years' residence at Southampton'—can be explained by the fact that the letters for that period (nos. 49–67 in *Letters*) went to Lady Knatchbull in the post-1845 division.

51 *The two following letters . . . written in November 1800*: these, amounting to over six pages, are both added in Ed.2. Ed.1 reads at this point: 'Her letters scarcely ever have the date of the year, and are never signed with her Christian name at full length. [new paragraph] The following letters must have been written in 1801, after the removal of the family from Steventon had been decided on, but before it took place.' Ed.1, then, has only the two short extracts of naval news from letters to Cassandra of 11 February and 26–7 May 1801.

Steventon, Saturday evening, Nov. 8th.: no. 25, in *Letters*, bequeathed by Cassandra to Caroline Austen in 1845. A comparison between the version in the *Memoir* and in *Letters*, 54–8, shows that JEAL repunctuated extensively, smoothed out grammatical awkwardnesses, and corrected JA's eccentric spellings. He also edited matter as well as style, silently omitting substantial sections of domestic detail and family gossip (e.g. the section in *Letters*, 56). This is his consistent policy with the letters he includes in the *Memoir*, and it extends elsewhere to the substitution of initials for full names and the suppression of details which he considers still likely to embarrass the families of those to whom JA makes occasional indiscreet or humorous reference. All further letters quoted by JEAL will be supplied with the relevant reference to the version in *Letters*, with which comparison should be made. I will note below only the most salient of JEAL's alterations or omissions.

Charlotte Graham . . . Harriet Bailey: Lady Georgiana Charlotte Graham, eldest daughter of the third Duke of Montrose (*Letters*, 529).

Mr. Chute's frank: William John Chute (1757–1824), Member of Parliament for Hampshire 1790–1806 and 1807–20 (*Letters*, 507). By an Act of 1763, MPs were entitled to free postage (expensive at this time) and often extended their frank to friends, by writing the address and date in their own hand.

one constant table: JA wrote 'our constant Table' (*Letters*, 55).

52 *Pembroke*: a small four-legged table with hinged flaps.

chiffonniere: a small cupboard with drawers.

Earle Harwood: (1773–1811), second son of John and Anne Harwood, the

Austens' neighbours at Deane House. He had joined the Royal Marines and in 1797 married Sarah Scott, 'a girl of apparently doubtful reputation' (*Letters*, 533).

52 *Marcau*: JA wrote 'Marcou' (*Letters*, 55). The islands of St Marcouf off the French coast at Normandy, then occupied by British forces.

53 *Mr. Heathcote*: See JEAL's note at p. 55.

Lord Portsmouth's ball: see JEAL's note at p. 54.

Sweep: the curved drive leading to the house.

maple: JA wrote 'Maypole', which makes better sense (*Letters*, 57).

Miss Lloyd: Martha Lloyd (1765–1843), eldest daughter of the Revd Nowis (or Noyes) Lloyd and his wife, and a close friend of the Austens. She became part of their household in 1805, living with them at Bath, Southampton, and Chawton. In 1828 she married JA's brother Frank as his second wife. The letter to Martha Lloyd is no. 26 in *Letters*, and it recapitulates many of the details in that to Cassandra of four days earlier. It remained in Frank Austen's possession after Martha's death and was given by him to an autograph hunter, Eliza Susan Quincy, of Boston, Mass., in 1852. She supplied JEAL with a copy for Ed.2 of the *Memoir*. In Chapter 9 below, JEAL includes under 'Opinions of American Readers' the letter from Susan Quincy to Frank Austen which elicited the sending of JA's letter to Martha to America. (See M. A. DeWolfe Howe, 'A Jane Austen Letter With Other "Janeana" From an Old Book of Autographs', *Yale Review*, 15 (1925–6), 319–35, for fuller details of the correspondence between Frank Austen and Susan Quincy. In sending the autograph, Frank wrote: 'I scarcely need observe that there never was the remotest idea of its being published' (ibid. 322). See, too, Farnell Parsons, 'The Quincys and the Austens: A Cordial Connection', *Jane Austen Society Report* (2000), 49–51.)

54 *Ibthorp*: JA writes here and elsewhere Ibthrop (*Letters*, 58), giving some indication of the pronunciation. It was Martha's home until 1805, and Cassandra and Jane were frequent guests there.

Manydown: the home of other close friends, the Bigg-Wither family, at Wootton St Lawrence, six miles from Steventon. Catherine and Alethea Bigg were particular friends of JA, and their younger brother Harris Bigg-Wither was to propose to her in 1802 (see note to p. 29 above).

55 *Henry's History of England*: Robert Henry, *History of Great Britain* (6 vols., 1771–93).

desultory: JA wrote 'disultary' (*Letters*, 59).

56 *battle of Trafalgar*: October 1805, when the British fleet under Lord Nelson defeated the French and Spanish. Frank Austen wrote to his fiancée, Mary Gibson, of his disappointment at missing the action (*Sailor Brothers*, 155).

My Dear Cassandra: written from Manydown, the home of JA's friends Catherine and Alethea Bigg, 11 February 1801. This is an extract only from a longer letter, for which see no. 34 in *Letters*. The autograph letter was bequeathed by Cassandra to Charles Austen whose daughter Cassy Esten made it available to JEAL. Cassandra was at the time of its writing staying in London with Henry and Eliza Austen, and JA is sending the latest news of Frank and Charles, both on recent active service in the Mediterranean, Charles on HMS *Endymion* and Frank now on his way home after distinguished action as commanding officer of HMS *Petrel*.

Sir Ralph Abercrombie: General Sir Ralph Abercromby (1734–1801), appointed in 1801 to command British troops in the Mediterranean.

jolly and affable: JA wrote 'fat, jolly & affable' (*Letters*, 80).

while Steventon is ours: the Austens left Steventon in May 1801, before which Edward, Frank, and Charles all made farewell visits to their old home (*Life & Letters*, 164).

later in the same year: a short extract from a much longer letter to Cassandra, written from Bath, 26–7 May 1801 (no. 38 in *Letters*). Again, JEAL was indebted to Charles's daughter Cassy Esten for it.

privateer: an armed vessel, owned and officered by private persons, but with a government commission to act against hostile nations.

gold chains and topaze crosses for us: according to Le Faye, the two topaz crosses remained with Letter 38 as it descended through Charles Austen's family and later into the auction rooms (*Letters*, 379, n. 4). (See G. H. Tucker, 'Jane Austen's Topaz Cross', *Jane Austen Society Report* (1978), 76–7.) The gift provided JA with the idea for the 'very pretty amber cross' which William Price brought from Sicily for his sister Fanny in *MP*, ch. 26. Charles Austen's experiences as a midshipman in the West Indies and his adventurous early career (*Sailor Brothers*, 21–2) are generally considered to be the originals for William Price.

58 *afterwards in Green Park Buildings*: the Austens arrived in Bath in May 1801, when they took the lease on No. 4 Sydney Place (not Terrace as JEAL writes), though they did not move in until the autumn, spending the intervening months with the Leigh Perrots (see notes below) or on holiday on the Devonshire coast and, for a short time, back in Steventon. They moved to 3 Green Park Buildings in October 1804 (*Fam. Rec.*, 117–20; 126).

Mr. Leigh Perrot: Mrs Austen's brother (see note to p. 37 above). He now divided his time between Scarlets, his Berkshire estate, and Bath, where he sought treatment for chronic gout. At this time he and his wife were renting 1 Paragon Buildings, Bath. On the death of Mrs Leigh Perrot in 1836 JEAL inherited Scarlets, with the proviso that he take the name of Leigh in addition to Austen.

Northleigh: Northleach in Ed.1. It was this Oxfordshire estate, inherited in 1751 (when he added Perrot to his name), which Mr Leigh Perrot sold to buy Scarlets.

59 *a niece of Sir Montague Cholmeley*: Jane Cholmeley (1744–1836), and according to *Life & Letters*, 134, he was her cousin. As Mrs Leigh Perrot she was another of JA's more colourful relations. In 1799 she was charged with shoplifting—stealing lace from a shop in Bath—and committed to Ilchester Gaol, facing the death sentence or, more likely, transportation, if convicted. Her trial took place in March 1800, when she was acquitted, though her innocence has subsequently been questioned. In *Life & Letters*, the first family biography to mention the incident, W. and R. A. Austen-Leigh include material which suggests that Mrs Austen offered to send either Jane or Cassandra to stay with their aunt while in gaol. The offer was declined, but they conclude with a melodramatic flourish: 'So Cassandra and Jane just escaped a residence in gaol and contact with criminals' (p. 135). None of these exciting events, occurring only a year before the Austens moved to Bath, finds its way into JEAL's account, though they must have continued to hang in the air and to affect the family's social standing in the city. (See *Fam. Rec.*, 106–10; and David Gilson's Introduction to the recent reprint of Sir F. D. MacKinnon, *Grand Larceny, Being the Trial of Jane Leigh Perrot, Aunt of Jane Austen* (1937); repr. in *Jane Austen: Family History* (5 vols., 1995); vols. not numbered.)

the Master of Balliol: the Revd Dr Theophilus Leigh (1693–1785), mentioned at pp. 11–13 above. For a possible example of Mr Leigh Perrot's skill with epigrams, see p. 37 and note above.

The unfinished story . . . residence in Bath: a sentence added in Ed.2, which prints for the first time *The Watsons* (so-called by JEAL 'for the sake of having a title by which to designate it') from the manuscript in Caroline Austen's possession. In Ed.1 the opening sentence of this paragraph reads: 'She does not appear to have had any work in hand during her four years' residence at Bath . . . ', suppressing at this time knowledge of the unfinished story.

fall of Louisa Musgrove: an incident in JA's last completed novel, *P*, ch. 12. The Cobb is the large, raised, stone breakwater, broad enough for walking on, skirting the harbour at Lyme Regis in Dorset.

then removed to Southampton: the time-scale was less compressed than JEAL suggests. The Revd George Austen died 21 January 1805; Mrs Austen and her daughters moved in March to No. 25 Gay Street, Bath; but they did not leave Bath finally until July 1806 or take lodgings in Southampton until October of that year, when they set up home with the newly married Frank Austen.

those four years: the period spent in Bath—May 1801 to July 1806—was five and not four years; but it was an unsettled time in JA's life, with much travelling. *Letters*, nos. 35–48, are recorded as belonging to this period—more than JEAL knew of, but still not many. Biographers have variously interpreted these unstable years: that they contributed to a conjectured depression which may have prevented JA from building on the intense fictional creativity of the later 1790s and may also have inclined Cassandra to destroy its evidence in letters; and that, on the contrary, these years propelled JA into a social whirl and a life of external stimulus which itself left no time for writing. The real point is that we simply do not know. (Cf., for instance, the divergent views of two recent biographers, Tomalin, *Jane Austen*, 173–5, and Nokes, *Jane Austen*, 350–2.)

Extract from a letter . . . to her Sister: no. 39 in *Letters*; bequeathed by Cassandra to Charles Austen's family. The extract is heavily and silently edited, omitting family news and gossip and some topics and expressions, presumably in the interests of good taste. For example, of the family housekeeping at Lyme, JEAL prints: '[I] keep everything as it was under your administration', but JA wrote: '[I] give the Cook physic, which she throws off her Stomach. I forget whether she used to do this, under your administration.'

not seeing the Royal Family: George III, the Duke of Gloucester, and other members of the royal family were staying at Weymouth in September 1804 at the same time as Cassandra Austen.

60 *offices*: the part of a house in which the domestic work was carried on—kitchen, pantries, dairy, etc.

But do not mention: JA wrote 'But I do not mention' (*Letters*, 94).

61 *Letter from Jane Austen . . . Cassandra*: added in Ed.2. The letter is no. 43 in *Letters*, and was probably bequeathed by Cassandra to Caroline Austen. It is again heavily edited.

riding-house . . . Miss Lefroy's performance: 'There were two riding-houses (i.e. riding-schools combined with livery stables) in Bath'; Miss Lefroy here is 'Lucy, now Mrs Henry Rice' (*Letters*, 382, n. 2).

62 *affidavits*: literally, a written declaration or oath; but JA is referring jokingly to visiting-cards.

as the exit we have witnessed: Mrs Lloyd died at Ibthorpe on 16 April 1805. Her daughter Mary, referred to later in this letter, had married James Austen as his second wife in 1797. Her eldest daughter Martha now joined forces with JA, Cassandra, and Mrs Austen. Presumably the 'peaceful and easy' end recently witnessed was that of JA's father on 21 January 1805.

hack postchaise: an enclosed four-wheeled carriage, hired from stage to stage of a journey.

63 *rambles . . . last summer*: when the Austens, with Henry and Eliza Austen, visited Lyme Regis.

From the same to the same: extracts from a long letter, written over several days from the lodgings in Gay Street, Bath, temporarily occupied by JA and her mother, to Cassandra then on an extended visit to Martha Lloyd at Ibthorpe. It is no. 44 in *Letters*, where it is dated Sunday 21–Tuesday

23 April 1805. The autograph was bequeathed by Cassandra to Charles Austen's family, on the strength of its references to Charles's services to Lord Balgonie, at that time a naval officer. Balgonie's parents were the seventh Earl of Leven and his wife. Several items of interest to Austen biographers are omitted from the extracts JEAL presents: in particular, JA's reference to the Austens' intention of joining households with Martha Lloyd whose mother had just died ('I am quite of your opinion as to the folly of concealing any longer our intended Partnership with Martha, & whenever there has of late been an enquiry on the subject I have always been sincere; & I have sent word of it to the Mediterranean in a letter to Frank.—None of *our* nearest connections I think will be unprepared for it; & I do not know how to suppose that Martha's have not foreseen it', *Letters*, 105); and her evident weariness at Bath society ('I shall be glad when it is over, & hope to have no necessity for having so many dear friends at once again', ibid. 106).

63 *Mrs. Stent*: See JEAL's note at p. 55.

a Mr.L., Miss B.: a misreading of the original, which has 'a M[r] & Miss B', though here and throughout the letter JA writes in full the names that JEAL signals by initials only. In this case, 'B' is 'Bendish'. See *Letters*, 103–6.

64 *Miss A.*: presumably the Miss Armstrong met at Lyme Regis during the previous summer and whose mother darned stockings during JA's visit (see p. 60 above). In Bath society, the connection is clearly less desirable.

I have been: JA wrote 'that we have been' (*Letters*, 105).

Lady Roden: Juliana Anne, Lady Roden, an aquaintance or connection, either through Hampshire society or the Navy (*Letters*, 383, n. 6).

to say himself what was untrue: JA wrote 'tell a lie himself' (*Letters*, 105).

65 *the Rev. George Leigh Cooke*: (1779–1853). His father had married JA's mother's first cousin and was JA's godfather.

Before the end of 1805 . . . Southampton: JEAL's dates are wrong here, with the result that he overestimates the length of the Austens' time in Southampton: it was closer to two and a half than four years. They moved there in October 1806, taking a lease on the house in Castle Square in February 1807. Here Mrs Austen, Cassandra, Jane, and Martha Lloyd remained until spring 1809, sharing for much of that time with Frank and his new wife.

I have no letters . . . at Southampton: see note to p. 50 above.

66 *I will record them*: Le Faye (*Fam. Rec.*, 149) conjectures a date of September 1808, when James Austen and his family visited Southampton, for JEAL's childhood memories. He would have been almost 10 years old.

The well-appointed . . . Embark his royalty: Shakespeare, *King Henry V*, III. Chorus, 4–5.

second Marquis . . . in the title: John Henry Petty (1765–1809), second

Marquis of Lansdowne, who bought the old ruined castle within Southampton city walls in 1804, enlarging it into a Gothic fantasy. The title and estates passed subsequently to Lord Henry Petty-Fitzmaurice (1780–1863), moderate Whig politician (for whom, see note to p. 113 below).

phaeton: an open, four-wheeled carriage.

67 *'like the baseless fabric of a vision'*: Shakespeare, *The Tempest*, IV. i, 151.

In 1809: the offer coincided with the death of Edward Austen's (he was only 'Knight' from 1812) wife, Elizabeth, on 10 October 1808, after giving birth to their eleventh child. The earliest mention of the move occurs in JA's letter of 24–5 October to Cassandra, now at Godmersham comforting Edward (*Letters*, 152). Anna Lefroy, more critical in this matter than her half-sister Caroline, thought Edward should have done more for his mother and sisters (*Fam. Rec.*, 155); and in her memories of JA she hints at the shortcomings of Edward's wife with regard to the Austens (see *RAJ*). The move to the house at Chawton (according to Caroline it was called 'Chawton Cottage' only 'in later years' (*MAJA*, 166)) occurred in July 1809.

Miss Lloyd: Martha Lloyd; see notes to pp. 53 and 63 above.

only a sojourner in a strange land: Exodus, 2: 22.

69 *A good-sized entrance . . . which supported it were not large*: apart from the clause 'and was capable of receiving other members of the family as frequent visitors', this section describing Chawton Cottage was added in Ed.2. As early as 20 November 1808 JA is writing to Cassandra of its 'six Bedchambers' and 'Garrets for Storeplaces' (*Letters*, 153); and in her letter in verse from Chawton on 26 July 1809, congratulating Frank on the birth of his son, she describes in passing the renovations to 'rooms concise' and 'rooms distended' (*Letters*, 178). This added section in Ed.2 owes much to Caroline Austen's memories, which JEAL absorbs almost verbatim (cf. *MAJA*, 167–8, in this collection). Caroline had spent considerable periods of her childhood at Chawton.

Cowper's unattractive house . . . Southey's edition of his works: *The Works of William Cowper, with a Life of the Author*, ed. Robert Southey, were issued in 15 volumes (1835–7), and included an engraved plate in volume 1 of Cowper's house in the village of Olney, Buckinghamshire.

The building indeed still stands: unlike Steventon rectory, pulled down in 1824. The Jane Austen Memorial Trust purchased Chawton Cottage in 1947 and they continue to administer it as a museum.

70 *Description of JA's person . . . and tastes*: JEAL draws heavily in this chapter on the memories of his sister Caroline and half-sister Anna, written out in 1867 and 1864, respectively, though not published until 1952 and 1988.

likeness prefixed to this volume has been taken: Cassandra's sketch, a lightly executed pencil-and-watercolour portrait, is the only authentic representation known to exist. It is dated *c.*1810, soon after the move to Chawton, and is held in the National Portrait Gallery, London. The steel-engraved portrait, the *Memoir*'s frontispiece, is taken from a Victorian likeness, executed by a Mr Andrews of Maidenhead, after Cassandra's original. The differences between the two are marked and provide the clearest indication of JEAL's purpose with regard to the selective account of his aunt that he chose to make public. He commissioned Andrews's enhancement of Cassandra's portrait and sanctioned the transformation of its sharp-faced, unsmiling original into something altogether softer and more compliant. Ed.2 was first issued without the portrait, but the reference to it at this point in the text led to enquiries for it, and it was included in later printings.

linger in my memory: compare with this the Revd Fulwar William Fowle's memory of hearing JA sing and play the piano: 'I well remember her singing—& "The yellow haired Laddie" made an impression upon me, which more than half a century has had no power to efface,' in a letter of 9 January 1870, acknowledging a copy of the *Memoir*. JEAL and Caroline were his cousins. For a fuller extract, see the Appendix (HRO, MS 23/M93/66/2/1). JA's letter of 27–8 December 1808 records her plan to have a piano when they move to Chawton, 'Yes, yes, we *will* have a Pianoforte, as good a one as can be got for 30 Guineas—& I will practise country dances, that we may have some amusement for our nephews & neices, when we have the pleasure of their company' (*Letters*, 161). There are music manuscript notebooks held by the Jane Austen Memorial Trust at Chawton Cottage containing music written out by JA.

knew something of Italian: JEAL owed this information to Anna Lefroy, in her letter of 16 April [1869?] (see the Appendix, p. 183).

71 *Goldsmith, Hume, and Robertson*: Oliver Goldsmith's *History of England* (4 vols., 1771) was in its full and its abridged form of 1774 his most successful history, and a popular schoolroom text. The unabridged 1771 edition is recorded among the books JA is known to have read, and a family copy, with the signature 'James Austen, Steventon', has been preserved in the family and includes marginal comments in JA's hand. David Hume, *The History of England* (6 vols., 1759–62), the front free endpaper of vol. 1 bearing the inscription 'Jane Austen 1797' (perhaps a gift from her uncle James Leigh Perrot), descended to JEAL and now has his bookplate. (see David Gilson, 'Jane Austen's Books', *Book Collector*, 23 (1974), 27–39). William Robertson was the author of many histories, including *History of Scotland* (2 vols., 1759).

his grandmother Mary: in her early spoof 'History of England from the reign of Henry the 4th to the death of Charles the 1st. By a partial, prejudiced, and ignorant Historian', written out according to her own dating in November 1791, when she was not quite 16, JA inverted the conventionally approved account of the past (as the gradual, Whiggish progress towards liberty and the defeat of Stuart absolutism) by setting up history as a pro-Stuart tragedy. Its climax and conclusion is the execution of Charles I in 1649, and its heroine is his grandmother Mary, Queen of Scots, 'one of the first Characters in the World', also executed, in 1587. (See 'The History of England', in *Catharine and Other Writings*, ed. Doody and Murray, 136; and Christopher Kent, 'Learning History with, and from, Jane Austen', in *Jane Austen's Beginnings*, 59–72.) JA's contrasted presentation of Mary and Elizabeth I, the one vulnerable, beautiful, and innocent, the other unattractive and severe, resembles that in Sophia Lee's *The Recess, or A Tale of Other Times* (1783–5). JEAL is unnecessarily po-faced in accounting for his aunt's hilarious exercise in political uncorrectness. In *MAJA*, his sister Caroline presents the same detail with less qualification.

the 'Spectator' downwards: see note to p. 16 above. In *MP*, ch. 16, Samuel Johnson's periodical papers, under the general title of *The Idler* (1758–60), are described as among the heroine Fanny Price's precious collection of books.

Richardson's works . . . living friends: Henry Austen in his 'Biographical Notice' (1818) recorded that his sister's 'favourite moral writers were Johnson in prose, and Cowper in verse', while Richardson, and particularly his last novel *Sir Charles Grandison*, ranked highest with her for fiction. JA's juvenilia are peppered with references to Richardson's novels; in 'Jack and Alice', in *Volume the First*, *Grandison*'s models of male and female perfection offer a precise point of departure for the parody. In 1977 a manuscript play 'Sir Charles Grandison', previously attributed to Anna Lefroy, though transcribed in JA's hand, was reassigned to JA. See *Jane Austen's 'Sir Charles Grandison'*, ed. Brian Southam (1980). In *Grandison*, members of the aristocracy (Lady L., Lady G.) are referred to by initials only, a convention of the novel-in-letters designed to suggest the authenticity of what was recorded and the consequent need to hide 'real' identities. Lady L. and Lady G. are Sir Charles's two sisters; the younger, Charlotte, marries Lord G. on April 11 (vol. 4, letter 16), while Caroline, the elder sister, is married to the Earl of L., an event narrated retrospectively at vol. 2, letter 25. The cedar parlour is at Selby House, one of the idealized domestic settings of the novel.

Johnson in prose . . . stood high: JEAL echoes his uncle Henry Austen's account (see previous note). Samuel Johnson is referred to as 'my dear Dr Johnson' in *Letters*, 121, while Fanny Price reads *The Idler* (see note above). George Crabbe's metrical *Tales* (1812) are among Fanny Price's reading (*MP*, ch. 16), and her name may be taken from Crabbe's earlier poem *The Parish Register* (1807), a moralistic study of various levels of village life, in which Fanny Price is a 'lovely' and 'chaste' young girl. William Cowper (see notes to pp. 37 and 69) is much quoted in JA's novels—by Marianne Dashwood, in *S&S*, ch. 3, where his 'beautiful lines . . . have frequently almost driven me wild'; and by Fanny Price, in *MP*, chs. 6 and 45; JA mentions her father reading 'Cowper to us in the evening', in *Letters*, 27.

71 *a sister novelist*: a reference to Fanny Burney, for whom see note to p. 20 above.

fancy being Mrs. Crabbe: see JA's letter to Cassandra, 21 October 1813: 'No; I have never seen the death of Mrs Crabbe. I have only just been making out from one of his prefaces that he probably was married. It is almost ridiculous. Poor woman! I will comfort *him* as well as I can, but I do not undertake to be good to her children' (*Letters*, 243). Sarah Crabbe had died on 21 September 1813. On her recent stay in London (September 1813) JA had joked about hoping to catch sight of Crabbe, known to be there too.

72 *Scott's poetry . . . merits of 'Waverley'*: Walter Scott (1771–1832), poet and novelist. Scott's medievalized verse tales were huge bestsellers between 1805 and 1815, setting a fashion for historical romance and extravagant adventure which would be continued in his novels, the first of which was *Waverley*, appearing in 1814, the same year as *MP*. In *MP*, ch. 9, Fanny Price quotes from Scott's poem *The Lay of the Last Minstrel* (1805), and in *P*, ch. 11, Anne Elliot and Captain Benwick argue the relative merits of Scott's two most successful poems, *Marmion* (1808) and *The Lady of the Lake* (1810). In both instances, JA uses an enthusiasm for Scott's poetry to signal the sensitivity and melancholy romanticism of the characters, and, more critically, to suggest their disinclination to reality. JA in fact lived to see five of Scott's novels published, not three: *Waverley* (1814), *Guy Mannering* (1815), *The Antiquary* (1816), *The Black Dwarf* (1816), and *Old Mortality* (1816), the last two appearing together as *Tales of My Landlord*. In 1816 Scott provided JA with her first major critical appraisal when he reviewed *E* for the *Quarterly Review* (see Ch. 8 below). From her letter to JEAL of 16–17 December 1816, it is clear that JA has read *The Antiquary* (*Letters*, 323).

no business to write novels: an extract from a letter of 28 September 1814, to Anna Austen (she became Lefroy in the November), no. 108 in *Letters*. Unlike his poetry, Scott's novels were published anonymously; hence JA's ready attribution of *Waverley* to him is interesting. How did she know? The novel appeared in a first edition in July 1814 and quickly went through three more editions before the end of the year. A notice of publication in the *Edinburgh Review*, 23 (Sept. 1814), 509, listed *MP* and *Waverley* together, which may possibly account for JA's jealous reference in this letter.

Mrs. ——'s: JA wrote 'Mrs West's Alicia de Lacy' (*Letters*, 277). The novelist was Jane West (1758–1852), a moral and conservative writer, and this her latest work was also published in 1814 and listed in the same notice in the *Edinburgh Review* as *Waverley* and *MP*.

Miss Edgeworth's, E.'s, and my own: JA wrote: 'Miss Edgeworth's, Yours & my own' (*Letters*, 278). The alteration is significant. All three of James Austen's children tried their hand at writing novels and turned to their aunt for advice. JEAL, who was called Edward in the family, is not likely to have made this alteration as a flattering reference to himself, but his half-sister Anna in copying her letter from JA for him to use in the *Memoir* may well have considered this a tactful or a modest change. Miss Edgeworth is Maria Edgeworth (1768–1849), Irish novelist and educational writer, much admired by JA. Her novel *Belinda* (1801) is one of the works described in the narrator's defence of the novel as a literary form in *NA*, ch. 5: 'only some work in which the greatest powers of the mind are displayed, in which the most thorough knowledge of human nature, the happiest delineation of its varieties, the liveliest effusions of wit and humour are conveyed to the world in the best chosen language.'

two of her nieces. One says: JEAL's half-sister Anna and his sister Caroline. The first two extracts are from Caroline's account (see *MAJA*, in this collection, where it appears with slight verbal differences).

two of her other nieces: named in Caroline's account as 'Mary Jane and Cassy' (*MAJA*, 174)—that is, Frank Austen's daughter Mary Jane (1807–36), and Charles's daughter Cassandra Esten (1808–97). This second extract from Caroline's account was added by JEAL to his *Memoir* in Ed.2.

73 *of another niece*: extracted from Anna Lefroy's account, but heavily edited, removing mention of the preference for Cassandra over JA in the intellectually insipid atmosphere of Godmersham Park, Edward Austen Knight's home. (See the fuller account in *RAJ* in this collection.)

A nephew of hers: identified by Deirdre Le Faye as Frank Austen's second son, Henry Edgar Austen (1811–54), who was only 6 years old when JA died ('Jane Austen's Nephew—A Re-identification', *Notes and Queries*, 235 (1990), 414–15). JEAL is at this point paraphrasing something recorded by his sister Caroline (*MAJA*, 170). The section 'A nephew of hers . . . her enlivening influence' was added in Ed.2.

quizzed: 'to quizz' is 'to make fun of'. 'She never abused . . . less prevalent now than it was then', was added in Ed.2.

74 *Mr. Gell to Miss Gill, of Eastbourne*: JEAL is the first to publish this verse. There are at least two surviving manuscripts (David Gilson, 'Jane Austen's Verse', *Book Collector*, 33 (1984), 28–9). In *Memoir* Ed.1 it was also reproduced as an apparently autograph manuscript facsimile, where it appears as two stanzas, with each of the four printed lines forming two short lines. In the manuscript version, 'eyes' and 'ease' are thus written out with the consequent loss of some of the playful punning of JEAL's printed 'iis' and 'ees'. *Minor Works*, 444, appears to base its text on this manuscript version. The illustration from Ed.1 is reproduced in this edition at p. 78.

On the Marriage . . . in her Youth: JA mentions this verse in a letter of 29 November 1812, jokingly referring to her brother James's 'great improvement' to it (*Letters*, 196–7). No surviving manuscript is presently known, and Chapman prints the version from the *Memoir* as the most authoritative text in *Minor Works*, 444. But a variant text suggests that two versions were in circulation in the family. In the other version:

> Camilla good humoured & merry & small
> For a Husband it happened was at her last stake;
> & having in vain danced at many a ball
> Is now very happy to Jump at a Wake.

This version is taken from the diary, now in Hampshire Record Office, of Stephen Terry, father-in-law to Anna Lefroy's fourth daughter Georgiana (printed in *Letters*, 409, n. 7). It is possible that James Austen's improvements included the changes, for discretion's sake, to 'Maria' and the more flattering 'handsome, and tall'. If so, his children kept both versions alive—one for private enjoyment and the other perhaps for more public circulation. The occasion of the verse was the engagement of Urania Wallop (her mother was Camilla) to the elderly Revd Henry Wake. The title is supplied in the *Memoir*.

at the play last night . . . in Isabella: an extract from a letter to Anna Lefroy, 29 November 1814 (no. 112 in *Letters*). JA is at this time staying in London at her brother Henry's. The play was David Garrick's *Isabella; or the Fatal Marriage* (1776).

'So, Miss B. is actually married . . . in print': again, from a scrap of an undated letter to Anna Lefroy, of February or March 1815 (no. 118 in *Letters*).

75 *In measured verse I'll now rehearse*: no manuscript of these verses is known, and all other printings derive from JEAL's. Caroline suggested in her letter of 1 April [1869?] (see the Appendix, p. 185) that her brother include the poem by way of 'stuffing', as a harmless piece unlikely to embarrass the family or compromise their aunt's mature reputation. It is taken to be written for Anna Austen (later Lefroy) and to reflect the 'mercurial and excitable' aspects of her character in youth (*Life & Letters*, 241). As such, the dating within the family is closer to 1810 than the 15 July 1817 (three days before she died) confidently but inexplicably attached to it by Doody and Murray in *Catharine and Other Writings*, 233. The geography of the poem—'Ontario's lake', in fact the smallest of the five Great Lakes, 'Niagara's Fall', and 'transatlantic groves' (groves beyond the Atlantic)—represents a popular, even hackneyed, setting for romantic adventure in the late eighteenth and early nineteenth centuries. See, for example, Charlotte Smith, *The Old Manor House* (1793) and Mary Brunton, *Self-Control* (1810), to which JA makes amused reference in a letter to Cassandra: 'I am looking over Self Control again . . . an excellently-meant, elegantly-written Work, without anything of Nature

or Probability in it. I declare I do not know whether Laura's passage down the American River, is not the most natural, possible, every-day thing she ever does' (*Letters*, 234).

76 *a niece . . . amusing herself by attempting a novel*: again, the reference is to JA's correspondence with Anna Lefroy, at this time still Anna Austen, who was writing a novel under the title 'Which is the Heroine?' In her manuscript 'Family History' (written *c.*1880–5), Anna's daughter Fanny Caroline Lefroy, looking back from old age to events before her own life, records of her mother's early attempt at fiction: 'With no Aunt Jane to read, to critic[i]se and to encourage, it was no wonder the M.S. every word of which was so full of her, remained untouched. Her sympathy which had made the great charm of the occupation was gone and the sense of the loss made it painful to write. The story was laid by for years and then one day in a fit of despondency burnt. I remember sitting on the rug and watching its destruction amused with the flame and the sparks which kept breaking out in the blackened paper. In later years when I expressed my sorrow that she had destroyed it, she said she could never have borne to finish it. but incomplete as it was Jane Austen's criticisms would have made it valuable' (HRO, MS 23M93/85/2/unpaginated). Although this early attempt was destroyed, Anna Lefroy subsequently published a novella, *Mary Hamilton*, in the *Literary Souvenir* for 1833 and two slight works for children—*The Winter's Tale* (1841) and *Springtide* (1842); she also attempted and later abandoned the completion of JA's unfinished novel *Sanditon*.

Chawton, Aug. 10, 1814: extract from a much longer letter full of critical comment and advice (no. 104 in *Letters*), written between 10 and 18 August. This portion is from 18 August.

Sept. 9: extract from a much longer letter, written 9–18 September 1814 (no. 107 in *Letters*).

Sept. 28: extract from a longer letter (no. 108 in *Letters*), already quoted from at p. 72.

77 *Hans Place (Nov. 1814)*: again to Anna, within the last few weeks married to Ben Lefroy—hence the appositeness of the joke about suitors being in love with aunts. JA writes from her brother Henry's London address (no. 113 in *Letters*).

your husband: JA wrote 'Ben' (*Letters*, 284).

spilikins . . . cup and ball: like the reference below to the neat appearance of her letters and her sewing, these examples of JA's dexterity are from Caroline Austen's recollections (*MAJA*, 171). In the game of spilikins, thin slips of wood were thrown in a heap and the player had to pull them off one at a time without disturbing the rest. In the game of cup and ball, the ball was attached by cord to a stick having a cup at one end and a spike at the other. The aim was to toss the ball in the air and catch it either in the cup or (more difficult) on the spike.

specimen of her . . . handwriting is here given: at this point in Ed.1 JEAL included a lithographic facsimile of the autograph manuscript of the verses on Mr Gell and Miss Gill. This was replaced in Ed.2 with the last few lines and signature of a letter to Anna Lefroy (*Letters*, no. 112), facing the opening of ch. 3. Here as elsewhere I have restored the Ed.1 illustration.

satin stitch: an embroidery stitch, repeated in parallel lines to give a satiny appearance.

79 *housewife*: JA gave the 'housewife' to her friend Mary Lloyd in January 1792 when the family moved from Deane parsonage to Ibthorp. Mary did not become Jane's sister-in-law until 1797. A 'housewife' was a cloth sewing case for needles, pins, thread, etc., and was a common home-made gift between women friends. 'Minikin' needles, as the word suggests, would be very small. The accompanying poem is dated 'Jan:ry 1792'. For a description of the manuscript and its slight variants from the text printed by JEAL, see David Gilson, 'Jane Austen's Verses', *Book Collector*, 33 (1984), 30. Both bag and manuscript are still in the Austen-Leigh family.

Two of her nieces were grown up . . . one of them was married: James Austen's elder daughter Anna was 24 and married since November 1814 at the time of JA's death in July 1817. Caroline, his younger daughter, and JEAL's other chief assistant in the *Memoir*, was only 12. But Fanny Knight, Edward Austen Knight's eldest child, a few months older than Anna, was also 24 and as yet unmarried. As Lady Knatchbull (she married Sir Edward Knatchbull in 1820), she inherited the bulk of JA's letters to her sister Cassandra.

her religious principles: it was her brother Henry Austen who in his 'Biographical Notice' (1818), first presented JA as 'thoroughly religious and devout' and with opinions according 'strictly with those of our Established Church'. The novels offer little evidence of this, but Henry's views were quickly absorbed into JA's nineteenth-century appraisal (see his 'Biographical Notice' in this collection). After several changes of career, Henry Austen had become a Church of England clergyman in 1816.

81 *so little*: Ed.1 reads 'nothing'.

was completed: Ed.1 reads 'was written'. Here and in the change noted above we see JEAL revising his text between editions to take account of the light shed by the unfinished manuscript of *The Watsons* on JA's presumed creative inactivity during her residence in Bath. See note to p. 59.

between February 1811 and August 1816: the dates are probably taken from Cassandra Austen's brief note on composition. See note to p. 44 above. What JEAL implies here has been of great significance to how critics have viewed JA's creative life. He suggests, in combination with his earlier statement at pp. 43–4, that the novels as we know them were the productions of two distinct creative periods—JA's early twenties and her late thirties—and that they were divided by a largely fallow interlude. But another interpretation of the same evidence and dates might be that, with the exception of *NA* (sold to a London publisher in 1803 under the title of 'Susan'), all the finished novels were the products of her mature Chawton years, and that this intense burst of creative completion was preceded by some twenty years of experimentation.

82 *She was careful . . . when anyone was coming*: an important detail on JA's working habits added in Ed.2. Cf. Caroline Austen's recollections, in *MAJA* 173.

Mrs. Allen . . . ' . . . to answer her or not': an edited and not wholly accurate quotation from *NA*, ch. 9.

Egerton . . . Murray . . . seven hundred pounds: Thomas Egerton, of the Military Library, Whitehall, London, was JA's first publisher, chosen partly perhaps from a connection established through James and Henry's much earlier publishing venture, *The Loiterer*, for which Egerton had been the London distributor. John Murray II (1778–1843) of 50 Albemarle Street, London, was a hugely successful publisher and businessman with a far more impressive imprint than Egerton. He was at this time at the height of his powers, as Byron's publisher and co-publisher of several of Scott's works. As well as issuing *E*, *NA*, and *P*, he brought out in 1816 a second edition of *MP*. During her lifetime JA received around £250 from *S&S* and *P&P* together, £310 from *MP*, and £71 partial profits on *E* and a second edition of *S&S*. These were nothing like the big profits some of her contemporaries were making, but nor were they unrepresentatively modest. (See Jan Fergus, *Jane Austen: A Literary Life* (1991), 193, n. 90, for totals of payments.)

no record . . . 'Sense and Sensibility': several letters descending from Cassandra Austen to her niece Fanny, Lady Knatchbull, and therefore unavailable to JEAL, mention the publication of *S&S*. They were first published in *Letters of Jane Austen*, ed. Edward, Lord Brabourne (1884). These are nos. 71, 95, and 96, in *Letters*. See also nos. 86 and 90, two letters to Frank Austen, both first published in *Sailor Brothers*, 233–50.

83 *Chawton . . . (1813)*: a discreetly edited extract, removing the gossip and homely detail about headache, jelly, and sweet pears that would undermine JEAL's representation of JA at this point as a serious novelist. The complete version is no. 79 in *Letters*, the original bequeathed by Cassandra to Charles Austen. '[M]y own darling child' is JA's first copy of *P&P*.

Falkener: JA wrote 'Falknor', possibly the local manager or coachman of the London to Southampton coach service. See the humorous reference to 'the Car of Falkenstein' in JA's letter to Anna Austen, 29–31 October 1812 (*Letters*, 195).

my stupidest of all: in January 1813, when this letter is written, *MP* was well on the way to being finished, though *E* was not yet begun. It is tempting to speculate that 'my stupidest of all' might refer to the recent revival (1809) of JA's hopes of buying back and seeing in print the novel eventually published after her death as *NA*.

83 *typical errors*: meaning 'typographical' or printing errors.

'I do not write for such dull elves': based on a couplet from Scott's verse romance *Marmion* (1808), canto 6, st. 38: 'I do not rhyme to that dull elf | Who cannot image to himself'.' JEAL spoils the wit of JA's free appropriation by failing to set it out as verse. See *Letters*, 202.

Chawton . . . (1813): an edited extract from a longer letter, no. 80 in *Letters*, again bequeathed to Charles Austen.

to you for all your praise: JA wrote 'to you all for your praise' (*Letters*, 203).

84 *The following letter . . . in February 1813*: what is presented here is an edited conflation of extracts from two letters, of 24 January and 9 February 1813 (nos. 78 and 81 in *Letters*), spliced together randomly and out of chronological sequence. For the correct ordering of the various sections, see *Letters*, 198–201, and 204–6. The letters, both to Cassandra, continue a discussion of the same people and books, which may account for JEAL's confusion of their details. Both were inherited by Charles Austen and lent to JEAL by Charles's daughter Cassy Esten.

Fanny's: Fanny Knight, JA's eldest niece.

the rejected addresses: [James and Horatio Smith] *Rejected Addresses: or, the New Theatrum Poetarum* (1812), a collection of parodies of well-known and contemporary poets. JA wrote 'M[rs] Digweed' and 'M[r] Hinton' (*Letters*, 199).

85 *Sir John Carr's . . . Capt. Pasley of the Engineers*: Sir John Carr, *Descriptive Travels in the Southern and Eastern Parts of Spain and the Balearic Isles, in the Year 1809* (1811); Sir Charles William Pasley, RE, *Essay on the Military Policy and Institutions of the British Empire* (1810). A 'Society octavo' is a book in octavo format (technically, one printed so as to produce eight leaves to each sheet, the commonest size at this time for new fiction and non-fiction) borrowed from the Chawton Book Society or Reading Club. In Letter no. 78 JA writes: 'The Miss Sibleys want to establish a Book Society in their side of the Country, like ours. What can be a stronger proof of that superiority in ours over the Steventon & Manydown Society, which I have always foreseen & felt?' (p. 199).

Clarkson or Buchanan . . . the two Mr. Smiths of the city: Thomas Clarkson, *History of the Abolition of the African Slave Trade* (1808); probably Claudius Buchanan's very popular *Christian Researches in Asia* (1811). For the two Mr Smiths, see note to p. 84 above.

'Mrs. Grant's Letters': Anne Grant, *Letters from the Mountains* (3 vols., 1810).

lie on her table: JA wrote 'lay in her House' (*Letters*, 206).

where you now are: JA wrote 'at Manydown', the home of their good friend Alethea Bigg, whom Cassandra was visiting.

I detest a quarto: a book size (see note to p. 85 above). A quarto is printed so as to produce four leaves to each sheet of paper and is therefore usually larger and more splendid than an octavo. The quarto is a size often reserved, as JA's joking comment suggests, for a scholarly and less portable work. Cf. Crabbe, *The Library* (1781), 'Then quartos their well-order'd ranks maintain, | And light octavos fill a spacious plain.'

no Government House . . . alter it to the Commissioner's: a reference to a detail in *MP*, ch. 24, the novel JA was then writing.

The following letter: from this point to the end of the chapter is an addition to Ed.2.

86 *curricle*: a light, two-wheeled carriage, drawn by two horses abreast and with a seat for the driver and one passenger.

Sloane Street . . . May 20 (1813): again extracted from a letter bequeathed to Charles Austen (no. 84 in *Letters*). JEAL's main omissions are of the homelier details of JA's London visit—of food eaten and plans for shopping trips.

the Hog's-back: 'A narrow ridge of bare chalk hills between Farnham and Guildford' with 'extensive views over six counties' (*Letters*, 416, n. 1).

87 *full of modern elegancies*: JA did not finish here, but continued: '& if it had not been for some naked Cupids over the Mantlepeice, which must be a fine study for Girls, one should never have Smelt Instruction' (*Letters*, 211).

Henrietta Street . . . March 2 (1814): no. 97 in *Letters*, again bequeathed to Charles Austen.

88 *different*: JA wrote 'very different' (*Letters*, 255).

the 'Heroine': Eaton Stannard Barrett, *The Heroine; or, Adventures of A Fair Romance Reader* (1813). As JA explains later in this letter, Barrett's novel was a burlesque on the style of Gothic romance made popular by Ann Radcliffe in the 1790s and later parodied by JA in *NA*.

peace was generally expected: March 1814 saw the fall of Paris to the allies; Napoleon abdicated in April.

the two-penny post: a reference to the local London letter post, dating from the late seventeenth century and doubled in price from a penny to twopence in 1801. In *S&S*, ch. 26, Marianne Dashwood uses it to send a letter to Willoughby.

M^{d} B.: Madame Bigeon, Henry Austen's housekeeper, to whom JA was to leave a legacy of £50 (see *Letters*, 339, JA's will).

89 *the rage for seeing Kean*: JA wrote 'Keen' (*Letters*, 256); Edmund Kean (1787–1833), Shakespearean actor. He made his first appearance at

Drury Lane in January 1814 and was an immediate huge success. JA is to see *The Merchant of Venice*.

little Cass . . . bed comfortable last night: JA's sentence goes on: '& has not filled it with fleas' (*Letters*, 256). 'Little Cass' (JA wrote 'little Cassandra') is Charles's daughter Cassy Esten (b. 1808), and in 1870 the letter's owner.

Dr. Syntax . . . Gogmagolicus: References included to amuse little Cassy Esten—William Combe, *The Tour of Dr. Syntax in Search of the Picturesque* (1812), a comic poem, hugely popular owing to its engravings by Thomas Rowlandson of the be-chinned cleric, Dr Syntax, in preposterous situations; and Gogmagolicus (JA wrote 'Gogmagoglicus'), a legendary giant who according to one tradition was captured and made to serve as a porter at the Guildhall in London, where his statue was still to be seen.

90 *Fanny Burney, afterwards Madame D'Arblay*: referred to already in this *Memoir*, as a novelist much admired by JA and as an important critical comparison for her growing reputation (see note to p. 20 above). Through her father Charles Burney, author and musician, as well as by her own early literary success (her first novel, *Evelina*, appeared in 1778 when she was 26), Burney was able to mix in London's intellectual circles. Hester Thrale (see note to p. 12 above) attracted many eminent figures to her social gatherings in Streatham, among them the actor and playwright David Garrick (1717–79) and the society painter and writer on aesthetics Sir Joshua Reynolds (1723–92). Himself a literary patron, Reynolds was a long-standing friend of Charles Burney. Samuel Johnson was Mrs Thrale's lodger at Streatham. An assiduous diarist throughout her life, Burney recorded her early meeting with Johnson and the Thrales in an entry for 27 July 1778. From the same time she has left a vivid account of her first visit to Reynolds's splendid house in Leicester Fields (now Leicester Square). (See *The Early Journals and Letters of Fanny Burney*, vol. 3, ed. Lars E. Troide and Stewart J. Cooke (1994), 66ff.)

Anna Seward: sentimental poet and letter-writer (1747–1809), known as 'the Swan of Lichfield', where she lived for most of her life. Despite rarely travelling, she managed, by tactical flattery and determined correspondence, to situate herself at the centre of an extensive literary circle, which included Johnson (born at Lichfield), the Edgeworths, Hester Thrale, and Walter Scott, to whom she bequeathed her literary works.

Joanna Baillie and Maria Edgeworth: Joanna Baillie (1762–1851), Scottish poet and dramatist, who enjoyed some commercial success and much educated admiration; she moved to London in 1784 and numbered Walter Scott and the intellectual Anna Barbauld among her friends. For JA's admiration of Maria Edgeworth, see note to p. 72 above. For most of her life Edgeworth lived in the family home at Edgeworthstown, County Longford, Ireland.

Crabbe . . . Campbell, Moore, and Rogers: for JA's admiration of the poet George Crabbe, see notes to p. 71 above. His best-known poetry was written in rural Suffolk and Leicestershire, where he was a clergyman. His acquaintance with the fashionable society poets Thomas Campbell (1777–1844), Thomas Moore (1779–1852), and the banker-poet Samuel Rogers (1763–1855), famous for his literary breakfasts, can be dated to 1817, when he absorbed himself for a time in the London social life of his publisher John Murray and the liberal circles of Lady Holland at Holland House, Kensington. He recorded his experiences in his 'London Journal', subsequently published in the posthumous *Life* (1834), by his son, also George Crabbe.

91 *Scott's guest . . . George IV . . . in that city*: Crabbe had met Scott in London, through John Murray, though the two were already correspondents. Crabbe visited Scott in Edinburgh in August 1822, coinciding with the ludicrous tartan extravaganza of George IV's triumphal state visit at which Scott was master of ceremonies.

a new term, 'Lakers': a term coined by Francis Jeffrey (1773–1850), the critic and chief voice of the influential *Edinburgh Review* (see issue 24 (1814)), to denote the coterie of Lake District poets Wordsworth, Coleridge, and Robert Southey.

Charlotte Brontë's life: Charlotte Brontë (1816–55), longest lived of the three Brontë sisters, all of whom were novelists and poets. After the remarkable success of her novel *Jane Eyre* (by 'Currer Bell') in 1847, she devoted herself to writing and remained much of the time in the isolated solitude of Haworth parsonage, West Yorkshire. Her fellow novelist, Elizabeth Gaskell, wrote her biography immediately after her death, making public its melancholy details. Brontë's 'kind publisher' was George Smith, of Smith, Elder, and Co., and the incident in Willis's Rooms, where Brontë attended a lecture given by Thackeray, is described in Gaskell's *Life of Charlotte Brontë* (1857), ch. 23. Gaskell's biography is a point of reference to which JEAL returns.

Miss Mitford: see note to p. 13 above. Her plays *Julian* (1823), *Foscari* (1826), and *Rienzi* (1828) were all performed in London. She had published her collected plays in 1854, with an autobiographical introduction.

Milman and Talfourd: both significant men of letters to JEAL's generation. Henry Hart Milman (1791–1868), minor poet, playwright, biblical and classical scholar; Sir Thomas Noon Talfourd (1795–1854), essayist, editor, and biographer of the poet and essayist Charles Lamb.

to know where she was buried: the incident is subsequently related in the *Autobiography of Mrs Elizabeth Fletcher, 1770–1858*, ed. Lady Richardson (1875), 299.

92 *one of the Prince Regent's physicians*: identified by Deirdre Le Faye as possibly Dr Matthew Baillie of Lower Grosvenor Street (*Fam. Rec.*, 202). Henry Austen's illness in October 1815 was serious enough for JA to fear

for a while that his life was in danger. It may have delayed the publication of *E*, for which she was negotiating with Murray at the same time as nursing her brother.

92 *Carlton House*: the magnificent London house of the Prince of Wales (Prince Regent, 1811; George IV, 1820) from 1783. It was demolished in 1827.

at that time in the press: permission to dedicate *E* to the Prince Regent was something of a two-edged compliment. JA hoped the knowledge might speed up production at the printers, but saw no evidence for this. On the other hand, she did become liable to costs which had to be paid out of her own pocket—an expensive red morocco presentation binding (see Gilson, A8, p. 68).

Mr. Clarke . . . Dr. Clarke . . . Bishop Otter: the Prince Regent's Librarian and Domestic Chaplain was the Revd James Stanier Clarke (1767–1834). His brother was Edward Daniel Clarke (1769–1822), a distinguished traveller (*Travels in Europe, Asia, and Africa* (6 vols., 1810–23)). William Otter (Bishop of Chichester in 1836) published *Life and Remains of E. D. Clarke* in 1824.

Nov. 15, 1815: a copy of JA's letter to J. S. Clarke descended to Charles Austen and his family. It appears in *Letters* as no. 125(D), a draft preserved by JA for her own reference.

93 *Carlton House, Nov. 16, 1815*: no. 125 in *Letters*, again descending from Cassandra to Charles Austen and his family.

Beattie's Minstrel . . . yet none knew why: from James Beattie, *The Minstrel; or, the Progress of Genius* (1771–4), book 1, st. 16, slightly misquoted by JEAL but not by Clarke in his original letter (see *Letters*, 297).

Goldsmith . . . 'Tableau de Famille': the reference is to the sentimental portraits of clergymen in Oliver Goldsmith, *The Vicar of Wakefield* (1766) and in the French translation (*Nouveaux Tableaux de Famille, ou la vie d'un pauvre ministre de village allemand et ses enfants* (1803)) of August Lafontaine, *Leben eines armes Landpredigers* (1801).

94 *no man's enemy but his own*: in the comic 'Plan of a Novel, according to hints from various quarters', which JA drew up in 1816 as a direct consequence of her correspondence with J. S. Clarke, she there proposes to describe 'a Clergyman, one who after having lived much in the World had retired from it . . . of a very literary turn, an Enthusiast in Literature, nobody's Enemy but his own . . . ' (*Minor Works*, 428–9). As she must have known when mimicking Clarke, his smugly self-referential phrase ('no man's enemy but his own') is filched from Henry Fielding, *Tom Jones*, book 4, ch. 5, where it is a description of the hero. (For the verbal closeness of the 'Plan' and Clarke's letters, see notes to pp. 97–9 below.)

Dec. 11: no. 132(D) in *Letters*, again part of Cassandra Austen's bequest to her brother Charles.

95 *Prince Leopold . . . Princess Charlotte*: Prince Leopold of Saxe-Cobourg (1790–1865) married the Prince Regent's daughter, the Princess Charlotte of Wales (1796–1817), in 1816.

'an historical romance . . . just now be very interesting': a loose extract from no. 138 in *Letters*.

Sir William Ross: (1794–1860), miniature-painter.

'My Dear Sir . . . honoured . . . ': no. 138(D) (JA's own draft) in *Letters*, where it is dated Monday 1 April 1816.

96 *But when his free course . . . With willing sport*: Shakespeare, *Two Gentlemen of Verona*, II. vii. 27–32, slightly misquoted ('free course' should be 'fair course').

97 *'should hardly like to live . . . confined houses'*: from Charlotte Brontë's correspondence with George Henry Lewes, an extract from a letter of 12 January 1848, quoted by Gaskell, *Life of Charlotte Brontë*, ch. 16.

'Plan of a novel . . . from various quarters': the manuscript, in JA's hand, is now in the Pierpont Morgan Library, New York. It clearly dates from the period of the Clarke correspondence (Nov. 1815–Apr. 1816). But to appreciate the full flavour and sharpness of JA's comedy, the 'Plan' needs to be read with the complete text of Clarke's letters. JEAL's selective extracting of both almost perversely obscures their interconnection, by omitting from the edited correspondence most of the points which appear in the 'Plan', and from the 'Plan' most of the suggestions incorporated verbatim from Clarke's hilariously self-preening letters. The 'Plan' along with Clarke's correspondence was in Cassy Esten's possession at this time and available to JEAL. Writing to her brother after the *Memoir*'s publication, Caroline Austen comments on his handling of these materials: 'I see you have been very merciful to Mr. Clarke in omitting the most ridiculous parts of his letter' (see the Appendix, p. 192). Clarke's letter, no. 132 in *Letters*, is the vital missing link and is itself as funny (in its complete misunderstanding of JA's novelistic talents) as anything in the 'Plan'. He advises her thus: 'Pray continue to write, & make all your friends send Sketches to help you—and Memoires pour servir—as the French term it. Do let us have an English Clergyman after *your* fancy—much novelty may be introduced—shew dear Madam what good would be done if Tythes were taken away entirely, and describe him burying his own mother—as I did—because the High Priest of the Parish in which she died—did not pay her remains the respect he ought to do. I have never recovered the Shock. Carry your Clergyman to Sea as the Friend of some distinguished Naval Character about a Court—you can then bring foreward like Le Sage many interesting Scenes of Character & Interest' (*Letters*, 307).

names of some of those advisers: see *Minor Works*, 428–30, for a complete text of the 'Plan', including JA's original marginal notes (there printed as footnotes), indicating the source of each suggestion.

98 *chaplain to a distinguished naval character about the court*: JA writes at this point in her manuscript the marginal note 'Mr. Clarke'. A comparison with the extract from Clarke's letter of 21 December 1815, no. 132, quoted in the note to p. 97 above, shows that JA is here drawing on it virtually verbatim. Clarke was, of course, weaving autobiographical details into his proposals—he had been a naval chaplain from 1795–1799.

tithes: literally 'tenths', the tithe being estimated at one-tenth of the produce of the land in a parish, to be paid for the support of its church and clergy. In practice, it was a specific assessment landholders paid to constitute the clergyman's income. It could lead to serious inequalities between rich and poor parishes and between curates, who might do most of the work but be paid very little, and the rector who enjoyed a good income. Again, see Clarke's letter quoted in note to p. 97 above.

99 *Often reduced to . . . work for her bread*: JA is glancing slyly at the fashion for sensational adventure in the contemporary female novel. Ellis-Juliet, the heroine of Fanny Burney's *The Wanderer; or, Female Difficulties* (1814), undergoes various sufferings in a downward spiral of poverty, trying to earn her living as a music teacher, performer, and seamstress. A more direct comparison can be found in Mary Brunton's *Self-Control* (1810), where the heroine Laura Montreville resolves somewhat impractically to earn a living for herself and her invalid father by selling sketches: 'Could she but hope to obtain a subsistence for her father, she would labour night and day, deprive herself of recreation, of rest, even of daily food, rather than wound his heart, by an acquaintance with poverty' (ch. 15). Laura's many sufferings eventually culminate in escape by canoe from a wilderness confinement in the region of Quebec. For JA's humorous response to this novel, see her letter to Cassandra, quoted in the note to p. 75 above.

Kamtschatka: modern Kamchatka, a peninsula at the eastern extremity of Asia, acquired by Russia in the eighteenth century. The setting is chosen for its improbability—even surpassing the remoteness of Quebec. Doody and Murray (*Catharine and Other Writings*, 361, note to p. 232) suggest that JA is here alluding to Madame Sophie Cottin's *Elizabeth; or, Exiles of Siberia* (1806), another tale concerned with the heroine's unlikely sufferings for the sake of her father. It was translated into English in 1809.

and living in high style: in Ed.1, Chapter 7 ends at this point.

Mr. Murray of Albemarle Street: John Murray III (1808–92), son of JA's publisher (for whom, see note to p. 82 above). JA's own estimate of Murray is somewhat more qualified than JEAL's. In her letter of 17 October 1815 to Cassandra, she describes him as 'a Rogue of course, but a civil one' (*Letters*, 291).

Hans Place . . . (1815): no. 126 in *Letters*, the original being in the John Murray Archive, 50 Albemarle Street, London.

100 *'Waterloo'*: Walter Scott's poem, *The Field of Waterloo*, jointly published by Murray in October 1815. It commemorated the allied victory against Napoleon in June 1815 and its profits went to the Waterloo subscription.

Hans Place, December 11 (1815): no. 130 in *Letters*, again in the Murray archive.

all unbound: that is, in publishers' boards, a temporary covering until the book should be leather-bound by the purchaser. Murray allowed JA twelve presentation copies of *E* in addition to the copy for the Prince Regent. His three-volume set was presented already bound in red morocco leather, at JA's own expense. JA published *E* on commission, a method she used for *S&S* and *MP*—that is, she as author was responsible for paying all the expenses of publication (paper, printing costs, etc.) out of profits, while the publisher distributed the copies and took a percentage commission on what was sold. In this way JA reserved copyright in the work to herself—hence her freedom to publish a second edition of *MP* with Murray rather than with Egerton, its first publisher, a detail mentioned at the end of this letter. But publishing on commission meant that she also took upon herself the risk of financial loss and, as this letter suggests, she still had to rely heavily on her publisher's sense of the market. The best account of JA's dealings with her publishers is to be found in Fergus, *Jane Austen: A Literary Life*. For precise details of the printing of *E* and *MP* (2nd edn.) see Gilson, 59–60 and 66–9.

101 *Hans Place, December 11 (1815)*: no. 131 in *Letters*. JEAL's copy in the *Memoir* is the source for all other printings, the original being untraced.

the proper place for a dedication: Murray must have pointed out immediately that dedications are not normally printed on title-pages.

Chawton, April 1, 1816: no. 139 in *Letters*, the original now in King's College Library, Cambridge.

Reviewer of 'Emma': this was JA's first major critical review. The anonymous reviewer was Walter Scott, in the *Quarterly Review*, 14 (dated October 1815, but published March 1816), 188–201. The *Quarterly* was Murray's own periodical and it was he who asked Scott to promote the novel: 'Have you any fancy to dash off an article on "Emma"?' (see Gilson, 69). We do not know whether JA knew that Scott was the 'clever' reviewer.

the late event in Henrietta Street: JA wrote, 'the late sad Event', a reference to Henry Austen's bankruptcy, declared 15 March 1816. 10 Henrietta Street, Covent Garden, housed the offices of the banking business of Austen, Maunde, & Tilson. The best family account of the circumstances surrounding the bankruptcy, and its effect on the Austen family and on JA's health, is to be found in Caroline Austen's *Reminiscences*, 47–8.

102 *the Countess of Morley*: Frances Talbot (1782–1857), second wife of John Parker, second Lord Boringdon, created in 1815 first Earl of Morley.

Lady Morley was a witty woman, with literary interests, and for a time was thought to be the authoress of both *S&S* and *P&P*. It is not known how JA became acquainted with her, but the likeliest explanation is that it was through her brother Henry's London society contacts. See W. A. W. Jarvis, 'Jane Austen and the Countess of Morley', *Jane Austen Society Report* (1986), 6–14. In Ed.1 this interchange of letters was placed at the end of Chapter 6. They are nos. 134(A) and 134(D) in *Letters*, and were bequeathed by Cassandra to Charles Austen. JA had sent the Countess one of the twelve presentation copies of *E*. See *Letters*, 302, where she jokes to Cassandra of her 'near Connections—beginning with the P.R. & ending with Countess Morley'. For the Countess's less favourable opinion of *E*, as expressed to her sister-in-law, see *Fam. Rec.*, 208.

Woodhouse family . . . Norrises: Emma Woodhouse and her father in *E*; the Bennets in *P&P*; the Bertrams and Mrs Norris in *MP*.

104 *Archbishop Whately . . . review of Madame D'Arblay's*: for Richard Whately, see note to p. 28 above. Thomas Babington Macaulay (1800–59), politician, essayist, and historian, and early JA enthusiast. He associates her talent for characterization with that of Shakespeare in his unsigned article, 'Diary and Letters of Madame D'Arblay', *Edinburgh Review*, 76 (Jan. 1843), 523–70 (at pp. 561–2). His claim is taken up and repeated by several major mid-century critics, including G. H. Lewes and Julia Kavanagh.

105 *Horace's 'satis est Equitem mihi plaudere'*: Horace, *Satires*, I. x. line 76: 'It is enough if the knights applaud me' (part of Horace's defence of an exclusive readership).

the following letter to Mr. Cadell: Thomas Cadell, of the reputable London firm Cadell and Davies, well established as novel publishers. In her letter of 1 April [1869?] offering materials to her brother for the *Memoir*, Caroline Austen provides a copy of the letter to Cadell, observing shrewdly: 'I do not know *which* novel he would have sent—The letter does not do much credit to the tact or courtesy of our good Grandfather for Cadell was a great man in his day, and it is not surprising that he should have refused the *favor* so offered from an *unknown*—but the circumstance may be worth noting, especially as we have so few incidents to produce. At a sale of Cadell's papers &c Tom Lefroy picked up the original letter—and Jemima [Anna Lefroy's daughter] copied it for me—' (see the Appendix p. 185, for a longer extract from this letter). The manuscript of JA's father's letter is now in St John's College Library, Oxford.

author's risk . . . the property of it: that is, publication on commission or through the author's sale of the copyright to the publisher. For JA's preferred method of publication, see note to p. 100 above. Fanny Burney's *Evelina* (1776) had been an unexpected runaway success; it is also mentioned in order to give some idea of the length of the offered manuscript and therefore the likely cost (in paper, type-setting, etc.) involved in publishing it.

to a publisher in Bath: though JA was at that time living in Bath, the manuscript of 'Susan', a version of which had been written, according to Cassandra's memorandum, in 1798 and 1799, was in 1803 offered to and bought by the small London publisher Crosby and Co. However, it seems likely that Crosby had provincial connections with booksellers in Bath (Gilson, 83); so JEAL's information is not necessarily inaccurate. JA enquired after her manuscript in April 1809 when Crosby informed her, somewhat oddly, that its purchase had not bound his firm to publish the manuscript, and that she might have it back on repayment of the £10 (see *Letters*, 174–5). It is not known exactly when JA bought it back—perhaps not until early in 1816. At this time she changed the heroine's name and the working title to 'Catherine'; but the novel was only published posthumously, under the title *Northanger Abbey*, which by family tradition Henry Austen gave it (*Fam. Rec.*, 210–11 and 233).

106 *old fishing-tackle in Scott's cabinet*: Walter Scott himself tells this story of the interrupted composition of *Waverley* (1814) in the 'General Preface' (1829) written for the collected edition of his novels. There he claims the work was begun in 1805 but 'laid aside in the drawers of an old writing desk', and only rediscovered several years later when he 'happened to want some fishing-tackle for the use of a guest . . . and, in looking for lines and flies, the long-lost manuscript presented itself' (*Waverley*, ed. Claire Lamont (1981), 352–4).

One of her brothers: Ed.1 reads 'Her brother Henry'.

for that which had cost her nothing: JEAL is here drawing on Henry Austen's words in his 'Biographical Notice' (1818). Writing to Frank Austen on 3–4 July 1813, JA noted with pleasure that the first edition of *S&S* had sold out and earned her £140 in profits (*Letters*, 217).

extracts from two of her letters: both to Anna Lefroy (nos. 111 and 118 in *Letters*). Both were given by Anna to JEAL for use in the *Memoir*, and both are since lost (see notes to *Letters*, 438 and 443).

Mr. C.'s opinion . . . in my list: in *Letters*, 282, 'Mr.C' reads 'M[rs] Creed'. The list, which survives, records 'Opinions of *Mansfield Park*', and is in *Minor Works*, 431–5, with Mrs Creed's preference of *S&S* and *P&P* over *MP* at p. 435.

a close imitation of 'Self-Control': for JA's anxious preoccupation with the success of Mary Brunton's *Self-Control* and the popularity of its highly decorous heroine, see note to p. 75 above and her own humorous 'Plan of a Novel' (pp. 97–9 above).

'Rosanne' in our Society: Laetitia Matilda Hawkins, *Rosanne; or, a Father's Labour Lost* (1814), a novel written to illustrate 'the inestimable advantages attendant on the practice of pure Christianity'. 'Our Society' is the Chawton Book Society or Reading Club.

107 *Two notices . . . in the 'Quarterly Review'*: see notes to pp. 28 and 101 above.

108 *'as tiresome in fiction as in real society'*: the three preceding references are to Walter Scott's anonymous review, in the *Quarterly Review*, 14 (Oct. 1815), 188–201, at pp. 194, and 200. Of Elizabeth Bennet's change of heart, he wrote: 'The lady . . . does not perceive that she has done a foolish thing until she accidentally visits a very handsome seat and grounds belonging to her admirer.'

Wilkie's pictures: the Scottish painter, Sir David Wilkie (1785–1841), noted like the Dutch painters of the Delft School for the high degree of realism in his domestic representations.

109 *'. . . full maturity and flavour without them'*: closing a long quotation from Whately's review, *Quarterly Review*, 24 (Jan. 1821), 352–76, at pp. 362–3.

110 *Southey . . . to Sir Egerton Brydges*: Robert Southey (1774–1843), poet and biographer, whose early revolutionary sympathies soon gave way to political and social conservatism. He was made Poet Laureate in 1813. In view of the comparison JEAL has already set up between JA and Charlotte Brontë, Southey's opinion of Austen's novels might be compared with the well-known advice he gave Brontë when she applied to him about publishing her writings: 'Literature cannot be the business of a woman's life, and it ought not to be' (included in Gaskell's *Life*, ch. 8). Southey records his views on JA in a letter of 8 April 1830, in Brydges, *Autobiography* (1834), ii. 269. For Brydges and his connection with the Austen family, see note to p. 44 above.

A friend of hers . . . Rev. Herbert Hill: JA's friend Catherine Bigg (see note to p. 54) had married Herbert Hill (1749–1828) in October 1808. Hill was Chaplain to the British factory or trading settlement in Oporto (not Lisbon), Portugal, between 1774 and 1801. Southey visited his uncle Hill there in 1775. Some of JA's later letters mention visits to Catherine at Streatham, where Hill became rector in 1810 (e.g. *Letters*, 274).

S. T. Coleridge: the poet and critic Samuel Taylor Coleridge (1772–1834). His opinion of JA's novels, to be found in *Specimens of the Table Talk of Samuel Taylor Coleridge*, ed. Henry Nelson Coleridge (2nd edn., 1836) (in *Collected Works*, 14 (2), ed. Carl Woodring (1990), 80 n.), is all the more remarkable in view of his open contempt for the modern female novelist. In Lecture 11 of his 1818 Lectures on European Literature he notes that 'Women are good novelists . . . because they rarely or never thoroughly distinguish between fact and fiction. In the jumble of the two lies the secret of the modern novel . . . ' (*Collected Works*, 5 (2), ed. R. A. Foakes (1987), 193).

Miss Mitford: see note to p. 13 above.

Sir J. Mackintosh: Sir James Mackintosh (1760/5–1832), political and moral philosopher and historian, author of *Vindiciae Gallicae* (1791), *History of England* (1830), and *Progress of Ethical Philosophy* (1830).

111 *Madame de Staël*: (1766–1817), born in Paris Anne Louise Germaine Necker, the daughter of a Swiss banker Jacques Necker, Louis XIV's

finance minister. A prominent intellectual and political opponent of Napoleon, she wrote two major works, *Corinne, ou l'Italie* (Corinne, or Italy (1807)) and *De l'Allemagne* (On Germany (1810)). In December 1808 JA can be found recommending an acquaintance to read 'Corinna' (*Letters*, 161). Subsequently, JA and de Staël shared a publisher in John Murray.

Mons. Guizot: François Pierre Guillaume Guizot (1787–1874), conservative French politician and historian and a prolific writer on general topics. He became French minister of education and prime minister. Susan Ferrier (1782–1854), an Edinburgh novelist whose first novel, *Marriage* (1818), was her most popular.

'Keepsake' of 1825: R. W. Chapman notes that this should be 1835. A popular annual miscellany, the issue for 1835 has at p. 27 the verses printed here. They form one of the earliest expressions of the sentimental enthusiasm that came to be known as 'Janeism'. Their author was George Howard, sixth Earl of Carlisle (1773–1848). Among the female novelists compared unfavourably to JA are Elizabeth Inchbald (1753–1821); Mary Brunton (1778–1818), already mentioned in this *Memoir* (see p. 106); and Amelia Opie (1769–1853); Susan Ferrier (see preceding note), was author of *The Inheritance* (1824).

112 *admiration felt by Lord Macaulay*: Macaulay's sister, Lady Hannah Trevelyan (1810–73), provided the information from her brother's journal entry of 1858, where he recorded: 'If I could get materials I really would write a short life of that wonderful woman, and raise a little money to put up a monument to her in Winchester Cathedral.' This subsequently finds its way into his nephew George Otto Trevelyan's biography, *The Life and Letters of Lord Macaulay* (2 vols., 1876), ii. 466.

Sir Henry Holland: (1788–1873), fashionable London physician, doctor to Queen Victoria, and cousin of Elizabeth Gaskell. He was unrelated to Henry Fox, third Lord Holland, here described. See Sir Henry Holland, Bart., *Recollections of Past Life* (1872), 231 n.

Sir Denis Le Marchant: (1795–1874), politician, had married in 1835 Sarah Eliza Smith, sister of JEAL's wife Emma.

Mr. Whewell: William Whewell (1795–1866), Professor of Moral Theology at Cambridge, 1838–55, and Master of Trinity College from 1841 to his death.

113 *Lord Lansdowne*: Lord Henry Petty-Fitzmaurice, third Marquis of Lansdowne, referred to at p. 66 above. In his edition of the *Letters of Jane Austen* (1884), i. 79, Edward, Lord Brabourne, Fanny Knight's son, records on the authority of his aunt Louisa Knight, now Lady Hill, that Lord Lansdowne was 'grieved and affected' to hear of JA's death.

Sydney Smith: (1771–1845), essayist and wit, one of the founders, in 1802, of the *Edinburgh Review*, a hugely influential periodical aimed at educating middle-class taste. He was a member of the great Whig political and intellectual salon of Lord and Lady Holland (Elizabeth and Henry Fox), at Holland House.

113 *'Catena Patrum'*: literally, 'chain of fathers', list of authorities.

finely written: Scott wrote 'very finely written'.

114 *list of criticisms*: for the 'Opinions of *Mansfield Park*' and 'Opinions of *Emma*', collections of comments with their authors, gathered and transcribed by JA, see *Minor Works*, 431–9. They were first printed, in part and less accurately, in *Life & Letters*, 328–32. The manuscripts, in JA's hand, are now in the British Library.

'Quot homines, tot sententiæ': 'as many opinions as there are men', Terence, *Phormio*, 454.

115 *a long letter of his sister's*: this is the letter to Martha Lloyd, Frank Austen's second wife, sent to the American autograph hunter Susan Quincy. It is included in Ed.2 of the *Memoir*, at p. 53 above, thanks to Susan Quincy, who returned a copy of it to JEAL. For the exchange of correspondence between the Boston Quincys and Frank Austen, see note to p. 53.

117 *'Northanger Abbey' in 1798*: according to Cassandra's memorandum, it was 'written about the years 98 & 99'. See note to p. 44 above.

118 *merely took a likeness of that actor*: Joshua Reynolds (see note to p. 90 above). He painted several portraits of his friend the actor David Garrick, but the more allegorical representation, 'Garrick between Tragedy and Comedy', was exhibited in 1762. Interestingly, Reynolds considered the same distinction in an address to the Royal Academy in 1786 (Discourse 13), where he contrasts 'all the truth of the *camera obscura*' and truth as 'represented by a great artist', interpreted and mediated, that is, by the imagination (Sir Joshua Reynolds, *Discourses on Art*, ed. Robert R. Wark (1975), 237).

drawn by Miss Mitford: see note to p. 13 above. 'The Talking Gentleman', like 'The Talking Lady', 'The Touchy Lady', and 'A Quiet Gentlewoman', is a character sketch from *Our Village*.

A reviewer in the 'Quarterly': this is Walter Scott, in his unsigned review of *E*, *Quarterly Review*, 14 (Oct. 1815), 194, where he writes: 'A friend of ours, whom the author never saw or heard of, was at once recognized by his own family as the original of Mr. Bennet, and we do not know if he has yet got rid of the nickname.'

by a friend: in October 1869 JEAL received a letter from the Revd G. D. Boyle, vicar of Kidderminster, with an account of a Mrs Barrett, now dead, who he claimed had, in her younger days, known and corresponded with JA. JEAL here includes extracts from Boyle's letter in which he apparently quotes the sentiments of JA as remembered by Mrs Barrett. (See the Appendix for the letter, from a transcript held in the NPG, RWC/HH, fos. 26–9.)

personal affection for Darcy and Elizabeth: in two letters to Cassandra of 29 January and 9 February 1813 (nos. 79 and 81). The relevant extracts are printed at pp. 83 and 84 above.

119 *'to see your Jemima'*: this was Anna Jemima, eldest daughter of Ben and Anna Lefroy, born 20 October 1815. JEAL here paraphrases no. 135 in *Letters*, a scrap only: 'As I wish very much to see *your* Jemima, I am sure you will like to see *my* Emma, & have therefore great pleasure in sending it for your perusal.' *Emma* was announced as published on Saturday 23 December 1815, and it is not possible to date the scrap of letter closer than December 1815 or January 1816.

'. . . no one but myself will much like': JEAL's *Memoir* is the source for this now famous authorial comment. The family view was that the character of Emma was, perhaps unintentionally, based on Anna Austen Lefroy (*Fam. Rec.*, 208, on the authority of Fanny Caroline Lefroy's 'Family History').

subsequent career of some of her people: these subsequent adventures of her characters are preserved from the memories of Anna Lefroy and JEAL. The anecdote relating to Mr Woodhouse was added in *Memoir* Ed.2. *Life & Letters*, 307, records a further example of the post-print continuations, spun for the amusement of JA's nieces and nephews: 'According to a less well-known tradition, Jane Fairfax [in *E*] survived her elevation only nine or ten years.'

120 *some family troubles*: apparently a discreet reference to Henry Austen's bankruptcy, which occurred in March 1816. But the letters from which JEAL goes on to quote date from April and May 1817 and refer to the disappointment felt in the Austen family at the will of James Leigh Perrot, Mrs Austen's brother, who had died on 28 March 1817. As he was childless, his sister's family reasonably expected immediate benefit under his will, and since Henry's bankruptcy had hit several members of the family hard they were much in need of this. However, although he made generous provision for the Austens in the longer term, Uncle Leigh Perrot left everything to his wife for her lifetime. For the Leigh Perrots, see notes to pp. 37, 58, and 59 above. As chief beneficiary on Mrs Leigh Perrot's death in 1836, JEAL would obviously be discreet in recording this disappointment as he was earlier in his omission from the *Memoir* of Mrs Leigh Perrot's prosecution for theft. But family tradition, as well as her own correspondence, suggest that the terms of the will were a considerable shock to JA and even exacerbated her illness (*Fam. Rec.*, 221–3).

a letter . . . to Charles: no. 157, where it is dated 6 April 1817. JEAL prints a severely edited extract. JA wrote: 'I have been suffering from a Bilious attack, attended with a good deal of fever.—A few days ago my complaint appeared removed, but I am ashamed to say that the shock of my Uncle's Will brought on a relapse . . . I am the only one of the Legatees [JEAL alters this to 'party'] who has been so silly, but a weak Body must excuse weak Nerves. My Mother has borne the forgetfulness of *her* extremely well;—her expectations for herself were never beyond the extreme of moderation, & she thinks with you that my Uncle always looked forward to surviving her' (*Letters*, 338–9).

to another correspondent: a short extract from no. 161, in *Letters*, where Le Faye conjecturally dates it 28/9 May 1817 and from College Street Winchester. JA and Cassandra had arrived there as recently as 24 May, in a last attempt to seek medical advice which might delay the progress of the illness. This is JA's last known letter and the first to be published: it is only known through Henry Austen's use of extracts from it in his 'Biographical Notice' (1818). Le Faye further conjectures that the letter's recipient was Mrs Frances Tilson, wife of Henry's partner in the now failed Austen, Maunde, & Tilson bank in London (see Le Faye, 'JA: More Letters Redated', *Notes and Queries*, 236 (1991), 306–8). In his 'Notice' Henry made it quite clear that the letter was written 'a few weeks before her death' (p. 142), which makes JEAL's insertion of it into a narrative of Spring 1816 the more surprising. R. W. Chapman, the first editor of the collected *Letters*, thinks, naturally enough, that Henry himself may have been the recipient (see *Letters* (1932; 2nd edn., 1952), note to Letter 147).

'My Dear E.': JA wrote 'My dear Edward'. This is no. 142 in *Letters*, and JEAL is now drawing on materials which do relate to Summer 1816. He is himself the recipient of the letter, the autograph of which is now on deposit in the British Library.

your mother: James Austen's second wife, Mary Lloyd. In her *Reminiscences*, 48, Caroline Austen records under the year 1816: 'My mother was very unwell [for a] great part of this summer, and in August she was advised to go to Cheltenham. Aunt Cassandra accompanied us.'

121 *finesse*: artifice, trick.

Mary Jane: Frank Austen's eldest daughter, then aged nine.

cleared off the rest yesterday: in JEAL's edited version of this letter a section is here omitted detailing various family comings and goings—trips to London and Broadstairs—in which JA is not included. It concludes with an interesting postscript mentioning a forthcoming journey to France by Henry and two of his Godmersham nephews. For the full text, see *Letters*, 315–17.

go to Oxford and not be elected: JA first wrote 'must not go to Oxford' and then cancelled 'not'. The election in question was presumably JEAL's award in 1816 of a Craven Founder's Kin Scholarship at Exeter College, Oxford.

122 *improvement*: JA wrote 'improvements', a precise term in landscape gardening at this time. Cf. *MP*, ch. 6, where the foolish Mr Rushworth is looking to improve the grounds on his estate.

Mrs. S. . . . Tangier: Mrs Sclater of Tangier Park, Hampshire, a seventeenth-century house near Manydown, home of JA's friends the Bigg-Wither family.

'My Dear E.': no. 146 in *Letters*, where JA wrote 'My dear Edward'. Again the autograph is on deposit in the British Library. In his 'Biographical Notice' of 1818 Henry Austen had slightly misquoted from this letter the now famous disclaimer about 'the little bit (two Inches wide) of Ivory on which I work with so fine a Brush'. JEAL omits a final paragraph in which JA alludes to the long-running family joke that she is to marry Mr Papillon, rector of Chawton: 'I am happy to tell you that Mr Papillon will soon make his offer, probably next Monday, as he returns on Saturday . . . ' (*Letters*, 323).

Charles Knight: Edward Austen Knight's eighth child, now 13 years old and a pupil at Winchester College.

123 *very superior sermons*: Henry Austen was ordained deacon in December 1816 and priest in early 1817, becoming curate at Chawton. See JA's letter to Alethea Bigg (24 January 1817), included at p. 126 below: 'Our own new clergyman is expected here very soon . . . '

Lovell is the reader: a reference to Walter Scott's novel *The Antiquary*, published in May 1816. The episode to which JA refers occurs in ch. 18. In Scott, the hero's name (a disguise) is Lovel (with one final 'l').

Two chapters and a half: In a letter of 4 September 1816, JA had informed Cassandra: 'Edward is writing a Novel—we have all heard what he has written—it is extremely clever; written with great ease & spirit;—if he can carry it on in the same way, it will be a firstrate work, & in a style, I think, to be popular.—Pray tell Mary [his mother] how much I admire it.—And tell Caroline that I think it hardly fair upon her & myself, to have him take up the Novel Line . . .' (*Letters*, 319).

vigorous sketches: it is so in Henry Austen's 'Biographical Notice', but JA wrote 'spirited sketches'.

how well Anna is: Anna Lefroy had given birth to a second daughter, Julia Cassandra, in September 1816, only eleven months after her first, Anna Jemima. Ben was her husband. Writing to Fanny Knight in March 1817, JA expresses concern at Anna's frequent pregnancies (she was at this time recovering from a miscarriage): 'Poor Animal she will be worn out before she is thirty' (*Letters*, 336).

'tell him what you will': a joking reference to a line from Hannah Cowley's *Which is the Man?* (1783), a play in the repertoire of the family theatricals at Steventon in the 1780s (*Austen Papers*, 126).

124 *Joseph Hall*: Mrs Austen's tenant at Steventon (*Letters*, 460, n. 4).

Dame Staples: a Steventon villager (*Letters*, 575).

importunities of a little niece: this is JEAL's sister Caroline, who tells the story of the three chairs in *MAJA*, 177, in this collection.

125 *brought to an end in July*: according to Cassandra's memorandum, *P* was 'begun Augt 8th 1815 finished Augt 6th 1816'. In its unrevised version the

final chapter (manuscript now in the British Library) is dated on the last page 'July 18. 1816'.

two others, entirely different, in its stead: the two concluding chapters of *P* were originally numbered 10 and 11 (that is, volume 2, chapters 10 and 11). What JA in fact did was to cancel the greater part of this first version of chapter 10 and substitute for it two new chapters, 10 and 11. The original chapter 11 was largely retained and became chapter 12. In most modern editions the three chapters are numbered continuously, without regard for the original two-volume division, as chapters 22–4. So, the final version of the ending was completed on 6 August 1816. What we have in manuscript are the drafts for the cancelled chapter 10 and the unrevised chapter 11 (which became volume 2, chapter 12, or chapter 24). The cancelled chapter was first printed by JEAL in Ed.2 of his *Memoir* but is not included in this edition because of its wide availability as an appendix to most modern editions of the novel. Along with the fragment of the unfinished novel (*Sanditon*), the manuscript chapters of *P* descended after Cassandra's death to Anna Lefroy.

The following letter: this marks the beginning of a long section (over four pages) added in Ed.2, comprising the letter to Alethea Bigg, the short extract from JA's letter to Caroline, and the quotation from Caroline's subsequent recollections. Ed.1 reads: 'the suppression of which may be almost a matter of regret. [new paragraph] In May 1817 she was persuaded to remove to Winchester . . . '

Miss Bigg . . . Robert Southey: JA's letter is to Alethea Bigg whose sister Catherine was married to Southey's uncle. See note to p. 110 above.

three days before . . . her last work: the reference is to the unfinished novel now known as *Sanditon*. According to the date at the top of the first page of the manuscript (now in King's College, Cambridge), JA began writing on 27 January 1817. The tradition in the family was that she intended to call it 'The Brothers', but Anna, who inherited the manuscript fragment, is calling it 'Sanditon' in a letter of 1862 (see Appendix). JEAL refers to it as 'The Last Work' and adopts that phrase for the title of ch. 13 of Ed.2 of the *Memoir*, in which he includes extracts amounting to about one-sixth of the total. As late as 1925, when R. W. Chapman first published the fragment in its entirety, it was still 'Fragment of a Novel'.

126 *'My Dear Alethea'*: extracts from no. 150 in *Letters*. JEAL omits other family news from the letter he prints in order to focus attention more steadily on JA's health.

I am convinced: JA wrote 'I am more & more convinced' (*Letters*, 326–7).

a good account of his father: Jane's eldest brother James was in poor health and died in December 1819.

127 *between Streatham and Winchester*: Alethea Bigg lived in Winchester with her widowed sister Mrs Elizabeth Heathcote, and was at this time visiting their other sister Mrs Catherine Hill in Streatham.

'Poet's Pilgrimage to Waterloo': 1816, by Robert Southey, nephew of Catherine (Bigg) Hill's husband, the Revd Herbert Hill. Southey's beloved son Herbert died aged 9 in April 1816, soon after the poem with its proem celebrating domestic contentment was completed.

to her niece: Caroline Austen. The extract is from the closing section of a longer letter (no. 149), where it reads: '*I* feel myself getting stronger than I was half a year ago, & can so perfectly well walk to Alton, *or* back again, without the slightest fatigue that I hope to be able to do both when Summer comes' (*Letters*, 326).

of the niece: again Caroline Austen, slightly altered in wording from her recollections printed here as *MAJA*, (178–9).

128 *Mrs Leigh Perrot . . . late husband's affairs*: see notes to p. 120. Caroline's father, James Austen, was to be the chief beneficiary of his uncle James Leigh Perrot's will, but subject to the widow's life interest; as it turned out, she survived him by sixteen years.

Mr. Lyford: Giles King Lyford (1764–1837), surgeon-in-ordinary at the County Hospital, Winchester. His father and uncle were also surgeons in Basingstoke and Winchester. Mr Lyford had already been called in and his treatment yielded some temporary relief while JA was still at Chawton (*Letters*, 340).

in College Street: at no. 8 College Street (still to be seen), where a Mrs David offered lodgings.

129 *There is no better way, my dearest E.*: no. 160 in *Letters*, to JEAL, then at Exeter College, Oxford. JA wrote: 'I know no better way my dearest Edward.'

Charles: Edward Austen Knight's eighth child, then a pupil at Winchester College.

William: William Heathcote, Elizabeth (Bigg) Heathcote's son and JEAL's boyhood friend.

130 *a letter . . . before printed*: no. 161, for which see note to p. 120 above. This extract, like the former, is known only from its earlier publication in Henry Austen's 'Biographical Notice' of 1818, where the wording is slightly different (see p. 142 in this edition).

her sister-in-law, my mother: Mary Lloyd Austen, whose memories of the deathbed are woven into Caroline's account in *MAJA*, 179–82.

two of her brothers . . . clergymen: James and Henry.

131 *she amused them even in their sadness*: a reference to 'When Winchester races first took their beginning', a set of comic verses written by JA three days before her death, and so her last literary work. Cf. Henry Austen: 'The day preceding her death she composed some stanzas replete with fancy and vigour' ('Biographical Notice', p. 138). The younger generation were uncomfortable with the idea of publishing such frivolous verses as JA's deathbed production, and Henry's embarrassing reference

to the verses, described by Caroline Austen, as late as 1871, as an unlucky allusion, was removed from his 'Memoir' of 1833, perhaps under family pressure. See Caroline's letter appended to this edition at pp. 190–1; and Deirdre Le Faye, 'Jane Austen's Verses and Lord Stanhope's Disappointment', *Book Collector*, 37 (1988), 86–91. The verses were first printed in *Sailor Brothers*, 272–3. R. W. Chapman includes them in *Minor Works*, 450–2, from a manuscript version possibly in James Austen's hand but under his own title 'Venta' (the Roman name for Winchester). Doody and Murray offer a version of the text, from a second manuscript (they speculate it is Cassandra's hand, from JA's dictation, now in the Berg Collection, New York Public Library), in *Catharine and Other Writings*, 246.

'a kind sister to me, Mary': these and JA's last words are recorded in Caroline's account, presumably from Mary Lloyd Austen's witnessing of the final moments (*MAJA*, 182). They are the more poignant for the reservations JA felt towards James's second wife, partly on account of her ungenerous treatment of Anna, James's daughter by his first wife. As recently as 22 May, JA had noted in her letter to her old friend Anne Sharp, former governess at Godmersham, that Mary 'is in the main *not* a liberal-minded Woman' (*Letters*, 340–1). Mary had been nursing JA for perhaps a month or more, as James's June letter to JEAL at Oxford makes clear (*Life & Letters*, 392–3). JEAL's restrained account of the deathbed, at which he was not present, can also be supplemented by Cassandra's stoical and tender letter, written only two days after, on 20 July 1817, to her niece Fanny Knight (*Letters*, 343–6). JEAL was presumably ignorant of this letter's existence.

132 *had actually destroyed . . . facilitated*: cf. Caroline Austen to JEAL, 1 April [1869?], writing to encourage him in compiling the *Memoir*: 'I am very glad dear Edward that you have applied your-self to the settlement of this vexed question between the Austens and the Public. I am sure you will do justice to what there *is*—but I feel it must be a difficult task to dig up the *materials*, so carefully have they been buried out of sight by the past generation' (see the Appendix, pp. 186–7).

the happiest individuals . . . have no history: cf. 'for the happiest women, like the happiest nations, have no history', George Eliot, *The Mill on the Floss* (1860), book 6, ch. 3; and Proverbs 49.

133 *prefixed to these pages*: a reference to the passage from Sir Arthur Helps, *The Life of Columbus* (1869), used as epigraph to the *Memoir*.

Miss Mitford . . . Life, vol. i. p. 305: see note to p. 13 above. Mitford in a letter of 3 April 1815, to Sir William Elford. The passage continues: 'and a friend of mine, who visits her now, says that she has stiffened into the most perpendicular, precise, taciturn piece of "single blessedness" that ever existed, and that, till "Pride and Prejudice" showed what a precious gem was hidden in that unbending case, she was no more regarded in society than a poker or a fire-screen, or any other thin upright piece of wood or iron that fills its corner in peace and quietness. The case is very different now; she is still a poker—but a poker of whom everyone is afraid' (*The Life of Mary Russell Mitford*, ed. L'Estrange (1870), i. 305–6). Mitford does, however, qualify the description a few lines later when she observes that the friend from whom she has it is, owing to a family legal dispute, not on good terms with the Austens. The further postscript, detailing Mitford's accusation and JEAL's rejoinder, appeared in Ed.1 but was omitted from Ed.2. R. W. Chapman restored it in his 1926 reprint of Ed.2.

HENRY AUSTEN, 'Biographical Notice of the Author' (1818)

The 'Biographical Notice' has a special importance as the first attempt to provide the public with the details of the novelist's life, presenting her by name in its opening page, though not on the title-page, as the author of *S&S*, *P&P*, *MP*, and *E*. Written within months of JA's death, it was prefixed to the posthumously published *NA* and *P* (issued late in December 1817, dated 1818). JEAL drew on details from this short notice in his *Memoir* as well as using it as the sole authority for one of JA's latest letters. The 'Biographical Notice' has remained widely known in the twentieth century, through its reprinting in R. W. Chapman's continuously available Oxford edition of *The Novels of Jane Austen* (1923).

Jane Austen's fourth brother, Henry (1771–1850), had a colourful and varied career. After St John's College, Oxford, he took up soldiering with the Oxford Militia, was later partner in a London banking firm, was declared bankrupt in March 1816, and in December 1816 became a clergyman in the Church of England. He acted informally as Jane Austen's literary agent. According to family tradition, he was Jane Austen's favourite brother.

137 *D'Arblay and . . . Edgeworth*: Fanny or Frances Burney (see note to p. 20 above); and Maria Edgeworth (note to p. 72 above), both contemporary women novelists much admired by JA.

138 *stanzas replete . . . and vigour*: Henry Austen's reference to the comic verses 'When Winchester races first took their beginning', written by JA on her deathbed, caused the next generation of the family much discomfort. This may explain why the reference is excised from his 'Memoir' of 1833. The verses were not published until 1906. See note to p. 130 above.

139 *her eloquent blood . . . her modest cheek*: paraphrasing John Donne, 'her pure and eloquent blood | Spoke in her cheeks', from 'Of the Progress of the Soul. The Second Anniversary' (1612), ll 244–5.

141 *Gilpin on the Picturesque*: William Gilpin (1724–1804), author of *Three Essays: on Picturesque Beauty; Picturesque Travel; and on Sketching Landscape* (1792).

Johnson in prose . . . Fielding quite so high: see notes to p. 71 above, where JEAL appears to be drawing on Henry Austen's 'Biographical Notice'.

142 *'What should I do, my dearest E.'*: from a letter to James Edward Austen, 16 December [1816]. For the full text, see *Letters*, no. 146. and *Memoir*, pp. 122–4 above, where JEAL quotes more extensively from the same letter, written to him by his aunt.

a letter . . . before her death: a letter known only from its publication here by Henry Austen. JEAL subsequently draws on it, at pp. 120 and 130 above.

HENRY AUSTEN, 'Memoir of Miss Austen' (1833)

This is a rewriting by Henry Austen of his 'Biographical Notice' of 1818. Much of the original information remains, but there are omissions, alterations, and additions. Henry Austen provided the new memoir to accompany *Sense and Sensibility*, published by Richard Bentley as No. 23 in his 'Standard Novels' series, dated 1833. Bentley had recently bought from Henry and Cassandra Austen, as joint proprietors, the copyrights of the five novels (the exception was *P&P*) which had remained in JA's ownership at her death (*Austen Papers*, 286–7), and he was now preparing the first edition of her works since 1818. Henry subjoins to the memoir the date 'October 5. 1832', and in a letter to Bentley of 4 October he describes it as 'A biographical sketch of the Authoress, which is to supersede that already publishd'. He continues: 'I heartily wish that I could have made it richer in detail but the fact is that My dear Sister's life was not a life of event. Nothing like a journal of her actions or her conversations was kept by herself or others.' (For the full text of the letter, see Deirdre Le Faye, 'Jane Austen: New Biographical Comments', *Notes and Queries*, 237 (1992), 162–3.) Bentley continued to issue Henry Austen's revised memoir in separate and collected edition printings of *S&S* until 1869, after which it was rendered redundant by his publication of JEAL's substantial *Memoir*. Intended to replace the 'Biographical Notice' of 1818, the fate of the 1833 memoir since the late nineteenth century has been quite the opposite. Regularly assumed by critics to be merely a reprint of the earlier piece (Brian Southam dismisses it as a 'slightly altered version', in *Jane Austen: The Critical Heritage*, vol. 1, *1811–70* (1968), 16), it saw no reprinting between the 1880s and 1997 and has largely dropped from critical view. But the 1833 text remains significant in several ways. The biographical details retained since 1818 have been pruned and rephrased, their lighter and more intimate touches ('She was fond of dancing, and excelled in it', the listing of her favourite writers, the mention of her deathbed comic verses) giving way to a greater formality and sobriety. The new material includes the anecdote recorded only here of JA's refusal of the invitation to meet Madame de Staël; finally, Henry supplements what he now feels to be an inadequate record 'of so talented a woman' with long passages extracted from 'a critical journal of the highest reputation'. As David Gilson has recently shown, the published criticisms Henry draws on are from two sources—Maria Jane Jewsbury in the *Athenaeum* and Richard Whately in the *Quarterly Review*. In effect, Henry's selection of their critical perspectives as the summation of his second biographical study set the terms on which readers encountered JA's writings in the mid-nineteenth century. (See David Gilson, 'Henry Austen's "Memoir of Miss Austen"', *Persuasions*, 19 (1997), 12–19, and 'Jane Austen and the *Athenaeum* Again', *Persuasions*, 19 (1997), 20–2.)

150 *Madame de Staël would be of the party*: Henry Austen is our only source for this story of JA's refusal to meet the French intellectual and novelist Germaine de Staël (for whom see note to p. 111 above). By 1815 JA and de Staël were both publishing with John Murray; but the date to which Henry Austen assigns the meeting that never was, summer 1814 ('soon after the publication of *MP*'), was after de Staël's departure from England. If we are to credit the story, then we must set it back a year, possibly to JA's London visit of October 1813.

151 *fastest since she died*: the whole of this long quoted paragraph is digested from Maria Jewsbury's article, 'Literary Women. No. II. Jane Austen', *Athenaeum*, 200 (27 Aug. 1831), 553–4, which Henry Austen selectively adapts (see Gilson, 'Jane Austen and the *Athenaeum* Again', 20–2). What looks like a grammatical error at p. 152 ('the fellows to whom may be met in the streets') is also to be found in the *Athenaeum* version.

153 *evidently a Christian writer*: this paragraph is taken from Richard Whately's unsigned review of *NA* and *P* in the *Quarterly Review*, 24 (Jan. 1821), 352–76 (at pp. 359–60). There are slight differences in the wording in the *Quarterly*, and Whately writes 'Miss Austin' throughout.

Cœlebs: a reference to Hannah More's *Cœlebs in Search of a Wife* (1808), a hugely popular moral novel setting out the duties of a model wife.

154 *Madame D'Arblay . . . Miss Porter*: For D'Arblay and Edgeworth, see notes to pp. 20 and 72 above. Amelia Opie (1769–1853) was the author of domestic novels, *Adeline Mowbray* (1804) and *Simple Tales* (1806); Jane Porter (1776–1850) contributed successfully to the vogue for the historical novel with *The Scottish Chiefs* (1810).

ANNA LEFROY, 'Recollections of Aunt Jane' (1864)

HRO, MS 23M93/97/4, 'Items found interleaved in the published works and related papers of R. A. Austen-Leigh, 1872–1961'. Anna Lefroy's letter to her brother JEAL is item 23M93/97/4/104, and described as 'found in p. 291'. It forms an irregular booklet of fourteen pages (approx. 16.5 × 10.8 cm), made up of three small sheets (pp. 1–6) and two larger sheets, folded down the centre to make pp. 7, 8, 13, 14 (sheet 4) and pp. 9, 10, 11, 12 (sheet 5). The left-hand edges of sheets 1–3 are wrapped round the centrefold and stitched lightly to the back at p. 14. I reproduce for this edition the text as it appears in this fair-copy manuscript, though for ease of reading I have not recorded erased words or page breaks. I have, however, retained irregularities of orthography and punctuation. JEAL took some details (JA and Cassandra walking in pattens in the sloppy lane between Steventon and Deane, JA's physical appearance, JA's accompanying Cassandra to the Abbey School) from Anna's recollections (*Memoir*, 18, 36, 70), and he quotes extracts from her letter, as 'the testimony of another niece' (p. 73), on JA's gift for storytelling and amusing young children. At some point Anna's third daughter, Fanny Caroline Lefroy, made copies of her mother's recollections, and these copies were used by the next generation of biographers. Constance Hill, in her *Jane Austen, Her Homes and Her Friends* (1902; 2nd edn., 1904), 194–6, quoted, with some discrepancies, perhaps derived from Fanny Caroline Lefroy's transcription, the central section of Anna Lefroy's letter (her long-running joke with JA over the novels of Mrs Hunter of Norwich); R. W. Chapman, from another copy made by Fanny Caroline, extracted Anna's reproduction of JA's spoof letter addressed to Mrs Hunter, and included it in his edition of JA's letters (no. 76 in *Letters*, ed. Le Faye). The Austen-Leigh archive holds the final autograph copy of Anna's 'Recollections', but she also wrote some draft notes for the letter and these stayed with her Lefroy descendants. They were sold, together with Anna Lefroy's attempt at a continuation of *Sanditon*, to America in December 1977 and have since been transcribed and edited, as *Jane Austen's Sanditon: A Continuation by her Niece; together with 'Reminiscences of Aunt Jane' by Anna Austen Lefroy*, ed. Mary Gaither Marshall (1983). It is clear from her transcriptions that Mary Marshall did not know of the final copy of the letter in the Austen-Leigh archive, though she speculates about the status of the drafts from which she works: '[a] number of deletions and additions have been made in the manuscript, both at the time of writing and after a later reading; therefore it is probably a copy of the letter she sent to Edward' (p. 149). Anna's two draft versions of the 'Recollections' differ in some respects from the Austen-Leigh copy, itself a conflation and reordering of the two, most particularly in elaborating on JA's trustworthiness as a confidant, as told to Anna by her cousin Fanny Knight. ('Time however, as it always does, brought new impressions, or modification of the old ones; in the latter years of Aunt Jane's life there grew up an especial feeling between herself & her eldest niece of that family [the Knights]—a confidence placed on one side meeting with sympathy & sound advice on the other—The particular circumstances were never fully known to me, & would not be to the present purpose but the matter was never really revealed to Aunt Cassandra—"To tell Aunt Jane anything I once observed is the same thing as to tell Aunt C. you are mistaken was the reply Aunt Jane is entirely to be trusted["]—They were so much to each other those Sisters! They seemed to live a life to themselves, & that nobody but themselves knew. I will not say their *true* but their *full* feelings & opinions upon any subject' (draft recollections, ed. M. G. Marshall, pp. 159–60).) This detail is omitted from the final copy of the letter in the Austen-Leigh archive, though it finds its way into Fanny Caroline's manuscript 'Family History' (HRO, MS 23M93/85/2). Deirdre Le Faye, 'Anna Lefroy's Original Memories of Jane Austen', *Review of English Studies*, NS, 39 (1988), 417–21, first provided a full transcription of the manuscript in the Austen-Leigh archive.

Anna (Jane Anna Elizabeth) Lefroy (1793–1872), daughter of James Austen and Anne Mathew, was born at Deane, Hampshire. Only 2 when her mother died, she spent much of the next two years, until her father remarried, at Steventon with her grandparents and aunts Jane and Cassandra. She married Ben Lefroy, the son of a neighbour, in 1814, and bore him seven children, but was widowed early (in 1829). She died in Reading. She was protective in later years of her special relationship to Jane Austen, who had encouraged her early attempts at writing fiction and, though the novel she was writing at Austen's death was later destroyed unfinished, she eventually earned a little money from a novella, *Mary Hamilton* (1833) and two small books for children—*The Winter's Tale* (1841) and *Springtide* (1842). At Cassandra's death she inherited Jane Austen's unfinished manuscript 'Sanditon' and tried unsuccessfully to finish it. In 1864 she wrote out for her half-brother her 'Recollections of Aunt Jane'.

158 *the Goodneston Bridgeses*: JA's brother Edward Austen Knight was married to Elizabeth Bridges of Goodneston Park, the sixth of Sir Brook Bridges's thirteen children. Lady Knatchbull, mentioned a few lines later, was their eldest daughter, Fanny Austen Knight (for whom, see note to p. 79 above).

159 *Mrs Hunter of Norwich*: Rachel Hunter (1754–1813). The novel here referred to is *Lady Maclairn, the Victim of Villany* (1806). (See Deirdre Le Faye, 'Jane Austen and Mrs Hunter's Novel', *Notes and Queries*, 230 (1985), 335–6.)

the note . . . weeks afterwards: no. 76 in *Letters*, where Le Faye tentatively dates it 29–31 October 1812. No original manuscript surviving, Le Faye takes her text from that in Anna Lefroy's 'Recollections', but adds a further sentence from a copy taken by Anna's daughter Fanny Caroline (see *Letters*, 407, n. 4).

Nicholson or Glover: Francis Nicholson (1753–1844) and John Glover (1767–1849), landscape painters.

160 *Car of Falkenstein*: a nonsensical name for the Alton coach, invented for a mock-heroic story which Anna was at this time writing with JA's encouragement. Caroline refers to it in *MAJA*, 172 ('it had no other foundation than their having seen a neighbour passing on the coach, without having previously known that he was going to leave home').

Dr and Mrs Cooper at Bath: The Revd Dr Edward Cooper and his wife Jane, Mrs Austen's sister and JA's aunt. See note to p. 26 above.

CAROLINE AUSTEN, *My Aunt Jane Austen: A Memoir* (1867)

Caroline Austen wrote her memoir of Aunt Jane apparently for family consumption, 'that *she* herself should not be forgotten by her nearest descendants', though as revisions to the text (noted below) show, she took some trouble in the crafting of it. It is described on the final page as 'Written out' 'March

1867'. JEAL drew on it extensively for his *Memoir*, especially in the enlarged second edition of 1871. Twelve years younger than her half-sister Anna, seven years younger than her brother JEAL, Caroline spent much of her childhood with her aunts Jane and Cassandra at Chawton: she was only 4 when the Austens moved there in 1809. To her we owe the description of Chawton Cottage and the intimate details of JA's daily routine there, together with the most touching of the accounts of her affinity with children, the little observations about her dexterity with cup and ball, her neat satin stitch, and the care she took with the look of her letters and the placing of the sealing wax on the envelope; so, too, the story of the three chairs which substituted for a sofa, and the record of JA's final illness, as reported by Caroline's mother, Mary Lloyd Austen, who witnessed it. JEAL incorporates Caroline's memories, deepening their effect in Ed.2 by further verbatim quotation and the addition of new details, like JA's warning to Caroline against writing too much while young (*Memoir*, 42, 67–74, 77, 124, 130–1). Caroline's account was again a source for the next generation of family biographers—for JEAL's youngest son and grandson, William and Richard Arthur Austen-Leigh, in *Life & Letters* (1913); and it was printed in almost complete form by Caroline's niece, Mary Augusta Austen-Leigh, JEAL's daughter, in her *Personal Aspects of Jane Austen* (1920), 139–47. It was not published independently until 1952, when R. W. Chapman prepared it for the Jane Austen Society. His edition received a brief mention in the *Times Literary Supplement*, 20 June 1952, p. 406. It was reissued in 1991. The present edition, based on Chapman's, has been corrected against Caroline's manuscript by Deirdre Le Faye. I am greatly indebted to Miss Le Faye for this generosity. The manuscript was presented to the Jane Austen Society in 1949 by Richard Arthur Austen-Leigh and now hangs, framed, in JA's House, Chawton.

Caroline Mary Craven Austen (1805–80) was James Austen's youngest child, born at Steventon. She did not marry, but lived with her mother Mary Lloyd until 1843, thereafter moving to be near her brother James Edward. From her mother she inherited 'pocket-books' recording family events and heard first-hand accounts of Aunt Jane. In adult life she spent much time with Aunt Cassandra.

166 *last long surviving Brother*: Admiral Sir Francis (Frank) Austen (1774–1865). The death of Frank Austen, her last surviving sibling, seems to have been one of the major factors in prompting the next generation to assemble a publishable biography of JA.

Cowper's dwelling place at Olney: see the note at p. 69 above, where JEAL draws extensively on this section of Caroline's memoir.

167 *The front door opened on the road*: Caroline first wrote 'The front door of the house opened on the road', subsequently crossing out 'of the house'.

170 *he had many children*: Charles Austen's first wife died in September 1814, leaving him with three daughters, Cassy Esten, Harriet Jane, and Frances Palmer. Frank Austen eventually fathered eleven children, the seventh

being born just before JA died. His eldest child, Mary Jane (1807–36), often stayed with her aunts, as did Cassy Esten. Both are mentioned a little later in Caroline's memoir, at p. [174]. On 8 January 1817, JA writes to Cassy Esten of a visit to Chawton Cottage made by Frank and his six children, then living, courtesy of Edward Austen Knight, at Chawton House (*Letters*, no. 148). They subsequently moved to nearby Alton.

One of my cousins: he has been identified by Deirdre Le Faye as Frank's second son, Henry Edgar Austen (1811–54). See note to p. 73 above.

'Behold how good . . . in unity': Psalm 132: 1.

the time came . . . forbearance and generosity: a reference to Henry's bankruptcy in March 1816, which hit several members of the family hard. See notes to pp. 101 and 120 above. Caroline's later *Reminiscences*, 47–8, contains the most detailed family account of the bankruptcy and its consequences.

171 *chiefly at work*: referring here exclusively to needlework.

172 *quizzed*: made fun of.

one of her nieces: Anna Austen Lefroy; a reference to the tale spun around the 'Car of Falkenstein', as described in Anna's 'Recollections'.

173 *History has charged her memory*: see note to p. 71 above.

174 *I dare say*: meaning, somewhat differently from nowadays, 'I am quite sure'.

should cease writing: Caroline first wrote 'should write no more'.

a volume of Evelina: Fanny Burney's first novel, published in 1778.

175 *her especial pride and delight*: her fourth brother, Henry.

176 *Two of the great Physicians*: Henry Austen was seriously ill during October and November 1815. He was first attended by Mr Charles Haden, who lived nearby in Sloane Street, but later, during the crisis of his illness, Dr Matthew Baillie was called in, one of the Prince Regent's physicians (*Fam. Rec.*, 202).

177 *afforded some amusement*: one consequence of this amusement was JA's 'Plan of a Novel', written late 1815–early 1816. See note to p. 97 above and Caroline's letter to JEAL in which she remarks on his 'very merciful' handling of the ridiculous Rev. Clarke in the recently published *Memoir* (see the Appendix, p. 192).

In a letter to me she says: no. 156 in *Letters*, written 26 March 1817.

178 *pocket books in my possession*: these were Caroline's mother's, Mary Lloyd Austen's, pocket books, in which she recorded brief, diary-type notes of events as they occurred. They formed the basis for Caroline's later *Reminiscences*, written in the 1870s.

They stayed: Caroline first wrote 'They stayed with us'.

Mr. Fowle's at Kintbury: the Revd Fulwar Craven Fowle (1764–1840), of Kintbury, Berkshire. He had been a pupil of JA's father at Steventon,

1778–81, and was married to Eliza Lloyd, sister of Martha and of Mary, Caroline's mother. Mary Jane Fowle was Fulwar Fowle's eldest daughter and Caroline's cousin.

a letter . . . dated Jany. 23rd–1817: no. 149 in *Letters*. JEAL quotes this extract in *Memoir*, Ed.2 (p. 127 above).

Mr. Leigh Perrot's death: JA's uncle died on 28 March 1817. For the distress caused in the family by the arrangements of his will, see note to p. 120 above.

179 *one of the eminent physicians of the day*: possibly Dr Matthew Baillie (see note to p. 176 above).

APPENDIX

183 *NPG, RWC/HH*: a file of correspondence between Henry Hake of the National Portrait Gallery and the Austen scholar R. W. Chapman, 1932–48. This includes a set of typed sheets, sent by Chapman to Hake, comprising copies of letters made by Richard Arthur Austen-Leigh of correspondence addressed to JEAL around the time of the preparation and publication of the *Memoir*. ('Copies of parts of various letters addressed to JEAL about the date of the composition & publication of the *Memoir* and preserved by him in an album—lent to me by RAAL 1926' RWC.) JEAL's album containing the originals of these letters is now lost or destroyed. The file consists of typed extracts of letters from Anna Lefroy (3 letters), Caroline Austen (4 letters), Catherine Hubback (Frank Austen's daughter) (2 letters), T. E. P. Lefroy (Tom Lefroy's nephew and Jemima Lefroy's husband)(1 letter), Cassandra Esten Austen (Charles Austen's daughter) (1 letter), Elizabeth Rice (Edward Austen Knight's daughter) (3 letters), Louisa Knatchbull-Hugesson (Fanny Knatchbull's daughter) (2 letters), Revd G. D. Boyle of Kidderminster (1 letter). It is not possible to determine whether errors or idiosyncratic features of orthography and punctuation are original to the lost manuscripts or were introduced at the typing stage.

Veneroni Grammars: Giovanni Veneroni, *The Complete Italian Master* (1763) and further editions in 1778, 1798.

184 *Lady Le Marchant*: wife of Sir Denis Le Marchant and JEAL's sister-in-law. See *Memoir*, 112–13, where JEAL records Sir Denis's anecdotes of famous opinions of JA's novels.

Mrs George Austen: wife of Frank Austen's son George. For Poll's letter, see note to *Memoir*, 44.

Cassandra Austen . . . Fanny: probably a reference to Charles Austen's daughters Cassandra and Frances. Another Fanny (Frank's daughter Frances Sophia) had letters from JA to Frank which she offered to JEAL on condition that he did not publish them, but the daughter referred to here as possibly objecting to handing over manuscript material is probably Frank's other surviving daughter Catherine, now Mrs Hubback, suspected of having copies of *The Watsons* and *Sanditon*. Portsdown Lodge, near Portsmouth, was Frank Austen's last home.

Herbert Austens: Frank Austen's fourth son Herbert and his wife.

185 *Mr. Austen's letter to Cadell*: used in the *Memoir*, at p. 105. Anna Lefroy's eldest daughter Anna Jemima was married to the purchaser of the letter, Tom Lefroy, usually distinguished as T. E. P. Lefroy, nephew of JA's former admirer of that name.

186 *to his daughter Maria*: a reference to 'Evelyn' from *Volume the Third*. See *Memoir*, 43 and note.

still living 'Chief Justice': a reference to Tom Lefroy, who died in 1869 months before the publication of the *Memoir*. See p. 48 and note.

187 *pocket book of 1817*: a reference to their mother Mary Lloyd Austen's diary for that year with its brief record of events, including JA's death.

the Manydown story: this and the following anecdote of JA's seaside admirer find their way into the second edition of the *Memoir* at p. 29 (see note).

189 *HRO, etc.*: Hampshire Record Office, Austen-Leigh archive, MS 23M93.

young Hastings: a reference to the infant son of Warren Hastings who died in the Austens' care in 1764. See *Memoir*, 13 and note. Other details recorded in this letter are included at *Memoir*, 11.

One Lime . . . by our father: HRO, MS 23M93/60/32 includes a poem by James Austen, copied in JEAL's hand, entitled 'To Edward, On planting a lime tree on the terrace in the meadow before the house. January 1813'.

W Knight: JEAL's cousin, William Knight, since 1822 rector of Steventon.

190 *HRO, MS 23M93/86/3b item 73*: Caroline is responding to the reception of the recent, expanded second edition of the *Memoir* in which JA's manuscript writings were first published. Lord Stanhope had written to the publisher Richard Bentley expressing disappointment at not finding JA's deathbed verses in the new edition. Bentley forwarded the letter to JEAL who shared its contents with his two sisters. We have only Caroline's defensive response. This extract is also quoted in Deirdre Le Faye, 'Jane Austen's Verses and Lord Stanhope's Disappointment', *The Book Collector*, 37 (1988), 86–91 (at pp. 89–90).

unluckily Uncle Henry . . . half a Century ago: the verses are those known as 'Winchester Races'. Henry Austen referred to them in his 'Biographical Notice' (1818) as an indication of his sister's cheerfulness of spirits only days before her death. The reference was deleted from his 1833 'Memoir'. But the comic verses and Henry Austen's tactless pride in them seem to have caused his nephew and nieces some embarrassment. See *Memoir*, 130 and note for further details.

191 *a very great gain*: Caroline is referring to the expansion of *Memoir*, ch. 6 in Ed.2, to include two letters from JA recording visits to London in 1813 and 1814. See pp. 86–9 above.

Charlotte Craven: Charlotte Elizabeth Craven (1798–1877), mentioned in *Letters*, 210–11 and 321, and in *Memoir*, 87.

Catherine Hubback: Frank Austen's fourth daughter and a novelist.

Mr Withers proposal: Harris Bigg-Wither, younger brother of Catherine and Alethea Bigg of Manydown Park. See *Memoir*, 29 and note.

Dr Blackall: the Revd Dr Samuel Blackall (1771–1842), Fellow of Emmanuel College, Cambridge, introduced to JA by Mrs Lefroy, at Christmas 1797, in the hopes of his replacing Tom Lefroy in her affections. JA found him pompous and loud and was unimpressed. (See *Letters*, 19 and 216.) The story of his interest in their aunt, handed down by Cassandra Austen, seems to have been confused in the minds of the next generation with Cassandra's other story of the seaside romance cut short so tragically by death. There is no evidence that JA was at all attached to Dr Blackall. See *Memoir*, 29.

192 *Mr. Clarke*: the Revd James Stanier Clarke, the Prince Regent's Librarian. See note to p. 97 above, which explains the 'mercy' JEAL showed to his memory.

The portrait: the steel-engraved portrait of JA, derived from a sketch by Cassandra Austen, which formed the frontispiece to the first edition of the *Memoir*. See note to p. 70 above.

193 *Her groves of green myrtle*: For identification of the songs, see Deirdre Le Faye, 'Three Missing Jane Austen Songs', *Notes and Queries*, 244 (1999), 454–5.

Rev. F. W. Fowle: Fulwar William Fowle (1791–1876) was the eldest son of Fulwar Craven Fowle, a one-time pupil of Jane Austen's father and brother of Tom Fowle who was engaged to Cassandra. See *Fam. Rec.*, 147, where F. W. Fowle's description of Jane's appearance, as remembered in 1838, is quoted, from Kathleen Tillotson, 'Jane Austen', *Times Literary Supplement*, 17 Sep. 1954, p. 591. Fulwar Fowle's mother was Eliza Lloyd, sister to Martha and Mary. Hence, James Edward, Caroline, and Fulwar Fowle were cousins.

194 *Marmion*: by Walter Scott. See note to p. 72.

195 *NPG, RWC/HH, fos. 26–9*: for a transcript of the letter and an investigation into the identity of Mrs Barrett and her relationship with JA, see R. W. Chapman, 'Jane Austen's Friend Mrs Barrett', *Nineteenth-Century Fiction*, 4 (1949), 171–4; and Deirdre Le Faye, 'Jane Austen's Friend Mrs Barrett Identified', *Notes and Queries*, 244 (1999), 451–4, where the letter is again reproduced. Le Faye identifies her as Ann Barrett, wife of an

attorney living in Alton and helping with the business of the Chawton estate during the period *c.*1813–16. JEAL draws on these recollections (as 'by a friend') at *Memoir*, 118.

197 *HRO, MS 23M93/85/2*: a substantial, unpaginated prose manuscript, written *c.*1880–5 by Fanny Caroline Lefroy (1820–85), Anna's fourth child, recounting the history of the Austen and Lefroy families. It contains copies of JA's letters to Anna Lefroy, transcribed extracts from Caroline Austen's manuscript books (published as *Reminiscences of Caroline Austen*, ed. Deirdre Le Faye, 1986), and extracts from the papers of other members of the Austen family. Though not the account of someone known to JA, it nevertheless became a repository for copies of primary documents of those who did know her. Included here are extracts from the 'Family History' describing the reaction to JA's death, in the words of her brother Frank Austen and of her mother, Mrs Cassandra Austen, Fanny Lefroy's great grandmother.

INDEX

The Oxford World's Classics Website

www.worldsclassics.co.uk

- Browse the full range of Oxford World's Classics online
- Sign up for our monthly e-alert to receive information on new titles
- Read extracts from the Introductions
- Listen to our editors and translators talk about the world's greatest literature with our Oxford World's Classics audio guides
- Join the conversation, follow us on Twitter at OWC_Oxford
- Teachers and lecturers can order inspection copies quickly and simply via our website

www.worldsclassics.co.uk

MORE ABOUT **OXFORD WORLD'S CLASSICS**

American Literature

British and Irish Literature

Children's Literature

Classics and Ancient Literature

Colonial Literature

Eastern Literature

European Literature

Gothic Literature

History

Medieval Literature

Oxford English Drama

Poetry

Philosophy

Politics

Religion

The Oxford Shakespeare

A SELECTION OF OXFORD WORLD'S CLASSICS

JANE AUSTEN	**Emma**
	Mansfield Park
	Persuasion
	Pride and Prejudice
	Sense and Sensibility
MRS BEETON	**Book of Household Management**
LADY ELIZABETH BRADDON	**Lady Audley's Secret**
ANNE BRONTË	**The Tenant of Wildfell Hall**
CHARLOTTE BRONTË	**Jane Eyre**
	Shirley
	Villette
EMILY BRONTË	**Wuthering Heights**
SAMUEL TAYLOR COLERIDGE	**The Major Works**
WILKIE COLLINS	**The Moonstone**
	No Name
	The Woman in White
CHARLES DARWIN	**The Origin of Species**
CHARLES DICKENS	**The Adventures of Oliver Twist**
	Bleak House
	David Copperfield
	Great Expectations
	Nicholas Nickleby
	The Old Curiosity Shop
	Our Mutual Friend
	The Pickwick Papers
	A Tale of Two Cities
GEORGE DU MAURIER	**Trilby**
MARIA EDGEWORTH	**Castle Rackrent**

A SELECTION OF OXFORD WORLD'S CLASSICS

George Eliot	Daniel Deronda The Lifted Veil and Brother Jacob Middlemarch The Mill on the Floss Silas Marner
Susan Ferrier	Marriage
Elizabeth Gaskell	Cranford The Life of Charlotte Brontë Mary Barton North and South Wives and Daughters
George Gissing	New Grub Street The Odd Woman
Thomas Hardy	Far from the Madding Crowd Jude the Obscure The Mayor of Casterbridge The Return of the Native Tess of the d'Urbervilles The Woodlanders
William Hazlitt	Selected Writings
James Hogg	The Private Memoirs and Confessions of a Justified Sinner
John Keats	The Major Works Selected Letters
Charles Maturin	Melmoth the Wanderer
Walter Scott	The Antiquary Ivanhoe Rob Roy
Mary Shelley	Frankenstein The Last Man

A SELECTION OF **OXFORD WORLD'S CLASSICS**

ROBERT LOUIS STEVENSON	**Kidnapped** and **Catriona** **The Strange Case of Dr Jekyll and Mr Hyde** and **Weir of Hermiston** **Treasure Island**
BRAM STOKER	**Dracula**
WILLIAM MAKEPEACE THACKERAY	**Vanity Fair**
OSCAR WILDE	**Complete Shorter Fiction** **The Major Works** **The Picture of Dorian Gray**
DOROTHY WORDSWORTH	**The Grasmere and Alfoxden Journals**
WILLIAM WORDSWORTH	**The Major Works**

TROLLOPE IN OXFORD WORLD'S CLASSICS

ANTHONY TROLLOPE

An Autobiography
The American Senator
Barchester Towers
Can You Forgive Her?
The Claverings
Cousin Henry
Doctor Thorne
The Duke's Children
The Eustace Diamonds
Framley Parsonage
He Knew He Was Right
Lady Anna
The Last Chronicle of Barset
Orley Farm
Phineas Finn
Phineas Redux
The Prime Minister
Rachel Ray
The Small House at Allington
The Warden
The Way We Live Now

A SELECTION OF **OXFORD WORLD'S CLASSICS**

HANS CHRISTIAN ANDERSEN	**Fairy Tales**
J. M. BARRIE	**Peter Pan in Kensington Gardens and Peter and Wendy**
L. FRANK BAUM	**The Wonderful Wizard of Oz**
FRANCES HODGSON BURNETT	**The Secret Garden**
LEWIS CARROLL	**Alice's Adventures in Wonderland and Through the Looking-Glass**
CARLO COLLODI	**The Adventures of Pinocchio**
KENNETH GRAHAME	**The Wind in the Willows**
ANTHONY HOPE	**The Prisoner of Zenda**
THOMAS HUGHES	**Tom Brown's Schooldays**

A SELECTION OF OXFORD WORLD'S CLASSICS

A SELECTION OF **OXFORD WORLD'S CLASSICS**

	Six French Poets of the Nineteenth Century
Honoré de Balzac	**Cousin Bette** **Eugénie Grandet** **Père Goriot**
Charles Baudelaire	**The Flowers of Evil** **The Prose Poems and Fanfarlo**
Benjamin Constant	**Adolphe**
Denis Diderot	**Jacques the Fatalist** **The Nun**
Alexandre Dumas (père)	**The Black Tulip** **The Count of Monte Cristo** **Louise de la Vallière** **The Man in the Iron Mask** **La Reine Margot** **The Three Musketeers** **Twenty Years After** **The Vicomte de Bragelonne**
Alexandre Dumas (fils)	**La Dame aux Camélias**
Gustave Flaubert	**Madame Bovary** **A Sentimental Education** **Three Tales**
Victor Hugo	**The Essential Victor Hugo** **Notre-Dame de Paris**
J.-K. Huysmans	**Against Nature**
Pierre Choderlos de Laclos	**Les Liaisons dangereuses**
Mme de Lafayette	**The Princesse de Clèves**
Guillaume du Lorris and Jean de Meun	**The Romance of the Rose**

A SELECTION OF OXFORD WORLD'S CLASSICS

Guy de Maupassant	A Day in the Country and Other Stories A Life Bel-Ami Mademoiselle Fifi and Other Stories Pierre et Jean
Prosper Mérimée	Carmen and Other Stories
Molière	Don Juan and Other Plays The Misanthrope, Tartuffe, and Other Plays
Blaise Pascal	Pensées and Other Writings
Abbé Prévost	Manon Lescaut
Jean Racine	Britannicus, Phaedra, and Athaliah
Arthur Rimbaud	Collected Poems
Edmond Rostand	Cyrano de Bergerac
Marquis de Sade	The Crimes of Love The Misfortunes of Virtue and Other Early Tales
George Sand	Indiana
Mme de Staël	Corinne
Stendhal	The Red and the Black The Charterhouse of Parma
Paul Verlaine	Selected Poems
Jules Verne	Around the World in Eighty Days Captain Hatteras Journey to the Centre of the Earth Twenty Thousand Leagues under the Seas
Voltaire	Candide and Other Stories Letters concerning the English Nation

A SELECTION OF **OXFORD WORLD'S CLASSICS**

John Buchan	**Huntingtower** **The Thirty-Nine Steps**
Joseph Conrad	**Heart of Darkness and Other Tales** **Lord Jim** **Nostromo** **The Secret Agent** **Under Western Eyes**
Ford Madox Ford	**The Good Soldier**
John Galsworthy	**The Forsyte Saga**
James Joyce	**A Portrait of the Artist as a Young Man** **Dubliners** **Occasional, Critical, and Political Writing** **Ulysses**
Rudyard Kipling	**The Jungle Books** **Just So Stories** **Kim** **War Stories and Poems**
D. H. Lawrence	**The Rainbow** **Sons and Lovers** **The Widowing of Mrs Holroyd and Other Plays** **Women in Love**
Katherine Mansfield	**Selected Stories**
Virginia Woolf	**Flush** **The Mark on the Wall and Other Short Fiction** **Mrs Dalloway** **Orlando: A Biography** **A Room of One's Own and Three Guineas** **To the Lighthouse**
W. B. Yeats	**The Major Works**